Folens

angles on psychology

for Edexcel A2 Level

Matt Jarvis
Julia Russell
Dawn Collis

United Kingdom: Folens Publishers, Water... House, Thame Rd, Haddenham, Buckinghamshire HP17 8NT.

www.folens.com

Ireland: Folens Publishers, Greenhills Road, Tallaght, Dublin 24.

Email: info@folens.ie

Project development: Rick Jackman (Jackman Publishing Solutions Ltd)

Layout artist: GreenGate Publishing Services

Illustrations: Barking Dog Art, GreenGate Publishing Services

Cover image: ErickN / Shutterstock

First published 2009 by Folens Limited.

British Library Cataloguing in Publication Data. A catalogue record for this publication is available from the British Library.

ISBN 978-1-85008-296-5

Contents

Introduction   1

1 Criminal psychology   3

Criminal psychology   4
Causes of criminal behaviour   4
Studying eyewitness testimony   19
Treating offenders   30
Summary and conclusions   36

2 Child psychology   39

Attachment   40
Deprivation   50
Privation   53
Atypical development   56
Daycare   62
Summary and conclusions   67

3 Health psychology: substance misuse   69

Health psychology   70
Drug action   70
Operant conditioning and drug use   73
Drugs and their effects   77
Biological explanations for drug misuse   88
Treating substance misuse   98
Drug abuse campaigns   104
Summary and conclusions   108

4 Sport psychology   111

Factors affecting sporting participation and success   112
Motivation and sport   117
Psychological techniques for improving performance   124
Summary and conclusions   130

5 Clinical psychology   133

Defining abnormality   134
Classification and diagnosis of mental disorder   136

Schizophrenia	139
Explanations for schizophrenia	140
Biological treatments for schizophrenia	146
Psychological treatments for schizophrenia	147
Unipolar depression	150
Biological explanations for depression	152
Psychological explanations for depression	154
Biological treatments for depression	156
Psychological treatments for depression	158
Phobias	160
Biological explanations for phobias	160
Psychological explanations for phobias	161
Drug treatments for phobias	162
Psychological treatments for anxiety disorders	163
Summary and conclusions	164

6 Issues and debates — 167

How do the approaches to psychology contribute to society?	168
How do the applications to psychology contribute to society?	177
Ethics in psychological research	184
Research methods	192
Psychology in today's society: the key issues	210
Debates in psychology	211
Summary and conclusions	222

7 Examination advice — 225

How is my A2 examined?	226
What to learn for Evidence in practice	228
What to revise	231
How to revise	235
Sample questions and answers	237
In the exam	247
References	248
Index	261
Acknowledgements	267

Introduction

This is the second edition of the hugely successful *Angles on Applied Psychology*, previously published in 2003 with our old publisher, Nelson Thornes. The new edition of *Angles* is tailor-made to the needs of students and teachers taking on the new A2 psychology from Edexcel. We know that many students have in the past found the *Angles* books useful for other A-level specifications as well. If you are studying AQA spec A, you might like to know that we now have books designed specifically for AQA, AS and A2 *Exploring Psychology*. You can see details of these at this at http://www.folens.com/page.cfm?&webpageid=74.

We were all heavily involved in the development of the current psychology specifications, Julia and Dawn at Edexcel and Matt as part of the Major Stakeholders Group that advised all the Awarding Bodies. This means that we have been in an excellent position to develop a textbook that really meets the changing needs of psychology students and their teachers. Since the last round of specs were written, psychology has been reclassified as a science A-level. For psychology students this means a whole new emphasis on *How science works* or research methods and on higher level thinking. This has suited the *Angles* ethos well and you can use our chapter features to develop your understanding of psychological thinking and research.

As well as updating our content, our major task in writing the third edition of *Angles* has been to keep as many as possible of the popular features of the last edition as possible, whilst making some changes in line with the requirements of the new specification.

Classic research: this feature identifies the studies named on the specification to be studied in detail. Some of these are compulsory and some are optional – this is clear on the boxed feature.

What's new? Although much of the research we quote is very up-to-date, the *What's new?* feature allows us to flag up examples of current research that are particularly interesting in themselves or which are particularly useful as examples of methodological choices or issues flagged up in *How science works*.

Media watch: this feature takes newspaper articles reporting real events and invites you to use the psychology you have been studying to explain why these events might have happened.

How science works: this is perhaps the biggest change from the previous two editions. The Edexcel AS spec now fully integrates research methodology into the approaches. We have placed the *How science works* boxes in the relevant chapters, linked to the rest of the chapter content.

Interactive angles: this is an interactive feature that gives you thinking, research or revision tasks to make sure you deeply process and fully understand the material you are studying.

Over to you: for each psychological approach you study at A2 you are required to undertake a piece of practical work. *Over to you* introduces you to this task.

Evidence in practice: an interactive feature designed to help you get to grips with the new specification requirements to summarise and content-analyse articles.

If you have previously used *Angles* books you'll be pleased to know that our basic principles haven't changed. We structure the book closely around the Edexcel specification so you won't spend a lot of time reading material you don't need to know. However, we also make an effort within the demands of the specification to provide you with as much interesting, up-to-date and relevant to real life material as possible. This is because motivation is incredibly important in learning; we want you to share the authors' love of psychology, work hard at it and do well. Happy angling!

Dedications

To Em with love, Julia

This book is dedicated to Ann Jarvis.

To Glyn for always being there for me, Dawn

What's ahead?

By the end of this chapter I should know about:

- what is meant by criminological psychology
- social learning theory as an explanation of antisocial behaviour
- the role of the media in modelling antisocial behaviour
- one other explanation of antisocial/criminal behaviour: either one from the biological approach or one from the social approach
- three studies into eyewitness testimony including
  - a laboratory experiment: eg Loftus & Palmer (1974) – car crash
  - a field study: eg Yuille & Cutshall (1985) – real life crime
  - one other, for example, Loftus & Zanni (1975), Kebbell *et al.* (2002) or Krackow & Lynn (2003)
- two studies in detail including:
  - Loftus & Palmer (1974)
  - either Yuille & Cutshall (1985) – witnesses in the field or Charlton *et al.* (2002) – St Helena TV
- token economy programmes as a way to treat offenders
- one other way to treat offenders, eg anger management
- either content analysis of an article or a summary of two articles relating to criminal psychology.

In addition I should understand:

- research methods used to investigate witness effectiveness, including laboratory experiments and field experiments
- the usefulness of such methods in criminal psychology and their reliability, validity and ethics

Where does criminal psychology take us?

- Should parents worry about what their children watch on TV?
- Are criminals just born bad?
- Do violent video games make kids aggressive?
- Why does ending a question '... didn't they?' matter to a witness?
- What can criminal psychology do for repeat offenders?
- Do humans have genes for aggression?

Criminal psychology

Criminal psychology, or, more correctly, criminological psychology, looks at the role of psychology in understanding the causes of **crime**, ways psychologists can help in the criminal justice process, for example in explaining factors which affect the identification and judgement of criminals, such as the accuracy of eyewitnesses, and in providing interventions to reduce criminal behaviour. We will explore each of these applications of criminal psychology in this chapter.

What do we mean by 'crime'? A criminal act is one which society forbids or punishes – but this definition is rather circular, and begs the question 'why is it forbidden?' The answer is not a simple one. What is deemed to be wrong in one society may not be in another. Some actions, such as killing people, are universally recognised as criminal. The illegality of other actions, however, such as drinking alcohol on the street, or below a certain age, is much more variable.

Regardless of the action, it can only be a criminal act if it was deliberate. Accidentally harming someone, such as pushing them under a passing car if you slipped up on the street, is not a crime because it is not done intentionally.

Hollin (1989) suggests three ways to define crime:

- **Consensus view** – an agreement amongst members of a society about which behaviours are unacceptable and therefore punishable. When crime is defined in this way, only acts forbidden by law are crimes. So, for example, **antisocial behaviour** would not be a crime unless the particular act was an illegal one. This definition has the advantage of being flexible. Crimes such as malicious wounding are typically unacceptable so are forbidden, whereas other actions can pass in and out of criminal law depending on the changing values of a society. Printing a book was once forbidden in the UK and incest was once legal.

- **Conflict view** – this suggests that criminal laws exist to protect the wealthy and powerful. Even when actions are forbidden in the common interest, they are defined in an unequal way so that the powerful tend to go unpunished. For example, until recently in English law the criminal offence of rape did not include

sexual coercion within marriage. A wife – typically the physically and economically weaker partner – had no legal right to refuse unwanted sexual intercourse.

- **Interactionist view** – this occupies the middle ground between the above approaches. It suggests there are no absolute values of right and wrong. Different meanings are possible. For example, killing is sometimes criminal but not always. During wartime, in the case of capital punishment or when acting in self-defence, it is not 'murder' and it is not criminal. Taking a life in the act of euthanasia is a criminal act in most societies, but one that some people would like to see decriminalised. The definition of crime according to the interactionist view is not dependent on a consensus, but is driven by those in power; it reflects both legal standards set by those in power and the changing moral values of the majority.

Interactive angles

For more information on antisocial behaviour, look at the following websites:

- http://www.respect.gov.uk/article.aspx?id=9066

- http://www.homeoffice.gov.uk/anti-social-behaviour/

- http://www.crimereduction.homeoffice.gov.uk/asbos/asbos9.htm

- http://www.antisocialbehaviour.org.uk/

1. How is antisocial behaviour defined?

2. What steps can be taken to control antisocial behaviour?

Causes of criminal behaviour

You will remember from your AS level that there are different approaches to psychology. These approaches can offer alternative, or sometimes complementary, explanations of behaviour. In this section we will consider explanations of the causes of antisocial and criminal behaviour from the learning, biological and social approaches.

The learning approach: social learning theory

In the learning approach at AS, you investigated several explanations of learning. One of these was social learning theory, which proposes that learning can occur when one individual (the learner) observes and imitates another, the model. For example, a young girl may watch an older one pinching another child and try to copy her. According to Bandura (1977), modelling will occur when the observer pays attention, is able to remember and reproduce what they have observed and when they are motivated to do so. This motivation may be an external reward or some inner drive. Internal motivation may

What's that?

- **crime:** actions deemed to be punishable by the majority and/or those in power

- **antisocial behaviour:** acting in a manner that causes or is likely to cause harassment, alarm or distress to one or more persons not of the same household as the perpetrator (Crime and Disorder Act, 1998). It includes aggressive, intimidating and destructive behaviour that reduces the quality of life within the community

be generated by the model and this can explain why there are differences in the effectiveness of models.

In other types of learning, such as classical or operant conditioning, the process of learning can be seen as the individual performs the behaviour. This is not necessarily the case in social learning. When a new behavioural potential is gained by observation, it is not necessarily demonstrated. A young boy may see his father hit his mother but not reproduce the behaviour until he is much older. Social learning also differs from operant conditioning because, in modelling, the learner's behaviour does not have to be reinforced in order for the behaviour to be acquired. However, reinforcement can affect performance. Children who imitate the antisocial behaviour of others, such as swearing or spitting, learn to reproduce the behaviour only in situations where it will be rewarded, such as to annoy their parents or teachers, or to impress friends.

The importance of modelling in the acquisition of aggressive behaviour in children was illustrated by Bandura *et al.* (1961), a study you may be familiar with from your AS. They compared three groups of children aged three to six years, who had been assessed for aggressiveness and spread equally between the groups. Two groups saw adult models being either aggressive or non-aggressive to a Bobo doll (sitting on it, punching it, throwing it and hitting it on the head with a mallet, as well as abusing it verbally). Half of the children saw a same-sex model, the others an opposite-sex model. A control group did not see any model. After being frustrated to increase the chance of aggressive behaviour being displayed, all the children were observed through a one-way mirror for 20 minutes whilst playing with toys including a Bobo doll.

Bandura *et al.* found that children exposed to the aggressive models imitated their exact behaviours and were significantly more aggressive – both physically and verbally – than the control group. This effect was greater for boys than girls, although girls were more likely to imitate verbal, and boys physical, aggression. Boys were also more likely to imitate a same-sex model as, to a lesser extent, were girls. These findings illustrate the potential risk for children exposed to antisocial models such as those displaying aggressive behaviours, and identifies one of the characteristics – the gender of the model – that makes imitation more likely. However, these were real models seen face-to-face and they were adults. Such findings may not indicate how children respond to models on television or to cartoon rather than human models.

Figure 1.1 The Bobo doll study.

Pennington (1986) identifies three categories of variable that affect imitation:

- characteristics of the model, such as gender, age, status
- characteristics of the observer, such as self-esteem
- the consequences of the behaviour for the model, such as reinforcement or punishment.

Interactive angles

Try searching 'Youtube' for segments of the footage from Bandura's original experiment.

Having watched the sequence, write a list of strengths and weaknesses of Bandura *et al.*'s experiment.

For the observer, their own level of self-esteem is an important determinant of imitation. Individuals with lower self-esteem are more likely to imitate the behaviour of models. This is important as low self-esteem is also associated with criminal behaviour (see page 18). One important consequence for the model is whether they are reinforced. If the observer sees the model receiving positive reinforcement for their actions, they are more likely to imitate them. This effect is called vicarious reinforcement. Aggressive behaviours may be seen to be successful – a child who bullies others for their pocket money reaps rewards, so is a potentially effective model for the antisocial behaviour of other children.

There may also be direct positive reinforcement for imitated violence. Children who are aggressive may be rewarded for their behaviour by obtaining benefits through threatening others, such as taking their sweets. Positive reinforcement

Interactive angles

1. Why was it important for Bandura *et al.* to test the children's aggressiveness before the study?

2. After watching the model the children were taken to a room full of nice toys then told they were for other children. This was done to frustrate the children. Why was this procedure necessary and what ethical issues does it raise?

may also be experienced through the feeling of power over others, or via increased status. Simply being able to imitate the actions of a popular TV villain may increase a child's popularity. Any of these examples would act as reinforcers and could increase the frequency with which such behaviours are performed. Bandura (1965) demonstrated that a child was more likely to copy an aggressive adult model if the child was reinforced, and less likely to if he or she was punished. In this sense, as well as in the provision of models, the social environment can influence the likelihood of antisocial behaviour.

Media violence

A different aspect of the social environment, the media – for example, television – is often claimed to be a cause of children's aggression. Bandura *et al.* (1961) demonstrated the modelling of aggressive behaviour by people in real life and, although media role models are not literally in front of the learner, they may have other characteristics that make them important.

The influence of television

When characters on TV use violence they are modelling aggression. There have been many assessments of the frequency of violent incidents on television which produce differing findings depending on such variables as the channel, type of programme, time of day and definition of violence used. One overwhelming similarity in the findings, however, is that there is a lot of violence on television. Estimates for the incidence of violence per programme range from approximately 50–90%, with some of the highest figures corresponding to children's programmes, especially cartoons.

Wilson *et al.* (2002) counted 14 violent acts an hour in children's television but less than four in adult TV. Children are also increasingly exposed to violent programmes designed for an adult audience. For example *The Professionals*, which was shown after the 9pm watershed when it was made 30 years ago, is now shown in the morning, including the school holidays! Films like *Saw* and *Hostel*, which feature graphic and extended torture, are highly fashionable. Consider as well the fact that children spend more time indoors than those of any previous generation (largely due to parents' fears for their safety) and they therefore tend to watch more television.

The number of violent acts and the duration within each programme may be increasing (see Table 1.1), although this is more evident in some programmes (such as films) than in others. A similar survey in 1997 found that 47% of programmes contained violent scenes (fewer than in 1994), but by 2001 the figure had risen again to 51% and violent scenes occurred at a rate of 5.2 per hour. This rise was attributed to the increase in violent scenes in the news due to the reporting of the September 11 attacks (Broadcasting Standards Commission, 2002). This raises questions about the validity and reliability of such data.

In each case the figures represent programmes analysed for only a short period of time (two seven-day blocks) and only for prime time television (5.30pm until midnight). One problem with this is that it excludes programmes specifically for children.

Figure 1.2 *The Professionals* was intended for after the 9pm watershed but is now part of daytime TV.

Table 1.1 Findings of research for the Broadcasting Standards Council (1996)

year	% of programmes containing violent scenes	number of violent scenes per hour	% of broadcast time that was violent
1992	43	2.9	2
1994	51	4	4

Figure 1.3 An increase in violent world events can increase the incidence of violent scenes on television as they appear regularly on the news, even during family viewing hours.

Interactive angles

To give yourself a better understanding of the huge variability in methods and findings of research into levels of media violence, use the Internet to find a range of different reports. You can download research documents from the Broadcasting Standards Commission and Ofcom from:

http://www.ofcom.org.uk/static/archive/bsc/plain/pubs.htm

http://www.ofcom.org.uk/find_document/

Recall Bandura's idea that, when behaviour is acquired by social learning, four processes take place: **attention**, **retention**, **reproduction** and **reinforcement** (see page 4). By watching TV and following a storyline, we are paying attention. If the violence seen is distinctive and arousing this means it is likely to be retained. Viewers may be impressed by the violence used, motivating them to reproduce it later. This is particularly true if the model is rewarded for their actions (vicarious reinforcement).

As films and TV programmes are designed to attract our attention and captivate us, the characters are designed to have the precise features that make them effective models. They have high social status, are powerful and are often likeable too. Cartoon 'baddies' are funny, film villains may be clever, attractive or strong. These same characteristics appeal to young people, so they identify with the models. This identification makes imitation even more likely.

Figure 1.4 The latest *Rambo* film has 236 killings – an average of 2.59 per minute.

Interactive angles

Think of a film or cartoon character that uses violence. Describe the characteristics of this individual that make it likely that they will be imitated.

Huesmann (1986) observed that children who identify more strongly with aggressive TV characters and perceive TV violence as more realistic are also more aggressive. If such observations can demonstrate a link between media violence and aggressive behaviour, then learning theory could explain the pattern. However, we need to think critically about the possible causes of such a link. If individuals who are exposed to an aggressive social environment are subsequently aggressive, this may be a causal effect, or there may be other influences such as genetics or personality.

Albert Bandura conducted many experiments investigating the effect of aggressive models on behaviour. In a study investigating the effect of filmed models, Bandura *et al.* (1963) compared the effect of an aggressive adult model and a film of the same adult, performing the same behaviours, dressed as a cartoon cat. Using a procedure similar to Bandura *et al.* (1961) – see page 5 – they found that aggressive behaviour modelled by the cartoon cat produced the highest levels of imitated aggression in children.

Figure 1.5 Aggressive cartoons affect children's behaviour.

Bandura *et al.*'s study used non-familiar filmed models. To investigate the effect of aggressive models from actual TV programmes, Boyatzis *et al.* (1995) assessed the effect of the *Power Rangers* on children's aggressive behaviour. Fifty-two boys and girls aged 5–11 were observed playing in their school classroom. Half were then shown an episode of *Power Rangers* and all were observed again. The level of aggression in the children who had seen the programme was seven times higher than in the control group. The increase in aggressive behaviour was much greater in boys than girls and they exhibited many behaviours like the Power Rangers' martial-arts style actions.

Laboratory experiments may not, however, produce very valid data about the effects of TV viewing. The measures of aggressive behaviour are very specific and may not reflect the range of behaviours that could be the product of media influence (such as social exclusion), especially as they are usually expressed towards an inanimate object. The participants may perceive that they are being invited or encouraged to behave in an aggressive manner, thus changes in behaviour may be the product of demand characteristics rather than modelling. Furthermore, the context in which their aggression is expressed is very permissive. There are no consequences to limit their behaviour as there would be in reality – such as sanctions from adults or retaliation by peers. The isolated nature of the experimental setting may produce uncharacteristic changes. For example, although Bandura *et al.* (1963) showed that rewarding an aggressive model produced greater imitation of the behaviour, this is not always the case. When Kniveton (1976) allowed children to play with toys in a room before exposing them to a model, they imitated much less. Although again artificial, this suggests that children do not respond to televised models in isolation from other influences. Experimental exposure to models is typically very short – just a few minutes, whereas a TV programme can last much longer. Similarly, the observation of the consequences is generally limited to the observation of immediate or short-term effects rather than longer term influences on behaviour.

One way to improve the realism of the findings of studies into the effect of media on criminal behaviour is to use correlational data gathered from self-reported information about exposure to media and evidence of antisocial behaviour. In a correlational study, Eron *et al.* (1972) measured the level of violence in TV programmes watched by 7–8-year-olds and measured their aggressiveness. They found a positive correlation between the two. By their teenage years, Eron *et al.* found an even stronger positive correlation of violence viewed and aggressiveness in boys (though not girls). And, the more violence the boys had watched on television as children, the more likely they were to be violent criminals as adults (Eron & Huesmann, 1986).

Clearly correlational studies of actual viewing habits and aggressive behaviour are more representative than laboratory experiments. However, they cannot demonstrate causality, merely whether the factors are related. The level of aggression may not be caused by the individuals' exposure to violent models on TV; it is possible that both the watching of violence and the aggressive behaviour may have been caused by some other variable, such as harsh parenting or an aspect of personality. This research is now several decades old. Although it is unlikely that the extent to which people *can* be influenced by violent models has changed, the nature of frequency of that violence has done so. Furthermore, most but not all of Eron *et al.*'s original sample were available to follow-up, which could lead to a bias in the results, making the findings less generalisable.

Interactive angles

1. Suggest two reasons why individuals from Eron *et al.*'s original sample might not be available to follow up and explain why such biases could be important in the research.

2. When Eron *et al.* collected information about the eight-year-old children's favourite TV programmes they asked the parents, whereas the same information was collected directly from the participants at age 18. How could this have biased the results?

An alternative source of real-world evidence comes from natural experiments. Williams (1981) conducted a natural experiment looking at the effect of the introduction of broadcast television to a remote community in Canada. The aggressiveness of children in a town (nicknamed 'Notel') which initially had no television was compared, over the same time span, to two other towns (one with just one TV channel and the other with many channels). Following the introduction of broadcast television, the level of physical and verbal aggression in the children in Notel almost doubled. Although levels of aggression in the other towns also increased over the same period, the change was less marked.

Unlike the findings of correlational studies, these results do seem to suggest that the change in behaviour was a direct result of TV viewing. This is particularly so as little change was seen in the comparison towns. This suggests that the change in Notel was not the product of some other influence in society, such as an increase in drug use. Furthermore, unlike the children describe in the Classic Research box on page 9, the children from these Canadian towns were not exceptional in their pre-TV behaviour. This suggests that the findings would generalise to other children.

Interactive angles

Consider the study conducted by Williams (1981).

1. If the introduction of TV resulted in parents spending more time watching television and less supervising their children, how would this influence your conclusions from the study?

2. After television was introduced, the children in Notel spent much less time than they had previously on other leisure activities. How could this, rather than the viewing itself, account for their change in behaviour?

3. Williams reports that the children's TV viewing patterns and level of aggression in Notel were not correlated. How could this observation be explained?

Not all evidence points to a link between exposure to media models and antisocial behaviour. For example, Hagell & Newbury (1994) found that young offenders watched no more violent television than a school control group. The delinquents were also less focused on television viewing, being less able to name favourite programmes or television character. They were more likely to be on the streets getting into trouble than indoors watching television. In a natural experiment, Charlton *et al.* (2000) showed that media violence does not necessarily lead to aggression (see Research Now).

Research now

Optional

Charlton, T., Panting, C., Davie, R., Coles, D. & Whitmarsh, L. (2000)

'Children's playground behaviour across five years of broadcast television: a naturalistic study in a remote community.' *Emotional & Behavioural Difficulties*, 54: 4–12

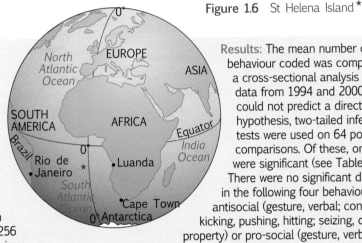

Figure 1.6 St Helena Island *

Aim: To investigate the effect of introduction of satellite TV on the aggressive behaviour of children.

Procedure: A naturalistic experiment was conducted using 3–8-year-olds on St Helena island who had not previously seen transmitted TV. Their aggressive behaviour was analysed in 1994 prior to the introduction of transmitted television in 1995. Children from two schools (with an average of 160 pupils on roll in total) were filmed in free play in the school playground and 256 minutes of video were taken. Their behaviour was assessed again in 2000 after satellite TV became available (totalling 344 minutes of video). Video recording was operated by a researcher in the playground but did not begin until the operator was no longer attracting the children's attention. School supervisors were also present and recording was not conducted in poor weather or when whole classes of children were absent.

A schedule of 26 playground behaviours was used which included aggressive behaviours such as pushing, hitting and kicking (as well as pro-social behaviours such as turn-taking and affection). The analysis of results was based on four antisocial and four pro-social behaviours and by gender and the number of children involved. A pair of independent coders scored each 60 seconds of video. Where they disagreed, the segment was replayed up to seven times to reach agreement. As the level of antisocial behaviour was so low, the results were combined into 30 minute periods for analysis.

Results: The mean number of each behaviour coded was compared in a cross-sectional analysis between data from 1994 and 2000. As they could not predict a directional hypothesis, two-tailed inferential tests were used on 64 possible comparisons. Of these, only nine were significant (see Table 1.2). There were no significant differences in the following four behaviours: antisocial (gesture, verbal; contact, kicking, pushing, hitting; seizing, damaging property) or pro-social (gesture, verbal). The initial level of aggressive behaviour displayed by the children was very low and remained so following the change in viewing opportunities. The children displayed almost twice as much pro-social behaviour as antisocial behaviour both before and after the introduction of broadcast television. Some increases and some decreases in aggressive behaviour were found, but the only two significant differences were *decreases* in incidence, although there were also five significant decreases in pro-social behaviour.

Boys were statistically more likely to engage in antisocial behaviour ($p \leq 0.01$ in a two-tailed test). Girls were somewhat more likely to be pro-social, but this difference was not significant.

Conclusion: Exposure to more violent TV does not necessarily result in an increase in aggressive behaviour. Importantly, no differences were found in the very behaviours most often associated with TV viewing, such as kicking, pushing and hitting.

Table 1.2 Frequency of playground behaviours

playground behaviour	participants	means pre-TV	post-TV	significance level (*p*)
antisocial				
non-compliant holding, forcing	one girl	1.11	0.83	0.05
non-compliant holding, forcing	mixed pair	0.78	0	0.05
pro-social				
hand holding, arm-in-arm	two girls	13.67	5.75	0.01
hand holding, arm-in-arm	group girls	5.22	1.58	0.05
hand holding, arm-in-arm	group boys	2.44	0.58	0.05
pro-social, consoling, affection	one boy	0.22	1.67	0.01
pro-social, sharing, turn-taking, helping	one boy	0	0.58	0.05
hand holding, arm-in-arm	mixed pair	2	0.58	0.05
hand holding, arm-in-arm	mixed group	1.89	0.58	0.05

Interactive angles

St Helena is an isolated island and the population is very small and cohesive. The children's parents and other members of the community are very watchful and supportive. For example, in another study (of secondary age children on St Helena) Charlton & O'Bey (1997) report a child saying 'Because everyone watches you ... everyone knows you ... you've just got to behave' (p134). How would this affect the impact of television on the children?

The procedure used by Charlton *et al.* was clearly highly valid in that, unlike studies such as Bandura, it used children in a real-life setting and pre- and post-experience to aggressive models to which the children were genuinely (rather than artificially) exposed. Their method was also rigorous, with good inter-observer reliability and efforts to ensure that the children's behaviour was unaffected by the presence of video cameras. Furthermore, any risk to the children from aggressive play or need for the operator to intervene was avoided by the presence of familiar school staff in the playground.

The reliability of the results in general is supported by the findings relating to gender differences. As shown by studies of gender from AS, you may recall that there are well-documented differences in aggression between girls and boys from a young age, as well as a tendency for females to be more nurturing. The research group also followed other cohorts of children, such as ones in nursery in 1993. These children, too, showed an absence of significant differences in aggression post-TV (Charlton *et al.*, 1999). Such additional evidence again suggests that the findings from Charlton *et al.* (2000) are reliable. Records were kept of the nursery cohort's viewing habits. No differences were found between children who did and did not watch television, nor were there any correlations between the amount of violent TV watched and antisocial behaviour.

However, St Helena is a very isolated, unusual environment and the findings may be unrepresentative of other western communities. Also, the programmes available to the St Helena children did not include some of the most violent that mainland children could view, such as *Mighty Morphin' Power Rangers* and *Teenage Mutant Ninja Turtles*. If the greatest influence of TV viewing on aggression is the product

Media watch

Clamp down on net's violent videos

Graeme Wilson

The Sun, 27 March 2008

A POWERFUL internet watchdog to guard kids from porn and violence will be demanded today.

Cinema-style ratings for video games will also be called for in a major report by TV child guru Dr Tanya Byron. PM

Gordon Brown summoned the star of *House of Tiny Tearaways* and *Little Angels* last autumn to investigate the online menace. And her final report today offers the most detailed analysis yet of the risks our kids face.

Figure 1.7 Reforms ... TV's Dr Tanya Byron.

Dr Byron will argue that parents, Ministers, internet firms and game producers must all do more to protect youngsters.

She wants cinema-style U, PG, 12, 15 or 18 ratings — with parents told if a game shows violence or sex scenes. And she will urge families to ban computers from kids' bedrooms — and put them in the lounge or kitchen.

A Whitehall insider said: 'She is not lecturing parents but is saying it's probably a good idea to keep an eye on what they're up to.'

And the TV doctor wants the sites to be monitored to check they are not showing 'happy slap' attacks or street fights.

1. How do the findings of Charlton *et al.* (2000) and Williams (1981) help to justify Dr Byron's comments about parents?

2. Describe two other pieces of evidence that suggest such measures are necessary.

Interactive
angles

1. Compare the procedures and findings of Charlton *et al.* (2000) and Williams (1981). To what extent do the differences in results relate to differences in the populations studied and what does that tell us about the importance of the social environment to levels of aggression?

2. Compare the findings of Charlton *et al.* (2000) with laboratory studies. Some differences might be accounted for by the measurement of long-term changes by Charlton *et al.*, but short-term changes in many laboratory studies. What other methodological differences might be important?

of just a few very aggressive programmes, this could be an important factor in the absence of an effect in St Helena. Indeed, Charlton *et al.* observe that without an investigation into the viewing habits of individuals, such as how much pro- or antisocial television they watched, it is impossible to draw any causal conclusions from this type of study.

The influence of video games and computers

In the last decade 'the media' has ceased to mean just film, television and radio and increasingly means computer technology. Computer use may have slightly different effects on human behaviour because it is a much more active process than simply viewing as is often the case with film and television. This is partly because they are interactive – the player participates in violent acts, albeit virtual ones – so they are more like 'real life' than simply watching, but also because regulation of use is more difficult.

Computer games and antisocial behaviour

Most non-gamers would probably be surprised by the level of violence in some popular games. Haninger & Thompson (2004) analysed the content of computer games rated as suitable for teenagers in the USA. Of the games sampled, 98% required the player to be violent; 90% required them to injure and 69% to kill; 42% showed the victim's blood.

Figure 1.8 Do computer games influence aggressive behaviour?

A glance at the best-selling games for Xbox in the week of writing this chapter (April 2009) shows that eight of the top ten games have overtly violent themes (see Figure 1.8).

At first, the evidence linking violent game-playing came from informal case examples. For example, many commentators were quick to point out that the two teenage boys who carried out the Columbine High School massacre in 1999 had spent many hours playing violent video games. This type of evidence on its own is a very limited basis for linking gaming and aggression.

Interactive
angles

1. Look up the Columbine High School massacre on the Internet. What games had the boys played and to what extent did their behaviour resemble their gaming?

2. Explain why we should not rely on one-off events like Columbine High as evidence for links between violent video games and real-life violence. You might want to look up information about other school killings such as at Virginia Tech.

Figure 1.9 Eric Harris and Dylan Klebold carried out the Columbine High School massacre after playing violent games. But is this really evidence to suggest that games cause violence?

Although the volume of research into the effects of violent games is much smaller than that concerned with film and television, the existing studies paint a worrying picture. Hopf *et al.* (2008) carried out a two-year longitudinal study on German teenagers, looking at both watching of violent films and playing violent games as predictors of violent crime at age 14. Both factors did predict involvement in violent crime but the stronger relationship was with violent video games. Research also supports a role for both social learning and desensitisation in the link between playing violent games and aggressive behaviours.

After an individual has acquired a behaviour by imitation, they may then internalise this learning such that it becomes part of their self-concept. This is called **identification** and is characterised by the behaviour becoming more automatic and likely to generalise to other situations. Konijn *et al.* (2007)

11

investigated whether aggressive behaviour after playing violent video games was greater when the player identified strongly with the game aggressor/character. In a study, 112 boys aged 12–16 years were randomly allocated to play either a realistic violent video game (*America's Army*, *Killzone* or *Max Paine*), a violent fantasy game or a non-violent game. After 20 minutes they had a reaction-time test and were told they were playing against an unseen partner. They were also told that the winner would give their opponent a loud blast of noise. The boys rated their identification with the game character by responding to the statement 'I wish I were a character such as the one in the game'. The boys who played the realistic violent games averaged the highest level of noise. Within this group, those who identified most strongly with the aggressor gave significantly higher noise levels than less identified individuals. These findings show that social learning from video games does increase aggressive behaviour and, importantly, that greater identification leads to higher levels of aggression.

Social learning alone may not be sufficient to explain the patterns found in research such as Konijn *et al.* (2007). They could equally be explained by exposure to violence

desensitising individuals to real-life aggression. Staude-Muller *et al.* (2008) conducted an experiment in which 42 men played either a high- or low-violence version of a 'first-person shooter' game, ie one in which the player takes the role of shooter. Participants then watched aggressive and generally unpleasant images whilst their heart rate and galvanic skin response were monitored. Those who had played the violent version of the game reacted less to the pictures, showing that, at least in the short term, they had been desensitised.

Violent video games may also increase criminality by reducing pro-social behaviour. Sheese & Graziano (2005) randomly allocated undergraduate students to either a violent or non-violent version of *Doom* (a multi-user game) in pairs. They were told they were competing with other participants but not each other. After the game the pairs were separated and each person was given a choice of whether to pool scores with their partner or keep them separate. If both partners opted to co-operate their combined score was multiplied by 1.5. If both chose to separate each lost half their points. If one person opted to separate while their former partner opted to co-operate they would have their score doubled and their partner would receive

Media watch

Video games warp brain

Jerome Starkey

The Sun, 9 January 2006

VIOLENT computer games alter your brain to make you aggressive, experts say.

New research shows gory games interfere with natural reactions to real-life violence.

Brain specialists found games such as *Mortal Kombat* and *Grand Theft Auto*, which include killings and street crime, desensitise players to genuine images of violence.

Figure 1.10
Game aggro ... dulls reaction.

It is the first research to show that violent games could CAUSE violent behaviour.

Studies have shown that people who play violent video games are more aggressive.

But critics claim this just means that naturally violent people enjoy playing violent games.

US psychologist Bruce Bartholow has shown that people who play violent video games have diminished responses to images involving violence. But they have normal responses to other distressing pictures, such as images involving sick children or dead animals. Scientists from the University of Missouri-Columbia carried out their research with the help of 39 experienced gamers.

1. How does this evidence help to separate the effects of cause and effect in viewing violence?

2. Comment on the sample used by Bartholow. To what extent would his findings be generalisable?

Figure 1.11 Fighting in *Doom* reduces co-operation, at least in the short term.

no points. Of the 24 people who had played the non-violent *Doom*, only one chose not to co-operate but seven people in the violent condition did so. This suggests that the participation in the violent game reduced the tendency to co-operate and share rewards.

The biological approach: born with a 'bad' personality?

Studies into the development of criminality often find that the children of parents with a criminal record themselves turn to crime. One explanation for this is the role of social factors. However, this is not the only possible cause. These individuals may be more at risk than average due to some biological difference. If this difference is heritable, then it would be possible for parents to pass on some tendency to their children and we should be able to identify patterns using twin or adoption studies, or find associations between particular genetic markers and aspects of behaviour such as aggression or lack of self-control. For example, Mason & Frick (1994) meta-analysed 12 twin and three adoption studies investigating the genetics of criminality. They estimated that nearly half (48%) of the variation in antisocial behaviour in the general population (including aggression and criminality) is genetically controlled.

The role of genes

For genes to have an effect on our behaviour they must act through a biological mechanism such as hormones, particular brain structures or neurotransmitters. If this is the case, it should be possible to investigate 'biological correlates of

Figure 1.12 The aggression in these twins is likely to be influenced by their genes.

behaviour', that is, to find differences in hormone levels, brain structure or neurotransmitters that are linked to the control of aspects of behaviour that relate to criminality.

Certainly there is evidence that behaviours such as aggression can be inherited. Lagerspetz (1979) bred 25 generations of mice. In each generation, she chose the least aggressive individuals to breed together and the most aggressive ones to breed together. The result was two very different strains. One group of mice were super-aggressive, the other very docile. Even when cross-fostered to non-aggressive mothers, mice from the 'aggressive' strain still demonstrated more aggression (Lagerspetz & Wuorinen, 1965). This showed that there is, at least in animals, a genetic component to aggressive behaviour.

Figure 1.13 Selective breeding experiments have shown that aggression, at least in mice, is partly genetically controlled.

Nobody is suggesting, however, that there is a single 'gene for aggression' in humans or animals. Nor is it likely that aggressiveness is simply the product of a combination of genes; the environment is clearly important too. Even so, how much genes matter and which genes are important is of great interest.

Lyons *et al.* (1995) looked at misbehaviour and juvenile crime in thousands of twins. The monozygotic twins (who share all of their genes) were not a lot more similar than the dizygotic twins (who only share 50% on average). This would suggest that the environment is important in determining criminal behaviour. However, records of criminal and aggressive behaviour in *adult* twins showed that monozygotic twins were indeed more similar. This suggests that genetic factors become more important in adulthood. One explanation for this is that, in childhood, the individual's environment is controlled; for example, exposure to violent television or being made to play with 'sensible' friends. As adults, however, individuals can make choices about how to behave.

Interactive angles

1. It would not be ethical to deliberately set up an experiment like Lagerspetz's using children, but a similar test could be conducted using existing information from children who had been adopted. Design such a study.

2. If you were asked to suggest ways to reduce adult aggressive behaviour, what advice would you give on the basis of the findings of Lyons *et al.* (1995)?

Cadoret *et al.* (1995) found that adopted children were somewhat more likely to show aggressive behaviours and have conduct disorders if either their adoptive home was disrupted, eg by marital disputes or drug problems, or if their biological parents had criminal records. However, when they were exposed to *both* of these factors, the risk was much greater. This illustrates how genes and the environment can interact.

What's that?

- **NOS**: a gene with many variants which has been linked to aggression. It is involved in the production of an enzyme with a role in the control of nitric oxide, which (among other things) acts as a neurotransmitter

- **Knock-out**: a term used to refer to animals which have a particular gene deleted

As evidence suggests there is a role for genes in human aggression, it should be possible to identify some of the genes involved. Research in this area has already identified genes in animals that are associated with aggression. The NOS gene has several variants that are involved in aggressive behaviour in rodents. Demas *et al.* (1999) found that deleting the eNOS2/2 gene eliminated aggression in male mice, even though they had extra-strong front legs! Conversely, Nelson *et al.* (1995) found that male mice with the nNOS2/2 gene deleted were *more* aggressive than normal.

What's new?

Research has begun to investigate the role of specific genes relating to aggressive and criminal behaviour in humans. In a study of 153 men attending psychiatric assessments in relation to criminal behaviour, Retz *et al.* (2004) looked at the relationship between violent behaviour and a variant gene called 5-HTTLPR. They found an association between a particular form of the gene and violent behaviour when the individuals had symptoms like ADHD in childhood, but not when they had symptoms of personality disorder or impulsivity. Retz *et al.* concluded that this gene (which controls aspects of the neurotransmitter serotonin) is associated with violent behaviour in male criminals.

Reif *et al.* (2009) investigated links between impulsivity (which could be a factor in aggression) and variants of the NOS1 gene in humans using a sample for psychiatric clinics which included 182 criminals. The gene variant was more frequent in adults with ADHD, some personality disorders and aggressive behaviour to the self and other people. They also explored the brain activity of these individuals and found that the gene variant reduced activity in the anterior cingulate cortex. This area processes information about emotion and reward, so the gene variant may affect the control of impulsive behaviour that is associated with aggression.

The role of hormones

As you may recall learning at AS, cross-cultural studies of gender differences show that males are typically more aggressive than females. Of course, this difference could be environmental – they are all affected by aggressive models or reinforcement – but it is likely that there are also biological differences, since the pattern is found in cultures with a diversity of social influences. One important biological difference between males and females is in the levels of the hormone testosterone. The hormone is found in both sexes, but adult males produce about 10 times more than adult females. In males, the testes produce testosterone from birth, the levels escalating at puberty – and males aged 15–25, with the highest levels of testosterone, are also the most likely group to commit violent crimes. The effect of testosterone on aggression is also well known from its role in animal behaviour. A castrated cat or dog is much less aggressive than an entire one.

Figure 1.14 Reducing testosterone levels by castration is often used to reduce aggression in pet, farm and zoo animals.

Roman emperors employed eunuchs – castrated males – to make them unlikely to rebel. Investigating the role of testosterone in human aggression using castration is not, however, an option. Instead, investigations rely on animal studies or on measuring testosterone levels and correlating this with reported or observed indicators of aggression.

Olweus *et al.* (1980) measured blood testosterone level in 16-year-old boys and assessed aggression using a questionnaire. Higher levels of self-reported physical and verbal aggression were associated with higher levels of testosterone. Whilst such differences are well documented, there are exceptions to this pattern. People with high levels of testosterone are not exclusively driven towards violence. Their energy and drive may alternatively be directed towards sport or success in their chosen career. If testosterone were the major force behind aggression, we would expect all men to be aggressive and for women not to be. This obviously isn't the case, as there are aggressive women and non-aggressive men. This suggests that the relationship between testosterone and aggression is not a simple one; other factors must clearly be involved. Since the relationship between testosterone and aggression is correlational, we cannot be sure that high testosterone levels are even *causing* aggressive behaviour or whether both high testosterone and high levels of aggression are the consequence of some other factor.

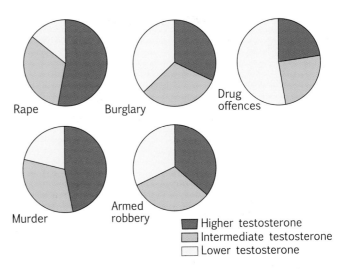

Figure 1.16 Testosterone levels in violent and non-violent male prisoners (based on Dabbs *et al.,* 1995).

Figure 1.15 Are boys biologically destined to be aggressive?

Experiments with male animals have shown that castration reduces aggression and that injecting testosterone reinstates aggressive behaviour (Beeman, 1947). Early castration generally has the lasting effect of reducing aggression, apparently changing the animal's predisposition permanently. If, however, testosterone is repeatedly administered to castrated animals they will eventually become aggressive. These findings suggest that testosterone has two roles, firstly to prime the individual for behaving aggressively (for example, by changing its nervous system) and secondly to initiate aggressive responses. This interpretation is supported by evidence showing that injected testosterone also increases aggression between females (Van de Poll *et al.*, 1988).

There is usually, but not always, a direct link between testosterone levels and aggression in animals. Is this the case in humans? Although men are typically more aggressive than women, and more likely to pick a fight for no apparent reason (Bettencourt & Miller, 1996), women do demonstrate as much aggression as men when they are seriously provoked. Unsurprisingly, Dabbs *et al.* (1995) found that male prison inmates who had committed violent crimes had higher levels of testosterone than those committing non-violent crimes (see Figure 1.16). Interestingly, Dabbs & Hargrove (1997) found the same relationship in female prisoners. These patterns, however, were not strong, indicating the other factors are also at work – the control of behaviour, including aggressive behaviour, is simply more complex in humans than in animals. In a series of experimental studies with students, Dabbs *et al.* (2001) demonstrated that individuals with high testosterone levels were more assertive, direct and confident in their interactions with other people. This finding could explain the prevalence of the most cold-hearted and premeditated murders among the prisoners with the highest testosterone levels.

The role of the brain

The findings from Van de Poll *et al.* (1988) suggest that testosterone affects early development and influences the tendency of an animal to become aggressive later. One way in which such an effect might operate is through the 'priming' of neural systems. Testosterone may influence brain development such that the individual is more inclined towards aggressive responses. A range of experimental evidence confirms that there are indeed specific brain areas involved in aggressive responses and that these may be sensitive to testosterone levels during development.

Early research into the control of aggressive behaviour indicated that the hypothalamus was important. Bard (1929) showed that decorticate cats (ones with their cortex removed) were overly aggressive, responding to the slightest provocation with arched backs, growling, hissing and bared teeth. This 'sham rage' could not, however, be elicited if the hypothalamus had also been removed. More recent research has shown that stimulation of the ventromedial hypothalamus leads to the spontaneous production of aggressive responses (Siegel & Pott, 1988). These findings suggested that the hypothalamus plays a role in the expression of aggressive behaviours.

The amygdala, an area of the brain close to the hypothalamus, is also involved in aggression. Direct stimulation of an area of the amygdala in hamsters produces aggressive behaviour (Potegal *et al.*, 1996b). This area is also involved in real aggression. When an animal attacks another (such as a hamster defending its territory) it stays on 'red alert' for about half an hour and is more likely to attack than it would be normally. Potegal *et al.* (1996a) found that the same area of the amygdala that produces aggression when stimulated was more active during this period of 'red alert'. People seem to respond in a similar way. We too are 'armed' to be more aggressive for 5–20 minutes after being provoked (Potegal, 1994).

Lesioning the amygdala in animals reduces aggressive behaviour. This finding led to attempts to control severe cases of human aggressive behaviour with a surgical procedure to remove the amygdala (amygdalectomy). Although moderately successful in reducing aggressive behaviour, Aggleton (1993) questions whether the operation can be justified, since it is not always effective and leaves patients so emotionally unreactive that they can appear sedated.

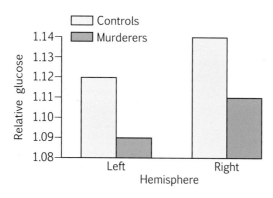

a

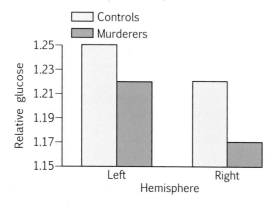

b

Figure 1.17 The level of brain activity indicated by the rate of use of glucose in murderers compared to controls.

Clearly experimental research on humans cannot use lesioning as a method. However, the role of different brain areas in criminal behaviour can be investigated using brain scanning. One of the studies you may have learned about at AS was Raine *et al.*'s (1997) investigation of brain abnormalities in murderers.

Raine *et al.* compared patterns of brain activity in murderers (who had been charged with murder or manslaughter and had been convicted) with a sample of non-murderers matched for age and sex. Of the 39 murderers, two were women and six had a diagnosis of schizophrenia; this was also matched in the control group. Using Positron Emission Tomography (PET), they identified differences in activity levels in several brain areas. In the lateral and medial prefrontal cortex the murderers showed much less activity (see Figures 1.17 a and b). Other areas showing differences included the amygdala, thalamus and hippocampus. In some areas, such as the thalamus and the area surrounding the hippocampus, there was a difference in lateralisation. In both cases the murderers' brains were more active on the right than the left. In the control participants' brains, there was equal activity in both sides of the thalamus and in the hippocampus the pattern was opposite to that of the murderers, that is, there was more activity on the left.

The areas identified as having abnormal activity are associated with a lack of fear, lowered self-control, increased aggression and impulsive behaviours, and problems with controlling and expressing emotions. All of these could lead to an increased risk of committing acts of extreme violence. They are also linked to problems with learning conditioned emotional responses and failure to learn from experiences which could account for the type of violent offences committed. Finally, effects on areas associated with learning could lower IQ, which links to lower chances of employment and a higher risk of criminality.

The role of neurotransmitters

As you will recall from AS, communication between neurones is achieved by neurotransmitters and particular groups of neurones often operate using the same neurotransmitter. One neurotransmitter, serotonin, is associated with aggressive behaviour. Specifically, low levels of serotonin turnover (how quickly it is recycled after use) are linked with higher aggression. In a laboratory experiment with mice, Valzelli (1973) showed that males with lower serotonin levels were more likely to fight when put together. Furthermore, Valzelli & Bernasconi (1979) demonstrated differences in serotonin levels between more and less aggressive strains of mice.

In a natural-environment study of rhesus monkeys, Higley *et al.* (1996) found that those males with the lowest serotonin levels were most likely to fight, had the most scars and wounds and were more likely to be dead by age six years than those with the highest serotonin levels. The aggressive monkeys were more likely to pick fights with opponents they could not possibly beat and to take other risks such as jumping from trees higher than seven metres!

Figure 1.18 Rhesus monkeys with low serotonin levels take risks such as jumping from great heights and picking more fights.

Serotonin seems to be important in people too. For example, Virkkunen *et al.* (1987) found that violent offenders had a lower than average serotonin turnover. They were also more likely to commit further violent crimes after their release from prison (Virkkunen *et al.*, 1989). Such findings link to genetic research. For example, Chen *et al.* (1994) found that mice with a mutation that caused reduced release of serotonin were more aggressive. However, the relationship is not a simple one. Brunner *et al.* (1993) studied a Dutch family, many of whom were aggressive. The antisocial behaviour of members of this family was linked to a mutation of the gene for monoamine oxidase type-A (MAO-A), the enzyme which breaks down serotonin. Since the mutation was associated with a *lack* of this enzyme, logically it should have produced a *reduction* in aggression as it would be more difficult for the body to dispose of serotonin.

Interactive angles

1. To what extent do you think it would be useful and appropriate for courts to use evidence from serotonin turnover to decide whether to give violent prisoners parole? Explain the reasoning behind your answer.

2. Serotonin levels can be altered by dietary control. Serotonin is manufactured in the body from the amino acid tryptophan but high levels of another amino acid, phenylalanine, make it difficult for the body to obtain tryptophan as they share a 'transporter'. Moeller *et al.* (1996) showed that young men on an unbalanced diet like this became more aggressive within hours of eating. The artificial sweetener aspartame (Nutrasweet) is high in phenylalanine and low in tryptophan. What would you recommend about suitable diets for people with aggressive tendencies?

Discussion of biological explanations of aggression

Early evidence suggested a role for genes in the control of aggressive behaviour, and subsequent research has confirmed this. However, this does not mean that genes *control* aggression but that there is a genetic influence on aggressive behaviour. We have neither identified all the genes involved in aggressive responses, nor concluded that genetic influences alone are the cause of aggressive behaviour – even in animals.

Whilst evidence relating to some of the probable routes through which genes may act, such as priming brain development or altering neurotransmitter levels, has been found, this is incomplete. Furthermore, some evidence, such as that relating to the role of genes controlling serotonin levels, is contradictory. Similarly, although testosterone undoubtedly influences aggressive behaviour, its relationship to levels of aggression is unclear. Finally, many brain areas have been identified which play a role in the expression of aggression, but the extent to which any one is responsible for aggressive behaviour is difficult to establish. This is especially so because there are different types of aggressive behaviour in both animals and humans and these are controlled in different ways.

The social approach: the self-fulfilling prophecy

You may recall from the social approach in your AS that people hold **stereotyped** beliefs that affect their behaviour towards other people. Since a stereotype is based on simplistic views about a group, the judgements they lead to are often incorrect. For example, believing that every young person in a hoodie top is a thug is clearly incorrect. However, holding such a belief would lead someone to respond negatively towards young people dressed that way, perhaps avoiding them, shouting at them or jumping to conclusions about their activities. So, as a consequence of holding stereotyped beliefs, a person may apply them and falsely label others.

The self-fulfilling prophecy (SFP) suggests that the stereotypes held by an observer can affect the behaviour of the observed. If an observer holds false beliefs about another person or group, these can affect the way the observer behaves towards them. The observer may respond in ways that are likely to elicit the expected behaviour from the observed individual. This would, of course, confirm their expectations and reinforce their stereotype.

What's that?

- **Stereotyping:** the tendency to apply commonly believed, oversimplified views, for example, from the media, to all members of a group

With regard to antisocial or criminal behaviour, the SFP suggests that this would arise if the observer expects others to behave in antisocial ways. This expectation causes them to behave towards the observed in ways that elicit such behaviour because their stereotyped beliefs change the way they interact socially. As a consequence, the anticipated antisocial actions are demonstrated, confirming the initial beliefs. For example, a new boy at a school seems to the teachers to be a real troublemaker. As a result, they come down on him hard at the first opportunity. He can see that he is being treated differently from the other children, so reacts badly. The teachers' initial response to him was the trigger for his subsequent antisocial behaviour.

Figure 1.19
When other people expect us to behave badly, we do.

The self-fulfilling prophecy can also explain recidivism. Once an individual has the label of 'criminal' it becomes hard to shift. As people reinforce the label by their behaviour, it becomes part of the individual's self-concept, producing further deviant behaviour. In this sense we should be wary of labelling a child as a 'problem' too early, as this may precipitate a worsening of their behaviour.

As with many areas of criminal psychology, it is difficult to obtain valid evidence in an ethical way. One approach is to observe the effect of naturalistic situations that could lead to self-fulfilling behaviours. Levy & Hartocollis (1976) compared the incidence of antisocial behaviour in two psychiatric units, one staffed by women, the other with both male and female staff. Over one year, the unit staffed by women had no instances of violence, compared to 13 in the unit with a mixed staff. This suggests that the expectation of violence, and the consequent use of male nurses, may have led to the violent incidents as patients' behaviour fulfilled expectations because staff on the units behaved differently towards them. However, this conclusion may be flawed if the differing staffing policies on the units were based on actual differences in risk of violence.

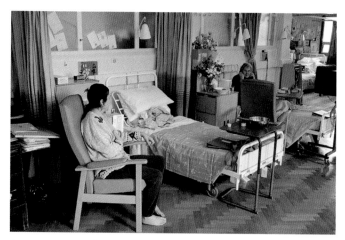

Figure 1.20 A 'heavy-handed' approach to controlling psychiatric patients can lead to violent behaviour.

In a more direct, but also naturalistic, study, Jahoda (1954) investigated the incidence of aggression in the children of the Ashanti people. It is traditional for them to give their male children 'soul names' according to the day of the week on which they were born. They believe that a boy's day of birth affects his character; 'Monday' boys being placid and 'Wednesday' boys being aggressive. Over five years, Jahoda found that 22% of violent offences were committed by boys with 'Wednesday' names but only 7% by 'Monday' boys. This suggests that the cultural expectations about the boys' natures and the explicit labels – their names – resulted in differential treatment of the boys. As a result, the boys fulfilled the expected differences.

Ageton & Elliott (1974) suggested that treatment of youth offenders by the police and courts could lead to further deviance. In a longitudinal study they found that of boys who exhibited delinquent behaviour, those who avoided apprehension had higher self-esteem and less delinquent views of themselves. This can be explained by SFP through the exposure of those boys who were caught to the negative responses of others (for example, from their families, the police or in court). Such responses from others would have led to the boys to exhibit behaviours in line with their 'criminal' label. Alternatively, the difference in self-esteem may be accounted for by the kudos allied to avoiding arrest, enhancing self-esteem in those who were not caught.

Figure 1.21 Negative experiences with the criminal justice service can lead to lowered self-esteem and further criminal behaviour.

In a more recent longitudinal study, Madon et al. (2003) assessed mothers' expectations of their teenage children's underage drinking. They found that when mothers held erroneous beliefs about their children's future drinking habits, these were likely to be fulfilled. Of course, it is possible that the mothers were simply very good judges of their offspring's likely future behaviour rather than being the cause of it.

Figure 1.22 If mothers expect their children to drink under age, they do.

In addition to the problems of alternative interpretations of the findings of those studies which appear to support SFP, there is also some evidence which contradicts it. Zebrowitz & Andreoletfi (1998) investigated whether baby-faced adolescent boys, who observers would stereotypically expect to be 'nice but weak', fulfilled this expectation. An analysis of their actual behaviour showed that, contrary to the predictions of SFP, they were *more* likely to commit crimes, suggesting other factors are also important in the development of criminal behaviour.

Interactive angles

Use the Internet to find out about the policy for making offenders on community service orders wear jackets which say 'Community Payback' on them.

To what extent does this seem like a good idea?

Figure 1.23

Gibbs (1974) investigated the potentially self-fulfilling effect of going to court and therefore being exposed to negative expectations. However, unlike Ageton & Elliott, the findings did not support this conclusion. Comparing people on criminal charges who had or had not appeared in court, Gibbs found little difference in self-esteem, suggesting that the responses of observers had not affected them.

Studying eyewitness testimony

Eyewitnesses are individuals who have (knowingly or unknowingly) seen a crime or a situation that could contribute to the apprehension of criminals. They report evidence to the police and may also do so in court. The reliability of these testimonies is crucial to the criminal justice system. Psychologists are therefore concerned with the accuracy of eyewitness reports, factors that can reduce their accuracy and procedures to improve their reliability.

Figure 1.24 Eyewitnesses to the shooting of Jean Charles de Menezes gave different reports.

The accuracy of recall is clearly of great importance to the criminal justice process. The reports given by victims of crime, eyewitnesses and the police are all vulnerable to error. For example, in 2005, Jean Charles de Menezes was mistaken for a terrorist by police officers and was shot dead at Stockwell Underground station in London. Many of the eyewitness reports of the events were contradictory, for example, reporting 3, 5, 8 or 11 shots being fired.

Interactive angles

Use the Internet to find reports about the death of Jean Charles de Menezes and identify some of the differences between testimonies.

You may wish to start with Wikipedia to find out a little more about the case or read reports such as:

- http://www.guardian.co.uk/attackonlondon/story/0,16132,1534138,00.html
- http://observer.guardian.co.uk/focus/story/0,6903,1548808,00.html
- http://www.theage.com.au/articles/2005/08/17/1123958126875.html?from=top5

For the evidence generated by psychological research to be of use to the criminal justice system, it must be valid and credible. There are a number of different ways to investigate eyewitness testimony, for example, using laboratory experiments, field experiments or case studies, each of which has advantages and disadvantages. In her research into the way eyewitnesses' memories can be altered by encounters with misleading information, Elizabeth Loftus has used mainly laboratory experiments to create situations that simulate aspects of crime scenes in order to find out how post-event information, that is, information provided after a memory has been encoded, can supplement, remove or change existing memories.

One such study, Loftus & Zanni (1975), explored the effect of leading questions on recall of car accidents. In the first of two experiments, 100 students watched a short film which included a multiple car accident in which a car makes a right-hand turn into the main stream of traffic causing a multiple car crash. Participants were then asked for a free recall report of the events on the film and filled in a 22-item questionnaire with six key questions. These used either the definite article 'the' or the indefinite article 'a'; for example, 'Did you see the stop sign?' or 'Did you see a stop sign?' Of these questions, three related to items present in the film and three to objects that were not present (for example, a broken headlight). Experiment 2 was identical, except that a different film and sample were used. The participants, aged 14–20, were selected from people in a public library. This film showed a minor collision between a car backing out of a parking space in a car park and a pedestrian with a bag of groceries. Again the participants were more likely to say 'yes' to definite article questions about non-existent objects. Overall, the participants were significantly more likely to answer 'yes', they had seen non-existent objects, to questions using the definite article 'the' (17%) than to questions using the indefinite article 'a' (7%). The definite article also resulted in fewer uncertain or 'I don't know' answers.

The findings of Loftus & Zanni (1975) and many other studies suggest that recall is not simply a process of retrieving the stored memory. Witnesses seem to *reconstruct* the event they have seen and, as a consequence, can incorporate additional 'post-event' information into their original memory of the scene. It is therefore possible that post-event information from discussion with other witnesses, reports in the media, or the wording of questions used in police interviews could affect the accuracy of eyewitness testimonies.

In another experiment investigating the role of leading questions, Loftus & Palmer (1974) explored the way in which a leading question can affect the recall of details *other than* those about which the leading question asked (see Classic Research).

Classic research

Compulsory

Loftus, E.F. & Palmer, J.C. (1974)

'Reconstruction of automobile destruction: an example of the interaction between language and memory'

Journal of Verbal Learning and Verbal Behavior, 13: 585–9

Aim: To investigate the effect of a leading question about a car accident that implies damage on subsequent recall of speed and of damage caused.

Procedure: *Experiment 1* A sample of 45 students were shown clips of traffic accidents. They were then asked a series of questions about the film including one that read 'About how fast were the cars going when they ... each other?' The missing verb was either *smashed*, *collided*, *bumped*, *hit* or *contacted*.

Experiment 2 A sample of 150 students were shown a short film that included a four-second scene of a car accident (which did not include any broken glass) and asked some questions. One third of the participants were asked the critical question 'About how fast were the cars going when they smashed into each other?' A third were asked the same question but with the word 'hit' and the final third were not asked about speed. A week later the participants were given another questionnaire including the critical question 'Did you see any broken glass?'

Results: *Experiment 1* Table 1.3 shows that more severe verbs resulted in higher estimations of speed. This difference was significant at $p \leq 0.005$.

Table 1.3 Speed estimates

verb	mean speed estimate (mph)
smashed	40.5
collided	39.3
bumped	38.1
hit	34.0
contacted	31.8

Experiment 2 Again the estimate of speed was higher for 'smashed' (mean 10.46 mph) than 'hit' (mean 8 mph), a difference that was significant at $p \leq 0.05$.

Table 1.4 Responses to 'Did you see any broken glass?'

	verb condition		
response	smashed	hit	control
yes	16	7	6
no	34	43	44

Table 1.4 shows that with a more severe verb, participants were more likely to report having seen (non-existent) broken glass. A chi-squared test on these data produced an observed value of χ^2 of 7.76 ($df = 2$, $p \leq 0.025$), a significant difference. The probability of saying 'yes' to the broken glass question is 0.32 [16/(16 +34)] for 'smashed' but only 0.14 [7/(7+43)] for 'hit'.

Table 1.5 Probability of saying 'yes' to 'Did you see any broken glass?'

	speed estimate (mph)			
verb	1–5	6–10	11–15	16–20
smashed	0.09	0.27	0.41	0.62
hit	0.06	0.09	0.25	0.50

An analysis was also conducted of the speed estimates of participants saying 'yes' to the broken glass question, that is those who were misled by the verbs, in order to find out whether the verbs were affecting more than just the speed estimates (see Table 1.5). If all the verb is doing is affecting the judgement of speed, then the probability of saying 'yes'

should be independent of the verb, that is, people giving the same speed estimates should be equally likely to say 'yes'. This is not the case. At each speed participants in the 'smashed' group were more likely to say 'yes', showing that the verb is also having some other effect.

Conclusion: The combined findings of the two experiments show that the leading information of the verb in the speed question affects the way in which the event was represented in memory. Over time, the misleading information from the question was integrated with the original memory so that, at retrieval, the memory was reconstructed to include this new information. This resulted in the inclusion of a false memory of the presence of broken glass as well as speed.

Table 1.6 Critical values for the chi-squared test

df	level of significance for a 2-tailed test			
	0.2	0.1	0.05	0.02
	level of significance for a 1-tailed test			
	0.1	0.05	0.025	0.01
1	2.706	3.841	5.024	6.635
2	4.605	5.991	7.378	9.210
3	6.251	7.815	9.348	11.348

Reconstructed Memories

About how fast were these cars going when they hit each other?

Average speed estimate 34 miles per hour 14% 'recalled' broken glass.

About how fast were these cars going when they smashed into each other?

Average speed estimate 40.5 miles per hour 32% 'recalled' broken glass.

Figure 1.25 People's recollections of car accidents are affected by how questions are worded.

Interactive angles

1. If Loftus & Palmer had conducted a chi-squared test on the data in Table 1.5, how many degrees of freedom (*df*) would there have been?

2. (a) Explain why Loftus & Palmer conducted a chi-squared test on the data in Table 1.4.

   (b) Using Table 1.6, find the critical value for the results in Table 1.4 and explain why this shows that they concluded there was a significant difference.

Loftus & Palmer's study had many methodological strengths. The aim of the study was disguised by 'hiding' the key (leading) question amongst others. This meant that participants would be less likely to guess the aim of the study, that is, it helped to reduce demand characteristics. Being a laboratory study, potential confounding variables, such as time allowed for learning and recall, could all be rigorously controlled, improving reliability. Although in many ways the task lacked mundane realism, by having a week-long gap between seeing the 'incident' and recalling it made the situation more realistic, as witnesses are unlikely to record what they have seen immediately. By combining studies 1 and 2, Loftus & Palmer were able to demonstrate that, not only could a single post-event item (for example, hearing the word *hit* or *smashed*) affect the memory of an object (the presence of broken glass), but also of events (the speed at which the car was travelling).

However, there are also several methodological weaknesses in Loftus & Palmer's study. The same factors that provide scientific rigour and improve reliability can also threaten realism. Eyewitnesses to actual crimes do not see them on video, or as several short excerpts, but as an ongoing part of day-to-day events. According to Moore et al. (1994) the median duration of exposure to a real crime scene is approximately 5–10 minutes. Experimental exposures average just six seconds – so the findings may not generalise well to memory for actual crime scenes where the witness has had longer to process the information and to transfer it to long-term memory.

Participants, especially as they are aware that they are in an experiment, may pay more attention than a witness would and certainly have fewer distractions. Conversely, participants in an experimental setting are likely to be less motivated and aroused than eyewitnesses seeing a real car accident, so their reactions may not be representative, especially as emotional state is known to affect recall. Consider also how the seriousness and consequences of a real crime differ from those of videoed simulation. Whilst this may be true, Loftus (1979a) failed to prevent the distortion of memories by offering participants a $25 reward if their recall about an incident was accurate.

Figure 1.26 Verbal labels, like 'chairs' and 'tables', help us to recognise what we have seen.

Finally, the participants used by Loftus were university students – a relatively narrow sample in terms of demographic characteristics such as age, education and cultural group. These issues raise doubts about the credibility of such research as the findings may not generalise well and, as such, are of questionable help to the criminal justice

system. Indeed, Clifford & Lloyd-Bostock (1983) suggest that in order for findings to generalise so that they are useful to the legal system, they should be reliable across different populations, testing situations, experimental materials and research methods.

However, Loftus & Palmer's findings are similar to those of many other studies both conducted in similar and different ways. For example, Carmichael et al. (1932) used verbal labels to change participants' recall of simple diagrams. More recently, Lupyan (2008) investigated the effect of verbal labels on memory for pictures of furniture from an IKEA catalogue. The participants were slower to recognise items they had seen amongst other pictures when they had been given a category name. Lupyan suggests that this is because it made it harder to remember the details which made the 'table' or 'chair' they had seen different from the others.

On the basis of evidence such as Loftus's studies, the Devlin Report (1976) recommended that the judges should tell the jury that convictions based on a single eyewitness testimony are generally unacceptable (for example, there should be substantial corroborative evidence). However, the report also observed that there was a gap between the academic research and the practical needs of the law and that psychological research was not sufficiently tailored to the requirements of the judicial process to form the basis for changes in procedures.

Many other studies using leading questions have reported similar findings to Loftus & Palmer supporting the general principle that misleading information can cause the reconstruction of memories. An alternative interpretation is that the participants' memories have not been permanently altered but that they are simply following the suggestions provided by the questions. This would account for some contradictory evidence showing that eyewitnesses cannot always be misled. For example, Loftus (1979b) failed to mislead 98 out of 100 participants with an incorrect suggestion relating to a slide of a man stealing a red purse from a woman's bag. Most of the participants who then read an account which referred to a brown purse still recalled the colour correctly.

Laboratory experiments and eyewitness testimony

The various studies of eyewitness effectiveness conducted by Loftus and her co-workers illustrate the use of the laboratory experiment as a research method. A laboratory experiment creates a situation in which one (or more) variable(s) are altered whilst all others are kept constant. This is possible as laboratory conditions allow the researcher to deliberately manipulate the independent variable (IV) – this is what makes a true experiment. The effect of the IV on the dependent variable (DV) can be measured accurately. In the case of studies of eyewitnesses, an aspect of the witnesses' experience is manipulated and the accuracy of their recall is measured. Other variables, such as the length of exposure to the 'crime scene', the ease with which each individual can see the events and the time over which they have to remember details, are kept the same. The deliberate manipulation of the IV and level of control mean that cause and effect relationships can be investigated.

In experiments on eyewitness testimony, the experimental design is usually independent groups. For example, in Loftus & Palmer (1974) different participants heard each of the verbs and in Loftus & Zanni (1975) they had questions using either the definite article ('the') or indefinite article ('a'). Participants would be more likely to guess the aims if they experienced each level of the IV. Demand characteristics are cues that give away what the study is about. Once participants are aware of this, their own opinions about what should happen will affect the results.

In addition to setting up experimental conditions it is also possible to have a control group – a condition in which the IV is absent. This acts as a baseline against which changes in the DV in the experimental group(s) are measured. Experiment 2 of Loftus & Palmer's study used a control group: two experimental groups were asked questions using 'smashed' and 'hit' but another group – the controls – were not asked about speed after seeing the film. All three groups were subsequently asked about broken glass. In all other respects the participants' experience was identical.

The DV is generally measured using questionnaires given to participants after viewing the film. These typically include a small number of short answer or yes/no questions that measure the DV and some filler questions. As a result they generate quantitative data which can be analysed using inferential statistics although qualitative data may also be collected.

The laboratory experiment is characterised by scientific rigour. Each level of the IV should be identical except for the variable being tested. This is achievable in a laboratory but would be much harder in a real-world situation. The researcher also aims to measure the DV objectively, that is, to record what is really there rather than what they expect or would like to find. By using measures such as answers to closed questions, the researcher removes the possibility of being subjective, that is, avoids the influence of their personal point of view. These aspects of a laboratory experiment gives the researcher greater confidence about the validity of their investigation – they are likely to be measuring what they set out to.

Other threats to validity include possible bias caused by experimenter effects (for example, when the experimenter has a strong expectation of what their study will show which they unconsciously communicate to the participants). This can be reduced using standardised instructions. Blind or double blind procedures also reduce experimenter effects, but these are rarely used in experiments on eyewitness testimony. The effect of demand characteristics can be minimised by giving participants as little information about the aims of the study as is possible ethically (or deceiving them about the aims), by using an independent measures design and by using filler questions to disguise the real purpose of the study.

The controls used in laboratory experiments and precise measures of the DV also contribute to reliability. By ensuring that participants are treated in the same way, researchers can be confident that their results are reliable. For example, the procedures can be easily repeated with other groups of participants. Indeed, the second experiment in Loftus & Palmer's study produced very similar findings to the first.

Ethically, participants should have enough information to give their real consent to participate. In practice it may be necessary to hide some aspects of the aim or the procedure in order to achieve high validity. To overcome this problem, participants should be given the right to withdraw at any time and be fully debriefed after the study. Furthermore, any procedure should be checked with an ethical committee to ensure that it is not expected to cause distress to the participants. Although the studies you have read about are unlikely to cause distress, using more realistic video footage or staging real crimes could be highly stressful.

An important practical disadvantage with using a laboratory experiment is that in unnatural conditions people may not act normally. This issue has two aspects. Firstly, watching a video and answering a small number of specific questions doesn't represent the challenge to witnesses presented by giving a statement to the police. In this respect such studies lack mundane realism, that is, the task is unrealistic. Secondly, the findings may not generalise beyond the laboratory setting, that is, there is a lack of ecological validity. This is in part due to a lack of mundane realism but also because the situation is unrepresentative. For example seeing a film in the safety of a lab doesn't produce the same level of arousal or motivation that a real scene would do. If levels of arousal and motivation are important to memory, then the findings may not generalise to real crimes.

Another possible problem with laboratory studies using an independent groups design is that of underlying differences between the participants in different levels of the IV. This could confound the results by obscuring or exaggerating differences between levels of the IV, for example, if the people in one group happen to be more observant, have better memories or get distracted more easily. A simple way to try to reduce this risk is to randomly allocate participants to each condition.

Interactive
angles

If you used *Angles on Psychology* for AS, look back at the descriptions of Loftus (1975) – the 'barn' study – and Paterson & Kemp (2006) on co-witness accounts. These were both laboratory experiments; evaluate them in terms of their strengths and weaknesses.

Lindsay (1990) pursued the criticism that, rather than actually altering memory, post-event information simply provides participants with a way to answer questions to which they have (or believe they have) forgotten the answer. First, participants were shown slides of a maintenance man stealing money and a calculator from an office while listening to a women's commentary. They then heard a misleading description of the events they had seen. This description was either

immediate and in the same voice as the original commentary, or delayed by two days and in a male voice. They were finally told (truthfully) that any information in the description was wrong and were given a test of memory. Being told that the information in the description was wrong should have prevented errors if the participants are simply using the post-event information to please the experimenter. However, the results showed that the misleading description could affect memory, but only if it was similar to the source (that is, in the same-day narrative/same-sex condition), suggesting that the effect of post-event information is genuine.

Many criticisms of studies such as Loftus & Palmer and Loftus & Zanni relate to the use of situations which lack realism – films of crimes and limited samples. Imagine how differently witnesses might feel at the scene and about reporting that they had actually witnessed a violent crime. This was the basis of Yuille & Cutshall's study (see Classic Research).

Classic
research

Optional

Yuille, J.C. & Cutshall, J.L. (1986)

'A case study of eyewitness memory of a crime'

Journal of Applied Psychology, 71(2): 291–301

Aim: To investigate the accuracy of recall in eyewitnesses to a real violent crime, over time and in response to leading questions.

Procedure: A sample of 21 witnesses to a real shooting were interviewed by the police. Of these, 13 agreed to a research interview four to five months after the event (aged 15–32, including three females). They saw a fatal shooting in which a thief entered a gun shop, tied up the owner, stole money and guns and left the shop. The owner freed himself and went out to take the thief's car registration. He was shot twice by the thief who was 6 feet (1.83m) away. The thief was killed by the owner with six shots from his revolver.

The accuracy of the witnesses' recall at the later date was compared to their initial testimonies and the effect of leading questions on their reports was assessed. They were asked questions that had been asked during the police interview and ones that had not (as they were not of forensic interest, such as the colour of the blanket over the body). In both the police and research interviews, the witnesses were asked first for a free recall account of what they had seen and were then asked specific questions. The content of these reports were scored for the number of accurate action, person and object descriptions (such as movements or gunshots, age or height and money or gun). The research interview also asked alternative versions of two questions relating to non-existent objects (a/the yellow panel on the car and, as is in Loftus & Zanni (1975), a/the broken headlight). Witnesses also self-rated the stress they had felt at the time on a 7-point scale.

Table 1.7 Accuracy of descriptions of people

detail	police interview	research interview
hair colour	77	80
clothing colour	66	59
weight, height, age	50	51
details excluding weight, height, age	82	80

Table 1.8 Average detail recalled

viewpoint	police interview	research interview	accuracy
central	72	24	85%
peripheral	104	55	79%

Results: The witnesses were very accurate and there was little change in the amount they recalled or their accuracy over time, although some aspects of their description, such as hair colour, age, weight and height estimations, did demonstrate errors (see Table 1.7). The amount of details recalled by the witness depended largely on their position in relation to the incident, with central witnesses recalling more than those with a peripheral viewpoint, especially in relation to action details. There was, however, no significant difference in the accuracy of these two groups (see Table 1.8). The make and colour of the car was fairly well remembered (reports being 83% accurate at the time and

56/57% accurate four to five months later). However, there were important differences between witnesses, for example:

- 12 were within ±1–9% accuracy over four to five months, but one witness's accuracy fell by over 20%

- although very few errors were reported in either the police or research interviews, two thirds that appeared in relation to the shop owner or thief were reported by just two witnesses and two thirds relating to the actions of others were reported by just three witnesses.

- most witnesses incorrectly reported the pattern or number of gunshots. The only accurate witness was familiar with guns and handled the shop owner's gun after the incident, so could have seen how many rounds had been discharged.

- only one witness correctly reported the date and time of the event during the research interview – the shop owner's wife, for whom it was a salient event.

Ten of the witnesses were unaffected by the leading questions (that is, said there was no yellow panel/broken headlight). Of the remainder, one witness had noticed nothing about the car so wasn't asked the question, one answered the control question 'Did you see *a* broken headlight?' by saying he hadn't seen it but thought there was one and the last said 'yes' to the misleading question – the only one to do so. Interestingly, three witnesses reported nonexistent events without misleading questions. Almost 3% of the action details from the police interviews were erroneous, for example, physical contact between the thief and shop owner. The witnesses whose reports included reconstructed memories had more limited viewpoints – they were further away or in a passing car.

Witnesses who reported being more stressed by the incident were more accurate than those who were less stressed (93% compared to 75% in the police interview and 88% compared to 76% in the research interview). However, the more stressed witnesses also had greater contact with the thief, shop owner or a weapon and reported sleeping problems following the event.

Conclusion: Eyewitnesses to real crimes are more accurate, and less influenced by leading questions, than laboratory research would suggest and very stable over time. Importantly, the findings show that a witness can recall one detail incorrectly but provide many other accurate facts so judges should not dismiss witness evidence on the basis of one inaccuracy alone – especially where that detail relates to features such as colours. Little reconstruction of the memory occurs except when the viewpoint is limited.

Figure 1.27 Are witnesses to real crimes as unreliable as mock witnesses?

The findings of Yuille & Cutshall clearly raise issues regarding the validity of evidence from laboratory experiments. The accuracy of Yuille & Cutshall's witnesses and the lack of reconstruction of their memories supports the criticism that laboratory studies lack ecological validity since the findings appear not to generalise to witnesses of real crimes. The witnesses in Yuille & Cutshall's study saw face-to-face action that had real consequences and was both emotional and motivating; these features are generally absent from laboratory studies where the participants are not involved and the events are less dramatic. The procedure of this study also highlights another problem with typical laboratory experiments – that the participants are usually limited to forced choice questions, that is, have to give simplistic yes/no answers. In real situations the witness can provide open answers and express uncertainties – as one of Yuille & Cutshall's eyewitnesses did to the question about the broken headlight.

The crime in Yuille & Cutshall's study was a very striking event – with life and death consequences. In this respect it is untypical of many crimes and, being so unusual, may in fact have elicited flashbulb memories. These are particularly vivid and accurate memories associated with key emotional events

(such as the death of Princess Diana or the events of 9/11). Another possible criticism is that, because it was a real crime, it was reported in the media and frequently repeated and this may have enhanced recall. This is unlikely, however, as the media reports included errors that were not incorporated into the witnesses' memories, the witnesses retained idiosyncratic details over time and their memories for irrelevant details that would not have been repeated, such as the colour of the blanket covering the body, also remained very accurate.

One disadvantage of field studies such as Yuille & Cutshall's is that it is much harder to achieve scientific rigour as variables cannot be so easily controlled. However, considerable efforts were made to ensure the validity and reliability of the data collected. Facts about the crime scene were ascertained using information from the police, witnesses, ambulance crew, forensic evidence and the research team's own observations. Three researchers independently reconstructed a logically possible sequence and these were combined into a verifiable description of the event. This was used to assess the accuracy of the participants' reports. This ensured a fair baseline for scoring and a high degree of reliability – the inter-rater variance was less than 2%. Since the researchers developed their own scoring system, it is possible that they inflated the witnesses' accuracy. However, this too is unlikely. The scoring system was very stringent and it is more likely that any errors in scoring reflected an *underestimation* of recall, for example they accepted a tolerance of only ± 2 inches or years for height and age estimations and none at all for the number of shots fired or the date of the incident.

An entirely different problem relating to the design of the study was that the research reports were not gathered until four to five months after the event. Whilst this was useful to see how the testimonies changed over time, by comparing immediate police interviews to subsequent research interviews, this introduces a possible confound – that the nature of the interviews and interviewers differed. Furthermore, it is possible that the absence of an effect of misleading questions arose because they were not used immediately after the incident, but in the research interviews

several months later, by which time the memories may have become more stable. Thus the conclusion that real witnesses are resistant to reconstruction may be flawed.

Whilst it is possible for the police to avoid using leading questions, not all sources of possible post-event information can be removed. The very fact that a witness is interviewed tells them that there have been serious consequences from the event they saw. Similarly, a witness may be affected by subsidiary information from the scene, such as the presence of ambulances (which may be called to accidents regardless of the certainty of any injuries). These sources of information may affect the individual's beliefs about the event and hence influence the way that their memory of the scene is reconstructed. Kebbell *et al.* (2002) investigated the effect of such beliefs on the accuracy of eyewitness testimonies (see Research Now).

Research now

Optional

Kebbell, M.R., Johnson, S.D., Froyland, I. & Ainsworth, M. (2002)

'The influence of belief that a car crashed on witnesses' estimates of civilian and police car speed'

Journal of Psychology, 136(6): 597–607

Aim: To investigate the effects of believing that a car crashed and whether it was a civilian car or a police car with flashing lights and sirens on the accuracy of estimates of vehicle speed by witnesses.

Table 1.9 Accuracy of recall of civilian car

detail	no crash	crash
speed (mph)	43	42
confidence	4.31	4.18
dangerousness	2.93	3.18
risk of crash	3.00	3.53
risk of fatality	4.18	4.18

Procedure: In Experiment 1, the participants were 33 prospective undergraduates, eight males, 25 females, aged 17–56. They watched a one-minute video, which they were told was from a security camera showing a street and a car being driven along it and past the camera. Half were then told that the vehicle subsequently crashed; the others that it came to a halt. They were shown a corresponding photograph of a car (from police files) which was either undamaged or with a damaged front that could have been caused by hitting another vehicle. Experiment 2 was identical except that different participants were used and the car in the video was a police car using its siren and flashing lights. The participants were 41 prospective undergraduates, six males, 35 females, aged 17–69. They were then shown exactly the same photos as above but the vehicle was a police car.

In each case, the participants were asked questions which they answered on a 10-point Likert-style scale. The questions asked were: 'How dangerous was the way that the vehicle was being driven?' (rated from *not at all dangerous* (1) to *extremely dangerous* (10)), 'How likely was a crash?' and 'How likely was the driver to kill someone?' (rated from *not at all likely* (1) to *extremely likely* (10)). They were also asked about their confidence in their judgements (rated from *pure guess* (1) to *absolutely certain* (10)). Finally, the participants were debriefed.

Table 1.10 Accuracy of recall of police car

detail	no crash	crash
speed (mph) *	51	64
confidence	3.47	3.13
dangerousness	4.12	5.13
risk of crash [†]	2.88	5.33
risk of fatality [†]	2.88	5.25

*significant difference at $p \leq 0.01$

[†]significant difference at $p \leq 0.001$

Results: In Experiment 1 there was no significant difference between the estimates of the vehicle's speed by the two groups (or any other variable).

In Experiment 2, however, participants who had been told that the car had crashed overestimated the police car's speed, the likelihood of a crash, and the likelihood of someone being killed. Participants who were not told that the vehicle crashed estimated the speed of the vehicle accurately (it was 49.7 mph). The participants' confidence in their estimates of speed were not significantly different between the two groups.

Conclusion: The effect of post-event information about whether a car crashes only results in an increase in speed estimation for police cars, not civilian ones, suggesting that beliefs about the differences between police and civilian drivers may be important. Specifically, that police drivers are highly trained so more safe under normal circumstances, so to have crashed they must have been driving more quickly. This is, however, only an inference. Alternatively, witnesses may associate sirens and flashing lights with high-speed chases, thus overestimate speed. Importantly, the results suggest that confidence is unrelated to accuracy.

Figure 1.28 Do flashing lights and wailing sirens affect our judgement of speed?

The findings of Kebbell *et al.* (2002) provide an interesting contrast to Loftus & Palmer, showing that post-event information that suggests greater severity in a car accident does not always result in higher estimates of speed. However, the results relating to the police vehicle do support the general principle of reconstructive memory and several of the findings have important applications. For example, the observation that a witness's confidence is unrelated to their accuracy could be crucial to the police. If an investigator is faced with different testimonies from witnesses and one says they are much more certain, this might be persuasive. However, they may not, in fact, be any more accurate. The findings on witness accuracy from this study should, however, be treated with caution since they were based on speed estimates from viewing a video tape. When viewing moving vehicles in real life there are many other factors (such as sound) which can affect the accuracy of an individual's estimate. Similarly, the course of the car – making progress in a straight line at a constant speed – may be untypical of a vehicle immediately before a crash. This may also reduce the extent to which the findings can be generalised beyond the experimental setting.

On the positive side, Kebbell *et al.* used a relatively naïve population compared to many studies on eyewitness testimony, since they were *prospective* undergraduates. This clearly matters, as psychology students may already be aware of the effects of leading questions, so would be more likely to be affected by demand characteristics. Indeed, Loftus (1979b) found that when participants identified that there were leading questions, they became more suspicious and the effect was much smaller.

Although Kebbell *et al.*'s findings show that knowing a car had crashed does not necessarily cause an increase in speed estimation, it does seem to do so in the case of police vehicles with flashing lights and sirens. This supports anecdotal evidence reported by Kebbell *et al.* that police accident investigators find that witnesses grossly overestimate the speed of police vehicles when flashing lights and sirens are used and a crash occurs. One reason this may arise is because, both in real life and on television, lights and sirens are used when a

vehicle is travelling at high speed. Clearly, the experimental evidence suggests that investigators should be cautious about using eyewitness testimonies in such instances.

So far we have only considered studies using adults as witnesses. However, children may also be required to give evidence, but their reliability is often doubted. If children are reliable, then they could provide a source of under-used eyewitness evidence. Sadly, children are sometimes the victims of crimes, such as sexual abuse, and finding ways to ensure that the evidence they provide is reliable is clearly of great importance.

According to Brennan & Brennan (1988), 6–15-year-olds failed to understand one third of questions asked by lawyers in court. Experimental studies also suggest that children's memories are unreliable. Lewis *et al.* (1995) investigated the effect of leading questions on children aged three to four years. They were shown photographs of adult males arranged like a line-up. One of these was labelled 'Daddy' (none was actually their father). When the children were subsequently asked 'Is this man your daddy?' in a sequence of pictures, 29% misidentified the previously labelled individual as 'daddy'. On one hand, this shows that child witnesses are susceptible to the effects of leading questions. On the other hand, it also shows that the number affected by this manipulation is relatively small.

Carter *et al.* (1996) looked at the effect of the style of spoken language used in the courtroom (legalese). Children aged five to seven were more likely to answer incorrectly if asked a question in legalese (such as 'To the best of your knowledge, X, in fact, kissed you, didn't she?') than if they were asked a simpler question (for example, 'X kissed you, didn't she?'). Note that the use of 'didn't she?' (a 'tag') in both of these questions makes them leading which, as we have seen, is likely to increase errors. These are clearly examples of the kinds of questions that could be used in cases of alleged child sexual abuse. The role of such tags in questions aimed at children in abuse cases was investigated by Krackow & Lynn (2003) (see *Research Now*).

Research now

Krackow, E. & Lynn, S.J. (2003)

'Is there touch in a game of Twister? The effects of innocuous touch and suggestive questions on children's eyewitness memory'

Law and Human Behavior, 27(6): 589–604

Aim: To investigate whether leading questions affect children's recall of real-life events.

Procedure: 48 children aged four years to five years ten months were recruited using advertisements in paediatrician's offices, pre-schools and birth announcements in local newspapers. They participated, with their parents' consent, in a field experiment in which they played Twister and a game called Shapes. There were two conditions in which children were either touched (on their hands, arms, calves or feet) or were not touched by an assistant ('Amy'). The children were randomly assigned to one of the four possible groups (touched/not touched, direct question/ tagged question). The parents, but not the children, were told it was a study about memory and asked not to tell the children. The children were asked if they wanted to play a game, so that they could give their consent. They also had their picture taken with 'Amy'.

One week later, the children were prompted to describe everything they could remember. These reports were analysed for content. The children were also asked 30 questions. There were abuse-related questions of two types, for example, either 'Did Amy touch your bottom?' (direct or non-leading) or 'Amy touched your bottom, didn't she?' (leading, because it has the tag 'didn't she?' on the end). They were also asked general forensic questions such as 'Amy took your picture, didn't she?', which were again either tagged (as in this example) or direct. All games and interviews were videoed for analysis.

Results: The children's reports were scored for the number of ideas the children recalled and whether or not these were complete. The inter-observer reliability on these was 0.87 and 1.00 respectively. Where differences arose between observers, they discussed these to resolve them.

In their free recall, the children who had heard tagged questions recalled significantly more ($p \leq 0.05$), but there was no significant effect of physical contact during play on the children's answers.

In the analysis of the answers to abuse-related questions, significantly more children said 'yes' to tagged questions than to direct ones (significant at $p \leq 0.0001$). Whilst the children hearing direct questions answered 98% of questions correctly, the children who were asked tagged questions appeared to be answering randomly (being correct only 44% of the time). Children asked tagged questions were also significantly more likely to incorrectly agree with general forensic questions ($p \leq 0.01$). As with the free recall evidence, there was no significant effect of touch on accuracy.

Conclusions: The use of tags on questions make child witnesses less accurate. Using direct questions leads to a higher degree of accuracy in both abuse-related and general forensic questions. This is important to ensure that interviews of children giving evidence in abuse cases do not use tagged questions. However, it also suggests that innocuous touch is unlikely to create false memories and therefore unlikely to lead to false accusations of abuse.

Figure 1.29 Playing Twister provides a realistic context.

Compared to laboratory experiments, Krackow & Lynn's field experiment is more realistic. Unlike experiments in laboratory settings, the children were unaware that they were participants in a study – they thought that they were playing a game with 'Amy'. Their responses would therefore have been more like those of real witnesses, as they would not have been affected by trying to do what they thought the experimenter 'wanted'. Even so, the events in experimental situations were very different from a child's actual experience of sexual abuse. The children were unafraid and unharmed, for example, and both fear and pain can influence the reliability of memory. This, of course, was essential in order

to protect the child participants and in this respect the study succeeded in investigating a socially sensitive area of research in an ethical way. Furthermore, the confederate 'Amy' was unknown to the children, whereas in reality the perpetrators of child abuse are often familiar people.

In dealing with a sensitive issue, Krackow & Lynn made many efforts to ensure the study was ethical. Both parents and children gave their consent and the parents saw the questions in advance, so they were in no doubt about the nature of the study. Three parents did refuse to allow their children to be asked about being kissed and being touched on the bottom.

These children were not asked those questions or were withdrawn from the study.

There were also methodological strengths to Krackow & Lynn's study. The children were randomly assigned to the four groups, to limit the effect of participant variables on the findings. Participation in the games (Twister or Shapes) was counterbalanced, as was the order of the questions about the games in the follow-up. This helped to ensure that any effects of the order of activities and questions did not influence the results. In the game of Twister, the moves were predetermined so that it was possible to ensure that every child in the *Touch* condition was touched in the same place on their body at the same point in the game. The movements were also identical for the children in the *No Touch* condition, but the experimenter's hand was put beside the child's rather than touching them. This controlled for the proximity between the experimenter and child. To ensure that the amount of touching that the children felt was the same, the female participants were asked to wear trousers.

Interactive angles

You can find out more about the work of Beth Loftus on eyewitness testimony from her websites. Try to explain the findings of other studies in terms of the effect of misleading information:

● http://faculty.washington.edu/eloftus/index.htm

Another source of information abut criminal psychology is Gary Wells' website. This includes an interactive eyewitness testimony simulation:

● http://www.psychology.iastate.edu/faculty/gwells/homepage.htm

Police officers have to interview witnesses who often can't seem to recall much about the perpetrators.

How might they try to elicit more, or more accurate, information?

how science works — Research Methods

Field experiments

An alternative to carrying out experiments on eyewitness testimony in the lab is to carry them out in participants' normal environment, that is, in a setting where they would expect to encounter the experimental situation. This research method is a field experiment. Like a laboratory experiment, it is a true experiment. The researcher sets up the levels of the independent variable (IV) and measures changes in the dependent variable (DV). The experimental design used can be independent groups or repeated measures. So, even though the researcher is working in the participants' natural setting for the behaviour being investigated, they are still deliberately manipulating the IV and imposing some controls, so cause and effect relationships can still be investigated.

Krackow & Lynn (2003) is an example of a field experiment because they manipulated the IVs of touching or not and asking direct or tagged questions. They used an independent measures design and collected both qualitative and quantitative data. Yuille & Cutshall (1986), in contrast, is not a field experiment but a field study – this is because they did not manipulate an IV.

Validity
In terms of experimental validity, field experiments are likely to be less valid than lab experiments as it is harder for researchers to control extraneous variables, so they can be less certain that they are measuring the variables they set out to. Changes in the DV could be caused by uncontrolled variables in the natural environment. Another factor affecting validity is the awareness of demand characteristics. In Krackow & Lynn's experiment, the children had given consent without knowing the purpose of the 'game' so there was little chance of them working out the aims. This avoided the

risk of the children responding to demand characteristics and improved validity. This does, however, raise a potential ethical issue in field experiments, that of informed consent. If a participant is unaware that they are taking part in a study they cannot give consent. In the case of the children in Krackow & Lynn's study, their parents had consented; however, this is not typical of most field experiments. Generally, participants are informed afterwards, debriefed and given the right to withdraw their data. For this to be sufficient it is important that participation is not very stressful, embarrassing or otherwise likely to mean that participants are less happy after the experiment than before. For this reason, experiments on eyewitness testimony in which a traumatic incident is staged are generally avoided.

Typically, field experiments have better ecological validity than lab experiments because they are carried out in the participants' normal setting. It is therefore more likely that the results will generalise from the experiment to real life. However, to have really good ecological validity, the experimental tasks need to be similar to those we encounter in real life too, that is, they must have mundane realism. Since children do play games like Twister, do have accidental contact with adults and are asked about what happened when they were playing, Krackow & Lynn's experiment is highly ecologically valid.

Reliability
A disadvantage of field experiments is their relatively low reliability compared to lab experiments. Such studies are hard to replicate because they require unique sets of circumstances that cannot be set up artificially.

Treating offenders

Once an offender has been apprehended and charged, psychologists can also contribute to their rehabilitation. The aim of these strategies is to reduce the risk of reoffending, that is, to prevent recidivism. Ideas from the learning approach and other areas of psychology have contributed here. We will now consider two ways to treat offenders, the use of token economy programmes and anger management interventions.

What's that?

- **recidivism:** repeat offending and the tendency to relapse into crime

Token economy programmes

You may have learned about token economy programmes at AS. It is a way to modify the behaviour that can be used with prison inmates, aggressive criminals on community orders and offenders in high security psychiatric hospitals. It uses operant conditioning to positively reinforce, and therefore increase the frequency of, desired behaviours. These can include non-aggressive and other socially acceptable responses such as helping. These are reinforced with tokens (secondary reinforcers) which can be saved up and exchanged for goods or opportunities such as cigarettes, watching TV or going into the exercise yard (primary reinforcers). Note that these are all 'privileges'; inmates are not required to 'earn' basic rights such as good food, comfortable accommodation or reasonable leisure time. Punishment, such as isolation, may also be used to reduce the frequency of non-desired behaviour such as aggression. Alternatively, tokens may be withheld if undesirable behaviours are demonstrated, which is described as a 'response cost'. In general, positive reinforcement is preferred over punishment as it indicates what to do rather than just what not to do and because it is seen as a more ethical option.

When a token economy programme is used in a prison, all prison officers should be involved. The aim is to give tokens as immediate rewards, which is more effective as they are more readily associated with the desired behaviour than if the reinforcement is delayed. It is also important to ensure that tokens are given consistently and appropriately. Bassett & Blanchard (1977) reported on the failure and subsequent success of a token economy programme through poor and

Box 1.1
Setting up a token economy

- **Tokens:** these have no intrinsic value and should be chosen so that they are easy to carry and give out and difficult to counterfeit. Although they are secondary reinforcers, if they in themselves are attractive, this helps. Commonly used tokens include toy money or poker chips, stickers, marks or punches on a card.

- **Target behaviours:** these should be explicitly defined for both staff and inmates and it should be clear how many tokens are earned (or taken away) for each instance. If possible, the definitions should indicate what behaviour is right, rather than what is wrong, for example, 'being polite and saying thank you' rather than 'don't be rude to others'.

- **Consistency:** there must be sufficient staff to see and respond immediately to behaviours and staff must do so consistently, providing the same value of tokens for the same behaviours. Staff also have a responsibility to ensure that tokens are not being stolen, traded or manufactured. A serious problem in prisons is that powerful prisoners may exert more effective rewards (such as approval) and punishments (for example, threats) than the token economy system can and this too must be monitored.

- **Primary reinforcers:** these must be desired by the inmates – the objects, activities or privileges they can access need to be meaningful if they are to provide motivation. Ideally, the inmates rather than the staff should decide on the primary reinforcers.

- **Exchange system:** secondary reinforcers should be redeemed for primary reinforcers at a set time and place and each primary reinforcer should be of known value and the cost should be relative to desirability. A balance must be reached between reinforcers being inaccessibly difficult versus too easy to earn, as either extreme is demotivating. However, the importance of a primary reinforcer to rehabilitation should also be considered. For example, if an earnable activity will contribute to good socialisation, the value should be lower so that it is more accessible.

- **Recording progress:** Prior to beginning the programme, each individual's baseline behaviour should be assessed. Daily records of behaviours, tokens and primary reinforcers can then be maintained to monitor the person's progress so that they can be given feedback and to evaluate the effectiveness of the system.

- **Schedules and shaping:** initially tokens are readily available (a continuous reinforcement schedule) and accompanied by verbal praise. Periodically, progress should be discussed and the goals (that is, the target behaviours) are reviewed, setting higher standards where possible and reverting to earlier targets if no progress is being made. This allows behaviours to be shaped. Tokens become progressively harder to earn, for example being replaced with just verbal praise (a partial schedule), so that the individuals become less reliant on artificial reinforcers and respond to social reinforcers that are more typical in society.

then improved consistency. Inmates carried a points card that was marked by prison staff according to pre-established behavioural categories to encourage self-management of behaviour. However, during a three-month period when there was no on-site supervision of staff, the points system was misused by staff. This resulted in less emphasis on positively reinforcing appropriate behaviours to one of punishing misbehaviour, partly through the introduction of many more response categories, which resulted in fines.

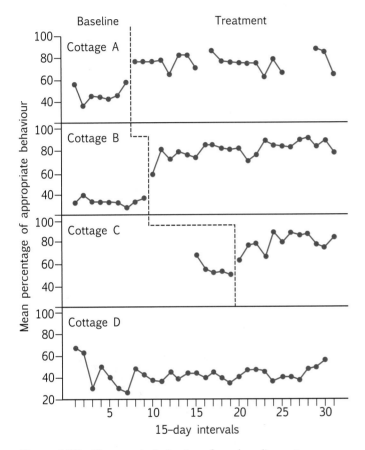

Figure 1.30 Changes in behaviour from baseline rates following a token economy programme. Cottages A, B and C were on the programme, D was the control.

Hobbs & Holt (1976) investigated the effectiveness of a token economy employed with 125 boys detained in a correctional institution for offences ranging from truancy to arson and homicide. Their average age was 14 years and most had six or more criminal charges. They compared boys living in separate accommodation units (cottages), three of which were on the token economy programme and one of which was not and was used as a control. Behaviours such as rule-following, co-operation, being non-violent and not destroying property were targeted. The 17 members of staff in the facility were well trained in the programme. They gave the boys tokens in a reliable way during the day and each evening the cottage supervisor counted up each boy's tokens. The tokens earned secondary reinforcers such as drinks, sweets, toys and cigarettes. They could also be saved in a bank, which paid interest, to exchange for more expensive

reinforcers, such as on- and off-campus recreational activities, trips to football and basketball games, or to purchase a four-day pass home. Release from the facility also depended on the total number of tokens earned. Hobbs & Holt found that the system improved the targeted behaviours in the participating cottages, whilst the behaviour of boys not on the programme remained fairly constant (see Figure 1.30).

The cost of the programme developed by Hobbs & Holt was almost $100 per boy per year, which translates to about £250 now. This reflects the general finding that, although the initial cost to set up a programme is quite high (for example, in terms of staff time, as they have to be present all the time), they are generally relatively cheap to administer, so reflect good value for money.

One criticism often raised about token economies is that they may be abused. Institution staff can choose to reward or punish behaviour in order to make their own lives easier, rather than for the benefit of prison inmates. Hobbs & Holt observed this about their own regime. One target response was 'line behaviour'. The boys earned tokens for good behaviour when they formed a line to walk from their cottage to dinner and back again (staying in a group and in a straight line). This was convenient for the staff but did not contribute to the rehabilitation of the boys. Such instances have been identified as unethical, as the institution is using its power inappropriately.

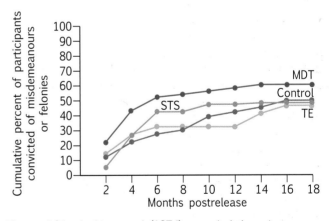

Figure 1.31 Jenkins et al. (1974) recorded the crimes committed by offenders over 18 months postrelease after different correctional options (see text for definitions).

Jenkins et al. (1974) studied young male offenders in the 18-month period after their release from American correctional centres following different programmes. Some were on a manpower development and training programme (MDT), for example, in training as butchers and welders; others in a State Trade School (STS), also directed at vocational training for prison inmates; another group were on a token economy programme (TE); and finally there was a control group (who had applied for training but had been refused). Although some differences in recidivism were found, these were largely nonsignificant. However, as can be seen from Figure 1.31, the token economy group had the lowest percentage of post-release offences. Jenkins *et al.* concluded that, whilst vocational training to enable offenders to work is essential, the training of interpersonal skills and money management (such as can be achieved on token economy programmes) is also critical to their future. One reason why this is important is that tokens can be given immediately, so are effective reinforcers for non-aggressive or co-operative behaviour, whereas the general effect of a prison sentence is far removed from the original act of violence.

Garrido & Morales (2007) conducted a meta-analysis to assess the impact of different behavioural strategies with juvenile offenders who had committed serious crimes (such as murder and armed robbery) and were serving sentences locked up in secure correctional facilities, or juvenile prisons. Studies looked at general recidivism (resulting in a court response, for example, parole) and serious recidivism (resulting in reincarceration) in young people aged 12–21. This covered the assessment of 6,658 juveniles from 30 studies in either treatment groups (3,685) or comparison groups (3,824). The median last follow-up was at 18 months, although the range was from six to 120 months. They found that receiving any intervention reduced recidivism (by 6.4% on average), but found few differences between treatments. In relation to serious recidivism, cognitive and cognitive-behavioural programmes, but not behavioural ones (including token economies), contributed more to a reduction in re-offending. It seems, therefore, that token economies are no more, and perhaps somewhat less, effective than alternative interventions, but better than nothing at all.

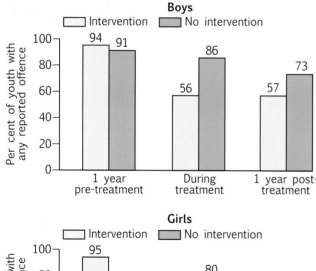

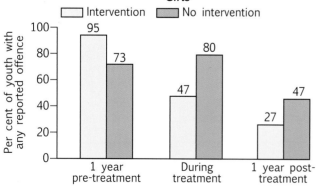

Figure 1.32 The effects of an intervention including a token economy are short-lived (Kirigin *et al.*, 1982).

Lipton *et al.* (2002) reviewed 69 studies of interventions with prisoners from 1968–1999 and, like Garrido & Morales, found that whilst behavioural strategies were effective at reducing recidivism, they were less so than cognitive interventions. Cohen & Filipczak (1971) reported the use of a token economy programme, after which the intervention group had lower re-offending for the next two years. However, after three years there were no significant differences between the groups. This supports a criticism of token economy programmes that their effects are short-lived. Whilst they may be able to modify behaviour within the institution, they can lead to reliance on extrinsic reinforcement rather than learning to rely on intrinsic rewards and this does not help individuals to cope in the outside world, that is, for response maintenance. Furthermore, a token economy programme only attempts to alter the outcomes – such as antisocial behaviour – not the causes of those problems. Thus, when the learned responses disappear, the original causes still motivate criminal behaviour.

Kirigin *et al.* (1982) reported on the effectiveness of the Achievement Place programme with young offenders including girls and boys with a history of crimes such as burglary, theft, assault and vandalism. The home-based programme included the use of a token economy. Those who participated in the programme were about half as likely to re-offend as those who did not. However, in the follow-up period, contact with the police and the courts was not different between groups (see Figure 1.32).

Rice *et al.* (1990) found that, although a token economy programme with 92 male offenders in a maximum security psychiatric hospital resulted in behaviour change, this was unrelated to their behaviour once discharged. They concluded that treatment programmes for such individuals need to emphasise skills that will help the individuals post-release.

In another study with patients in a maximum security psychiatric hospital, Quinsey & Sarbit (1975) found that some aspects of their behaviour changed as a consequence of a token economy programme, such as co-operation. However, there was no reduction in fines for misbehaviour, suggesting that a token economy may not be sufficient to promote change.

Some studies show that token economies are ineffective or even damaging. Ross & MacKay (1976) studied the use of a token economy programme with delinquent girls. This was ineffective at reducing their behaviour problems when directed at either reducing antisocial behaviour or increasing social acts. Nor was a token economy combined with peer training effective, yet peer training alone did improve their behaviour. These findings suggest that using a token economy may, in some situations, be disadvantageous in terms of improving behaviour.

A range of criticisms of token economies have already been considered. Corrigan (1995) raises one other, that making adults submit to a token economy is humiliating and infantilising. If the economy required inmates to earn basic rights, such as food, the system would be degrading, but this is not the case. Tokens are used to obtain additional, not necessary, goods and services. Furthermore, whilst exchanging behaviours for privileges may seen infantilising, this is the nature of the social world – people work to earn money, students study hard to get good grades.

In a review of ten years of use of token economies in institutional settings (such as psychiatric hospitals and prisons), Kazdin (1982) suggested several ways that token economies could be made more effective. These include:

- tailoring the value of tokens and responses required for each individual
- allowing individuals to 'sample' the primary reinforcer so that it is motivating
- managing the system more like an 'economy', for example, allowing saving and having 'sales' of primary reinforcers
- ensuring response maintenance after the programme by reinforcing behaviours under a variety of situations, so they are not limited to a small range of cues; they can thus generalise to new settings, substituting natural reinforcers such as praise especially from peers, altering the schedule and delaying reinforcement so that extinction is slow and removing the token economy gradually, so that behaviours are retained without direct reinforcement.

In addition, the report identified some other benefits of token economies, such as the value of staff modelling good behaviour. This is important not only as an additional route to behaviour management, but also because it achieves behaviour change without reliance on direct reinforcement. The behaviour of trainers themselves is also seen to improve, with more positive attitudes to, and interaction with, individuals on the programme.

Anger management

One possible trigger for criminal behaviours such as aggression, violence and damage to property is anger. Anger management programmes aim to reduce such behaviour by enabling individuals to learn ways to recognise and control emotions, which should enable them to avoid aggressive encounters that lead to violent behaviour. The technique is based on cognitive-behavioural principles, that is, it involves the individual thinking about their behaviour, as well as applying behavioural techniques to changing those responses. The ultimate goal is that the individual learns to control their anger and hence avoid engaging in criminal behaviour.

Anger management strategies involve three key steps:

- **cognitive preparation:** group members are helped to recognise their own anger patterns and so identify situations that trigger aggressive behaviour
- **skill acquisition:** individuals learn behavioural and cognitive coping strategies, such as relaxation, which will help them to control the feelings of anger and replace these emotions with acceptable responses

- **application and practice:** individuals try out the skills in role plays and actual situations (such as minor but genuine provocation) and are positively reinforced for appropriate, non-aggressive responses.

The National Anger Management Package, developed by the Prison Service in England and Wales, is one example of the technique as used in Britain. Keen (2000) describes the use of the course in a young offender institution with males aged 17 to 21 years. The course is based on eight 2-hour sessions, seven of which are given over two to three weeks, followed by the final session a month later. The aims of the course are to:

- raise members' awareness of how they become angry
- raise members' awareness of the need to monitor their behaviour
- educate members in the benefits of controlling their anger
- improve techniques of anger management
- allow members to practise anger management in role plays.

Keen found that the participants felt that they had a better awareness of their anger management difficulties and had improved their ability to control their anger after the course. Similarly, Hunter (1993) reported considerable reduction in impulsiveness and interpersonal problems following an anger management programme, although Law (1997) found that only one individual who completed an 8-session course showed any improvement. Just because an individual feels that they are able to control their anger does not necessarily mean that this will be reflected in a reduction of aggression. How effective are anger management programmes at changing behaviour?

Figure 1.33 If offenders can control their anger this may reduce recidivism.

Valliant & Raven (1994) measured the aggressiveness of male inmates who had committed assault, property offences or a combination of the two. A sample of 57 participants received anger management training for two hours per week over five weeks. The inmates' aggression levels were significantly lower after the intervention. Blacker *et al.* (2008) also reported success with an anger management course that was supplemented with drama-based cognitive-behavioural techniques. The 'insult to injury' programme aimed to encourage offenders to identify and generate strategies for potentially volatile situations and to offer a safe and supportive environment in which to practise and evaluate the techniques learned. The programme also explored issues such as power and control, pride and shame and victim awareness. A group of 62 violent adult male offenders took part in a 9-day course. Significant reductions in anger were found between the pre- and post-course measures.

In both the studies by Valliant & Raven and Blacker *et al.*, a comparison was made between each individual's pre- and post-treatment score. Factors other than the intervention could have therefore affected their behaviour over this time period. This problem was overcome in a study by Ireland (2004), which assessed 50 young male prisoners in an anger management course and 37 control prisoners who were also suitable for the course.

The groups used by Ireland had committed similar offences and did not differ in their level of angry behaviours. Angry behaviours were assessed two weeks before and eight weeks after the course for the anger management group and at the same time for the control group who stayed on the waiting list. She found that 92% of the prisoners in the experimental group showed an improvement between the two times, but no reduction in the angry behaviours of the control group was seen. One reason that such an intervention may be effective is that they provide individuals with greater insight into the causes of their behaviour and offer alternative ways of responding to provocation.

Holbrook (1997) also used anger management successfully with prisoners. The sample had been selected specifically because their aggression was reactive. Following the course, they were less likely to engage in revenge. This raises an important issue about the causes of aggression. For anger management programmes to be effective, the cause of aggression must be anger but this is unlikely to be the case for all offenders – consider those criminals who are cold and calculating in their violent behaviour.

Zamble & Quinsey (1997) argue that there is a relationship between anger and violent crime and suggest that uncontrolled anger is a risk factor in predicting violence and recidivism. However, Loza & Loza-Fanous (1999) dispute that anger is a primary cause of violent criminal acts. They suggest that many of the research findings linking anger with violence and rape were based on laboratory studies using students (for example, Zillman, 1993) or offenders' own explanations of their violent acts (Zamble & Quinsey, 1997).

Stewart (1993), however, found that female arsonists had deficits in control of anger.

To investigate the link between anger and violent crime, Loza & Loza-Fanous studied 271 Canadian male offenders, comparing a group of violent offenders with non-violent ones and a group of rapists with non-rapists. Violent offenders had committed crimes such as murder, assault and robbery with violence, whereas the non-violent ones had committed property offences, such as fraud and so on. Using several measures of anger, they found no difference between violent offenders and non-violent offenders or between rapists and non-rapists on anger measures. Loza & Loza-Fanous argue that anger treatment programmes are ineffective with violent offenders, since this is not the cause of their criminality. Furthermore, they suggest that such programmes could potentially be harmful as they encourage the offender to attribute his violent actions to anger for which he cannot be blamed, rather than taking full responsibility for his actions.

Figure 1.34 Crimes other than aggression may also be linked to anger-management problems.

Even if we assume that, for some offenders at least, anger management may be of use, findings such as Ireland and Holbrook only demonstrate short-term changes. These effects may not persist after the course or release from prison, so are unlikely to reduce recidivism. Furthermore, some research studies test only prisoners deemed suitable for the course, so the strategy may not generalise to other aggressive offenders, for example if they cannot self-evaluate.

Over to you

Evidence in practice

Your task for this section of the course is to either produce summaries of two news articles or conduct a content analysis. This section will guide you through examples of these tasks and give you examples to try for yourself. In order to summarise or analyse an article effectively, you need to be sure that you understand the content. Return to earlier parts of the chapter to help you where necessary. If you can, try to track down any original research that the article refers to, but be sure not to muddle up what is actually in the resource you are using and what you have found out as background material.

Media watch

Report points to dramatic fall in TV violence

Rhys Williams

The Independent, 22 August 1995

Violence accounts for just 1 per cent of airtime on terrestrial and satellite television in Britain, according to research published yesterday.

Figures gathered by the University of Sheffield on behalf of the Independent Television Commission and the BBC also showed that incidents of violence on the four terrestrial channels had nearly halved since 1986.

The study, which represents the most comprehensive review of its kind in this country, involved content analysis of more than 4,700 hours of programming over four weeks on BBC, ITV and Channel 4, as well as four satellite channels – Sky One, UK Gold, Sky Movies and the Movie Channel.

It found that violence on terrestrial television accounted for 0.61 per cent of output, compared with 1.53 per cent for satellite. While 37 per cent of programmes contained violence of some kind, the report said the general level of violence was inflated by a small number of programmes which contained exceptionally large quantities. For example, 2 per cent of programmes monitored – mainly feature films and drama – accounted for nearly half of all screen violence.

Marmaduke Hussey, chairman of the BBC board of governors, welcomed the study as 'an authoritative independent piece of academic research' which proved that the corporation took concern over screen violence 'very seriously'.

Yesterday's publication follows demands last month by the Department of National Heritage on the BBC to accept a clause on taste and decency which would curb violence in programmes in its new charter.

Virginia Bottomley, Secretary of State for National Heritage, said the study was 'a constructive step forward in informing public debate', adding: 'I am pleased that both the BBC and ITC have given this issue high priority.'

A detailed assessment of the nature and possible impact of the violence will be completed in the autumn in time for a BBC seminar on how public standards of taste and decency have changed.

Sir George Russell, chairman of the ITC, said that the commission had asked television companies last year to reduce the levels of screen violence. 'The fall in the amount on terrestrial channels is a move in the right direction.'

The research, completed by Dr Barrie Gunter, also found that a fifth of violent acts appeared in children's programmes, but these were mainly in cartoons and animation. Otherwise, the bulk of violence occurred after the watershed suggesting, the report concluded, that it was 'an effective turning point in the schedule'.

Exercise

Content analysis exercise

The author of this article is discussing statistics relating to the appearance of violence on TV and whether the prevalence matters. Your task is to carry out a content analysis of the article. You need to explore the language being used and the psychological evidence being employed. Most importantly, you need to relate your conclusions to your understanding of criminal psychology.

1. Identify the categories of words that have been used, such as 'violence', and more positive terms such as 'curb' and 'watershed'.

2. Draw up a tally chart and record the frequency of each word, phrase or idea.

3. Looking at your chart, is the article mainly positive or negative about the level of violence on TV?

4. Write out an explanation of the psychological principles that underpin the article, showing how the author's views can be justified.

5. Find another article about media violence. Carry out the same procedure. Do the two articles use the same or different approaches to making their argument? Can you account for the ideas in your second article using the same psychological explanations as you used for the first?

Exercise

Summary exercise

1. (a) Find out about the film *Anger Management*. Watch the film and decide on the extent to which it accurately portrays anger management strategies.

   (b) Find an article about the use of anger management in prisons, such as at:

   http://www.guardian.co.uk/society/2003/nov/15/mentalhealth.crime

   http://www.guardian.co.uk/uk/2006/apr/24/ukcrime.prisonsandprobation1

   http://www.hmprisonservice.gov.uk/prisoninformation/prisonservicemagazine/index.asp?id=5237,18,3,18,0,0

2. Summarise the ideas that two of these sources provide about why and how anger management is used with offenders and how effective it is.

3. Use psychological theory and/or empirical research to defend and contradict the ideas put forward by each of the sources you have chosen.

REALlives

Key

You may be asked to describe one key issue from criminological psychology. You can choose this yourself from this chapter. Suitable examples include:

● Are criminals born or made?

● How reliable are eyewitnesses?

● Who does a prison token economy help?

● Does anger management work?

Make sure that for whatever you identify as your key issue you can pose a question and draw on psychological theory and/or research to answer it.

Summary and conclusions

Psychological explanations can help us to understand why people engage in criminal behaviour. The social learning approach suggests that individuals are more likely to perform behaviours such as aggressive acts if they observe and imitate aggressive models. These models may be seen in real life, such as parents, or in the media, for example on TV or films. Evidence from correlations and lab and natural experiments supports a relationship between exposure to aggressive models and aggressive behaviour. A more recent source of models is from video games. These may be an even more effective source of modelling, as they are interactive and highly motivating, which is a cause for concern. However, not all evidence supports the relationship between media violence and aggression, for example Charlton *et al.*'s (2000) study of children on St Helena.

Biological explanations of criminality are supported by evidence from animal and human studies and suggest that some genes are linked to aggressive behaviour. This does not suggest, however, that there is one or more specific 'genes for aggression'. For genes to affect behaviour they must have an influence on a biological mechanism, such as hormones or the brain. The hormone testosterone has been linked to increased levels of aggression in animals and in humans. However, men have higher levels of testosterone than women and not all men are aggressive. The amygdala is a brain area associated with aggressive behaviour and low levels of the neurotransmitter serotonin are associated with higher levels of aggression.

An alternative explanation of criminal behaviour is the self-fulfilling prophecy. This suggests that if we believe that someone is a criminal, this affects the way that we behave towards them. This in turn is likely to make them respond in the way that we expect. They therefore end up changing their behaviour to fit the label we have for them. Some evidence suggests that this is another factor that can contribute to criminality.

After a crime has been committed, psychology can help to understand how best to use information from witnesses. Evidence such as Loftus & Palmer's (1974) laboratory experiment has shown that memory is reconstructive, so if witnesses are exposed to post-event information this can distort their recall. Such findings indicate that leading questions should be avoided in interviewing witnesses. However, case studies such as Yuille & Cutshall (1986) show that in real-life incidents, eyewitnesses can be very accurate and resistant to the effects of leading questions. Finally, psychologists can help with the rehabilitation of criminals. Evidence suggests that both token economies and anger management can help to improve offender behaviour and reduce recidivism.

What do I know?

1. (a) Define antisocial behaviour. [2]

   (b) Evaluate research into the causes of antisocial behaviour. [8]

2. (a) Describe the laboratory experiment as used in research into criminological psychology. [4]

   (b) Evaluate the laboratory experiment as used in research into criminological psychology. [4]

3. Compare and contrast **two** explanations of criminal behaviour. [12]

4. (a) Describe the procedure of Charlton et al. (2000). [4]

   (b) Evaluate Charlton et al.'s (2000) study. [6]

5. Imagine that you have been asked to advise on ways to reduce recidivism in offenders in a prison.

   (a) Describe **one** technique that you could recommend. [6]

   (b) Explain why you would expect this technique to be successful. You are advised to use evidence in your answer. [6]

Chapter 2 Child psychology

What's ahead?

By the end of this chapter I should know about:

- what is meant by child psychology
- the evolutionary basis of attachment
- Bowlby's theory of attachment
- measuring attachment by means of the Strange Situation test
- Ainsworth's attachment types including cultural variation
- deprivation, in particular Bowlby's maternal deprivation hypothesis
- reducing the effects of deprivation
- privation, including the case of Genie
- the reversibility of privation
- the characteristics and effects of either autism or ADHD
- two explanations for the disorder I have chosen
- evidence for both positive and negative effects of daycare on children's development
- one of the following studies: Bowlby (1946), Rutter & the English & Romanian Adoptees Study Team (1998) or Belsky & Rovine (1988)
- one key issue of your choice from child psychology
- either content analysis of an article or a summary of two sources provided in this chapter

In addition I should understand:

- structured and unstructured observations including their strengths and weaknesses
- cross-cultural studies
- longitudinal studies including their strengths and weaknesses
- case studies including their strengths and weaknesses

Where does child psychology take us?

- Why do parents love their children?
- Is criminality down to the parents?
- Can children bounce back from early trauma?
- Does ADHD really exist?
- What causes autism?
- Should we put children in day care?

Child psychology forms part of the broader field of developmental psychology. Developmental psychologists are concerned with human development from before birth right through the lifespan including young adulthood, middle age and old age. Child psychologists are concerned specifically with the development of children and adolescents. It is sometimes convenient to separate child development into the cognitive domain (concerned with mental processes such as thinking, language and memory) and the social–emotional domain (concerned with relationships). In this chapter we look at the possible impact of early events on both cognitive and social–emotional development, and in the case of atypical development the likely role of genetic factors. One of the ideas that has most interested child psychologists is that early development affects later development. In some areas such as attachment, there is considerable evidence for this idea. In other areas it has sparked controversy, and we look in this chapter at arguments over whether the use of daycare can affect children's development and whether parenting skill can affect the development of conditions such as autism and ADHD.

Attachment

An **attachment** is a close two-way emotional relationship between two people. We form attachments throughout our lives, but psychologists are particularly interested in our earliest attachments, formed in infancy with our main carer or carers (most commonly the biological mother). We tend to behave in particular ways towards our attachment figures, regardless of our age. We tend to want to be physically close to them (psychologists call this **proximity seeking**). We get distressed when we are separated from them and we tend to use them as a 'secure base'. **Secure base behaviour** involves exploring the world but regularly visiting our attachment figures, taking our sense of security from contact with them. Some attachment behaviours are age-specific. For example, young children show **stranger anxiety**, fear and distrust of unfamiliar adults, and **separation anxiety**, a dislike of being apart from the attachment figure.

The evolutionary basis of attachment

Evolutionary psychologists study the possible evolutionary basis of human behaviour, often by looking at related behaviour in other species. The most basic principle of evolutionary psychology is that a behaviour that increases the chance of an individual living long enough to reproduce is likely to be passed on to future generations. Such behaviours are described as 'adaptive'. By studying mother–infant interaction in a range of species psychologists have come to see attachment as adaptive. Bowlby (1957) pointed out that the close emotional bond between parents and children in humans and some other species is adaptive, increasing the probability of the children surviving to adulthood.

What's that?

- **Attachment:** a close two-way emotional bond between two people
- **Proximity seeking:** staying close to an attachment figure
- **Secure base behaviour:** regularly returning to an attachment figure when exploring
- **Stranger anxiety:** anxiety in the presence of strangers
- **Separation anxiety:** anxiety at being apart from an attachment figure
- **Evolution:** the processes whereby species change over generations
- **Critical period:** a time during the development of a child or animal when an event must happen if normal development is to take place
- **Innate:** an inborn tendency to behave in a particular way

In the first half of the twentieth century, a number of biologists studied the behaviour of mothers and infants in a range of animal species. Konrad Lorenz (1935) described the process of imprinting, in which newly hatched birds attach themselves to the first moving object they see (most commonly their mother) and follow it wherever it goes. This allows them to keep relatively safe. Lorenz identified a **critical period** in which imprinting needs to take place. If imprinting does not occur within the critical period, chicks will not attach themselves to a mother figure. Lorenz also investigated the relationship between the nature of the adults that young animals encountered and their preferences as adults. Most dramatically, Lorenz (1952) described the case of a peacock reared in the reptile house of a zoo. As an adult this bird would only direct courtship behaviour towards giant tortoises!

Figure 2.1 This child is showing classic attachment behaviour.

Figure 2.2 These ducklings imprint on their mother and then stay close to her, keeping them relatively safe.

Imprinting carries a clear evolutionary advantage to birds because chicks that remain close to the mother are less vulnerable to predators. However, imprinting is not true attachment because it is a one-way process, only really occurring in the chicks. In mammals, mothers and infants develop a two-way attachment. This carries a further evolutionary advantage because not only will young and vulnerable individuals seek close contact with adults, but those adults will be motivated actively to nurture and protect the young (Bowlby, 1957).

Interactive angles

Consider the dangers children face in the modern environment. What dangers can be reduced if:

(a) the child seeks proximity to a parent, cries at separation and exhibits secure base behaviour?

(b) parents actively intervene to keep children safe?

Figure 2.3 This baby monkey is safer if it stays close to its mother.

The basic applications of evolution to understanding attachment were established half a century ago. However, evolutionary psychology is a big part of modern psychology, and some ideas about attachment are still being developed. It is clear why secure attachment behaviour (proximity seeking, separation anxiety and so on) might have survival value. However, why should we have evolved the possibility of insecure attachment? Jay Belsky (1999) has suggested that insecure attachment (normally regarded as poor quality attachment) can actually be an advantage in particular circumstances.

Belsky's theory begins with some well-established facts about attachment. We know that stress influences parenting style and that this in turn affects the quality of attachment. We also believe that insecure attachment is associated with starting sexual activity at a young age and a tendency to form emotionally less intense adult relationships. Belsky suggests that parenting styles are adaptive in preparing individuals for their environment. High levels of environmental stress are associated with a dangerous environment. Dangerous environments therefore lead to relatively harsh and inattentive parenting styles and to insecure attachment. For an adult living in a high mortality environment where there is a high probability that anyone they attach to is going to die young, it is actually an advantage to have an insecure attachment. The insecure adult with less intense attachments to their loved ones will cope better with losing them and so have a better chance of survival themselves than will securely attached people.

Bowlby's theory of attachment

John Bowlby was a child psychiatrist and psychoanalyst who also had an interest in animal behaviour. Combining these interests, he put together ideas from Freudian and evolutionary approaches to create a theory of attachment. From Freud he took the idea that the mother or main carer has a unique role in a child's development and that the quality of the first relationship will affect future relationships (see *Angles on Psychology for AS Level*, p95). Bowlby called this special focus of attachment towards a particular individual **monotropy**. From early studies of animals like Lorenz's geese, he took the idea of a critical period in which attachment needs to develop and a role for attachment in keeping infants close to the main carer and therefore safe. Based on both Freud and animal research like that of Lorenz, Bowlby proposed that attachment behaviour is instinctive and that normal psychological development requires the development of a secure attachment between a baby and its main carer.

The role of evolution

Because attachment behaviour can be seen in a range of species, Bowlby (1957) proposed that it has developed through a process of evolution. The purpose of attachment behaviours is to keep the young person or animal safe. A million years ago early humans lived in small settlements and faced real threats from predators like wolves and big cats. By seeking proximity with a larger, stronger adult, signalling distress when left alone and returning from exploring for regular visits to its parents, a Stone Age child would greatly increase its chances of survival. Attachment of adults towards children further increases the chances of the child's survival because attached adults would be motivated to keep them close and defend them from predators.

Figure 2.5 Babies' smiles have evolved to make adults care about them.

Figure 2.4 Stone Age children were less at risk of being eaten if they sought proximity, signalled separation distress and displayed secure base behaviour.

Social releasers

Bowlby suggested that babies are born programmed to behave in ways that encourage attention from adults. These 'cute' behaviours include smiling, cooing, gesturing, gripping and sucking. Bowlby called these behaviours **social releasers**, because their purpose is to release instinctive parenting behaviour in adults (see Figure 2.5). He famously said that

> Babies' smiles are powerful things, leaving mothers spellbound and enslaved. Who can doubt that the baby who most readily rewards his mother with a smile is the one who is best loved and best cared for?
>
> Bowlby (1957, p237)

What's that?

- **Monotropy:** the tendency to direct infant attachment behaviours towards a single main attachment figure
- **Social releasers:** innate behaviours designed to stimulate interaction from adults
- **Internal working model:** a mental representation of the first relationship. This acts as a prototype for future relationships
- **Interactional synchrony:** the synching of adult and baby actions so that they take turns and imitate each other's movements

The interplay between infant social releasers and instinctive parenting responses gradually builds the attachment between infant and carer. There is a sensitive period of around two years when the baby is particularly oriented towards trying to interact with adults. If the mother or main carer does not respond to social releasers during this sensitive period, then the main opportunity is lost and it will be much harder for the child to form an attachment later. This means in practice that during a child's infancy, a main carer has to be present and attentive much of the time.

Internal working models

Attachment has consequences for the later development of the child. Recall Freud's idea that a child's first relationship serves as a prototype for later relationships. Bowlby (1969) developed this idea, proposing that each child forms a mental representation of its first attachment, called an **internal working model**. This mental representation is called to mind in forming later relationships and particularly influences their own parenting behaviour. If the child internalises a working model of attachment as attentive, loving and reliable, then this is what they will expect from and bring to future relationships. If, on the other hand, they are neglected or abused, there is an increased probability that they will seek out or display these behaviours themselves as an adult.

Discussion of Bowlby's theory

Bowlby's theory is thorough, explaining both *why* and *how* we form attachments. It also explains some of the consequences of the nature of individual attachments through internal working models. There is research to support the existence of social releasers and the importance of parenting responses. Brazleton *et al.* (1975) observed mothers and babies during their interactions. They noted that mothers and babies took turns in beginning interactions and that both imitated each other's movements. They called this **interactional synchrony**. The researchers also undertook an experiment. Mothers were asked to ignore the babies' social releasers. They found that the babies quickly became distressed. Some even curled up and became motionless, exhibiting signs of depression. These findings support Bowlby's ideas about social releasers and the importance of responding to them.

Bowlby's idea of internal working models predicts that patterns of attachment will be passed on from one generation to the next. Bailey *et al.* (2007) tested this idea. They questioned 99 teenage mothers with one-year-old babies about their attachment to their own mothers. They also observed the attachment behaviours of their babies. Those mothers who reported insecure attachments to their own parents were much more likely to have children whose behaviour implied insecure attachments. This suggests that, as Bowlby proposed, a pattern of insecure attachment was being passed from one generation to the next.

Figure 2.6 It seems that as Bowlby said, parents who have good relationships with their parents find it easier to form an attachment to their babies.

Exercise

1. Using Bowlby's ideas about attachment formation, explain why the toddlers might have become attached to Qrio.

2. What parallels can you see between this research and Harlow's?

Media watch

Children bond with their robot playmate

The Guardian
6 November 2007, page 10

Child-like robot playmates are being developed for nursery schools after researchers found that toddlers learn to regard them as human. The Japanese-built prototype silver robot, Qrio, possesses an 'impressive array' of mechanical and computational skills, according to the researchers. It can interact with humans, walk, sit down, stand up, move its arms, turn its head and even dance and giggle.

Scientists discovered that the children's social contact with the robot increased over time. The children found Qrio more interesting when it behaved in a more 'human' interactive way than when it was programmed to dance randomly. Initially, the toddlers touched the robot on its face and head, but later only on its hands and arms, mimicking the behaviour of children to other humans.

Care taking behaviours were shown toward the robot, but not towards a 'huggable' soft toy that was also placed with the children. The scientists wrote 'Our results suggest that current robot technology is surprisingly close to achieving bonding and socialisation with human toddlers.'

What sort of questions could you ask an adult to get an idea about their quality of attachment?

One approach is to ask about proximity to parents, distress at separation from them and secure base behaviour. Put together a short questionnaire (5–10 questions) that asks questions about these attachment behaviours.

Although much of Bowlby's theory is supported by modern psychology, it has some limitations. The idea that we have evolved attachment behaviour to enhance children's safety has good *face validity*, that is, it seems to make sense. However, like many evolutionary ideas it is extremely difficult to test directly, so there is a lack of firm evidence. Another limitation concerns Bowlby's emphasis on the role of the mother. There is evidence from modern studies to suggest that in two-parent heterosexual families, the quality of attachment with a father can also have an effect on children's development, for example in later criminality.

Mary Ainsworth's attachment types

Bowlby distinguished between secure and insecure attachments and used the idea of internal working models to understand individual differences in attachment. However, it was his student – and later colleague – Mary Ainsworth who developed the system of attachment types most commonly used today. Ainsworth (1967) observed children's behaviour in their own homes as they interacted with their main carers and strangers. She proposed that babies and toddlers divided fairly neatly into three attachment types, according to the degree of independence shown by playing infants, the anxiety they displayed when left alone or with a stranger and their response to being reunited with the primary carer. Ainsworth & Wittig (1969) developed a laboratory procedure designed to simulate these everyday events in order to classify attachment types. This is called the **Strange Situation**, and it is still the most popular procedure for classifying attachments.

Measuring attachment: the Strange Situation

This is a laboratory procedure designed to measure the security of attachment a child displays towards its primary carer. Secure base behaviour, proximity seeking, separation anxiety, stranger anxiety and response to being reunited with the primary carer are all assessed. The *Strange Situation* gets its name from the fact that the baby is placed in an unfamiliar, that is, strange, room. The procedure has eight episodes, the seven key stages of which last three minutes each. These are shown in Table 2.1 and Figure 2.8.

Table 2.1 The Strange Situation

Stage	Situation	Designed to measure
1	The child and carer are placed in an empty room	
2	The child is free to explore (encouraged if necessary)	Proximity seeking and secure base behaviour
3	A stranger enters, greets the mother and attempts to play with the child	Stranger anxiety
4	The carer leaves the child with the stranger	Stranger anxiety and separation distress
5	The carer re-enters and the stranger leaves	Reuniting response
6	The carer leaves the child alone	Separation distress
7	The stranger re-enters	Stranger anxiety
8	The stranger leaves and carer re-enters	Reuniting response

Figure 2.7 Bowlby probably underestimated the potential importance of infant–father attachment.

Ainsworth's attachment types

Based on the Strange Situation, Ainsworth proposed three types of attachment. Type B is secure attachment; types A and C are types of insecure attachment.

Type A: **avoidant** – these children do not seek proximity with, nor display secure base behaviour towards, their carer. They show no distress when she leaves, nor do they make contact when she returns. In the order of 20–25% of British 12–18-month-olds are classified as type A.

Type B: **secure** – these children play independently but seek proximity and regularly return to see the carer (secure base behaviour). They typically show moderate separation distress and stranger anxiety. They require and accept comfort from the carer in stage 8; 60–75% of British 12–18-month-olds are classified as type B.

Type C: **resistant (or ambivalent)** – these children explore less in stage 2 than others, intensely seeking proximity. They get very distressed on being left alone and with a stranger, but they resist comfort when reunited with their carer. Around 3% of British infants are classified as type C.

Interactive angles

As well as forming attachments to their carers, children can also become attached to toys, especially cuddly ones like teddies. Think about the Strange Situation and devise a test that a researcher could do to measure how attached a child was to a particular toy.

Figure 2.9 Children display attachment behaviour towards soft toys.

Figure 2.8 The eight stages of the *Strange Situation*.

Observational research always involves watching people or animals in a particular situation and noting in some way what takes place. Naturalistic observation takes place in the usual environment of the individual or individuals being observed. For a child this means in their home, nursery, school, park and so on; not in a psychologist's laboratory. Observation may be overt (the observee knows they are being observed) or covert (the observee is unaware of the observation). Naturalistic observation has been important in child psychology, often as a first stage of research prior to structured observation. For example, in her early work Mary Ainsworth observed mothers and their babies interacting in their own homes. This allowed her to see how children typically behaved when left alone and with a stranger and how they responded to being reunited with their primary carer. Naturalistic observation has the strength that it takes place in the observee's natural environment, so it tends to capture natural behaviour. However, it is no use as a test for a psychological characteristic because the researcher cannot control when or how often, or in what sequence, the situations they are most interested in will take place. This in turn means that it is very difficult to generate numerical data from naturalistic observation.

Structured observation takes place when the researcher defines in advance exactly what behaviours they are looking for and sets up a situation in which the opportunity to display those behaviours is standardised for anyone being observed. A coding system is needed so that all observers note the same behaviours in the same way. A good example of a structured observation procedure is Ainsworth's *Strange Situation*. This measures attachment type in children by setting up a sequence of events in each of which we can note the child's attachment behaviour. In Stage 2 the child is with their primary carer but in an unfamiliar room. This allows observers to note to what extent the child explores the room and how often they return to see the primary carer (two ways of coding secure base behaviour). Later stages are set up to measure separation anxiety, stranger anxiety and reunion response.

The advantages of structured observations are that they generate numerical data and so allow us to use the procedure as a psychological test. A good structured observation procedure recreates the conditions of a naturalistic observation, so that natural behaviour is being observed while at the same time being controlled enough to collect standard information about each participant. The *Strange Situation* comes out well on both of these criteria. The risk of a highly structured observation is that it can be too artificial and ceases to represent the natural situation it aims to recreate.

Reliability and validity

A procedure is said to be reliable when it consistently produces the same results, and valid when it measures what it sets out to measure. Naturalistic and structured observation have different strengths as regards reliability and validity. Naturalistic observation is likely to have problems with reliability. Two people watching mothers and infants interacting in their own home without an agreed way of coding behaviour may come to different conclusions. Structured observations like the Strange Situation are more reliable because the situation is clearly defined and so is what observers are looking for. Two people watching the same child in the Strange Situation are very likely to classify it as the same attachment type.

Validity is slightly more complex. Structured observations like the Strange Situation tend to have good predictive validity. By this we mean that we can predict something about how a child will turn out based on the results of the observation. We will see later in this chapter (page 47) that children classified as type B by the Strange Situation tend to be advantaged in several aspects of their development. Unstructured observations tend not to have good predictive validity. On the other hand, they may have good ecological validity. This means that they represent well what happens in real-life situations. Structured observations may or may not have good ecological validity. The Strange Situation by definition takes place in an artificial setting, but its episodes are meant to replicate everyday situations of brief separation and reuniting between infant and primary carer. Its ecological validity is therefore up for debate.

Ethical issues

Observations raise ethical issues. For naturalistic observation the main issue is privacy. Before we watch people in their own home we need to be sure they have given real consent – that is, that they fully understand the procedure and do not feel under pressure to allow the observation. Before we can watch someone in public without their knowledge we need to be sure that they will be carrying out only activities which they would be happy to have observed and recorded. Structured observations like the Strange Situation, which put people in particular situations, raise the additional issue of distress. We are deliberately causing mild stress to a baby in the Strange Situation, and we need to consider the balance between this stress and the benefits of the procedure and whether the child would reasonably expect to experience this kind of stress in their everyday life anyway. The Strange Situation procedure takes account of stress for the children being assessed. Mothers monitor the children through a two-way mirror and are told they can stop the procedure at any time if they are concerned that the child is becoming too distressed.

Explaining attachment types: maternal sensitivity hypothesis

Mary Ainsworth proposed that variations in attachment type are chiefly the result of the behaviour of the mother or main carer towards the child. Most importantly, high levels of **sensitive responsiveness** are associated with secure attachment. Carers who are skilled at picking up and responding to the child's signals tend to have type B children. According to Ainsworth, type A and C attachments are the result of insensitive parenting. Type A and C patterns of behaviour in the Strange Situation represent different coping strategies for dealing with the anxiety of the situation. Type A children avoid contact with adults in order to not be disappointed by them. They are emotionally distanced from the situation. Type Cs, on the other hand, cope using anger and control. They maintain very close proximity in order to keep their carer 'on a short leash' and display considerable anger when left alone and when reunited with her.

Modern research has supported the importance of sensitive responsiveness in developing secure attachments. However, it has also shown that other factors are involved. Fuertes *et al.* (2006) followed up 48 babies and their mothers from birth to one year. They assessed the babies' temperament (their genetically influenced personality) at one and three months, maternal sensitivity at nine months and attachment security (using the Strange Situation) at one year. Both maternal sensitivity and temperament were found to be associated with attachment type. Thus both a child's temperament and their primary carer's sensitivity affect attachment.

Even if we accept Ainsworth's idea that sensitivity is important, there is a problem with the word 'insensitive'. This is normally used as an insult, so it implies here that the mothers of insecure children are of bad character. However, there are many reasons why a mother might not pick up infant signals. Donovan *et al.* (2007) tested whether in fact so-called 'insensitive' mothers may simply have difficulty processing the sort of information that would allow them to interpret correctly their babies' signals. They looked at mothers' ability to judge emotion from pictures of baby faces. They found that mothers who found this task hard when their babies were six months old were more likely to display insensitive behaviour and to have insecurely attached babies at two years. This means that 'insensitive mothers' may simply have a cognitive disadvantage rather than a character flaw.

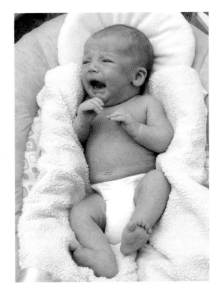

Figure 2.10 Mothers with poor perceptual skills and difficult babies may have a hard time forming a secure attachment.

Interactive angles

Various psychologists and other professionals such as social workers offer attachment training for mothers and other main carers in order to help them form secure attachments with their babies. Using ideas from attachment theory, in particular sensitive responsiveness, explains how attachment training might work.

Attachment type and later development

Ainsworth (1989) believed that attachment type as classified by the Strange Situation would remain fairly constant throughout the child's life and that it would lead to particular patterns of behaviour in adulthood. For example, as we have already seen (page 43), securely attached people are advantaged in their ability to parent their own children. Ainsworth also believed that securely attached adults would find it easier to have successful friendships and romantic relationships. These advantages have been confirmed by modern research.

What's that?

- **Sensitive responsiveness:** the ability of the adult carer to pick and respond to non-verbal signals from the baby

Figure 2.11 Ainsworth suggested that people with secure attachments have better friendships.

Research has consistently shown that, as Ainsworth believed, securely attached adults are advantaged in their friendships and romantic relationships. Banse (2004) looked at the relationship between attachment type and marital satisfaction in 333 German couples. Satisfaction of each partner was associated with type B attachment in themselves and their partner. In other words, where both partners were secure, satisfaction was greatest. Scores of secure attachment correlated strongly (coefficients of 0.43 for wives and 0.37 for husbands) with marital satisfaction. Scores for each of the insecure attachment types correlated negatively with satisfaction.

Interactive angles

There is a large body of research linking insecure attachment to mental health problems. Go to http://www.pubmed.gov or http://scholar.google.com and search for studies linking insecure attachment to particular mental health problems. Use 'attachment' as a search term and try combining it with 'depression' or 'eating disorders'.

Some research has also shown that attachment type is associated with criminality. Smallbone & Dadds (2000) assessed 162 male students for attachment to parents and aggression, antisocial behaviour and sexual coerciveness (likelihood of forcing someone into a sexual act against their will). Insecure attachment was associated with higher levels of aggression, antisocial behaviour and sexual coerciveness. Sexual coerciveness was most strongly associated with insecure attachment to the father than to the mother. This has important implications for the ideas of Bowlby and Ainsworth, who both placed their emphasis on the role of the mother.

Figure 2.12 Research suggests that couples where one or more partners have an insecure attachment may have the most relationship problems.

Longitudinal studies

Whenever we research children's development over time, we have to consider how we will obtain children of different ages or different stages of development. The quickest and easiest way to compare children of different ages is to take a sample of different children at each age and compare them. This is called a cross-sectional design. However, although this approach is quick and easy it has important limitations. Because different children are used in each condition, individual differences between them will affect the results.

A better way to study children of different ages is by means of a longitudinal design. This involves following up a group of children over an extended time. Longitudinal designs are particularly useful for following up children who fall into particular categories at a young age, for example, attachment type. If we know the attachment classification of a group of babies we can follow the development of that group and see how they turn out, for example, in terms of their adult relationships. We can of course assess attachment type retrospectively in adulthood, but we cannot assume that attachment type always remains the same throughout life, so this is a less valid method for measuring infant attachment.

The major problem with longitudinal designs is the time they require, typically several years. This means that if you have an idea now for a longitudinal design, you may not get your results for decades! The time needed for longitudinal studies creates a further problem: *attrition*. Attrition means the loss of participants during the course of a study. If a study runs for several years some participants may die. Others may move away and not leave contact details. Yet others may simply decide they don't want to be part of the study any more. Where studies run for a long period, attrition rates can be so high that the study has to be abandoned.

Cultural variations in attachment

Studies of infant attachment conducted in different **cultures** have revealed some variations in the proportions of securely and insecurely attached infants. In a classic study, Van Ijzendoorn & Kroonenberg (1988) carried out a **meta-analysis** of the combined results of published studies of attachment type in a range of cultures. Studies were selected on the basis that they used the Strange Situation to classify infant attachment type into types A, B and C. Results were meta-analysed. This means that their results were combined and weighted for sample size. A total of 32 studies conducted in eight countries were included in the meta-analysis. In all countries, secure attachment was the most common classification. In most countries (except China, Japan and Israel) anxious resistant (type C) was the least common. There were, however, some big variations in the percentages of types A, B and C. These are shown in Figure 2.13.

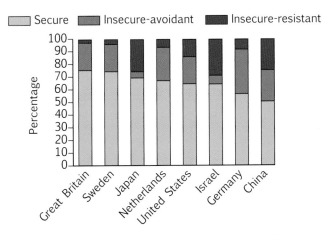

Figure 2.13 Percentages of attachment types in different cultures. Based on Van Ijzendoorn & Kroonenberg (1988).

Explaining cultural variations

There is a range of possible explanations for the sort of variations in attachment seen in studies like that of Van Ijzendoorn & Kroonenberg. Grossman & Grossman (1990) suggest that the idea of 'attachment' has subtly different meanings to different cultures. Take type A, avoidant attachment; in Britain, we are uncomfortable at the idea of emotionally disengaged children. However, what we call 'avoidant' in Britain and America might be called 'independent' in Germany, where independence is valued more highly. If this is the case, then we would expect there to be a higher proportion of type As in Germany than in Britain. Looking at Figure 2.13 this is in fact the case.

An alternative explanation for apparent cultural variations in attachment is that the Strange Situation, which was developed in the USA, simply doesn't work in some cultures. For example, Takahashi (1990) suggests that the procedure is not appropriate for testing Japanese mothers. In Japan the cultural norm is for mothers and babies to be rarely separated. This means that we would expect to see very high levels of separation anxiety. Japanese mothers also tended to spoil the stages of the Strange Situation assessing response to reuniting by rushing straight to the child and scooping it up. In the absence of a reuniting response to observe it is quite likely that the severe separation anxiety of the Japanese children led to a falsely high number being labelled type C.

Figure 2.14 The final stage of the Strange Situation is difficult in Japan because mothers are rarely separated from their babies and tend to rush straight to them and scoop them up, making it hard to assess the response to being reunited.

A third possible explanation comes from Belsky (1999). Belsky developed Bowlby's ideas about the evolutionary origins of attachment further, suggesting that different attachment types are useful for people living in different environments. We know that insecure attachment is associated with early onset of sexual activity and a tendency to form less deep adult relationships. Belsky has proposed that parenting behaviours that lead to insecure attachments and so to early sexual activity and shallow adult relationships are actually *helpful* in environments where mortality rates are high and so people need to reproduce young and not invest too much emotion in relationships with partners who are likely to die young. Belsky also suggests that the stress of life in a high-mortality environment naturally leads to low levels of maternal sensitivity and hence high rates of insecure attachment.

Cross-cultural studies

Cross-cultural research involves comparing people in different cultures. A culture is a set of norms, values, beliefs and practices that characterise a community. The community can be as large as a national, religious or ethnic group or as small as a family. In practice, cross-cultural researchers most commonly compare people of different nationalities. This is important because otherwise we could end up with either a discipline of psychology that is only relevant to people in Europe and USA, or alternatively, separate psychologies for different parts of the world.

Cross-cultural studies look at both the differences and similarities between people in different communities. Culture-specific practices, beliefs, values and so on are called emics. Universals that occur in a wide range of cultures are called etics. In cross-cultural studies, culture is treated as an independent variable, and the focus of the study (which can be emic or etic, and range from child-rearing practices to visual perception) as the dependent variable. Some research has revealed some surprising etics. For example, the features males and females find sexually attractive are surprisingly similar across a range of cultures.

A classic example of cross-cultural research is the work of Van Ijzendoorn & Kroonenberg (1988), who looked at the proportions of infants of different attachment types in a range of countries. Here nationality is an independent variable and attachment types the dependent variable. The study revealed wide variation in the proportions of type A, B and C children in each country, suggesting that child-rearing practices vary across cultures.

Cross-cultural research has been useful in helping us to understand what aspects of human behaviour are universal and which are a product of culture. However, the approach is not without its critics. Psychologists from the *cultural* tradition (as distinct from *cross-cultural*) believe that culture is too complex to be treated as an independent variable. There are also serious methodological obstacles to effective cross-cultural research, most seriously matching samples from different communities. If we compare a sample from one country that is wealthier, more liberal, more religious and so on than the sample from another, then we are not comparing like with like. On the other hand, if one of those countries is overall more wealthy, liberal, religious and so on, finding two groups representative of those cultures means that we cannot compare like with like and there will always be confounding variables.

Deprivation
Bowlby's maternal deprivation hypothesis

Bowlby's most basic idea was that the development of an attachment in early life is an essential aspect of a child's development. Before going on to develop attachment theory properly, Bowlby (1951) initially proposed the **maternal deprivation hypothesis**. This stated that a child requires the continuous presence of a primary carer throughout a sensitive period lasting at least the first 18 months to two years. Bowlby identified two particularly serious consequences of the failure to form an attachment, or serious disruption to the attachment during this sensitive period (for example, prolonged separation from the primary carer).

- **Affectionless psychopathy:** this is the inability to experience guilt or deep feelings for others. Naturally this interferes enormously with one's relationships in later life. It is also associated with criminality, as affectionless psychopaths find it difficult to appreciate the feelings of their victims and so lack remorse.

- **Developmental retardation:** Bowlby proposed that there is a critical period for intellectual development and that if children are deprived of a maternal relationship for too long, they would suffer retardation, that is, very low intelligence.

Bowlby provided evidence for the link between affectionless and psychopathic behaviour and early experience in a classic study conducted at the child guidance clinic where he worked. This study is described in detail on page 51.

Taken at face value, the '44 Thieves' study provides powerful evidence for a link between early disruption to attachments and later emotional impairment. However, there are some important flaws in the design. First, information about early separations was collected during interviews. This relies on the participants' honesty and accuracy of recall, so it does not carry the same weight as information obtained from an objective source, such as medical records. Second, Bowlby himself carried out both the interviews and the psychiatric assessments. As he knew what he was expecting to find, he may have been biased in his assessments. In modern research it is standard procedure for researchers to assess participants without knowing any details that might predispose them towards bias. This is called a *double blind* procedure.

Contemporary psychologists generally believe that, whilst early relations with the primary carer are very important, Bowlby overstated his case in his early work, and that children are more resilient to early experiences – for example, temporary separation from their primary carer – than he gave them credit for. In fairness to Bowlby, he did later acknowledge this.

Classic research

Optional

Bowlby, J. (1946)

Forty-four juvenile thieves

London: Bailliere, Tindall & Cox

Aims: To see whether teenage criminals who displayed affectionless psychopathy were more likely to have had an early separation than those who had not.

Procedure: 44 of the teenagers referred to the Child Guidance Clinic where Bowlby worked were selected on the basis that they were involved in criminal activity and that they were living with their biological parents. Bowlby interviewed them in order to assess whether they exhibited signs of affectionless psychopathy. This was identified by lack of affection to others, lack of guilt or shame at their actions and lack of empathy for their victims. Bowlby also interviewed the families of the adolescents in order to establish whether the children had had prolonged early separations from their primary carers in their first two years. Bowlby then matched up those young people who had been classified as affectionless psychopaths with those who had had prolonged maternal deprivation in the first two years. A control group of non-delinquent young people was established in order to see how commonly maternal deprivation occurred in the non-delinquent population.

Findings: Of the 14 children identified as affectionless psychopaths, 12 had experienced prolonged separation from their mothers in the first two years. By contrast, only five of the 30 delinquent children not classified

as affectionless psychopaths had experienced similar separations. Of the 44 people in the non-delinquent control group, only two had experienced prolonged separations.

Conclusions: The young criminals who had a prolonged separation in their first two years were several times more likely to exhibit affectionless psychopathy than those who had no such separation. This provides strong support for Bowlby's maternal deprivation hypothesis.

Figure 2.15 Bowlby found that violent criminals who do not show guilt or shame are more likely to have had prolonged separation from their mothers in early childhood.

One way in which our ideas have changed since Bowlby's time is that most psychologists would make a distinction between **deprivation** and **privation**. Privation occurs when no attachment is formed, whereas deprivation takes place when a child is separated from an attachment figure after an attachment has been formed (Rutter, 1981). Bowlby did not distinguish between deprivation and privation, and nowadays psychologists tend to associate the very serious effects of affectionless psychopathy and retardation with *privation* rather than deprivation. It is also important to distinguish between short- and long-term deprivation. We can therefore separate out three types of early experience:

- short-term deprivation: separation from an attachment figure for a few hours or days
- long-term deprivation: separation from an attachment figure for extended periods or permanently
- privation: prevention from forming a normal attachment to a carer, for example, because of severe abuse or institutional care.

What's that?

- **Deprivation:** separation from an attachment figure
- **Privation:** the failure to form a normal attachment

Short-term deprivation

Children are separated from their main attachment figures for short periods for various reasons. The most common is probably daycare, in which working parents use professional childcare services such as nurseries or childminders. We return to daycare later in this chapter, but here we can look briefly at hospitalisation as a reason for short-term separation.

Before Bowlby's work became influential, the conventional wisdom surrounding children in hospital was that, provided their physical care was good, they would experience few difficulties. It was thus standard practice for parents to be allowed very little access to their children when they were in hospital. Robertson & Bowlby (1952) caused a stir when they filmed a two-year-old girl called Laura when she went into hospital for eight days for a minor operation. Laura's emotional state deteriorated visibly throughout the eight days and by the end of her stay she was severely withdrawn and no longer showed any affection towards her visiting mother. Robertson & Bowlby filmed several more children in hospital and, based on their observations, proposed three stages children go through when experiencing this type of separation:

● **protest:** children at first were often panic-stricken and upset. They cried frequently and tried to stop their parents leaving

● **despair:** after a time, children cried less frequently, but became apathetic and uninterested

● **detachment:** children eventually began to take an interest in their surroundings. However, if they reached this stage, children frequently rejected their primary carer.

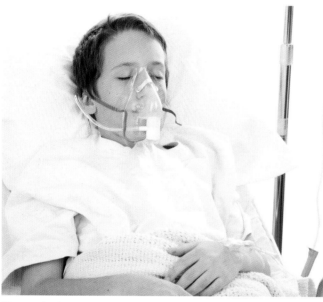

Figure 2.16 Separation from parents makes hospitalisation a frightening experience for children.

Later research has revealed that not all children go through the stages described by Robertson & Bowlby. There are, in fact, wide variations in children's reactions to being in hospital. Kirkby & Whelan (1996) reviewed research into the effects of hospitalisation on children. They concluded that, although it *can* have negative consequences, there are many variables that impact on the effects. These include the age of the child and the quality of their parental attachments, the seriousness of the condition and the severity of the medical intervention.

Long-term deprivation

Some of you will have parents who are separated or divorced. It is important as we look at the possible consequences of divorce to keep in mind that there are a number of factors that determine the effects divorce has on children. The differences reported between children of divorced and intact couples are typically quite small and do not apply to all children. Richards (1995) has identified a number of typical effects of parental separation on children.

1　Lower levels of academic attainment.

2　Higher rate of behavioural problems.

3　Earlier average ages for beginning sexual relationships, leaving home, cohabiting and marrying.

4　More distant relationships with family as an adult.

5　Lower socio-economic status and psychological well being as an adult.

An important question you might ask is whether children are more affected by parental conflict or **discord** within an intact family, or by parental separation/divorce/remarriage, collectively called **family reordering**. This is important to families in discord who have to make a decision whether to reorder or remain together, based partly on their beliefs about the effects on the children. The results of studies seeking to find out whether reordering or discord is worse for a child are mixed. A classic study by Cockett & Tripp (1994) aimed to compare directly the effects of discord with those of reordering. A sample of 152 children and their parents were divided into intact, reordered and discordant groups. Reordered families were defined as those who had at least one change to the family structure through separation, divorce and so on. Discord was defined as serious argument within the family. Children were assessed on their self-image, social life, school success and health. On all measures the reordered group came out worst and the intact group best. How well families had dealt with reordering was also assessed, and most parents came out extremely badly. Only a small minority of children had been prepared in advance for parental separation and fewer than half had regular contact with the absent parent.

A problem with using this type of study to compare the effects of reordering and discord is that it is impossible to truly match the groups. It is possible that the reordered group's greater incidence of problems was due to some form of greater conflict or lesser reason for staying together that triggered the family split, rather than the split itself. Logically, there *must* be something different in the reordered and intact groups, because something led one group of families to remain intact while the others separated. Also the reordered group had experienced discord before the parents split up, so really they made up a discord and reordering condition, not simply a reordering condition. This type of design may therefore overestimate the effects of family reordering.

Other studies have suggested that parental discord can cause more problems for children than family reordering. Fergusson *et al.* (1992) used a different approach to try to tease out what factors in family problems affect children most. They examined a group of 1,265 children who had been studied each year, up to the age of 13. The rates of parental separation, reconciliation, arguments, violence and sexual problems were recorded each year. At 13 years the rate of criminal offending was noted and the rates of offending were looked at in relation to each of the above variables. Significant associations with offending were found for all the variables measured, apart from parents' sexual problems. The most significant factor was parental discord, measured by the number of arguments.

Figure 2.17 It is unclear how serious the effects of family discord are as compared to family reordering.

Reducing the effects of deprivation

We can take the lessons from both studies of short- and long-term deprivation to see how the effects of deprivation can be reduced. Hospitalisation is already stressful for children because of their condition, the unfamiliar environment and perhaps frightening medical procedures. This is particularly the case where an operation is involved. These things are to some extent unavoidable. However, separating children from their attachment figures is an extra stress that can be avoided. Modern hospital procedures are very different from those in Bowlby's time when parents were restricted to seeing their children in visiting hours. Now parents are generally allowed unlimited visiting time with children and may even be provided with a bed so that they can stay with a child 24 hours a day.

The effects of family reordering can also be tackled. We have already seen from the Cockett & Tripp study that most parents neither prepare children adequately prior to separation, nor make proper arrangements for children to keep in regular touch with the absent parent. It is likely that these two simple strategies would help children considerably. Cockett & Tripp also found that the worst effects of family reordering came from multiple reorderings. For example, when a separated parent soon moves in with another partner and perhaps their children, children have a further transition to adjust to, and perhaps further problems of getting on with the new family. One approach to reducing the effects of reordering is therefore to take some time before forming a new family unit and prepare the child in advance for additional reorderings.

Privation

Privation takes place in extreme circumstances where children do not have an opportunity to form a normal attachment. This may take place where there is extreme neglect and/or abuse or when children are brought up in institutional care with a large number and high turnover of carers. Researchers are interested in precisely what the effects of privation are and to what extent it can be reversed. However, studying privation in humans is methodologically tricky. Clearly, for ethical reasons we cannot deliberately 'prive' human children just to see how they turn out. We are therefore limited to existing cases where children have been abused/neglected. We can also look at large numbers of institutionalised children, but this is a very different situation to that of the isolated 'prived' child and appears to lead to different problems.

Privation has been largely studied by means of case studies. Case study research involves detailed recording of real-life instances. The problem is that real-life cases are each unique, and it is hard to draw conclusions. We consider here the case of Genie.

Classic research

Compulsory

Curtiss, S. (1977)

Genie: a psycholinguistic study of a modern day 'wild child'

London: Academic Press

Background: Genie was born in Los Angeles in 1957. When Genie was 20 months old a doctor told her family that she might have learning difficulties. In response to this, her unstable father kept her isolated in her bedroom. She was kept tied to a potty by day and tied into a sleeping bag at night. Genie was beaten whenever she tried to communicate, and she had only the most basic interactions with her father. Her mother and brother were not allowed to communicate with her or leave the house.

Case history: Genie was rescued at the age of 13 when her mother ran away and took her to social services. At

this point she had very little speech and was afraid of adults. She was initially fostered by a special needs teacher and then by one of the psychologists studying her. At first she showed progress and developed limited language (a steadily increasing vocabulary but no grammatically correct sentences) and attachments to her carers. However, she continued to display extreme anxiety. When the research funding was terminated, the psychologists returned her to social services and she was cared for in a succession of foster-homes. In one of her foster placements she was physically abused again and regressed to the state she was in when first rescued. At this point, Genie was briefly reunited with the psychologists, to whom she displayed considerable anger. Genie was then settled with an adult foster-carer who (understandably) did not wish her to have anything to do with psychologists again. We therefore have no up-to-date information on her progress.

Interpretation: Genie suffered privation as the result of being forcibly separated from her mother and being kept isolated from all human interaction, except with her abusive father. This led to damage to both her emotional and cognitive development.

A case with a better outcome

Koluchova (1972, 1991) described the case of two severely abused twin boys. The twins were born in 1960 in the former Czechoslovakia (hence they are commonly known as the 'Czech Twins'). Their mother died shortly after they were born and they spent a year in an institution and were then fostered by an aunt for six months. Their father remarried and the twins were reared by their stepmother, who is believed to have had serious mental health problems. She kept them locked in a dark closet and regularly beat them severely. The boys were rescued at the age of seven years. They were severely retarded, had no speech and were very afraid of adults. They received two years of intensive hospital care including physiotherapy, speech therapy and psychotherapy, then a pair of sisters (said to be extremely sensitive and loving) fostered the boys. At 14 years they had normal speech, social behaviour and IQ. At 20 they had above average IQ and were working and experiencing successful romantic relationships. Both are reported (Clarke & Clarke, 1998) to have successful romantic relationships and careers.

Interactive angles

The cases of Genie and the Czech Twins are in some ways very similar. However, they had very different outcomes. Although our information is not complete, the twins are believed to have no long-term after-effects, whilst Genie is believed to remain severely affected.

1. Identify three differences between the two cases that might have contributed to the different outcomes.

2. What do these studies tell us about the limitations of case studies?

To learn about further cases of privated children, visit http://www.feralchildren.com. What sort of picture emerges overall from these cases about the effects of privation?

Case study method

Genie and the Czech Twins are classic examples of case studies. In a case study we look in detail at a particular person or small group of people who have experienced particular circumstances, such as privation. Case studies involve the gathering of as much data as possible about the circumstances and what happened to the individuals involved, and an interpretation being made of how the circumstances link to the outcome. For example, in the case of Genie we make the interpretation that her developmental problems are the result of her experience of privation. In some cases we can gather data as events happen. However, in cases of privation this is not possible. If we knew that child abuse was taking place we would be bound to intervene. We therefore tend to work by piecing information together retrospectively.

Reliability and validity

Case studies have problems of reliability. We cannot replicate a case study – every case is different – and so it is very difficult to tell using the case study method whether particular situations reliably lead to particular outcomes. For example, based on the very different outcomes of the Genie and Czech Twins cases, we cannot say that privation reliably leads to a particular outcome. On the other hand, real-life cases have good validity. Ethical issues mean that we cannot recreate the real stress of privation, and the sort of mild short-term stress we can create in the laboratory has poor validity – it is simply nothing like the stresses people suffer in real life. Using cases like Genie and the Czech Twins, we are at least studying real privation.

Ethical issues

Case studies have the great ethical strength that we are simply recording events that have happened. We have not set up the situation and so cannot be held responsible for the harm suffered by the people involved in the case. However, case studies do raise some important issues. One issue is balancing the gathering of data against the welfare of the individual. In the case of Genie, for example, researchers fostered her and were responsible for both providing aftercare and studying her. Some critics have argued that by returning her to the State system after their research grant ran out, Genie's psychologists failed in their duty of care. Another issue concerns privacy. Normally we try to preserve the privacy of people studied in case studies, for example by referring to them by initials and by not publishing photographs. However, Genie's photograph was published and she may be recognisable now. It is very difficult to know how as an adult, probably with some degree of learning difficulty, she feels about the publication of her picture, along with many intimate details of her early life.

Institutionalisation

Institutionalisation occurs when children spend a substantial period living in an institution, such as an orphanage or children's home. We can think of this sort of experience as privation if children do not have the chance to form attachments or deprivation if they do. Often institutions will contain a mixture of prived and deprived children. Most research has shown that children who enter full-time care institutions at a young age and who spend extended periods there are disadvantaged in particular aspects of their development.

A large-scale if grim opportunity to study the effects of poor quality institutional care came about in Eastern Europe in the early 1990s. In Romania under President Nicolai Ceaucescu, it was a legal requirement for women to have five children. In many cases, parents could not afford to keep their children and they were handed over to the State, where they were kept in massive, very poor quality orphanages. Following a revolution in 1989, conditions were improved and many of the children were adopted. This allowed psychologists to look in depth at the effects of institutionalisation and adoption. We can look at one study of the Romanian orphans in detail in Classic Research.

Classic research

Optional

Rutter, M. & the English & Romanian Adoptees Study Team (1998)

'Developmental catch-up, and deficit, following adoption after severe global early privation'

Journal of Child Psychology and Psychiatry, 39: 465–76

Aim: To assess the extent to which good care can compensate for early privation.

Procedure: 111 children adopted in Britain from Romanian orphanages were followed up and their progress was compared to that of 52 British children adopted in the same period. All were under two years of age. Most of the Romanian children had been in institutional care since close to birth, but a subgroup had spent only a few weeks in an orphanage. Their IQ was tested as soon as the infants arrived in the UK, and the average score for the Romanian orphans was 63. For those over six months old the average IQ was 45. Physical development was also poor, 51% being in the bottom 3% of the population for weight. The children were assessed again at four years.

Results: At age 4 the average IQ of the Romanian orphans had increased from 63 to 107. For those adopted after six months, it increased on average from 45 to 90. Physical development was also average and on a par with that of the British children adopted at the same time. There was a negative correlation between age when adopted and

measures of physical and psychological development, that is, the younger the child when adopted the better they did.

Conclusion: In terms of intellectual and physical development, early privation can largely be compensated for by good later care. However, early intervention is much more effective than later intervention and should ideally take place before a child reaches six months of age.

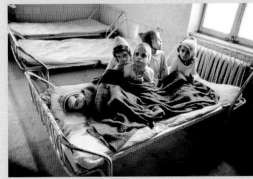

Figure 2.18 Images of the conditions in Romanian orphanages shocked the world.

The study by Michael Rutter and the English Romanian Adoption team suggests that many of the effects of privation are reversible, particularly with early intervention. However, later research on Romanian orphans has highlighted a high rate of attachment problems, and it seems that these are harder to tackle. A particular pattern of attachment behaviour called **disinhibited attachment** is particularly common in institutionalised children. Disinhibited attachment involves clingy, attention-seeking behaviour and indiscriminate social interaction with adults, that is, social behaviour directed towards all adults as opposed to a small number of attachment figures. One possible explanation for this sort of behaviour is the large number of carers young children typically see whilst in an institution (typically over 50 per week). Children in this situation may simply not see enough of any one carer for it to be possible to direct their attachment behaviour towards them in particular. There can also be considerable competition for adult attention in institutional care, so we can see how children might get into the habits of attention seeking and indiscriminate sociability. Rutter (2006) suggests that disinhibited attachment may be the result of the child adapting to multiple carers at a **sensitive period** of development. Zeanah *et al.* (2005) set out to see how strong the association is between institutional care and disinhibited attachment. A sample of 95 children aged 12–31 months who had spent most of their lives in institutions was assessed for attachment using the Strange Situation, whilst their carers were questioned about indiscriminate attachment behaviour; 19% of the institutional group as opposed to 74% of a control group were classified as securely attached by the Strange Situation. On a scale of 0–6, 44% of the institutional group scored 3+ for signs of disinhibited attachment, as opposed to less than 20% of the control group.

Is privation reversible?

We can draw on both case studies of abused children and follow-ups of institutionalised children to help answer this.

- The case of Genie suggests that privation cannot be entirely reversed. However, remember that Genie was rescued extremely late at age 13 and that she may have had developmental problems prior to her abuse. In addition, she did not receive the best care when rescued and there is no recent data available regarding her progress.

- The case of the Czech Twins suggests that privation can be reversed. However, they were an unusual case because they suffered institutionalisation, then family fostering, then severe abuse, but throughout this they maintained an attachment to each other.

- Rutter & the ERA team's (1998) study of Romanian orphans suggests that the effects of privation can be reversed. However, this study focused on physical and intellectual development. Other studies of Romanian orphans adopted in Britain have highlighted a higher than usual incidence of problems of emotional development.

- The Zeanah *et al.* (2005) study suggests that privation may not be reversible, as most children assessed had insecure attachments. However, this study did not follow up the children long term and so it may well be that many of those children will have gone on to develop secure attachments later.

The evidence for the reversibility of privation is thus very mixed. Certainly good quality care leads to vast improvements in children's progress and it appears that in some cases this may completely compensate for early experiences, in particular in intellectual and physical development. However, this is not always the case and it may be that effects on emotional development are harder to reverse. We are not entirely clear on exactly why one child might do so much better than another after early privation, but one important factor seems to be the age at which they are provided with good quality care – the earlier the better.

Atypical development

There are a number of mental disorders that are usually first diagnosed in childhood. We therefore associate them with child development, although they are in fact lifelong conditions. We can look in this chapter at two conditions in particular: ADHD and autism.

ADHD

ADHD stands for attention deficit hyperactivity disorder. As the name suggests, the main characteristics are poor attention and hyperactivity. Over the last 20 years, there has been a rapid rise in the number of cases diagnosed. ADHD is controversial for several reasons. One is that there are different systems for diagnosis, and the likelihood of receiving a diagnosis of ADHD varies considerably according to which system is used. According to the International Classification of Disease (ICD), around 1–2% of the population suffer from ADHD, but according to the other major system for classifying and diagnosing mental disorder, the Diagnostic and Statistical Manual of Mental Disorders (DSM), up to 9% of the population meet the criteria for diagnosis. This means that if you are assessed under the DSM system you are much more likely to receive a diagnosis of ADHD. The DSM criteria for diagnosing ADHD are shown in Box 2.1.

Box 2.1

Diagnostic criteria for ADHD according to DSM-IV-TR

ADHD or ADD is characterised by a majority of the following symptoms being present in either category (inattention or hyperactivity). These symptoms need to manifest themselves in a manner and degree which is inconsistent with the child's current developmental level. That is, the child's behaviour is significantly more inattentive or hyperactive than that of his or her peers of a similar age. Persisting for at least six months to a degree that is maladaptive and immature, the patient has either inattention or hyperactivity–impulsivity (or both) as shown by:

Inattention. At least six of the following often apply:

- fails to pay close attention to details or makes careless errors in schoolwork, work or other activities
- has trouble keeping attention on tasks or play
- doesn't appear to listen when being told something
- neither follows through on instructions nor completes chores, schoolwork, or jobs (not due to oppositional behaviour or failure to understand)
- has trouble organising activities and tasks
- dislikes or avoids tasks that involve sustained mental effort (homework, schoolwork)
- loses materials needed for activities (assignments, books, pencils, tools, toys)
- easily distracted by extraneous stimuli
- forgetful.

Hyperactivity–impulsivity. At least six of the following often apply:

- squirms in seat or fidgets
- inappropriately leaves seat
- inappropriately runs or climbs (in adolescents or adults, the may be only a subjective feeling of restlessness)
- has trouble quietly playing or engaging in leisure activity
- appears driven or 'on the go'
- talks excessively.

Impulsivity

- answers questions before they have been completely asked
- has trouble awaiting turn
- interrupts or intrudes on others
- begins before age seven
- symptoms must be present in at least two types of situations, such as school, work, home
- the disorder impairs school, social or occupational functioning
- the symptoms do not occur solely during a Pervasive Developmental Disorder or any psychotic disorder including Schizophrenia
- the symptoms are not explained better by a Mood, Anxiety, Dissociative or Personality Disorder.

There are further subtypes of ADHD, in which the major symptoms are either inattention or hyperactivity, as opposed to both. Of course children can become hyperactive or inattentive for any number of reasons, and the symptoms of ADHD are similar to those shown by children in emotional distress. Guidelines from the National Institute for Health and Clinical Excellence (NICE) (2008) state that a diagnosis of ADHD should only be made after an assessment of the child's 'social, familial and educational or occupational circumstances, and physical health' (2008, p21). In other words, if there is good reason why a child might display symptoms as a response to their circumstances, for example, becoming upset at their parents separating, it may be unwise to assume that they have ADHD. NICE guidelines also emphasise that the child should be observed in several situations before a diagnosis is made. If they appear hyperactive or inattentive in school but not elsewhere, then the problem may lie with their education rather than a clinical condition.

Effects of ADHD on development

Although it seems to be possible to treat ADHD with strategies ranging from drugs to psychotherapy, untreated or unsuccessfully treated ADHD is associated with both cognitive and social problems.

Figure 2.19 Maths can be hard for children with ADHD because it requires good short-term memory.

Problems in cognitive development

Children with ADHD often have a lower than average verbal IQ and typically underachieve at school. There are various reasons why this might be the case. It may be that the ADHD makes it hard for children to have the sort of quality interactions with others that stimulate the development of verbal intelligence. Alternatively, it may affect children's ability to concentrate on IQ tests or educational assessments, meaning that these tests do not give a true picture of the child's abilities. A third possibility is simply that children with very high IQ and ADHD cope with school and so are never diagnosed. This would mean, of course, that these children never appear in the statistics for IQ in children with ADHD, leading us to underestimate their abilities.

Although all the above are likely to be true, in some cases research has found that ADHD is associated with specific difficulties with particular cognitive tasks. Children with ADHD may, for example, struggle with arithmetic and reading (both aspects of verbal IQ) whilst their factual knowledge is unaffected. Westerberg *et al.* (2004) suggest that the problem lies with mental tasks that require short-term memory. Short-term memory is needed for reading as we visualise or verbalise a sentence whilst extracting meaning from it, and for arithmetic as we similarly visualise or verbalise numbers. In a series of experiments, Westerberg *et al.* confirmed that 27 children with ADHD did worse on a range of short-term memory tasks than a control group. Some standard tasks in IQ tests similarly rely on short-term memory, so it seems likely that it is these tasks that lead to lower IQ scores in children with ADHD.

Problems in social development

Maedgen & Carlson (2000) compared the social status and behaviour of children with a diagnosis of ADHD with peers. Parent and teacher ratings were gathered and the children were observed in a frustrating task designed to assess their ability to regulate their emotions. Of the ADHD group, 16 had both attention and hyperactivity problems; 14 were predominantly inattentive. On a range of measures, the ADHD groups came out worse in their social functioning. Those with attention and hyperactivity problems were most aggressive and were least able to self-regulate emotions. The inattentive group tended to be passive in their interactions with peers. Social status was related to aggression and self-regulation, so the children with attention and hyperactivity problems tended to have the lowest social status with their peers.

Unfortunately, confidence and competence in social situations requires practice and experience of successful interaction. If ADHD makes it harder for children to have early successful interactions because of difficulty in keeping their attention on another child or in restraining impulsive behaviour they cannot easily go through the processes in which most children learn social skills. There is, therefore, a case for social skills training in the treatment of ADHD. However, research has not consistently supported the effectiveness of social skills training for ADHD. Abikoff *et al.*

(2004) followed up 103 children aged seven to nine who either received Ritalin or Ritalin and social skills training. Although Ritalin was associated with improved social skills, those who had social skills training as well did no better. Antshel & Remer (2003) looked at a programme of assertiveness training for 120 children aged eight to 12. They found that, although assertiveness skills improved, this did not lead to an improvement in general social skills.

Explanations for ADHD

There have been a number of explanations for ADHD, ranging from the biological to the social. It is widely believed that true ADHD as opposed to ADHD symptoms is a biological condition, perhaps influenced by genetic make-up or the result of brain injury. However, there are also radical social explanations that suggest that ADHD is simply a social construct.

The brain damage hypothesis

One explanation for ADHD is that it results from early brain injury. Levin *et al.* (2007) noted that children with a history of recorded head injury are statistically more likely to go on to develop ADHD. In the light of the fact that we know mild brain injury is associated with changes in behaviour, this has led to the brain damage hypothesis; that ADHD is the result of mild brain injury caused by physical trauma in early childhood. The major evidence for the brain damage hypothesis comes from the greater incidence of ADHD in children with a history of head trauma. In addition, there is evidence that head injury can make existing ADHD worse. Yeates *et al.* (1997) investigated the effects of concussion in children and found that in several cases, symptoms in patients already diagnosed with ADHD became considerably worse. This line of research further supports the idea that there is a link between head injury and ADHD symptoms.

There is, however, an alternative explanation for the link between head injury and ADHD. If children with ADHD have poor attention and are highly impulsive, they are perhaps more likely to have accidents than most children. Their head injuries may be a *result* of ADHD rather than a cause. This was investigated by Keenan, Hall & Marshall (2009). They followed up 2,782 children who had a head injury in the first two years, along with 1,116 who had a burn. As expected, the children with the head injury were twice as likely to be diagnosed with ADHD as a control group with no history of accidents. However, so were the burned children. This suggests that the relationship was between ADHD and accidents in general, rather than head injury. This in turn suggests that ADHD is not the result of brain injury.

The genetic basis of ADHD

An alternative biological explanation for ADHD is that it has a genetic basis. Kirley *et al.* (2002) have summarised the evidence for this by looking at twin, family and adoption studies. All point towards a genetic vulnerability. For example, Kirley *et al.* calculate that if one identical twin has ADHD there is a 68–81% chance that the other twin will also suffer from it. This figure suggests that genes are more important than environmental factors in the development of ADHD. The likelihood of sharing ADHD decreases among family members as genetic similarity decreases, and adopted children are more likely to share ADHD with a biological parent than an adopted one. Although all these sources of evidence can be criticised, taken together they make a powerful case for genetic vulnerability to the condition.

How might genes lead to the symptoms of ADHD? Genes do not code for behaviour directly. They code for physical characteristics including those of the developing brain. In particular, we know that variations in genes affect the biochemical functioning of the brain. Neurotransmitters are chemicals that pass between one neuron and another, allowing information to be passed through the brain. Different neurotransmitters are important in different parts of the brain and are involved in different mental functions. Because we know that the drug Ritalin, properly called methylphenidate, works on the dopamine system, research has focused on genes that affect this system.

There are various genes involved in coding for aspects of brain development that affect the dopamine system. For example, the gene DRD4 affects the uptake of dopamine after it has crossed a synapse, the gap between two neurons. A particular variation on the DRD4 gene leads to a reduced response to dopamine. Several studies have looked at the association between DRD4 variations and ADHD. A meta-analysis by Faraone et al. (2001) found a small but significant relationship, suggesting that DRD4 is one of the possible genes involved in ADHD. So far, we have found a number of genes like DRD4 that are modestly associated with ADHD, but no single gene that can explain a large percentage of cases. This suggests that ADHD can be caused by several different genetic variations.

The social constructionist perspective

Until now we have assumed that ADHD is a real phenomenon. However, this is actually a controversy and many professionals question the reality of ADHD. If ADHD is not real then how can we explain its apparent existence? One answer is that it is a social construct. Social constructs are ideas that are thought up for social reasons. They might, for example, serve the interests of a particular group or they might ease society's collective guilt about an injustice.

Timimi (2004) has launched a devastating attack on the existence of ADHD, co-endorsed by 33 professionals. Whilst the symptoms of ADHD are associated with particular genetic variations and respond to drugs like Ritalin, Timimi points out that the genes are also involved in several other disorders and Ritalin has similar effects on children regardless of their diagnosis. Most children diagnosed with ADHD also have another diagnosis. Taken together, these arguments weaken the case for the existence of ADHD. Timimi suggests that to understand the labelling of a set of behaviours such as ADHD, we need to understand society's views on what is normal childhood.

We live in a historical period where there is considerable anxiety around childhood and child rearing. Parents and teachers are under social pressure to turn out children that behave in particular ways, and are acutely aware that the State can intervene when they fail to do so. Meanwhile, medical research has been increasingly funded by drug companies with a vested interest in 'discovering' a biological basis for abnormal behaviour that can be treated by drugs. Timimi suggests that drug companies have cashed in on parental and teacher anxieties about children's behaviour and together they have socially constructed a disorder where none exists.

The social constructionist perspective on ADHD is helpful in reminding us that all psychological ideas exist in a social context and that it is possible for a diagnosis like ADHD to become mainstream without being scientifically valid. The main problem is that, like all social constructionist explanations, Timimi's is very hard to find direct evidence for or against. Analyses of the way we speak about childhood (for example, Danforth & Navarro, 2001) have confirmed that we do indeed use medical language to describe children's behaviour when it worries us. This, however, is not the same as evidence that we should not do so! Parents of children with ADHD show higher levels of stress and less successful coping than others (Dupaul et al., 2001). This is consistent with the idea that ADHD is a social construct influenced by parental guilt; however, it is just as likely that the parents were struggling *because* of their children's ADHD. Debates about the role of drug companies in sponsoring ADHD research (for example, Baldwin & Cooper, 2000) have not reached firm conclusions.

Autism

Generally we now speak of the autistic spectrum rather than autism. This is because individuals who suffer autistic-related symptoms vary so much in their abilities and problems. People are now typically described as having an autistic spectrum disorder (ASD) rather than being autistic. Generally people on the autistic spectrum suffer from problems in three areas:

- Communication – some people on the spectrum have speech difficulties. Others may struggle more to read body language, or they may have difficulty with informal use of language such as jokes.

- Social interaction – because people on the autistic spectrum find it hard to understand others' emotions or express their own, they can find interacting with other people difficult.

- Social imagination – people on the spectrum often find it hard to imagine what is going to happen next in a situation. They therefore find new or unpredictable situations frightening and may not anticipate danger.

A formal diagnosis using the DSM (Diagnostic and Statistical Manual of Mental Disorders) system requires the symptoms shown in Box 2.2.

Box 2.2

DSM-IV criteria for a diagnosis of autistic disorder

I **A total of six (or more) items from (A), (B), and (C), with at least two from (A), and one each from (B) and (C)**

   A Qualitative impairment in social interaction, as manifested by at least two of the following:

   1 marked impairments in the use of multiple nonverbal behaviors such as eye-to-eye gaze, facial expression, body posture, and gestures to regulate social interaction

   2 failure to develop peer relationships appropriate to developmental level

   3 a lack of spontaneous seeking to share enjoyment, interests, or achievements with other people (for example, by a lack of showing, bringing, or pointing out objects of interest to other people)

   4 lack of social or emotional reciprocity (note: in the description, it gives the following as examples: not actively participating in simple social play or games, preferring solitary activities, or involving others in activities only as tools or 'mechanical' aids)

   B Qualitative impairments in communication as manifested by at least one of the following:

   1 delay in, or total lack of, the development of spoken language (not accompanied by an attempt to compensate through alternative modes of communication such as gesture or mime)

   2 in individuals with adequate speech, marked impairment in the ability to initiate or sustain a conversation with others

   3 stereotyped and repetitive use of language or idiosyncratic language

   4 lack of varied, spontaneous make-believe play or social imitative play appropriate to developmental level

   C Restricted repetitive and stereotyped patterns of behaviour, interests and activities, as manifested by at least two of the following:

   1 encompassing preoccupation with one or more stereotyped and restricted patterns of interest that is abnormal either in intensity or focus

   2 apparently inflexible adherence to specific, nonfunctional routines or rituals

   3 stereotyped and repetitive motor mannerisms (for example, hand or finger flapping or twisting, or complex whole-body movements)

   4 persistent preoccupation with parts of objects

II **Delays or abnormal functioning in at least one of the following areas, with onset prior to age three years:**

   A social interaction

   B language as used in social communication

   C symbolic or imaginative play

III **The disturbance is not better accounted for by Rett's Disorder**

There are some misleading and unhelpful stereotypes around autistic spectrum disorders. People on the spectrum are not unemotional; they simply find it hard to express and understand emotion. Some individuals are more interested in things than people, but this is not the case for everyone and many people on the spectrum crave friendships but lack the confidence and perhaps the social skills to form them.

Effects of autism on development

Autism is a pervasive disorder. This means that it affects many aspects of a person's development. We can look at cognitive and social development.

Cognitive development

People on the autistic spectrum vary tremendously in their intelligence. On average IQ is lower than in the general population; however, many people with ASD have average or above average IQ. Asperger syndrome is an autistic spectrum disorder characterised by average or above-average intelligence. Occasionally people with ASD have extremely well-developed specific mental abilities and are called *savants*. Savant syndrome was popularised by the film *Rain Man*, which concerned a character (based on two real-life savants) with remarkable memory abilities. There is considerable debate about how common savant syndrome is because it may be that many people with ASD never discover the extent of their mental abilities.

Figure 2.21 Mathematicians are particularly likely to be on the autistic spectrum.

Figure 2.20 The film *Rain Man* portrayed a savant with remarkable memory abilities.

Baron-Cohen (2008) suggests that autism results in two distinctive differences in children developing cognitive abilities. These are in the areas of empathy and hypersystematising. Children with autism generally have poor empathy, the ability to understand emotional states in others. They also tend to hypersystematise, that is, to perceive patterns in information. Children on the autistic spectrum often show obsessive interests, in which they pursue knowledge and expertise in particular areas. To Baron-Cohen this is an example of hypersystematising behaviour. According to Baron-Cohen this makes people with ASD particularly suited to science, where there is an emphasis on perceiving relationships between variables and formulating rules to understand them.

Children on the spectrum are disadvantaged in typical educational settings because of the complex social interactions of the classroom and playground. Many individuals also have low IQ. However, high-functioning people with ASD are well suited to success in science and maths because these require hypersystematising. Baron-Cohen et al. (2001) compared the scores of scientists and non-scientists on a standard questionnaire called the Autistic Spectrum Quotient, or AQ, and found that scientists averaged significantly higher scores. In another study Baron-Cohen et al. (2007) surveyed 378 maths undergraduates and a control group from a range of disciplines about their own and family members' autism. Maths students were over seven times more likely to have a diagnosis of autism themselves and five times more likely to have a close relative with a diagnosis.

Problems in social development

The distinctive cognitive strengths and weaknesses that characterise the autistic spectrum make it hard for children to have successful social interactions. Obsessive interests can be uninteresting to others and lack of empathy can lead to other children seeing those with ASD as uncaring or insensitive. Typically people with ASD fare less well in forming friendships than do most of us. Baron-Cohen & Wheelwright (2003) tested 68 adults with an ASD diagnosis with the Friendship Questionnaire. Out of a maximum score of 135, the ASD group averaged 53.2 (males) and 59.8 (females) as compared to 70.3 (males) and 90 (females) in a control group.

As we might expect given their problems with social skills, children with ASD often have low social status with their peers. Campbell et al. (2005) found that popular children did not respond to information about autism with more positive attitudes towards children with ASD. However, unpopular children did, meaning that informing classmates about the needs of a child with ASD may only help them socialise with unpopular children, who often have poor social skills. This in turn means that the child with ASD has limited opportunity to learn better social skills. In another study Campbell & Marino (2009) asked 293 children from two schools to select peers to be 'buddies' for new children, with and without ASD. Whereas those nominated to buddy a new child without a diagnosis were characterised by high social status, those chosen to buddy a new child with ASD were those with lower status.

This sounds very gloomy; however, there is evidence to suggest that, whilst people with ASD do not naturally understand others well and so do not naturally acquire good social skills, they can still learn them with the right intervention. Owens et al. (2008) tested the effectiveness of LEGO therapy on social skills. Building LEGO is a highly structured activity that should appeal to the hypersystematising brain. This provides a motivating environment for the child with ASD. LEGO therapy involves teams of mixed ASD/non-ASD children working together on a construction project, perhaps with adult help. The co-operative nature of the task forces the already motivated child to engage in trying to understand the rest of their team. In the Owens *et al.* study, maladaptive behaviour decreased sharply after 18 sessions of LEGO therapy and the quality of social interactions increased.

Figure 2.22 Co-operative tasks involving LEGO construction can be effective for teaching social skills to children on the autistic spectrum.

Explanations for autism

As compared to the highly controversial diagnosis of ADHD, there is a general consensus that autism is real and that it is a biological condition. We can consider here evidence that autism is genetic in origin and that it is the result of having an extreme male brain.

The genetic basis of autism

How might genes lead to the symptoms of autism? Genes do not code for behaviour directly. They code for physical characteristics including those of the developing brain. It may be that particular genetic variations combine in some individuals to produce ASD. Bailey *et al.* (1995) looked at 27 pairs of identical and 20 of non-identical twins, at least one of which had a diagnosis of ASD. Where one identical twin had ASD, the other received a diagnosis 60% of the time; 90% of the identical twins of a person with ASD showed significant symptoms even if they had never had a diagnosis. In no case did any non-identical twins share autism. This suggests that autism is largely genetic in origin.

There have been a number of attempts to link autism to particular genetic variations. Farzin *et al.* (2006) looked at a possible link with Fragile-X syndrome. Fragile-X syndrome is the most common cause of mental retardation. It is caused by a variation on a gene necessary for the production of dendrites and synapses, which allow brain cells to communicate with one another. Farzin and colleagues investigated the possible link between a pre-mutation and ASD. A pre-mutation occurs when a form of a gene is found that is somewhere inbetween the normal form and a known mutated form. In this case the pre-mutation was in the FMR1 gene, abnormal but less so than the form leading

to retardation; 79% of the sample as opposed to none of a control group without the pre-mutation were assessed as having ASD. The sample was not a representative one, therefore we cannot generalise and say that 79% of all people with the pre-mutation have ASD. Nor can we speculate, based on this study, about what proportion of ASD cases this might explain. However, the results do suggest that this is at least a partial explanation for autism.

Extreme male brain (EMB) theory

Baron-Cohen (2005) has pointed out that the key cognitive aspects of autism – low levels of empathy and high levels of systematising – are features of the male brain. Typically, men score higher on tests of systematising, while women score higher on tests of empathy. This has led to the hypothesis that autism is the result of having an extreme male brain. Certainly there is plenty of evidence for the idea that men and people with ASD share some cognitive strengths and weaknesses – both men and people with ASD tend to be more systematic and less empathic than others. There is also evidence for what Baron-Cohen calls a 'broader autistic phenotype', that is, a set of characteristics that would not lead to a diagnosis but which are related to autism: scientists, mathematicians and engineers with poor social skills. Interestingly, these occupational groups are particularly likely to have children on the autistic spectrum, suggesting that the extreme male brain runs in families.

There are problems with the extreme male brain theory. Ellis (2005) suggests that it provides a better explanation for Asperger's syndrome than for other forms of autism because it cannot explain the language problems that many people with ASD show. Also, the theory focuses narrowly on the two characteristics shared by males and people with ASD. There are also many differences. Men are, for example, more physically aggressive than women; however, people with ASD are not generally physically aggressive. Clearly, we cannot be talking about the complete male brain, just aspects of it.

What's that?

- **Daycare:** non-parental care, for example, provided by nurseries or childminders

Daycare

The most common circumstance in which babies and toddlers are separated for short periods from their main carers is **daycare**. Economic and social factors mean that it has become the norm for both parents in British families to work, at least part time. Many children thus spend a substantial part of the week apart from their main carer or carers. Recall Bowlby's maternal deprivation hypothesis (page 50). This suggests that separation of child and main carer risks disruption to the attachment process. If we take this to include daycare, then we might expect the use of daycare to have negative effects on children's development. On the other hand, Bowlby's work was generally concerned with longer-term separations. Recall as well Rutter's conclusion that the most serious effects of separation identified by Bowlby were true of privation rather than deprivation. Daycare is certainly not privation, nor is it long-term separation.

Figure 2.23 Many children now spend substantial time in daycare.

The debate over the alleged effects of daycare on children's development is one of the most bitter in psychology, so much so that Karen (1994) has called it the 'Child Care Wars'. On one hand, opposing daycare – or at least long hours in it – are psychologists and parents concerned about a potential risk to children's development. Also on this side of the argument are fundamentalist religious and politically right-wing groups. Some of these groups are probably motivated as much by the opportunity to discourage mothers from working as concern for children's welfare. On the other hand, in the pro-daycare camp are equally concerned psychologists and other professionals who see potential *positive* effects for children using daycare. Allied to this point of view are feminists horrified by the thought of anyone putting pressure on mothers not to work. Also on this side of the debate are governments who perhaps see an opportunity to reduce the money paid out in benefits to non-working mothers by encouraging them to return to work as early as possible. This is a complex picture where people with radically different views and priorities all seek to claim the moral high ground.

Evidence for negative effects of daycare

Jay Belsky (1986) sparked off the daycare debate by suggesting that there was worrying evidence to suggest that babies cared for in daycare settings during their first year were at higher risk of developing insecure attachments and displaying aggressive behaviour than those cared for at home. This appeared to be especially the case where daycare was full time or close to it. Since then, a huge number of studies have been published in this area and the majority have supported Belsky's view. We can look at one such study in detail in Classic Research.

Figure 2.24 It seems that long hours in daycare early in life can increase the risk of insecurity in some children.

Classic research
Optional

Belsky, J. & Rovine, M.J. (1988)

'Non-maternal care in the first year of life and the security of infant–parent attachment'

Child Development, 59: 157–67

Aim: To compare the rates of insecure attachments in babies whose parents used full-time and part-time daycare with those with full-time mothers.

Procedure: 149 12–13-month-old babies (90 male, 59 female) with two married heterosexual parents were assessed for attachment to both their mothers and fathers using the Strange Situation. Special attention was paid to Stage 8 which measures the child's response to being reunited with their carer. Mothers of the infants were interviewed about their work and classified according to whether they worked and used daycare, and if so for how many hours a week. Rates of insecure attachment to mothers and fathers were calculated in relation to mothers' working hours.

Results: There were higher rates of insecure attachment in children whose mothers worked 20 hours a week or more. In particular, these children showed more resistance to being reunited in Stage 8 of the Strange Situation. Babies whose mothers worked more than 35 hours a week were more likely to have an insecure attachment to their father.

Conclusion: Using daycare for more than 20 hours per week during the first year of life increases the risk of a child developing an insecure attachment to the mother and more than 35 hours a week increases the risk of developing an insecure attachment to the father.

Limitations of the evidence

Although the volume of research suggesting a risk of negative effects for children using daycare is quite large, as with all things size isn't everything! One serious problem is that comparisons between children who experience daycare and those who do not are not necessarily comparing like with like. These studies are not true experiments because we can never randomly divide children into daycare and no daycare conditions. It therefore remains possible that some other difference between the groups accounts for differences in the social behaviour observed. One possible difference was explored in a study by Koren-Karie (2001). She compared 38 Israeli mothers who returned to work with a control group matched for age and income for their own attachment status. Far more mothers with insecure attachments to their own parents opted to return to work and use daycare. Because patterns of secure and insecure attachment tend to be passed on from one generation to the next, any disadvantages in the social development of the daycare group might well be due to having insecure mothers, rather than to using daycare.

Evidence for positive effects

A rather smaller but still respectable body of research has found that returning to work and using daycare can have positive effects on children's social development. Andersson (1996) followed up 128 Swedish children who had been in daycare from infancy to 13 years, when they were assessed for social skills and peer relations. As compared with a control group who had had full-time maternal care, the daycare group were judged to be more popular and socially skilled. In another study Harrison & Ungerer (2002) questioned 145 Australian mothers about their work behaviour and attitudes and assessed their babies for attachment at 12 months using the Strange Situation. Mothers who returned to work when their baby was less than five months old were the most likely to have babies classified as secure. Working mothers in general were more likely to have secure babies. Commitment to work and comfort with using daycare also predicted secure attachment.

Another body of research supports the benefits of daycare for children whose families are economically disadvantaged and so have a harder time providing optimal care. This is a very controversial idea (Kagan *et al.*, 1980), because it suggests that the middle classes make better parents and because it

suggests a double standard – daycare is good for one group of children but not for another. However, the evidence is strongly supportive; in a recent meta-analysis of daycare studies Ahnert *et al.* (2004) found a strong positive correlation between socio-economic status and attachment security in children who did not have daycare. However, there was no such correlation in children who had daycare. This suggests that daycare was of benefit to poorer children.

Asking the right questions: what makes good and bad daycare?

Looking at these conflicting findings, it is clear that in some cases daycare appears to have harmful effects on children's social development. In other cases it seems to have beneficial effects. We *could* unpick some methodological differences between studies and decide to take sides in the debate, based on the quality of research. However, in the last few years there has been some valuable research into what factors affect the outcomes of daycare. This has allowed us to say that asking whether daycare is a good or bad thing *per se* is simply the wrong question. It appears that daycare *can* have harmful effects on social development, but probably only under particular circumstances. The age at which daycare commences, the time spent in daycare, the quality and **stability** of the daycare, the management of the **transition** to daycare and the pre-existing attachment type of the child may all mediate the effects of daycare.

Starting age and dose effects

Virtually all the research into daycare has involved children commencing daycare prior to one year. Note that in his 1986 publication, Belsky himself only claimed that daycare starting in the child's first year may have a harmful effect. There is no evidence and no serious suggestion that later daycare, for example in the form of pre-school nursery sessions, is bad for children. The amount of time spent in daycare may also be significant. Belsky (2002) explored this '**dose effect**'. Looking at a national **longitudinal study** of the development of 1,083 children across the USA, he noted that children who had averaged less than 10 hours of daycare in their first 4.5 years were 5% more likely to have higher than normal levels of aggression, whereas those averaging 30 hours or more showed a 16% increased probability of elevated aggression. This suggests strongly that the amount of time spent in daycare is important.

- **Stability:** the extent to which a child keeps to the same daycare arrangements
- **Transition:** the process where a child used to full-time care at home is introduced to daycare
- **Dose effect:** the idea that long hours in daycare have more of an effect than a few hours
- **Longitudinal study:** one in which people are followed up over long periods to study their development

Figure 2.25 Some research suggests that children who spend long hours in daycare have a higher probability of behaving aggressively.

The transition to daycare

Some but not all parents introduce children to daycare gradually, for example, by staying with them in the daycare setting and by leaving them at first only for short periods. The effect of this practice on attachment was tested in a recent German study. Ahnert *et al.* (2004) followed 70 German children in their first year as they entered daycare, assessing attachment before and three months after daycare began using the Strange Situation. A substantial number of children who started daycare abruptly changed attachment type from secure to insecure. On the other hand, where mothers spent time introducing the child to daycare, the secure babies maintained their attachment and some insecure babies changed type, becoming securely attached. This study suggests that the stress of starting daycare may affect children, but also that this can be avoided by making a gradual transition. It may be that some children find the transition from full-time maternal care to daycare much more stressful than others. Belsky & Fearon (2002) assessed children's attachment type prior to starting daycare and followed up after they had begun. They found that the negative effects of daycare were associated only with children with type A attachments. Types B and C were unaffected.

Quality of daycare

Leaving aside what we know about attachments, common sense suggests that the better a child is looked after, the better they will develop. Allhusen & NICHD (2003) carried out a sophisticated study of the effects of quality of daycare. A sample of 985 children and their professional carers were observed twice for half a day in their daycare setting. Observers rated carers for sensitive responsiveness (page 47), positive attitude towards the child and the amount of stimulation they provided. These combined quality measures correlated significantly with the child's social competence (+0.2), quality of interactions with a friend (+0.12) and behavioural problems (−0.16). This suggests that the quality of daycare is important, as well as the amount of time spent in it.

Figure 2.26 Childcare professionals need to be sensitive and positive towards children.

Media watch

Evidence in practice

The Guardian
8 July 2004

Your task for this section of the course is to either produce summaries of two news articles or conduct a content analysis. In this section, we will guide you through examples of these tasks and give you examples to try for yourself. In order to summarise or analyse an article effectively, you need to be sure that you understand the content. Return to earlier parts of the chapter to help you where necessary. If you can, try to track down any original research that the article refers to, but be sure not to muddle up what is actually in the resource you are using and what you have found out as background material.

Five beautiful, plump babies sit in their high chairs in a semi-circle, waiting for lunch. They are eerily quiet. Two nursery staff move around preparing bowls, bibs and spoons. As I stand there, I am fixed upon by ten huge round eyes. Is it my imagination or does it seem that their eyes are begging for interaction, for an adult smile? Maybe it is just that they are hungry? Meanwhile, a little four-month-old baby, recently fed and changed, has been put in a bouncy chair on the floor where she is just out of sight, momentarily, of a carer; she begins to cry plaintively. After a little while, a member of staff comes to cuddle her and settle her in a cot. Did she get her reassurance quickly enough? As quickly as a mother or father would have given it?

I don't know the answers — nor do many thousands of other mothers and fathers who take the decision every day to place their babies, from as young as four months, in a nursery. Even here, in this nursery in leafy Caterham, Surrey, with its clearly dedicated staff, those eyes make me feel uncomfortable. Instinctively, it doesn't feel quite right. But I question my response: perhaps it is simply because I belong to a transition generation. For most mothers in their 30s and 40s, our earliest years were firmly tied to our mother's apron strings, but we are abandoning that model of motherhood in droves — more than half of us now hand over the care of our baby to others for many hours a day, before they reach their first birthday.

In the past two decades, we have revolutionised how we care for children in the first three years of life. In 1981, only 24% of women returned to work within a year of childbirth, while in 2001 it was 67%, and the proportion is expected to continue rising. Childcare has become a boom industry. The vast bulk of that expansion has been in private day nurseries; since 1997 alone, the number of places has doubled, and it has quadrupled in a decade. Just over 200,000 children under three now attend a day nursery. It comfortably outstrips all other forms of non-family care for under-threes.

But the popularity of this revolution is at odds with what the experts are saying. Over exactly the time period that the sector has boomed, research on both sides of the Atlantic has reached remarkably similar conclusions; namely, that large quantities of care in a day nursery before the age of three increases the incidence of insecurity and aggression in children, and that these damaging effects are still evident years later. What is extraordinary is how little impact this research has had, so far, on either public perception or government policy. This is partly because most of the experts have preferred to keep their heads below the parapet, well aware of the kind of panic headlines that their findings could produce. They are terrified of thousands of already anxious parents waking up to a *Daily Mail* splash — 'Day nurseries make children violent'. They have preferred to lobby government from the inside. Meanwhile, the private-sector day nurseries mushroom unchecked, and government ignores the negative findings.

Exercise

Content analysis exercise

The writer of the above article is clearly uncomfortable with the widespread use of daycare. Your task is to carry out a content analysis of the article with the aim of showing how the writer has used language to make their argument convincing.

Identify the uses of language you will be looking for in the article. You might, for example, look for words like 'expert' and 'research' which can be used to make the writer sound logical and those like 'cry' and 'distress' that are designed to provoke an emotional response.

Draw up a tally chart and record the frequency with which each of these key words are used.

Looking at your chart, has the writer used mostly logical or emotional devices to make their point?

Get surfing and find another article on daycare. Carry out the same procedure. Do the two articles use the same or different approaches to making their argument?

Exercise

Summary exercise

1. Visit the following two websites:

    http://www.fulltimemothers.org/index.htm

    http://www.daycaretrust.org.uk

    Summarise the points each organisation makes about daycare.

    What conclusions are reached by each organisation?

    What theory and/or research might each organisation draw upon to make their arguments?

    What other factors might influence each organisation (political, religious, commercial etc)?

You may be asked to describe one key issue from child psychology. You can choose this yourself from this chapter. Suitable examples include:

- Does daycare harm children's development?
- Is privation reversible?
- How can we reduce the effects of deprivation?
- Is autism a biological condition?
- Can mothers be held responsible for insecure attachments?

Make sure that for whatever you identify as your key issue, you can pose a question and draw on psychological theory and/or research to answer it.

Summary and conclusions

A child's first attachment to their adult carer or carers seems to be extremely important in affecting their later development. It is likely that our tendency to form attachments is an evolutionary mechanism, increasing the probability that a child will survive to adulthood. Attachment can be of different quality, and a secure attachment is associated with better later development. A standard procedure for assessing infant attachment type is Ainsworth's Strange Situation. This classifies children into types, type B being secure. Type Bs have been shown to have better adult relationships and better mental health than others.

Children's development can be affected by separation from their attachment figures (deprivation) and, more seriously, by the failure to form a normal attachment (privation). Separation can be short-term, as in hospitalisation, or long-term, as takes place in family re-ordering. Long-term separation is associated with some developmental problems; however, it is not clear whether this is due to family re-ordering itself, or the inadequate ways in which most families handle re-ordering for children.

Some children are affected by developmental conditions. One such condition is ADHD. ADHD is diagnosed when a child has problems with attention and/or hyperactivity. These symptoms are associated with problems in cognitive and social development. Some professionals believe ADHD is a neurological problem. However, this is controversial and some social psychologists suggest instead that it is not a real condition at all, but a label applied to children whose behaviour challenges parents and teachers.

Daycare, which is perhaps the most common situation in which young children are regularly separated from their attachment figures, is highly controversial. Some studies have found that daycare is associated with high rates of insecure attachment and other social-emotional problems such as increased aggression. However, not all studies support this finding, and a closer look at the research shows a number of factors that mediate the possible effects of daycare; for example, starting age, time in daycare, quality of daycare and how the transition from full-time parental care to daycare is handled.

What do I know?

1. (a) Define deprivation. [3]

   (b) Evaluate research into the effects of privation. [7]

2. (a) Describe **one** research method used in child psychology. [4]

   (b) Evaluate the method you described in (a). [6]

3. (a) Describe the symptoms of **one** child disorder you have studied. [3]

   (b) Identify **two** effects this disorder may have on the child's development. [2]

   (c) Evaluate **one** explanation for this disorder. [6]

4. (a) What is meant by the term 'separation anxiety'? [3]

   (b) Evaluate the use of structured observations to study children's development. [5]

5. Amina is nine months old and her mother is considering returning to work and using daycare. Based on psychological research, what could you advise her about the possible effects of daycare? [12]

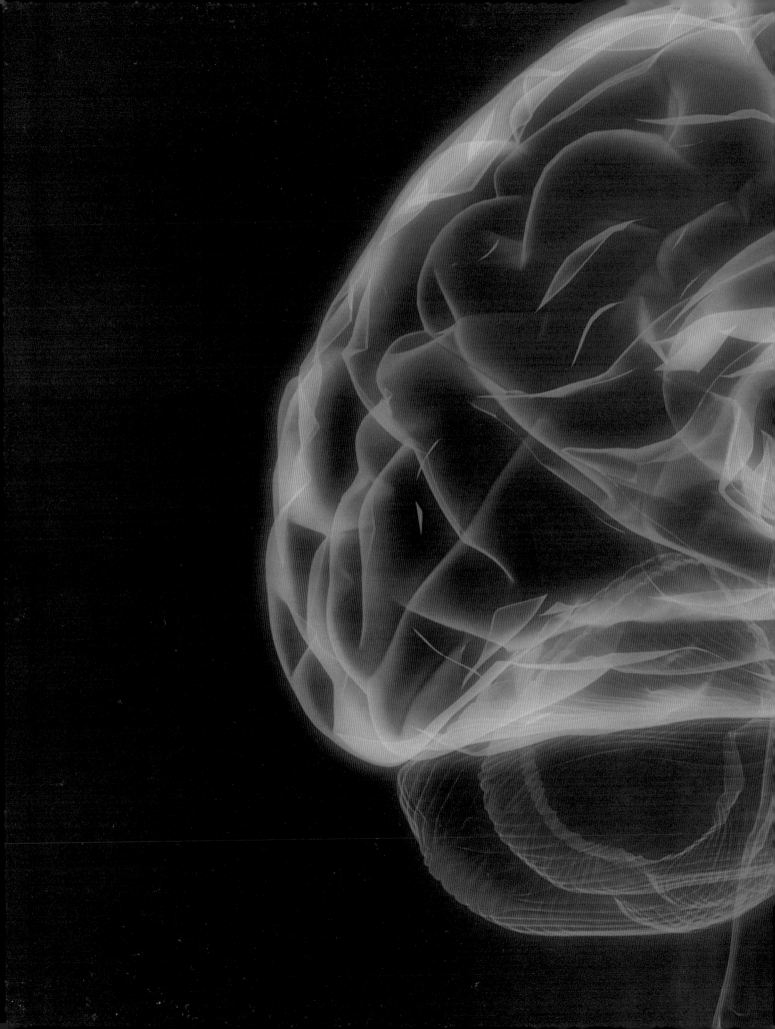

What's ahead?

By the end of this chapter I should know about:

- what is meant by health psychology
- two explanations of substance misuse: one from the biological approach and one from the learning approach
- the mode of action, effects, tolerance, dependency and withdrawal of heroin and one other drug eg cocaine or marijuana
- two ways to treat substance misuse including drug treatment of heroin dependence and one other
- one campaign to reduce recreational drug use
- two studies about drugs: Blätter *et al.* (2002) and one other
- one key issue from health psychology
- either a content analysis or a summary of two articles relating to health psychology

In addition I should understand:

- the use of animals in laboratory studies for drug research
- the practical and ethical issues relating to the use of animals in research
- two research methods which use humans to investigate the effects of drugs
- issues relating to the use of humans in research including issues of reliability and validity

Where does health psychology take us?

- Is addiction 'all in the brain'?
- What can health psychology do for drug misusers?
- Why would *Coca Cola* ever have contained cocaine?
- Is alcoholism inherited?
- Are bungee-jumpers more likely to take drugs?
- Should we pay heroin users to stay clean?
- Are people who like sweets more likely to be alcoholics?

Health psychology

Health psychology is the application of psychological knowledge to the promotion and maintenance of health, the avoidance, diagnosis and treatment of illness and the improvement of health care provision. There are many areas of health psychology and in this chapter we will consider the role of health psychology in understanding drug misuse.

One way to study health psychology is to use a biological approach. This allows psychologists to explain problems such as how drugs act and to understand their effects using physiological concepts. Social, cognitive and learning theory approaches can also help psychologists to account for aspects of healthy and unhealthy behaviour and understanding these factors can help us to promote good health. In this chapter we will consider biological explanations for the action and effects of drugs and look at the ways in which other approaches can help to explain why people take drugs and ways to prevent them from starting to use drugs or to help them to stop. In Chapter 5 we will consider the use of drugs for medical purposes in the treatment of mental illness, but in this chapter we will be focusing on substance *misuse*, that

is, the use of legal or illegal drugs or other substances, such as glue and solvents, that results in damage to physical or mental health of the user, or to the welfare of others.

Drug action
Drugs, neurotransmitters and the synapse

To understand how drugs work you will need to recall some details from the biological approach which you studied at AS. Particularly, you need to understand the processes that occur at the synapse – the gap between neurones across which a chemical signal is sent. As you can see in Figure 3.1, an impulse travels along the axon of a neurone and when it reaches the synaptic knobs, it causes neurotransmitters to be released into a gap called the synaptic cleft. The neurotransmitters attach to receptor sites on the post-synaptic neurone, the edge of the next cell. These are specially shaped to allow only particular neurotransmitters to attach to each one. When sufficient neurotransmitters have attached to the receptor sites, an impulse is transmitted along the second neurone. The neurotransmitters fall out of the receptor sites and are recycled. They are broken down by enzymes in the synaptic gap and are reabsorbed into the pre-synaptic membrane to be re-used.

Types of neurotransmitters

In this chapter, and in Chapter 5, you will encounter several different neurotransmitters. Dopamine, noradrenaline and serotonin are from a group called monoamine neurotransmitters – they are quite similar in structure. The endorphins are another key group of neurotransmitters. Finally, GABA (gamma-aminobutyric acid) is different from all those listed above as it works in a different way (see page 71).

Figure 3.1a A neurone.

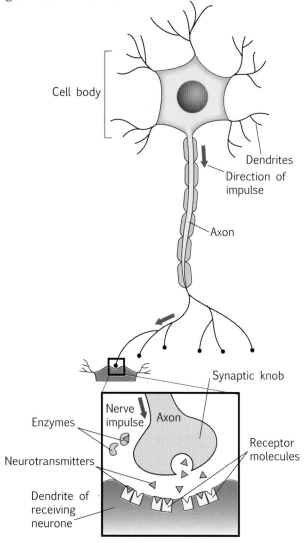

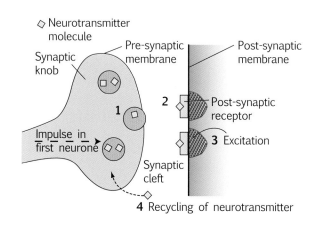

1 Neurotransmitters are released from the pre-synaptic membrane in response to an impulse.
2 They cross the synaptic cleft and attach to post-synaptic receptors.
3 This causes a response in this neurone, for example, excitation.
4 The neurotransmitters are broken down in the synaptic cleft (by enzymes) and recycled or are taken back into the synaptic knob and re-used (re-uptake).

Fig 3.1b Normal synaptic functioning.

Inhibitory synapses

Many synapses work in the manner described above. The action of neurotransmitters at such synapses is called 'excitatory' because they increase the probability of nerve impulses. In some situations, however, the role of the neurotransmitter is to *reduce* the frequency of impulses. These are called inhibitory synapses. One example of an inhibitory neurotransmitter is GABA.

What's that?

- **Synaptic cleft**: the gap between two neurones, bordered by the pre- and post-synaptic membrane. It is normally crossed by neurotransmitters but is also a site of action for drugs

- **Antagonist**: a drug that limits the effect of a neurotransmitter and reduces post-synaptic activity, for example, by blocking post-synaptic receptors or preventing recycling or release of neurotransmitters

- **Agonist**: a drug that mimics the effect of a neurotransmitter and increases post-synaptic activity, for example, by stimulating post-synaptic receptors

Drugs and the synapse

There are several different ways that drugs can interfere with processes at the synapse (see Figure 3.2). They can:

- block the receptors so that neurotransmitters cannot fit into them

- attach to the receptors and have the same effect as a neurotransmitter

- prevent the recycling of neurotransmitters so that they stay in the synapse and can re-attach to receptor sites.

In the first of these, the drug molecule is a similar shape to a neurotransmitter and will fit into the receptor site. By doing so, it prevents neurotransmitters from attaching so they cannot stimulate the post-synaptic neurone. This reduces the frequency of nerve impulses and drugs that act in this way are called 'antagonists' – they have the *opposite* effect from the neurotransmitter. Drugs such as naloxone (see page 81) act in this way.

In the second two situations, the frequency of nerve impulses will be increased. Drugs that act in this way are called 'agonists' – they have the same kind of effect as the neurotransmitter. This is because they either mimic it or they prevent it being taken back into the pre-synaptic membrane so, once released, neurotransmitter molecules can re-stimulate the receptors. Drugs such as heroin act by mimicking neurotransmitters (called endorphins). Some drugs used to treat depression (which you will encounter in Chapter 5) work by preventing the re-uptake of the neurotransmitter serotonin – they are called selective serotonin re-uptake inhibitors (or SSRIs).

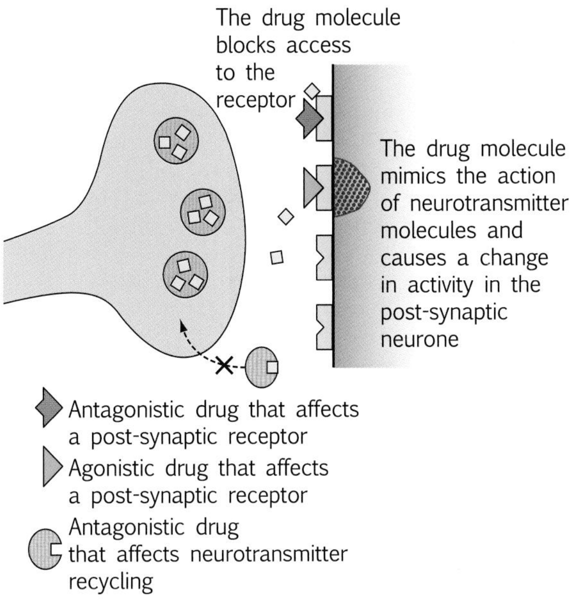

The drug molecule blocks access to the receptor

The drug molecule mimics the action of neurotransmitter molecules and causes a change in activity in the post-synaptic neurone

◆ Antagonistic drug that affects a post-synaptic receptor

▷ Agonistic drug that affects a post-synaptic receptor

Antagonistic drug that affects neurotransmitter recycling

Figure 3.2 Effects of drugs on neurotransmitters and synaptic functioning.

What's that?

- **Psychoactive drug**: a chemical compound taken for its effect on mental processes, for example, affecting cognitions (including perception), emotions or behaviour

- **Psychological dependence**: a compulsion to take a drug for the pleasant effects it has, such as feelings of exhilaration or self-confidence. It may lead to misuse, as the compulsion can result in uncontrolled drug taking. It does not produce withdrawal effects

Drugs and the user
Dependence

Taking a drug has both immediate effects on the user and longer term ones. We will be looking at these in detail for specific drugs (see pages 77–88) but there are several consequences that are typical for many drugs that we will consider here. These effects can arise in the use of both prescribed, medically required drugs and through the misuse of psychoactive drugs, that is, drugs that are taken 'recreationally' purely for their mind-altering effects. Many drug users display uncontrolled drug use. They feel a compulsion to take the drug for its effects. This is an example of positive reinforcement – the user is operantly conditioned to continue their drug-taking habit in order to gain the experiences they desire (see page 74 for a detailed explanation). They may believe that they need a drug in order to function, although physiologically this is not the case. Such users are described as psychologically dependent. Interestingly, people may develop a **psychological dependence** upon other things, such as work or other people, and may be at a loss to cope in the absence of the focus of their dependency.

What's that?

- **Physical dependence:** refers to a compulsion to keep taking drugs in order to avoid withdrawal symptoms. Continued use of the drug is required for the user to feel normal

- **Withdrawal symptoms** or the **abstinence syndrome:** the experience of physically painful and unpleasant symptoms suffered by a physically dependent user as the effects of the drug wear off. These may include vomiting, shaking, headaches and convulsions, although they vary from drug to drug

No smoking It is against the law to smoke in these premises

Figure 3.3 Physical dependence leads to a compulsion to take the drug and can affect social relationships or work commitments and lead to illegal behaviour.

Box 3.1

The Diagnostic and Statistical Manual (DSM-IV) criteria for disorders of substance misuse

For a diagnosis of the chronic problem of **substance dependence**, an individual must show three of the following at any time in a 12-month period:

- tolerance

- withdrawal symptoms

- increasing doses

- unsuccessful attempts to cut down intake

- considerable time spent obtaining, using or recovering from the use of the substance

- important social, occupational or recreational activities are given up (for example, being too hung over to turn up for work)

- continuation of use despite recognition that this causes physical or psychological problems

For a diagnosis of the acute or episodic problem of **substance abuse** an individual must experience one or more of the following in a 12-month period:

- interference with obligations in their major role, for example, at work, home or school (such as missing lessons)

- recurrent use in potentially hazardous situations (for example, drink-driving)

- legal problems related to drug use

- continued use, despite social or interpersonal problems caused by substance use

Users of some drugs become strongly dependent upon them. In the state of **physical dependence**, the user is compelled to continue to take the drug in order to avoid the unpleasant effects they experience when they stop. These unpleasant effects, such as sweating, shaking, vomiting or depression, are called **withdrawal symptoms**; together they are described as the **abstinence syndrome**. In general, withdrawal symptoms are the opposite of the effects the drug itself has. For example, if the drug makes the user euphoric, withdrawal is likely to include depression; if the drug induces sleep, a withdrawal symptom is likely to be insomnia. Taking the drug again removes these withdrawal symptoms. As a consequence, the user is compelled to re-administer the drug in order to avoid the unpleasant experiences. This is an example of negative reinforcement – the user is negatively reinforced to continue their drug-taking habit because removing the withdrawal symptoms makes them feel better (see also page 74).

Substance dependence, like other mental illnesses, is diagnosed using the Diagnostic and Statistical Manual or DSM (see Box 3.1). You will study this in more detail in clinical psychology (see page 136). Diagnostic criteria for substance misuse disorders include the concept of compulsive drug use (for example, continuation even when the user recognises that it is damaging). Compulsion can exist even when the other criteria are not met. For example, a smoker will not be dangerously intoxicated by nicotine, nor (assuming they are old enough and smoking at home or out of doors) be in breach of the law. Nevertheless, a dependent smoker will find a day at work intolerable if they cannot have a cigarette.

Tolerance

Down regulation: changes to receptors

Drug users often need greater doses of the drug over time in order to achieve the same effects as they did at first. This is called tolerance. There are several explanations for why this arises. One important explanation for tolerance reflects the way that the nervous system responds to the presence of a drug. Each drug type attaches to a particular class of receptor sites (see Figure 3.2). With drug molecules, in addition to the normal neurotransmitters, entering the synapse the body adapts. The number of receptor sites (or their sensitivity) is reduced – a process called down regulation. As a consequence, larger doses of the drug are needed to reach the same level of stimulation of the neurones, as there are fewer receptors for the drug molecules to attach to.

Drug removal by enzymes

Another explanation for tolerance is related to the way that drugs are disposed of by the body. Drug molecules are broken down by enzymes in the liver. In response to the presence of some drugs, the liver produces more of the enzymes responsible for removing that drug. As a consequence, a body which has been repeatedly exposed to a drug can break it down more quickly than one which has not. This is because the user's liver is more efficient at processing the drug molecules, so the user needs more of the drug to reach the same level in the body.

What's that?

- **Tolerance:** is the development of a need for greater amounts of a drug with repeated use in order to achieve the same effect. It occurs with many drugs, such as alcohol, heroin and cocaine

- **Down regulation:** the reduction in the sensitivity or number of receptor sites on the post-synaptic membrane in response to long-term exposure to a drug

Classical conditioning: the compensatory reaction hypothesis

A final explanation of tolerance, sometimes referred to as the 'homeostatic theory' of tolerance or the 'compensatory reaction hypothesis', is based on classical conditioning. It suggests that, when users often take drugs in the same context, aspects of that situation become environmental cues. The body responds to these cues (such as familiar procedures, locations or people) by preparing the body for the incoming drug. The response, however, is to compensate for the drug presence – by making the body *less* sensitive. In classical conditioning terms, the environmental cues – initially neutral stimuli (NS) – become associated with the unconditioned stimulus (UCS) of the drug. After repeated pairings during drug-taking, these cues become conditioned stimuli. The conditioned response is in the opposite direction to the effect of the drug itself, so counteracts the drug's effect. This learned effect can readily explain tolerance as more drug (UCS) + environmental cue (NS) pairings result in a stronger conditioned response of reduction in sensitivity.

This hypothesis can also account for some instances of drug overdose. When familiar environmental cues are missing, such as if a user is in a group of strange people, or alone when they usually take drugs in a group, the compensation response does not occur. In the absence of the bodily preparation for the incoming drug, the effects are much more intense, which can lead to a fatal overdose.

Cross-tolerance and cross-dependence

Within some drug categories such as the opiates (heroin, morphine etc), prolonged use of one drug in the group results in the development of tolerance to the others. This is called **cross-tolerance**. It occurs because the drug molecules are very similar and attach to the same receptor sites. The effect of cross-tolerance is that a user of one drug in the group would need a higher dose of another, similar drug to produce an effect than would a non-user. This effect can be readily understood in the light of the down regulation explanation of tolerance. Since all the related drugs in a chemical group attach to the same receptors, changes in the number of those receptors on the post-synaptic membrane caused by misusing one drug will have the same effect on sensitivity to related drugs. One consequence of this relationship is **cross-dependence**. This is when the symptoms of withdrawal produced by physical dependence on one drug can be reduced by the use of another drug. This underlies the medical use of drugs in rehabilitation of users. For example, benzodiazepines (the drug group which includes Valium) are used clinically to relieve the symptoms of withdrawal from alcohol.

Operant conditioning and drug use

You will have learned about operant conditioning in your AS course. This theory suggests that a behaviour will increase in frequency if it is often followed by a pleasant consequence, called a reinforcer. If reinforcement follows a behaviour immediately, or closely, it is more likely to affect the frequency than if there is a pause between the individual performing the behaviour and the arrival of the reward. For example, Logan (1965) found that hungry rats would learn to run through a maze for food. Given two paths, one leading to a small but immediate food reward and the other to a larger but delayed reward, they would choose the former – immediacy is preferable to quantity.

There are two kinds of 'reward': positive reinforcement and negative reinforcement. A positive reinforcer increases the frequency of a behaviour because its effects are pleasant. For example, nice food is a positive reinforcer. It is important to remember that a negative reinforcer also increases the frequency of a behaviour because its effects are pleasant. In this case, however, the pleasant effect is the removal of something nasty. For example, the stopping of an annoying sound would be a negative reinforcer. These concepts can be used to explain some aspects of drug misuse.

A learning theory explanation for drug misuse: positive reinforcement

Many laboratory animals, such as rats and monkeys, will self-administer drugs. This can be demonstrated using a Skinner box, in which a bar-press leads to the dispensing of either an intravenous dose or the opportunity to drink dosed quantities of a drug such as alcohol. Such experiments have shown that rats will press the bar for cocaine in a similar pattern to the way that they work for food. For example, in a fixed ratio schedule, as the ratio rises the number of responses per hour increases, thus the animal receives roughly the same number of reinforcements per hour. However, the rat's ability to respond becomes impaired by the effects of the drug itself at high doses of cocaine, preventing them from pressing the bar (Pickens & Thompson, 1968 – see *Angles on Psychology*, pages 170–2).

Figure 3.4 Drug self-administration. Animals such as rats and monkeys will learn to self-administer drugs in a Skinner box.

As we saw above, immediate reinforcers are more effective than delayed ones. Drugs such as heroin that are injected or smoked pass very quickly into the brain, so have an almost instant effect. Their reinforcing properties are therefore particularly powerful because the user can readily form an association between the drug-taking behaviour and the positively reinforcing experience. This applies to animals too; rats will learn more quickly to press a bar for an intravenous dose of cocaine than for a sip of alcohol. This is partly because alcohol is slower to have an effect. The importance of the relative speed of reinforcement helps us to understand how a user can become addicted to a drug which has unpleasant or even life-threatening effects. Such risks are long term, whereas the effects of positive reinforcement are short term. Thus, an individual is more powerfully affected by the immediate rewards than by the delayed consequences of withdrawal, imprisonment or death.

Of course, people (and animals) can also become addicted to drugs with slower-acting effects. In the case of animals, they need to be 'taught' the association (for example, by flavouring alcohol, which rats do not spontaneously like, with a sweet taste, which they do). People, however, can make the cognitive connection which bridges the gap between taking the drug and experiencing the desired effects. A human can, for example, link the effects of ingesting a pill to the later psychoactive effects, thus positive reinforcement can still operate.

The exact neural mechanism of this reinforcing effect differs between drug types. However, many drugs seem to act through the dopamine reward system (see Box 3.2 on page 89). For example, Wise *et al.* (1995) found that dopamine levels in the nucleus accumbens of rats rose by 150–300% in response to lever presses for injections of heroin. Using a different technique, White & Hiroi (1993) tested rats on their preference for a location where they previously had or had not received drug doses intravenously. They found that the rats developed a 'place-preference' for the testing compartment where they had received amphetamine injected directly into the nucleus accumbens, but not if it was injected into other brain structures (see page 79).

A learning theory explanation for drug misuse: negative reinforcement

The effects of withdrawal are potentially powerful negative reinforcers. Dependent users may be reinforced to continue drug use in order to avoid unpleasant effects such as nausea, anxiety and depression, which they experience in the absence of the drug. Negative reinforcement can thus provide a reason for the maintenance of drug use. Furthermore, this explanation is able to account for the observation that many dependent users no longer experience the positively reinforcing effects for which they originally took the drug. For example, a dependent heroin user feels little of the euphoria or well-being that a non-dependent user would experience. They do, however, need to continue to take the drug to ward off withdrawal. However, this explanation is clearly incomplete. A dependent user who achieves a period of abstinence will no longer experience withdrawal symptoms, yet often feels compelled to resume their habit (that is, to **relapse**). Indeed, when their habit becomes too costly some dependent heroin users deliberately employ the strategy of a period of abstinence in order to reduce the dosage they need. They would not to do this if the avoidance of the unpleasant effects of withdrawal was the sole factor maintaining their habit. Furthermore, some addictive drugs do not produce physical dependency and users do not experience particularly unpleasant withdrawal symptoms. Again, this suggests that negative reinforcement is insufficient as an explanation of continued drug use.

On the basis of the explanation above, negative reinforcement appears only to be able to explain the

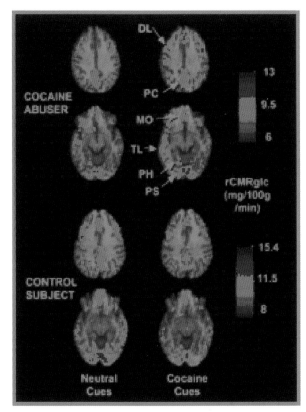

Figure 3.5 Pet scanning shows more activation in cocaine users' brains in a situation designed to induce craving than in non-users.

continuation of drug use, not its initiation. One situation in which negative reinforcement could account for an individual starting to take a drug is in order to reduce some pre-existing psychological symptoms. This idea, referred to as 'self-medication', would offer a reason for an anxious person misusing alcohol or someone suffering low self-esteem taking cocaine. In each case, the user is seeking to remove or reduce unpleasant feelings by taking the drug. Thus, even their initial drug use would be negatively reinforcing.

What's that?

- **Relapse:** the return to drug use by a previously dependent user after a period of abstinence
- **Self-medication:** the use of a non-prescribed drug to reduce pre-existing psychological symptoms (such as depression, anxiety or low self-esteem)

Another role for negative reinforcement is in the reduction of craving. According to Robinson & Berridge (1993), this is not simply a desire to remove the unpleasant effects of withdrawal – indeed, there may be none – but a motivation to satisfy an urge to take the drug. The removal of this longing offers relief, so is a negative reinforcer. A physiological correlate of craving has been illustrated using PET scans of the brains of cocaine users and non-users. Grant *et al.* (1996) exposed participants

to two sets of stimuli. In the control condition, participants were shown craft-related items including a paint brush, paints, clay and a leather punch. They also saw a video of a person handling seashells. In the experimental condition, participants saw drug-related items such as some cocaine, a mirror, a razor blade, a straw and a glass pipe and a video of people sniffing and smoking a white powder. The participants who had a history of cocaine use were told they would be allowed to sniff the cocaine after the experiment. The brain scans showed increased activity in some areas of the cocaine users' brains (for example, the amygdala) in response to the drug-related stimuli. This did not occur in the control participants, nor in either group when presented with the non-drug-related stimuli.

Craving may be induced, in animals or humans, by giving the user a 'taste' of the drug or exposing them to something associated with it. For example, a rat which has learned to self-administer cocaine can be prompted to bar press for more of the drug if it is given a small 'priming' dose. Self *et al.* (1996) found that this cocaine-seeking behaviour could also be triggered by stimulating a single type of dopamine receptor (D_3). Dopamine (see page 88) is intimately involved in the reward system that reinforces drug taking (and other behaviours). This priming effect is also seen with electrical brain stimulation (see page 89), again suggesting that the reinforcement associated with drug taking may be satisfying a need rather than strictly being a 'positive' experience.

Stress can also act as a prime that induces craving. Under stress, an abstinent user is more likely to relapse. This can also be understood in terms of negative reinforcement – the drug helps to reduce the avoidable discomfort of craving. The same effect can be demonstrated in rats that have been conditioned to self-administer cocaine or heroin. When a stressor is introduced, their response rate increases. Shaham & Stewart (1995) linked this craving to dopamine levels in the nucleus accumbens. The response of rats trained to self-administer heroin was extinguished (by replacing the heroin infusion with saline) and they were then stressed using electric shocks. Following this, the rats increased their bar-pressing rate, as did the level of dopamine in the nucleus accumbens.

One way to study the effects of withdrawal experimentally is to induce it in a dependent animal by using drugs which block the effects of the drug under investigation. This can be achieved with an antagonist (see page 71), so the procedure is called antagonist-precipitated withdrawal. Investigations using an antagonist for heroin, called naloxone, are discussed on page 81.

Interactive angles

How does the priming effect explain the risks associated with a single drink for a recovered alcoholic?

Human research methods for investigating drugs: brain scanning

MRI scanning

Magnetic resonance imaging (MRI) can be used in two ways; either as a structural technique or a functional one (fMRI). Although the techniques are somewhat different, both provide detailed images on a computer monitor. Standard MRI scans look like a photograph taken of a slice through the brain and are highly detailed. MRI scanning uses a powerful magnetic field that affects the positively charged particles (protons) in hydrogen atoms. These respond like compass needles, so align when the magnetic field in the scanner is turned on. Radio waves are then passed through the head by the scanner. As the protons return to their original positions, they emit radio waves that are detected by the scanner. Different areas of the brain emit differing amounts of radio waves causing different densities (shades of grey) on the image. If there are lots of hydrogen atoms, the area appears white; if there are very few it is dark.

In fMRI, a similar technique is used, but the chemical responding to the magnetic field is haemoglobin – the oxygen-carrying molecule in the blood. As oxygen is needed for brain activity, more and less active brain areas look different. This technique is sometimes referred to as BOLD (blood-oxygen-level dependent) fMRI. It produces images with different colour densities (or colours) indicating differing levels of brain activity. From this, specific areas which are more or less active can be identified.

An MRI scanner is a large machine with a narrow central tube. The participant lies on a bed which slides inside the scanner. The environment is both very noisy (because of the powerful magnet) and confined. The participant can, however, hear and speak to the researcher through a headset. For good scans to be obtained, the participant must remain very still.

MRI is of value to psychologists because it allows us to compare the structure of brains that are functioning normally and abnormally. For example, structural scans can be used to compare brains of drug users and non-users to investigate whether physical differences exist. However, if differences are identified, researchers cannot be sure whether those differences existed before drug use or are a product of it. fMRI can be used to study brain events during drug use and to investigate differences in brain function between users and non-users.

PET scanning

Positron emission tomography (PET), like fMRI, is a functional technique. It involves injecting a radioactive tracer molecule into the participant's blood, which is then detected as it undergoes decay. Tracers are radioactive versions of chemicals used up during brain activity, such as water (containing radioactive oxygen ^{15}O) or glucose (containing radioactive carbon ^{11}C). The tracer reaches the brain after about one minute and takes 10–15 minutes to decay, releasing minute amounts of radioactivity initially in the form of positrons (these collide with electrons and produce gamma

rays). The emission of gamma rays detected by the scanner is used to produce a record of the levels of activity in different brain areas by determining where most blood is flowing to. The scanner itself consists of a doughnut-shaped ring which surrounds the participant's head. As with an fMRI, greater levels of brain activity appear on the scan as different colours.

The participant is generally scanned several times in two conditions. One set of recordings is taken when they are inactive, as a baseline. Another set of records is made when they are performing a particular task. The difference between the scans tells us which parts of the brain are involved in that activity. This technique has enabled researchers to investigate active brain areas involved in tasks which can be useful if deficits such as in information processing or memory are suspected following drug use. For example, Galynker *et al.* (2000) used brain scanning to compare brain function in people with no history of drug abuse, those receiving methadone treatment and another who had received methadone treatment and had not abused opiates for four years. Using radioactive glucose, differences were identified between the entirely drug-free and non-user groups. Ex-users had more activity in the anterior cingulate gyrus than the non-user controls (with those on methadone treatment intermediate between the two). There are two possible explanations for these findings. Either opiate use increases activity in this brain area, or this pattern of activity reflects a predisposition to take addictive drugs such as opiates. The cause, however, cannot be distinguished using brain scanning.

Evaluation

Modern scanning techniques are useful because they provide such clear, accurate and detailed images. The techniques have good reliability, although their validity depends on the interpretation of the findings and this can be difficult. Although changes or differences may be observed, understanding their meaning is difficult. For example, differences between drug users and non-users may indicate changes due to drug use or pre-existing differences which underlie a need for self-medication. Another threat to validity in such studies is the truthfulness of participants. Those in 'non-user' control groups may have drug experiences they are not revealing and drug users may be taking more, or different, drugs than they have declared. These problems are compounded by relatively unreliable drug-testing methods. Nevertheless, functional scanning methods allow researchers to see what is happening during brain activity, so valid differences in use/non-use situations can be readily obtained. One further advantage of scanning methods over self-reports of drug effects is that they are more objective. Users may be poor judges or untruthful sources of information about drug effects, even when they are not intoxicated. Using objective methods such as scanning overcomes some of these subjectivities although, of course, only brain activity can be detected and this cannot be directly correlated to psychological experiences such as thoughts or emotions.

There are also practical and ethical considerations to brain scanning. The environment within a scanner is very different from most situations in which people find themselves, thus the recordings may not be representative of day-to-day life. This may be particularly so for drug users; for example, if they are overly anxious, thus introducing a possible confound. Both the noise and confinement of an MRI scanner may be particularly threatening, as may be the prospect of an injection for PET scanning for some drug users. An ethical issue, in addition to potential distress, is the question of protection of participants from exposure to greater risk than everyday life. PET scans, as they use radioactivity (albeit in minute amounts), carry a risk so the frequency with which participants can be scanned is limited. One final practical issue relates to the physical limits imposed by scanning. It is only possible to test a small range of activities on participants while they are being scanned, simply because they must be relatively still.

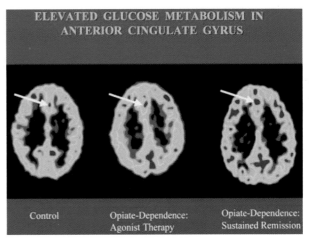

Figure 3.6 PET scans from Galynker *et al.*

Drugs and their effects

In this section we will look at different drug types before returning to explanations for drug use.

Classifying drugs

As we saw on page 71, drugs can be divided into types on the basis of the way they act at the synapse. There are, however, several other ways they can be classified (including the legal classifications, which are not of interest here). Psychologists commonly classify on the basis of their effect on neural activity, thus they can either be **stimulants** (which increase the frequency of neural impulses), or **depressants** (which decrease the frequency of neural impulses). In addition, drugs can be grouped according to the effect that they have; for example, **sedatives** produce sedation, that is, make the user calm and sleepy, and hallucinogens produce **hallucinations**, that is, they cause the user to experience perceptions without a stimulus. Finally, drugs can be grouped chemically, such as the **opiates** – drugs similar in structure to those derived from the opium poppy.

Heroin

Heroin, or diamorphine hydrochloride to use its medical name, is an opiate drug. It is a chemically altered form of morphine, an analgesic (painkiller). Although used medically as it is a powerful analgesic, heroin is a commonly used drug of abuse. It may be taken in different ways (for example, orally or by inhaling vapours when burned), but is most often injected. The chemical alteration that converts morphine into heroin makes it three times as powerful. This is in part because it is more soluble in lipids (fats), so passes into the brain more quickly. This means the speed and intensity of its effect is greater than morphine if it is smoked or injected. Many analgesic drugs, such as codeine and morphine, are derived from the opium poppy, hence this group of drugs is

Figure 3.7 For many years, heroin was believed to be useful for curing a range of ills.

called opiates. Pert & Snyder (1973) identified the receptors to which opiate drugs attach. These receptors exist to receive input from endogenous (internal) opioids called endorphins (**end**ogenous m**orphin**es). The key roles of endorphins are to reduce the experience of pain and to provide reinforcement.

Mode of action: heroin

Heroin acts by stimulating opioid receptors and mimics the effects of endorphins, the natural opioids; it is therefore an agonist. The attachment of either an endorphin or heroin molecule to a receptor inhibits the release of another neurotransmitter, GABA (gamma-aminobutyric acid). Because GABA serves to prevent dopamine release, the effect of heroin is to facilitate the release of dopamine. So, indirectly, heroin causes an increase in the amount of dopamine in the synapses of affected brain areas. One key brain area where this occurs is the nucleus accumbens, which is important in the brain reward system (see page 88).

- **Stimulants:** drugs which increase the frequency of nerve impulses
- **Depressants:** drugs which decrease the frequency of nerve impulses
- **Sedative:** a drug that induces calmness or sleep
- **Hallucination:** an apparent sensory experience that arises in the absence of an external stimulus
- **Opiate:** a drug from the group containing morphine and heroin. The original source of these drugs was the opium poppy, although some, such as methadone, are synthetic

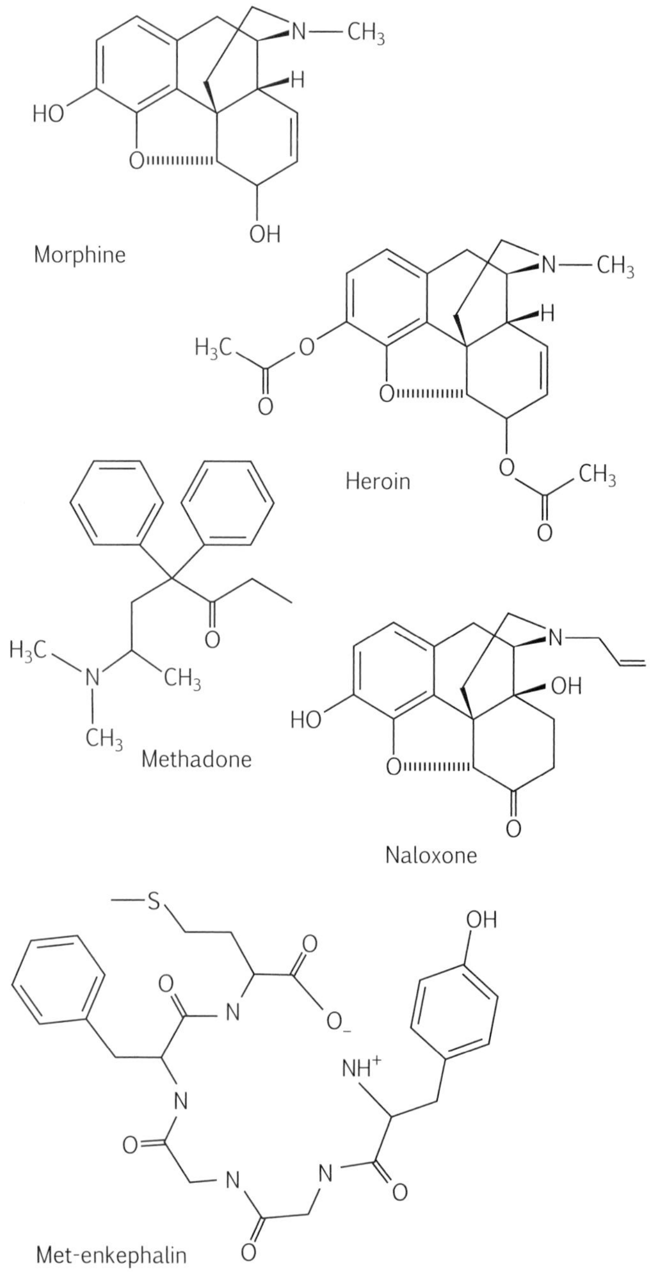

Matthes *et al.* (1996) used genetically modified mice to demonstrate that heroin (being closely related to morphine) has its effects by attaching to opioid receptors. They produced a targeted mutation (called a 'knockout') of the gene which produces one class of opioid receptor (the 'mu' receptor). When given morphine as adults, the knockout mice appeared to gain neither analgesia nor reinforcement from the drug. Unlike normal mice given morphine, who were slow to withdraw their tails from a source of heat as they had been numbed to the pain, the knockout mice remained sensitive and removed their tails quickly at both doses of morphine tested – see Figure 3.9. When tested on their place-preference, the knockout mice showed no sign of a conditioned preference for the location where they received heroin, unlike the control mice. (See also page 79 for explanations and other examples of the place-preference technique.) Finally, in response to a period of abstinence, the normal mice shook themselves vigorously. This 'wet-dog' shake is characteristic of rodents experiencing withdrawal, but was no more frequent in the knockout mice treated with morphine than when they were given saline solution as a control.

Figure 3.8 Five related molecules: met-enkephalin (an endorphin), morphine, heroin, methadone and naloxone.

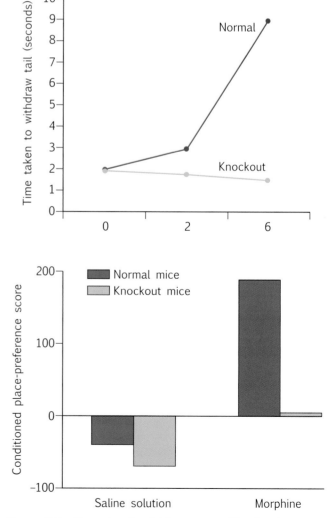

Figure 3.9 The role of opioid receptors. 'Knockout' mice, lacking the gene to produce mu opioid receptors, are insensitive to the analgesic and reinforcing properties of morphine (Matthes *et al.*, 1996).

Skinner boxes and drug self-administration

Many of the studies described in this chapter use Skinner boxes (see Figure 3.17, page 84). These have a number of uses in drug research. Firstly, they can be used to investigate whether a drug which is misused by humans also acts as a reinforcer for animals. If so, then animals can be trained to self-administer the drug and dependent animals can then be used as models for human dependent users. The drug is given in small doses via a tube that is surgically attached to the animal's head. It is connected to a dispensing mechanism that is activated when the animal presses a lever. The tube is able to rotate at the top of the cage, allowing the animal to move around inside the box.

For some drugs, such as cocaine, animals will discover the reinforcing effects and learn to self-administer the drug in a similar way to their learning of a bar press for a food reward. For other drugs, however, animals such as rodents do not learn spontaneously: rats don't like the taste of alcohol, so need to be given sweetened alcohol first to induce them to become dependent.

A dependent animal can model the nature of drug dependence, for example, how quickly dependence is acquired for one drug compared to another, or how resistant the habit is to extinction. They can also be used to model the withdrawal process, by removing access to the drug or by inducing withdrawal using an antagonist (antagonist-precipitated withdrawal). The withdrawal effects exhibited by animals differ from those seen in humans, but some symptoms can be readily observed and measured so the process can be monitored. For example, mice show a characteristic jumping during cocaine withdrawal and rats withdrawing from heroin display 'wet dog' shaking.

In a shuttle box, the animal runs between two ends or boxes – it 'shuttles' backwards and forwards. At each end there may be a lever to press. The floor of the box over which the animal must run can be electrified. This can be used to measure the strength of an animal's motivation. For example, a hungry animal will run across a grid that inflicts a mild electric shock, but not a strong one. The animal's behaviour may be recorded either by sensors which detect its movement across the grid, or by counting bar presses at each end. The strength of the electric shock an animal will endure to gain a self-administered dose of a drug can be used as an indicator of its dependence or craving.

Priming

Within the Skinner box technique, priming may be used when the conditioned lever-pressing response has extinguished. The animal is given an incentive to begin lever pressing again by supplying a single dose of the drug in the absence of a lever press. This causes the animal to resume responding.

Brain recording

In addition to the drug-delivery tube, micro-electrodes can be placed in the animal's brain to record from (or stimulate) very localised brain areas. This can be used to record neural activity immediately before or after receiving drug reinforcements. The electrodes give a precise record of the activity in the brain, which is passed out to a computer that can record and analyse relative activity levels in different areas of the animal's brain.

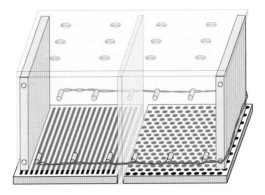

Figure 3.10 The conditioned place-preference test. A rat is reinforced with a drug in only one of two compartments. When drug free, the rat is allowed to choose between the compartments and its movements are accurately recorded using photocells so it does not have to be observed by a researcher.

Conditioned place-preference

This technique removes the influence of incentive as the animal is simply given doses of the drug without lever-pressing. A cage is used containing two locations that are visually different (see Figure 3.10), between which the animal can move freely. The drug is given in only one of these two possible environments. If the animal does not show a preference for the environment in which it received the drug, this suggests that the drug is not positively reinforcing. If the animal does show a preference for the location where it received the drug, even when no drug is provided, this indicates that the drug was reinforcing. The animal's preferred location is recorded automatically by sensors in the cage.

Evaluation
For:

● All of these techniques rely on automated processes for administration of rewards and measuring of responses (as lever presses or movements). This avoids the need for human presence or recording. This has three advantages:

• it is highly objective: whereas a human observer may make subjective judgements about an animal's response, a machine will not

- it is highly reliable: a machine will record the same value each time an animal responds in a particular way

- it avoids the possibility that an animal will react to the human experimenter.

- By starting with drug-naïve animals, such studies control for the possible influence of drug interactions. Many volunteers for human drug experiments are poly-drug users, that is, they have a history of using more than one drug. This can be an important confounding variable.

- By keeping animals in highly controlled situations, researchers can be certain of the dosage size, strength and frequency. None of these are possible in field research with people, as they may be taking additional drugs to those being monitored (particularly as drug testing of urine or blood, for example, can be unreliable) and the strength and dosage of street drugs will vary.

- Measures such as frequency of drug self-administration by animals and willingness to run over electrified grids give objective measures of drug reinforcement and craving that would be practically and ethically difficult to investigate using human participants.

Against:

- Animals as models for human drug-taking are imperfect. They exhibit differences, such as not spontaneously self-administering drugs which are commonly misused by people, for example, alcohol.

- Furthermore, many effects of psychoactive drugs used by people are cognitive or emotional (such as hallucinations or euphoria). They are characteristically human responses so are very difficult to investigate using animal models.

- Animals as models for human withdrawal are also imperfect. They exhibit different withdrawal symptoms, such as wet-dog shakes and jumping, that are not shown by people and other symptoms, such as depression, cannot be effectively measured in animals.

- The procedures for drug studies are in themselves traumatic, so the best-controlled studies also include a sham group, that is, a group on whom the same procedures are conducted but without the variable of the drug (for example, they are operated on or given saline injections). This means that more animals are used than is strictly necessary in order to control for the potential effects of the procedure.

- Drug studies necessarily lead to dependence and therefore the distress of withdrawal. Some also employ strong electric shocks, which are painful for the animal subjects. Yet others allow animals to self-administer lethal quantities of drugs. These procedures raise significant ethical issues with regard to their value compared to the suffering caused.

The effects of heroin

When users take heroin, they seek various effects. It is a powerful analgesia (hence it is used medically). Like morphine, its analgesic effect is central (that is, on the brain rather than the site of the pain) and it makes the individual feel more comfortable so they aren't bothered about pain. Heroin also produces intense euphoria – a feeling of well being – and withdrawal from reality and sleepiness (sedation). Being three times more potent than morphine, this is much more apparent with heroin. Under medical supervision as a painkiller, diamorphine hydrochloride is rarely dependence forming, but is readily so when used in an uncontrolled way. One reason for this is that heroin, like endorphins, acts on the brain's reward system. Rats will readily learn to press a lever in a Skinner box in order to receive a dose of heroin. When given unlimited access to self-administered heroin, many experimental animals die from overdoses (Bozarth & Wise, 1985).

In addition, there are biological effects such as pupil constriction and reduced breathing rate. This is the most important side effect of use that is responsible for death from overdoses – the user simply stops breathing. Heroin also causes nausea and slows the movement of food through the intestines. Constipation can therefore become a significant problem for dependent heroin users.

Figure 3.11 Heroin is a powerfully addictive drug.

The incidence of heroin addiction in Britain is high. In the British Crime Survey 2007–08, 0.1% of adults reported having used heroin in the last year. Whilst this percentage is low, it represents huge numbers of people country-wide. Figures from the Home Office for 2005–06 estimate that there are in excess of 280,000 problem opiate users aged 15–64 in England alone (Hay *et al.*, 2007). This is all the more startling when the long-term effects are considered. As an illegal, dependence-forming drug, it has many associated costs.

Most obviously, heroin use carries the risk of death, since overdosing on heroin can be fatal. There were an estimated 829 deaths involving heroin/morphine in 2007, a 16% rise compared to 2006, although lower than in 2005 (Office for National Statistics, 2008). This potential risk is increased if the drug is 'cut', that is, mixed with other chemicals, such as talcum powder, by the dealer. In some cases, the additive itself may be harmful or even fatal; in others, it makes the strength of the drug unpredictable, which can lead to accidental overdose. Heroin use also increases the risk of injury and infection, as judgement is affected by intoxication and dependent users are less resistant to disease. This risk is worsened through unhygienic use of needles (for example, most users fail to sterilise needles and often share them), so infection rates with illnesses such as HIV and hepatitis are high.

Users are more likely to experience mental health problems, such as depression, even after prolonged abstinence (Brooner *et al.*, 1997). Both possession and dealing of heroin are against the law, so users also risk criminal prosecution; for example, the estimated 280,000 people who use heroin in Britain are breaking the law. As the price of heroin is governed by illegal trade, it is expensive. This, in turn, leads users into criminal behaviour to support their need (which increases because of tolerance), especially as they become less able to hold down a job.

The development of tolerance to heroin results in cross tolerance to all other opioids, both natural and synthetic. Thus, a dependent heroin user would need to take more of the opiate drug Fentanyl (which is also misused) to experience the same effects as a non-user. Similarly, in a medical situation, a dependent heroin user would gain less pain relief from a post-operative injection of morphine.

Heroin tolerance, dependence and withdrawal

Following the brief sensation of euphoria there is a relatively lasting feeling of well being – initially. However, as tolerance develops rapidly and equivalent doses merely maintain the user in a bearable condition, these pleasant effects are short-lived. The immediate symptoms of withdrawal include pain, nausea, diarrhoea, sweating, extreme anxiety and depression. During prolonged abstinence, dependent users suffer continued depression and anxiety, decreased self-esteem, abnormal responses to stress and an increased incidence of other psychiatric

disorders (Brooner *et al.*, 1997). In addition they experience physical symptoms such as sweating, fever, vomiting, cramping, diarrhoea and pain. They also have an intense craving for the drug.

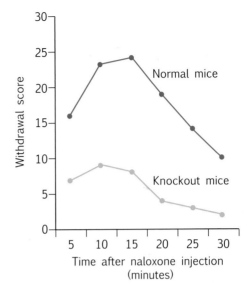

Figure 3.12 Knockout mice without the gene for a chemical called CREB gain pain relief from taking morphine but do not experience withdrawal.

The physiological mechanism responsible for withdrawal seems to be related to the process of down regulation. Following repeated morphine use, the number of opioid receptors remains the same but they become less sensitive to opioids (both natural endorphins and opiate drugs). A chemical called CREB (cyclic AMP-responsive element binding protein) is activated by the binding of opioids to mu receptors (see page 78). In a study using knockout mice which lacked the ability to produce CREB, Maldonado *et al.* (1996) showed that, although the mice responded normally to injections of morphine (that is, it produced analgesia and increased physical activity), they did not exhibit withdrawal symptoms. When given the opiate antagonist naloxone, normal mice experience antagonist-precipitated withdrawal; the knockout mice, however, did not (see Figure 3.12). This finding suggests that the processes controlling withdrawal are at least in part different from those responsible for the effects of opiate drugs.

Cocaine
Mode of action: cocaine

Cocaine blocks the re-uptake of the neurotransmitter dopamine, and also of noradrenalin and serotonin. This leads to an accumulation of dopamine in the synaptic cleft so it can re-stimulate the post-synaptic receptors. In particular, cocaine causes an increase in dopamine levels in the nucleus accumbens, which is central to the brain reward system. Figure 3.13 shows the marked similarity between the number of cocaine self-administrations by an animal and the brain dopamine levels (Di Ciano *et al.*, 1995).

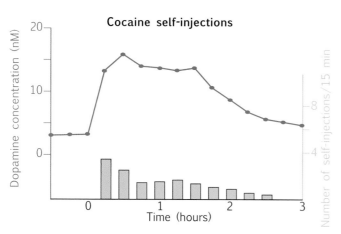

Figure 3.13 Di Ciano *et al.* (1995) demonstrated that cocaine levels and dopamine levels are closely linked.

In humans, the link between cocaine, euphoria and dopamine has also been demonstrated. Schlaepfer *et al.* (1997) used a radioactive molecule that occupied dopamine receptors which could be detected with a PET scan. When given cocaine, the participants reported feeling euphoric and the PET scans showed that the radioactive chemical had been displaced from the dopamine receptors by cocaine molecules.

The link between the reinforcing properties of cocaine and the nucleus accumbens was also shown in an elegant experimental study by Caine & Koob (1994). They destroyed the dopamine-producing neurones of the nucleus accumbens in rats using a specific chemical. The rats, which had previously self-administered cocaine, stopped doing so. The rats did, however, continue to press a lever for food. This cleverly shows that the damage caused to the dopamine-releasing neurones did not affect the ability to press the lever, or to respond to motivating situations in general, but specifically to the rewarding effects of cocaine.

Although most research has focused on the role of dopamine, this alone cannot account for the reinforcing effects of cocaine. Rocha *et al.* (1998) studied mice with a genetic mutation to the dopamine system that should have caused a loss of the reinforcing effects of cocaine, but that was not the case – they still self-administered the drug. This suggests that another process must also be involved. Rocha *et al.* also found that mice with altered serotonin receptors were even more motivated to self-administer cocaine. It thus seems likely that serotonin is also involved in the reinforcing role of cocaine.

The effects of cocaine

Cocaine is powerfully reinforcing. Unlike other drugs that are abused by humans, every animal species that has been tested will self-administer cocaine to excess. This includes baboons, rhesus monkeys, pigtail macaques, dogs, squirrels and rats (Julien, 2001). This is good evidence for its strength as a positive reinforcer. Furthermore, like rats given heroin, allowing rats free access to cocaine results in them self-administering so much that they die and are much more likely to do so than those self-administering heroin (see Figure 3.15).

Figure 3.14 Until 1903, Coca Cola contained cocaine – little wonder it relieved mental and physical exhaustion!

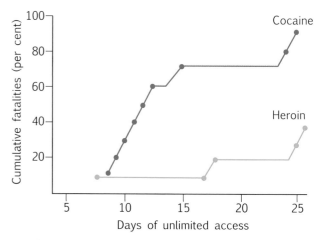

Figure 3.15 Animals self-administering cocaine are more likely to drug themselves to death than those self-administering heroin. (Adapted from Bozarth & Wise, 1985.)

The effects that users seek include a powerful sensation of euphoria, increased self-confidence, alertness and energy and a reduction in tiredness, boredom and hunger. When cocaine is injected, or vapourised and smoked, the effects are rapid and intense, peaking quickly (in seconds or minutes respectively) and lasting about half an hour. However, the user also experiences unpleasant effects, such as anxiety, irritability and insomnia. At high doses, anxiety becomes intense and the individual may become psychotic, meaning that their view of reality and their personality become distorted. Psychosis can include experiences such as hallucinations, mood disturbances, feelings of persecution and repetitive behaviour. These symptoms are also characteristic of the mental illness schizophrenia (see pages 139–140). This similarity further supports the belief that the effects of cocaine are mediated by the neurotransmitter dopamine as high dopamine levels are linked to schizophrenia.

Alongside these psychological effects, biological effects include pupil dilation, increased heart rate and blood pressure and a diversion of blood to the muscles. All of these changes are also those which occur in exciting or stressful situations.

Following the period of pleasant effects, the user experiences a 'crash', during which they suffer a depressed mood with symptoms roughly opposite to those of the 'high', which lasts several hours. Other effects include tremors, loss of co-ordination and seizures. This 'crash' occurs because the high levels of dopamine in the synapses inhibit the release of further neurotransmitter molecules. Thus, once the dopamine has been removed, the relative levels are lower than they were prior to taking the drug, which results in the dysphoric mood state.

Long-term use leads to social and sexual dysfunction, as well as a risk of mental illnesses such as cocaine psychosis, depression and personality disorders. Because cocaine is a vasoconstrictor (it narrows blood vessels) it can reduce oxygen levels and cause brain damage. The consequences of this include strokes, movement disorders and seizures. Even abstinent users may suffer lasting effects such as memory loss. For example, Rounsville et al. (1991) studied a sample of 300 cocaine users and found that 56% met the criteria for a mental illness. One reason why the mental and physical consequences of cocaine addiction are so severe is that cocaine users often misuse other drugs, including alcohol and heroin.

Cocaine tolerance, dependence and withdrawal

Frequent cocaine use leads to tolerance and to physical dependence. This arises from at least two effects: the down regulation of dopamine receptors (making them less sensitive to dopamine) and a reduction on the number of these receptors (White & Kalivas, 1998). Cocaine demonstrates a strong tolerance effect, so dependent users may take very large doses, as much as 150 milligrams (effects are apparent at 8 milligrams). For a dependent user, breaking a cocaine habit is extremely difficult. Cocaine users are also highly likely to relapse once abstinent.

When a user stops taking cocaine they experience a 'crash'. The withdrawal symptoms include depression, insomnia, nausea or vomiting, anxiety, hallucinations and seizures. The user has an intense craving to take more cocaine. They may also experience intense guilt, anger or suicidal feelings. Childress et al. (1999) investigated the role of craving in cocaine dependence. A comparison was made between a group of abstinent cocaine users and a control group of

Figure 3.16 Cocaine is a highly addictive drug.

non-users. They were shown a video of cocaine-relevant stimuli. The cocaine users reported subjective craving, whereas the non-users did not. Furthermore, brain scans showed that only in the users was there an increase in blood flow to the limbic system. This area of the brain is involved in motivation, thus providing a biological indicator of craving.

The problems of cocaine misuse are magnified by the effects on the family and financial concerns. These threats contribute to the user's fears, so exaggerating the symptoms of withdrawal.

Marijuana
Mode of action: marijuana

The drug marijuana, or cannabis, contains a psychoactive chemical from the cannabis plant, *Cannabis sativa*, delta-9-tetrahydrocannabinol (THC). Receptors for this molecule are found in various brain regions, including the hippocampus and cerebellum. Their absence from areas such as the medulla, that control vital functions (breathing, heart beat and so on), accounts for the fact that even large doses of the drug are not lethal. As with the relationship between opioids and opioid receptors, natural or 'endocannabinoids' (endogenous substances that attach to the same receptors as THC) exist.

Attachment of THC to receptors in different parts of the brain, with different roles, can account for the various effects of cannabis. In the cerebellum, THC affects movement and posture, producing a tendency to sit still. In the frontal cortex it affects cognitive processing, creating sensory distortions and affecting concentration. In the hippocampus, THC is responsible for the disruption of memory.

When cannabinoids attach to their receptors on the pre-synaptic membranes of neurones, they inhibit the release of other neurotransmitters. This applies to both THC and natural cannabinoids, such as anandamide. Although not very similar in chemical structure, THC and anandamide are sufficiently alike for THC to occupy the cannabinoid receptors and have the same inhibitory effect. This is more limited, however, so it is called a partial agonist. The similarity between the molecules can be seen in Figure 3.17. One of the roles of anandamide is to inhibit a type of serotonin receptor that is involved in mediating nausea (Fan, 1995). This accounts for the efficacy of cannabis in combating nausea such as experienced by cancer patients receiving chemotherapy.

Figure 3.17 a THC, **b** Anandamide

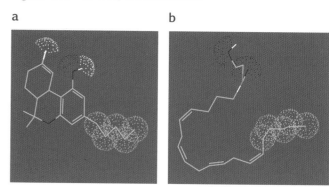

a   b

Practical and ethical issues raised by using animals in research

Practical

Many of the studies described above have involved deliberately inducing drug dependence. This is clearly not something we could perform on randomly selected humans. And, if we ask for volunteers, the sample is likely to consist of those already taking drugs. The practical benefit here is the availability of drug-naïve animals which can be artificially manipulated. Furthermore, humans are unlikely to volunteer for studies which will induce the unpleasant symptoms. With animals, however, it is possible to test the effects of withholding drugs or reversing their effects with an antagonist to study the biological and psychological effects of withdrawal. The reliability of the results of such studies is high as they can use many animals. The validity is also high as important variables such as previous drug use, drug doses and access to other reinforcers are rigorously controlled.

Many studies into drug effects are conducted on rodents such as mice and rats. Whilst there are clear biological similarities which make them good models for human drug dependence, there are also significant differences. For example, opiate withdrawal in rodents leads to characteristic 'wet dog' shaking – a symptom not seen in humans. Perhaps more importantly, it is very difficult to assess the psychological effects, such as anxiety, experienced by animals in response to drug use or abstinence. Nor can the complex cognitive and social effects of drug use be mirrored in animal studies. They therefore lack some important influences and consequences present in the human drug-taking experience.

Ethical

One of psychology's key aims is to improve the human condition. This aim can be used to justify the use of animals in experiments to better our understanding of processes such as drug action. In order to obtain valid and reliable evidence, experiments should be well controlled. Such a high level of control can be exercised over animals but would not be acceptable for human participants. For example, deliberately making people dependent on a drug would be unethical.

Such studies are, however, possible with animals. When used in such experiments, an animal which is enduring prolonged and significant pain can (and should) be killed. This would not be acceptable with human participants, so animals provide a means to test wider applications of drug research than would be ethically possible with human participants.

The very thing that makes animals good models for human drug responses, the similarity in our nervous systems, also serves to raise questions about the ethics of conducting such research on non-human animals. Since withdrawal from drug dependence is unpleasant for us, so it will be for animals. In order to reduce the suffering of animals, guidelines and legal provisions ensure that the minimum number of animals are used, that their suffering is reduced as much as possible and that studies conducted which will induce pain or distress are likely to result in medical benefit. It can still be argued, however, that it is the human population who benefit but the animal population which suffers.

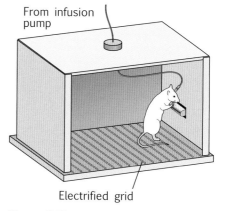

From infusion pump

Electrified grid

Figure 3.18 Many animal experiments cause pain or distress. A rat which has learned to self-administer cocaine will endure a more painful electric shock in order to receive another dose than a hungry or thirsty animal will for food or water.

Ledent *et al.* (1999) used knockout mice which lacked the gene to produce the cannabinoid receptor. These mice did not respond to cannabinoid drugs, confirming the association between the receptors and the action of THC.

What's new?

One of the well-documented side effects of cannabis is as an appetite stimulant – a property that is used to stimulate eating in cancer and AIDS patients. Logically, a cannabis antagonist should suppress appetite. Natural cannabinoids have been detected in human milk and it is believed that they may play a role in the early development of newborns. Fride *et al.* (2001) investigated the effect of cannabinoids on feeding in newborn mice. The mice were injected with a cannabinoid antagonist, and some were then injected with the active component in cannabis – in a dose sufficient to swamp the receptors and counter the effect of the antagonist. The mice treated with the antagonist failed to feed from their mothers and died within four to eight days. This effect was not as pronounced if the antagonist was given later than the first day after birth. The mice treated with the cannabis derivative fed and grew normally. Fride *et al.* concluded that natural cannabinoids trigger the ingestion of food and are important for very early growth.

Figure 3.19 Baby white mice and mother mouse.

Fride *et al.* (2003) went on to demonstrate the importance of endocannabinoids in the initial suckling using mice which did not have cannabinoid receptors. These 'knockout' mice lacked the gene to produce receptors for one type of cannabinoid receptor. As a result, even if endocannabinoids were present, they could not respond to them. The newborn mice, like those treated with the antagonist, failed to suckle. Unlike the antagonist-treated mice, however, the behaviour of the knockout mice could not be reversed by an agonist. Injecting them with cannabis did not stimulate eating. Interestingly, the pups did begin to feed slowly after day one. At this stage, using the antagonist had little effect on feeding behaviour. In combination, these studies confirm the role of endocannabinoids in the initial stimulation of suckling after birth and suggest that a different mechanism of appetite stimulation follows quickly.

Hampson & Deadwyler (2000) tested rats on a memory task in different situations: with THC, with a synthetic cannabinoid drug (WIN-2), with a cannabinoid antagonist and with the antagonist given prior to the THC or WIN-2 drug. The antagonist alone had no effect on memory. THC impaired memory, and WIN-2 was even more powerful in this respect. However, when the rats were given the antagonist before the cannabinoid drugs, the memory impairment was not seen. They also measured the activity levels in hippocampal neurones and found that, in both THC and WIN-2 conditions, there was a reduction in activity. This confirms the role of cannabinoids in disrupting the laying down of new memories.

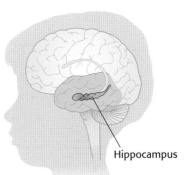

Hippocampus

Figure 3.20 This diagram shows two brain areas that have receptors for cannabinoids, the cerebellum and hippocampus. The hippocampus plays a role in the consolidation of memories, which may account for memory losses associated with cannabis use.

The effects of marijuana

Medically, cannabis produces effects such as analgesia, sedation, appetite stimulation (used with cancer patients) and reduction of pressure in the eye (for glaucoma patients). However, it also has effects such as interfering with attention and perception (including time) and affects mood, movement, learning and memory.

Similar short-term effects of cannabis on memory are seen in humans as have been found in animals (see page 86). Kurzthaler *et al.* (1999) used a double-blind design to test the effects of cannabis on participants smoking either a normal cigarette or one containing 290 micrograms/kg of body weight THC. They tested the participants on perceptual and motor skills. Their speed and accuracy was impaired when tested immediately, but not after 24 hours. Kurzthaler *et al.* concluded that using cannabis would significantly disrupt the user's performance on tasks requiring vigilance and fast reactions, such as driving.

Pope (1998) reported little effect of daily cannabis use on memory. They did find that frequent users were somewhat poorer on a test where they had to mimic simple card-matching rules demonstrated by the experimenter, adapting whenever the rule changed. Whilst slight, such an impairment could be significant in a rapidly changing environment such as on the road. The findings were from well-controlled samples, but even these results raise issues of validity. Why, for instance, did they find smaller performance decrements in female participants than in males? Fletcher *et al.* (1996) compared chronic users and non-users over a 20-year period. The users demonstrated greater impairment of memory and attention, but the differences were subtle and the chronic users' abilities were still within the normal range. They concluded that 'no evidence exists for the severity of health risks associated with the use of other drugs'. These results conflict with other studies which demonstrate impaired ability to attend to tasks and filter out irrelevant information (for example, Lunddqvist, 1995 and Solowij, 1995).

Figure 3.21 Driving under the influence of cannabis is unsafe.

More recent evidence has explored cognitive deficits in adolescent and adult samples in which use of other drugs, such as alcohol, has been controlled and where longer abstinence before testing has been required. Harrison *et al.* (2002) compared heavy and light lifetime use of cannabis and tested participants after 0, 1, 7 and 28 days' abstinence. The heavy smokers showed memory deficits on word lists within the first week, but by day 28 there were few differences between users and non-users or associations between cognitive problems and total lifetime cannabis consumption. Harrison *et al.* concluded that there was little evidence for irreversible effects.

In contrast to Harrison *et al.*, Medina *et al.* (2007) studied adolescents (aged 16–18 years). They were tested on cognitive tasks after a month of abstinence. They found that the cannabis users were slower at psychomotor tests (such as number and letter sequencing) and had poorer complex attention, story memory and planning and sequencing abilities compared with controls. The findings of Medina *et al.* support the idea that cannabis use in adolescence may be more damaging than in adulthood. For example, Ehrenreich *et al.* (1999) found that of present age, age of first use, degree of intoxication and total lifetime use, only earlier adolescent cannabis use predicted later adolescent cognitive impairment, with the earliest users having the poorest reaction times to visual stimuli.

It has been suggested from research into the effect of cannabis on the brain development of young animals that cognitive deficits in adolescents who begin using cannabis early may arise because of damage to their developing brains. This would explain why studies on adults show relatively less impairment. Studies using brain scanning on humans offer some support for this view. For example, Matochik *et al.* (2005) found structural differences in the brains of young adults who were heavy cannabis users and those of non-users. They found significantly less grey matter and white matter in several brain regions among the cannabis users.

Interactive angles

1. Describe the evidence suggesting that cannabis does, or does not, cause cognitive impairments.

2. To what extent should psychologists insist that laws against driving under the influence of cannabis are necessary?

Chronic cannabis use is associated with 'dropping out'. Musty & Kaback (1995) found that as many as 50% of adolescents on a substance abuse treatment programme had depressive symptoms. It is not clear, however, whether this is a consequence or cause. Are depressed teenagers more likely to use cannabis? Estimation of the problem arising from cannabis dependence is hindered by the way statistics are gathered. For instance, the number of people receiving treatment for cannabis use in the USA is inflated by those arrested or who test positive in random checks at work. They may opt for rehabilitation as an alternative to prosecution or being fired.

Evidence from many sources has linked cannabis use to mental disorders. A meta-analysis conducted by Semple *et al.* (2005) evaluated the findings of seven controlled studies of cannabis use and psychotic symptoms. Psychosis is a symptom of mental illness in which the individual has a poor and distorted view of reality, such as is found in schizophrenia (see page 139). They concluded that early cannabis use increases the risk of psychosis and that this was related to the amount taken. Especially for adolescent users and those who had already experienced psychotic symptoms, cannabis use was associated with an increased risk of developing schizophrenia.

In a recent review, Sewell *et al.* (2009) evaluated evidence from a range of sources relating cannabis to psychotic symptoms. These included controlled studies, cross-sectional and longitudinal studies and pharmacological research. Such studies demonstrate that the effects of cannabis on healthy individuals produce a range of short-term symptoms that resemble the positive, negative and cognitive symptoms of schizophrenia (see page 139 for a description of these symptoms). They concluded that only a very small proportion of individuals who use cannabis are likely to develop a psychotic illness in the long term and cannabis use alone cannot account for the development of psychotic symptoms. However, they also concluded that use of cannabis in young people produces an almost two-fold increase in the risk of developing schizophrenia.

Oh, what a tangled web they weave

The Daily Express
28 April 1995

Spiders on drugs can't spin straight.

Stoned spiders produce way-out webs, scientists have discovered. On marijuana they spin only so much, then decide it doesn't matter anymore. On Benzedrine, a well-known upper, the results are, to say the least, hallucinatory.

Give the little arachnids a spot of caffeine and they can do no more than throw a few threads together at random.

The insect spins with terrific speed but without any clear thought given to planning. The result is a tangled web indeed – a spaghetti-like mess which leaves great holes through which its intended victims can fly.

One recruit, fed a dose of chloral hydrate, a well-known soporific, dozed off before it had got started.

The information was gathered by scientists from NASA, America's space programme.

... The researchers, from NASA's Marshall Space Flight Center in Alabama, think spiders could replace other animals in testing the toxicity of chemicals.

By analysing the state of the webs after the spiders have been fed certain substances, they believe they can better predict the toxicity of new medicines.

... NASA spokesman Jerry Berg denies the research is frivolous. For one thing, spiders are cheaper to use than higher-order animals like rabbits and less likely to engender complaints from the animal welfare lobby. 'It follows a long tradition of using lower life-forms like insects and even bacteria in research,' he says.

Figure 3.22a Web of spider exposed to caffeine.

Figure 3.22b Web of spider exposed to marijuana.

Research the effects of marijuana (cannabis), Benzedrine (a benzodiazepine or drug, like Diazepam, used to reduce anxiety), caffeine and chloral hydrate (a now rarely used hypnotic that induces sleep). Using this information, the comments in the text and your knowledge of animal experimentation on drug use, develop reasoned arguments for and against the use of animal models to explore the effects of drugs on humans.

Marijuana tolerance, dependence and withdrawal

Traditionally, cannabis use was believed to be habit forming rather than dependence causing as users do not experience intense symptoms of withdrawal. One reason is because cannabinoids dissolve into body fat where they are stored and released slowly. There are three consequences to this. Firstly, any subsequent doses of cannabis add to existing levels. This is a possible explanation for the apparent 'reverse tolerance', that is, the need for lower rather than higher doses with repeated use. Secondly, it means that the onset of withdrawal is slow and therefore more tolerable and thirdly users may test positive for the drug long after they last used it.

Recent research, however, has identified both an abstinence syndrome and evidence for the development of tolerance. One physiological mechanism for tolerance is the down regulation of cannabinoid receptors. Sim-Selley & Martin (2002) used mice to test the effect of long-term exposure to cannabis. Both THC and the more powerful artificial agonist WIN-2 (see page 85) produced tolerance over 15 days of the high doses. For example, the mice became less affected by the reduced tendency to move around and the analgesic effects. When the mice brains were examined, they had fewer cannabinoid receptors, supporting the belief that cannabis tolerance is the result of down regulation. The receptors were also less likely to bind cannabinoid receptors, so desensitisation had also occurred.

Haney *et al.* (1999) describe the symptoms of cannabis withdrawal including agitation, irritability, anxiety, depression, insomnia and nausea. More recent evidence supports these observations. For example, Bolla *et al.* (2008) compared sleep in 17 recently abstinent cannabis users and 14 non-user controls. The ex-users slept for less time, were slower to get to sleep and their sleep did not improve on the second night of testing.

Milin *et al.* (2008) described the progress of 21 adolescents entering substance abuse programmes. They reported their withdrawal symptoms to be greatest during the first two weeks of abstinence but continuing into the third week. The most severe symptoms were restlessness, appetite change and craving. Other problems included twitching, shaking, irritability, depression and sweating.

Biological explanations for drug misuse

We have already considered learning theory explanations of drug misuse. Now that you understand how two drugs act, you can consider the role of biology in dependence.

A clear piece of evidence for biological explanations of drug abuse is the prevalence of cocaine self-administration throughout the animal kingdom (see page 82). This suggests that there is something fundamentally pleasurable about cocaine use – rather than misuse being due to some problem within the user. This supports the idea of a biological system through which dependence acts. A clear candidate for this is the dopamine reward system.

The dopamine reward system

Although the dopamine reward system appears to be the mechanism by which positive reinforcement affects the frequency of behaviour, drug studies have indicated that the biology of the system is not that simple. On the one hand, it is true that those behaviours which lead to positive reinforcement are certainly associated with increased activity in the dopamine reward system (be they eating, drug-taking or electrical self-stimulation). On the other, this does not mean that the experience is necessarily pleasurable: reinforcement and pleasure are not synonymous. This is obvious in the case of negative reinforcement – the relative comfort gained from the cessation of something painful or nasty cannot be called 'pleasurable'. However, it may also be erroneous to describe the positive reinforcement associated with drug craving 'pleasure'. Lamb *et al.* (1991) looked at the lever-pressing rates of ex-heroin users receiving injections of either morphine at different doses, or a placebo. Consider their results – see Figure 3.23 – remembering that reinforcement *increases* the frequency of a response. The findings show that, even at undetectable levels, morphine increased lever-pressing rates, suggesting that the overt sensation of pleasure is not necessary for heroin to have a reinforcing effect.

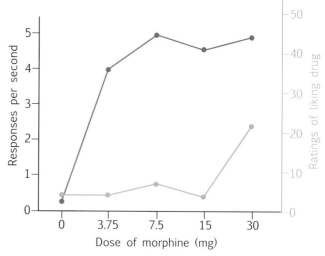

Figure 3.23 Lamb *et al.* (1991) found that ex-heroin users soon stopped pressing a lever if it only dispensed an injection of a placebo. However, their lever-pressing rates were high for all doses of morphine, even when these gave no subjective pleasure.

So, what do we know about the biological process behind this reinforcement? Reinforcers all share one physiological effect: they increase the release of dopamine in the nucleus accumbens. This effect can be produced by addictive drugs with widely differing actions, such as cocaine, opiates, cannabis, nicotine, alcohol and amphetamine, as well as natural reinforcers such as food, water and sex and, unsurprisingly, electrical self-stimulation of the nucleus accumbens (see Box 3.2).

When dopamine is released by neurones in the nucleus accumbens, it travels across the synaptic cleft and attaches to dopamine receptors on the post-synaptic membrane. Its exact action depends on at least two factors. Firstly, whereabouts in the nucleus accumbens it is released (in the middle or around the edge) and secondly, to which type of dopamine receptor it attaches. At least five, possibly more, different types of dopamine receptors are known to exist and their roles, with regard to reinforcement and craving, are probably different. For example, Khroyan *et al.* (2000) found that squirrel monkeys with a history of cocaine self-administration could be primed to reinstate their drug-seeking behaviour by agonists for D_2 type dopamine receptors, but not by stimulation of the D_1 type. Clearly, dopamine plays a central role in reinforcement of behaviour in general and in drug dependence in particular, but as yet the precise role is unclear.

The effects of tolerance

As we saw on page 73, tolerance leads to the need for increasing dose sizes to achieve the same effect, but this need can arise via at least three different routes. The major biological one is down regulation, which is a biological response to the incoming drug. It results in reduced numbers of receptor sites on the post-synaptic membrane of neurones, or a reduction in their sensitivity to the drug. In either case, more of the drug would be needed for the user to experience the same level of effect.

Box 3.2

The nucleus accumbens and brain self-stimulation

An accidental discovery by Olds & Milner (1954) helped to explain how reinforcement works. They were investigating whether brain stimulation could make a rat turn left or right. While searching for a way to affect the rat's choice, Olds & Milner stumbled upon an area which, when stimulated, caused the rat to respond by looking around and sniffing as if responding to something pleasant. When rats could self-stimulate this area by pressing a bar in a Skinner box, they did so. Olds (1958) reported that a rat would press the bar as many as 2,000 times per minute and would do so for hours, continuing until it collapsed from exhaustion. Although a number of brain areas have now been identified, the nucleus accumbens is one of the most important. Two neurotransmitters, noradrenaline and dopamine, are also associated with this system. It is likely, therefore, that this 'brain reward' system plays a role in the reinforcing properties of addictive drugs since many act at dopamine synapses.

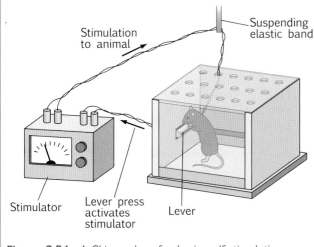

Figure 3.24 A Skinner box for brain self-stimulation

An alternative biological explanation for tolerance suggests that, with exposure to a specific drug, the body responds with changes in the liver. One of the roles of the liver is to detoxify chemicals in the body, for which purpose it can produce a huge variety of enzymes. Production of enzymes by the liver is affected by a positive feedback system – the more of a toxic chemical that is present, the more enzyme the liver produces to dispose of it. Hence, as the intake of a drug increases, so too does the liver's capacity to destroy it.

Genetic predisposition

As the biological systems operating in different individuals are almost identical, it is difficult for these explanations to account for individual differences in drug taking. Why should some individuals be more likely to take drugs or become addicted to them if we all share the same biology? Several different strands of research have explored this question.

One line of investigation has explored the role of genes in controlling drug dependence in animals. Klein *et al.* (2008) compared the withdrawal symptom of jumping in ten different strains of mice. The mice were inbred, so individuals within any one strain would be highly genetically similar and differences between strains could therefore be assumed to be due to genetic factors rather than individual differences. Each strain was tested with both acute and chronic doses of heroin, followed by antagonist-precipitated withdrawal. The range of jumps was 0–104 for acute heroin injection and 0–142 for chronic injections. However, between strains, the responses were very different indicating a strong genetic link.

Figure 3.25 Breeding experiments with mice suggest that genetic factors influence heroin dependence.

Different patterns of responses to drugs also seem to relate to genetic differences in humans. Nielsen *et al.* (2008) compared samples of DNA from 104 former heroin addicts and 101 controls. They found significant associations between heroin addiction and several gene variants. One genotype pattern identified was significantly associated with heroin addiction and accounted for 27% of the risk for the individuals in the experimental group. A second genotype pattern appeared to confer some protection for developing heroin addiction and the absence of this factor accounted for 83% of the risk.

Finally, a different approach to this question has been taken by looking at family patterns of drug misuse. This is a difficult area to research as it is hard to separate the risk factors of genetics from upbringing. If an individual whose parents took drugs are also drug-dependent, this might be due to aspects of their environment or a genetic predisposition. To separate out these two factors, twin and adoption studies as well as family studies have been used. For example, Fowler *et al.* (2007) looked at possible causal factors of problem drinking in 862 twin pairs aged 11–17 years in England and Wales. They found that genetic factors were important and that environmental factors, such as best friend's alcohol use, were also important. However, as Fowler *et al.* observe, even choice of friends may have some genetic component, so it is likely that the two influences of genes and the environment do not act independently. Certainly, other studies have identified both components to be important.

Maes *et al.* (1999) investigated the genetic component of risk in tobacco, alcohol and other drug use by adolescents. In their study of 1,412 monozygotic (MZ) and dizygotic (DZ) twin pairs aged 8–16 from the Virginia Twin Study, they found a significant genetic influence in all three. However, from comparison of 327 MZ and 174 same-sex DZ twins from Minnesota, Han *et al.* (1999) concluded that the environment was the major contributor to risk of alcohol abuse. Using a different technique, Kendler *et al.* (2000) compared reared-together and reared-apart twins. They investigated 778 MZ twin pairs born between 1890 and 1958 using the population-based Swedish Twin Registry. In common with some other studies, they found a gender difference. For men, they found that there was a large genetic component to regular tobacco use. For women, the pattern appeared to change with social factors. For women born prior to 1925, few used tobacco and twin similarity was environmental in origin. For women born after 1940, both rates of tobacco use and the importance of genetic factors increased, resembling those of males. Kendler *et al.* concluded that, as social restrictions of female tobacco use relaxed over time, so the influence of genetic factors became apparent.

Figure 3.26 Identical twins are more likely to have the same habits regarding the use or non-use of drugs than non-identical twins.

Studies such as Maes *et al.* and Han *et al.* which compare MZ and DZ twins can be criticised, as the relative differences in environments between the two twin types is difficult to ascertain. Although separated twin studies overcome this particular problem, they are not without flaws. For example, Kendler *et al.* treated twins as 'reared apart' if they were separated by age 11 years (although more than two-thirds had been separated by age two years). Clearly, this offers considerable time for the environment to work in the same way on both individuals.

Evidence for a genetic predisposition to substance abuse of a range of drugs exists; for example, Dick & Bierut (2006) estimated the heritability of alcohol dependence to be around 50–60% based on evidence from family, twin and adoption studies. Agrawal *et al.* (2004) found evidence for genetic factors affecting cannabis and other drug use, although they found environmental factors to be important too. Finally, Kendler *et al.* (2003) investigated use of and dependence on six drugs, cannabis, cocaine, hallucinogens, sedatives, stimulants and opiates, in male twins. They found a strong link between twins in many categories and concluded that both genetic and environmental factors are important.

In addition to looking for genetic patterns in the incidence of use and dependence, researchers have investigated other biological indicators of heritability. Families with a history of addiction also have some characteristic brain wave patterns in common with each other. For example, a particular wave form called P300 is an 'event-related potential', that is, it occurs in response to specific visual stimuli. Iacono *et al.* (2003) found that the amplitude ('height') of P300 waves was lower in individuals with a family history of substance use and substance use disorders. Interestingly, this difference could be seen before substance use disorders became apparent. Remember, however, that it is only an indicator – not all individuals with low amplitude P300 waves go on to receive a diagnosis of substance abuse disorder.

Gene markers associated with alcoholism have been identified. For example, the gene DRD2 is found in 42% of people with alcohol dependence. Lou *et al.* (2005) have even found a link between different forms of this gene and different alcoholic behaviours (for example, early onset drinkers and 'benders'). Whilst this is clearly important, the gene is not found in all people with alcoholism and is found in people without. It is clear, therefore, that genes do not offer the whole answer for the explanation of substance misuse.

One way in which genes might act to influence drug misuse is by affecting the individual's personality. **Sensation seeking** is a personality characteristic which is associated with high-risk behaviours such as bungee-jumping that has also been linked to drugs (Zuckerman, 1979). This is explored in detail in Classic Research.

What's that?

- **Sensation seeking:** a personality trait, assumed to be at least partly genetic, is linked to high-risk behaviours including drug use

- **Cognitive motivation:** the reasons for a person's behaviour, for example, why they choose to drink alcohol, based on the outcomes that they anticipate

Interactive angles

Research such as Iacono *et al.* and Lou *et al.* have identified genetic markers for drug misuse.

1. How might it be useful for individuals to be made aware if they are genetically at risk of addiction?

2. Under what circumstances might such an awareness be disadvantageous?

Classic research

Optional

Stacy, A.W., Newcomb, M.D. & Bentler, P.M. (1993)

'Cognitive motivations and sensation seeking as long-term predictors of drinking problems'

Journal of Clinical & Social Psychology, 12(1): 1–24

Aim: To investigate long-term predictors of alcohol use and drinking-related problems (such as driving while intoxicated or physical problems). Specifically, they looked at the way drinking-related problems link to personality factors including sensation seeking and to 'cognitive motivation', and whether these two factors are related. Finally, they were interested in whether particular negative outcomes of drinking were specific to particular reasons for drinking; for example, are people who drink for social reasons more likely to end up with family problems than work problems?

Procedure: This study used a longitudinal design. The participants were being followed up as part of a wider investigation into drug use. The sample was 64% white and 71% female. The mean age was 17.95 years at the start of the study and 26.95 years at follow-up. The sample was initially obtained from 11 junior high schools in Los Angeles. There were more schools from lower socioeconomic areas in order to fairly represent the United States as a whole. The drop-out rate was very small and did not relate to drug-use. Data was obtained from participants by self-report using confidential questionnaires to provide measures of:

Sensation seeking: four 4-item scales were rated on a scale of 1 (never) to 5 (always):

- *experience seeking* (for example, 'I would like to explore strange places')

- *thrill and adventure seeking* (for example, 'I would like to try parachute jumping')

- disinhibition (for example, 'I like wild parties')

- *boredom susceptibility* (for example, 'I get restless when I spend too much time at home')

Cognitive motivation: four scales of 3, 4 or 5 items each answered with either 1 (no), 2 (not sure) or 3 (yes).

Figure 3.27 High sensation seekers are more likely to take drugs.

- *reduction of negative affect* (for example, 'get rid of anxiety or tension')

- *enhancement of positive affect* (for example, 'enjoy what I'm doing more')

- *social cohesion* (for example, 'feel good around people')

- *addiction* (for example, 'feel bad when I don't use it')

Alcohol use:

Questions asked about:

- how often beer, wine and spirits were drunk (rated on a 7-point scale from 'never' to 'more than once a day')

- how many drinks were consumed (the number of drinks in an average day on a 9-point scale from 'did not drink' to 'more than 6')

Problem-drinking consequences:

There were 29 questions that identified personal, physical, social and work-related negative consequences including: 'missed work' and 'hurt relationships with friends or family'. These were rated on a 3-point scale as occurring 'never' to 'more than once' in the past year.

Driving while intoxicated (DWI):

This measured frequency in response to items such as 'drove a car while drunk' and arrest and conviction record.

The first three measures were assessed at the start (adolescence) and at follow-up (adulthood); the last two just at follow-up.

Results: Cognitive motivation and alcohol use in adolescence both predicted problem-drinking consequences in adulthood. Alcohol use predicted DWI; both the frequency of drinking wine (significant at $p \leq 0.05$) and drinking beer (significant at $p \leq 0.001$) were important. In addition, the cognitive factor of positive affect in adolescence also predicted later DWI behaviour (significant at $p \leq 0.001$), as did the sensation seeking factor of disinhibition (significant at $p \leq 0.01$). Work-related problem consequences were predicted by thrill and adventure seeking and by social cohesion (both significant at $p \leq 0.05$). There was also a link between adolescent personality and adult cognitive motivation. Adolescents with higher sensation seeking scores grew up to become adults with greater cognitive motivation for alcohol use (significant at $p \leq 0.05$).

Conclusions: This information can be used to identify adolescents who are at risk of future alcohol-related problems. Two possible actions could be to reduce the effects of high sensation seeking needs or the strong expectation that the effects of alcohol will be positive.

The influence of cognitive motivation on alcohol misuse may result from many factors, such as social learning, personal experience and genetic predisposition. In contrast, sensation seeking is generally assumed to be the product of a genetic predisposition. However, the link between adolescent personality may not have a direct effect on adult motivation, but could result from a third factor. For example, responses to reinforcement may affect both the desire for high sensation experiences and the motivation to drink alcohol.

Attempts to change adolescents' sensation seeking level are unlikely to be successful if it is a biologically determined predisposition. It may therefore be more effective to try to develop alternative outlets for sensation seeking that are more healthy than alcohol use. Furthermore, cognitive and behavioural habits need to be developed that will be effective at the specific times when the individual is at risk from problem drinking. Particular situations, such as difficult social contexts, or emotional states such as anger or frustration, could be targets for intervention. One problem with these instances is that they have high cue dependence, so memories of alcohol use could trigger further drinking. The key, therefore, is to help the individual to re-learn new information relating to those cues.

Ethically, there is an issue with labelling adolescents. For a vulnerable adolescent, knowing that they have been identified as 'at risk' may result in them being more inclined to follow this future path. This could be explained by a self-fulfilling prophecy – the individual would be more likely to engage in negative behaviours because they feel that other people expect them to fail in this respect anyway.

Interactive angles

1. Look at the statistics for problem drinking in England and Wales at http://www.ias.org.uk/resources/factsheets/drinkinggb_excessive.pdf.

   How important do you think it is that psychologists try to help to reduce the scale of the problem?

2. Suggest how you might divert the sensation-seeking needs of a high sensation-seeking adolescent in order to reduce the risk of them developing a drinking problem later in life.

Figure 3.28 Why might high sensation seekers be particularly at risk?

Human research methods for investigating drugs: questionnaires

Questionnaires are a common source of self-report data and are frequently used to obtain information about drug use, dependence and experiences as well as demographic data.

Questionnaires are generally given to the participant to answer on paper (or sometimes on a computer), although occasionally a questionnaire format is used in a structured interview. Different question techniques can be used to generate different kinds of data. Closed questions allow the participant to give only a small selection of different answers, such as indicating which drugs from a list they have ever used, or stating in months/years how long they have smoked. Open questions give the participant an opportunity to provide fuller answers, giving depth and detail. These therefore tend to generate qualitative data, whilst closed questions produce quantitative data. Most questionnaires are structured, with fixed questions in a pre-determined order. Occasionally, there are semi-structured options (of the type 'if the answer to question 9 is "no", please move on to question 16').

Questionnaires have the advantage that they are relatively cheap to produce once they have been designed and validated, so if participants can be found many can be distributed. Of course, the validation process takes time and appropriate participants may in fact be difficult to locate, unwilling to participate or impossible to find at follow-up. This is particularly true of dependent users whose employment and housing circumstances may be unreliable. This can lead to bias in the sample, as only the less problematic users can be traced. However, if a large sample can be obtained findings are likely to be generalisable, as they will be more representative of the target population than a necessarily smaller sample used in a more time-intensive method, such as individual interviews.

In terms of analysis of data, the use of closed questions is helpful to allow the data to be easily collated, scored and analysed statistically. In contrast, when open questions are used, detailed data can be obtained. This can provide greater insight, for instance into the reasons for drug use or reluctance to abstain. Open questions can also supply information that it is difficult to obtain through direct observation, for example, the emotional experiences during euphoria or withdrawal. Questionnaires can be checked for reliability using methods such as split-half or test–retest methods. When standardised, questionnaires can be highly reliable.

One difficulty with using questionnaires is that they lack flexibility. Closed questions do not allow participants to say exactly what they mean, so important information may be lost and results may not truly reflect opinions or feelings. In any questionnaire, responses may reflect social desirability, that is, the tendency for participants to respond in the way they think people ought to, thus reducing the validity of the findings. This is especially problematic in drug research, as drug use is generally frowned on by society and illicit drug users are also breaking the law. These influences may reduce the truthfulness of responses. Answers to repetitive questionnaires may also be affected by response biases, where participants respond in a set way, for example an adolescent might always give answers that indicate excessive drug use.

In terms of ethical issues, questionnaires can be readily made confidential, for example, coding individuals using individual demographic characteristics so that they can be re-matched at follow-up without using a name. They also allow participants a ready option to withhold information. If a participant in an interview is unwilling to answer a question they may feel more pressured to do so than one who is only face-to-face with a piece of paper.

Learning theory explanations for drug misuse

We have already looked at the one learning theory explanation of drug misuse. On pages 73–75 we considered operant conditioning and the importance of positive reinforcement in initiating and maintaining drug use through its pleasurable effects and the role of negative reinforcement in maintaining drug use through the avoidance of withdrawal. In addition, we looked at the role that classical conditioning plays in explaining tolerance. Here we will explore social learning theory, another further learning theory explanation of drug misuse.

Social learning theory

In contrast to the ideas already explored, social learning suggests that the family may influence an individual because it offers a source of role models rather than genes. If you remember from your AS the key characteristics of role models, you will see that family members could be powerful influences for social learning. They are present for children and adolescents to observe – and they are likely to command attention. There may be opportunities for imitation, such as being offered a glass of wine or beer, or stealing a cigarette from an adult. Adults, especially parents, are familiar and have high status within the family. These two characteristics increase the likelihood of being imitated. Finally, there is the influence of vicarious reinforcement. A child may see a parent returning from a hard day at work relaxing with a cigarette. They may be exposed to family gatherings at which adults appear to enjoy themselves more when they drink. They may see the extreme mood changes of a parent who is dependent on heroin. These are sources of vicarious reinforcement for the observing child.

Figure 3.29 Social learning may account for early drug use.

Evidence relating to the predictions of social learning theory and parents is contradictory. Some studies have shown, as would be expected, that parental drug use is linked to child drug use. For example, Dielman et al. (1991) found that parental norms for alcohol use predicted adolescent alcohol use and Courtois et al. (2007) found that adolescent smoking and cannabis use was linked to parental use. They also found associations between parental and adolescent use of other psychoactive drugs. However, whilst such patterns could be the result of social learning, they could equally be explained by heredity.

In terms of parental influence, it seems unlikely that parental norms are of great importance in adolescent drug use. There are two reasons for this conclusion. Firstly, that studies such as Dielman et al. (1991) find that parental influences are secondary to peer influences. Secondly, where parental influences are important they have the potential to be protective against drug use, rather than encouraging. Simons-Morton et al. (2001) found that more involved parenting was linked to lower risk of drug use. Similarly, Best (2005) observed that cannabis users were less likely to spend time regularly with their mothers and fathers, compared to non-users. This may be related to parenting style – authoritative parenting tends to lead to lower rates of drug use than authoritarian, neglectful or indulgent parenting (Courtois, 2007). Eitle (2005) looked at the risks of a child using alcohol, tobacco or illicit drugs. Living with two natural parents reduced the risk, but only when exposure to deviant peers was low. This suggests that observing drug-taking in people of the same age may be more important than observing adult role models.

Lucchini (1985) observes, in relation to role models in the 'drug scene' for heroin or cocaine users, that for young people some addicts may be perceived to have high status – another key characteristic of an effective model. This again suggests that peers could act as role models for drug use in young people. Bahr et al. (2005) investigated drug use in a sample of 4,230 American adolescents. Peer drug use had a strong effect and they concluded that social learning between peers was important. This explanation is supported by Dielman et al. (1991) who found that peer norms were more important than parental norms as predictors of alcohol use and Best (2005) who studied 2,078 young people aged 14–16 in London. Those who spent more of their free time with friends who smoked, drank alcohol and used illicit drugs were more likely to use cannabis themselves. A similar pattern was seen in the findings of Simons-Morton et al. (2001) in relation to drinking – adolescents who spent more time with deviant peers were more likely to drink. Of course, such findings do not necessarily mean that the peers are acting as role models. Individuals with a predisposition for substance misuse may seek out friends with similar behaviour.

In a study of 428 adolescents, Donohew et al. (1999) found that friends' use of alcohol and marijuana was linked to the individual's own use. Interestingly, the adolescents were all scored for sensation seeking – a measure of 'adventurousness' – and were asked to name up to three peers. An analysis of this data showed that there was a link between the peers' sensation seeking and the individual's own use of both marijuana and alcohol two years later. This suggests that peers may have an ongoing influence on substance use rather than just being chosen for their particular current characteristics. The influence of friends on drug use is explored further in Classic Research.

Interactive angles

A full report of the drugs taken by children, which includes a discussion of their own reasons for drug use, can be read at: http://www.ic.nhs.uk/webfiles/publications/sdd07/SDD%20Main%20report%202007%20%2808%29-Standard.pdf. It is a National Health Service report on drug use, smoking and drinking among young people in England, 2007.

Summarise the key findings.

Classic research
Optional

Morgan, M. & Grube, J.W. (1991)

'Closeness and peer group influence'

British Journal of Social Psychology, 30(2): 159–69

Aim: To investigate how peers affect the initiation and continuation of cigarette smoking, drinking alcohol and the use of other drugs.

Procedure: Anonymous questionnaires were given to secondary school children in Dublin. The sample was stratified for gender, size and type of school. The number of males and females was approximately equal and the mean age was 15.8 years. The initial very large sample of 2,927 was retested after approximately two months and had fallen to 2,782, due largely to school absences. By follow-up a year later, the sample had shrunk again to 2,057 because many students had left school. Those who left the sample were more likely to smoke, drink and use drugs, but only very slightly.

The self-report questionnaire asked (at each test time):

- whether they had ever smoked a cigarette, drunk alcohol or taken any of a list of 12 illicit substances

- how many cigarettes they smoked a day on average

- how many times during the previous month they consumed alcohol

- how many times during the previous month they used illicit drugs.

At the initial testing, participants were also asked about drug use of:

- their current best friend

- other good friends

- most young people of their age.

For the best friend and other good friends the participants were also asked to rate how likely they would be to approve of the respondent's substance use.

Questionnaires were administered in the students' normal classroom without the teacher present (except in one school where several classes were brought together and another where disciplinary problems were anticipated, so the teacher was present but interacted very little). Confidentiality was maintained without using names by matching questionnaires using a code based on information including gender, date of birth and number of older brothers and sisters. Of the questionnaires 77% were matched at follow-up and there

were no significant differences in substance abuse between matched and unmatched participants. The internal reliability of items measuring substance abuse was high (0.7 to 0.91). The test–retest reliability between the two initial testing sessions was 0.83 for smoking, 0.72 for drinking and 0.59 for substance abuse.

Results: The relationship between drug use by the best friend is stronger than to other friends and its importance remained constant while other friends became less influential over time. Perceived use by friends was found to be a more important influence than perceived approval (for both best and other friends). However, whilst the best friend was most important in the maintenance of drug use, several good friends were influential in the initial use of drugs, through both example and approval.

Conclusion: Friends play an important role in drug use throughout the teenage years, being important in the initiation and continuation of drug use.

Figure 3.30 When starting drug use, close friends matter, but the best friend is most important to maintenance of the habit.

Role models for drug misuse may also exist in the media. You may recall from your AS that children are affected by what they see on television. Does this extend to influencing their drug use? Media personalities certainly have characteristics that could make them effective models, such as being high status, powerful or likeable. These features may apply to celebrities, characters in films or TV programmes, or to people in advertisements.

Exposure to television advertising for alcohol has been linked to teenagers' consumption of alcohol (Atkin & Block, 1981). The demonstrated effects, however, were very small with other factors being far more influential in their behaviour, such as the individual's vulnerability to the influences of advertisements or the attitudes of their peers or friends. Many products, such as new sweets, with incessant advertising directed at children fail to succeed in the market (Smith & Sweeny, 1984). So, what factors might be more important than mere exposure?

Figure 3.31 Advertising has a limited effect on early drug use.

One possibility is that advertising promotes the positive values of legal drugs such as tobacco and alcohol. Supporting this idea, Charlton (1986) found that British children aged 9–13 who could name a favourite cigarette advert were more likely to claim that smoking led to looking grown up, calmed the nerves, gave confidence or was useful in controlling weight. However, these children were no more likely to smoke the brand they preferred.

Evidence relating to television programmes, rather than advertisements, suggests that media influences may affect children's behaviour. In a correlational study of 400 adolescent boys, Tucker (1985) found that those who watched more television also consumed more alcohol and this pattern was evident even when potential demographic factors had been excluded. However, not all studies have demonstrated this relationship. For example, Hanssen (1988) found no indication that TV viewing was linked to higher alcohol consumption.

Since the evidence is contradictory, it is interesting to see the results of experimental studies. Rychtarik et al. (1983) investigated the influence of television viewing on children aged 8–11 years. Each child viewed an episode of *M*A*S*H*, the same episode with the drinking scenes deleted, or did not see the programme. The children who had seen the full programme were more likely to choose alcohol than water to serve to a 'parched' adult. This, of course, does not tell us about the children's own drinking habits.

Some of the most potentially influential models in the media are celebrities. Boon & Lomore (2001) found that 75% of young adults reported having had, at some time, a strong attachment to a celebrity and 59% reported that these idols had affected their attitudes and beliefs. When numerous celebrities are reported to use illicit drugs, and this is often glorified in the press, such observations suggest that they may influence drug-taking. Gunsekera et al. (2005) investigated the way drugs were represented in 200 high-earning films. They found that, whilst the drug use depicted did not include injected illicit drugs, the portrayal of drug use was very positive and without negative consequences. The drugs used were primarily tobacco (68% of films included at least one character smoking), alcohol (32% included intoxication) and cannabis (8% of films), the latter typically being used by a background character.

In an experimental investigation of the power of celebrity endorsement, Ross et al. (1984) studied children's views about advertisements. When a famous presenter endorsed a toy racing car, children believed that they were experts and exhibited greater preference for the product. So, if celebrities are perceived to be better informed, as well as high in status, it is likely that they would influence children's attitudes and behaviours. Since Gunsekera et al. found that drug use was positively portrayed in film media – providing a source of vicarious reinforcement – these two effects could combine to produce highly effective role models.

Figure 3.32 Do musicians act as role models for drug use?

Another possible source of powerful models for young people is through popular music. Roberts *et al.* (2002) surveyed 300 music videos appearing on television in the USA. They found that visual depictions of illicit drugs and references to them in lyrics were rare (appearing in nine and 51 videos respectively). References to alcohol and smoking were more common (37% and 21% of videos respectively). Unlike Boon & Lomore's findings with respect to films, Roberts *et al.* argue that drugs in music are depicted in a neutral manner, being common elements of everyday life. Whilst this could be seen as better than presenting drugs as highly desirable, it could equally be argued that this makes drug use acceptable, promoting a social norm of drug use rather than non-use.

Classic research

Optional

Brook, J.S., Richter, L., Whiteman, M. & Cohen, M. (1999)

'Consequences of adolescent marijuana use: incompatibility with the assumption of adult roles'

Genetic, Social & General Psychology Monographs, 125(2): 193–207

Aim: To investigate the link between adolescents' marijuana use and both their later use and the way that they move into adult roles. In addition, the influence of delayed or problematic transition to adulthood on subsequent marijuana use was explored.

Procedure: Informed consent was obtained and confidential interviews were used to complete structured questionnaires, which were administered five times from childhood to early adulthood. This measured marijuana use and variables relating to adult roles. The participants were obtained by random sampling of families with children aged between one and ten years in New York in 1975. Some of the initial 976 families had dropped out by the second test (in 1983) leaving 703 participants. They were replaced by families with children aged 9–12 years, giving a total of 756 participants with a mean age of 14 years. The numbers and mean ages for subsequent follow-ups were 1986 (739, mean age = 16 years), 1992 (749, mean age = 22 years), 1996 (623, mean age = 27 years). The sample represented a range of socioeconomic groups, were approximately half female and 91% were white.

From 1983 the participants were asked about the frequency of their marijuana use at each follow-up, so lifetime use could be judged. In 1992 and 1996, they were also asked about their adult roles, specifically whether they:

- were employed (part time, full time or not)
- were married
- had children
- lived with their parents, spouse or had other living arrangements.

These variables were measured as 'yes' or 'no' answers.

Results: Adolescents who used marijuana were more likely to adopt unconventional adult roles such as unemployment, late marriage and having children out of wedlock. Specifically, compared to infrequent users, frequent marijuana-using adolescents were, by their late 20s:

Figure 3.33 Teenage cannabis use has lasting effects.

- 1.8 times more likely to be unemployed (significant at $p \leq 0.05$)
- nearly twice as likely to be cohabiting, living with friends or living alone rather than with parents or spouse (significant at $p \leq 0.001$)
- less likely to be married (significant at $p \leq 0.001$)
- more likely to be a single parent (significant at $p \leq 0.01$).

In addition, young adults (aged approximately 22) who were unmarried were more likely to be marijuana users in their late 20s (significant at $p \leq 0.01$). No relationship was found, however, between living arrangements or employment status at this age and later marijuana use. These effects were independent of gender and socioeconomic status.

Conclusion: Frequent marijuana use in adolescence may adversely affect successful transition to adult roles. This has implications for drugs education, identifying the need to inform adolescents about the wider risks of marijuana use in terms of successful adult functioning.

Interactive angles

1. Comment on the following with regard to Brook *et al.*:

   (a) Ethics

   (b) The sampling method and sample.

Brook *et al.* (1999) suggest that one explanation for these findings is that marijuana has a negative effect on motivation, for example, resulting in apathy, uncertainty about future goals and dropping out of education. Such consequences may be linked to the effects marijuana has on attention and cognitive functioning. Additionally, marijuana use may affect emotional functioning and the ability to cope with the demands of adult roles. Interestingly, drug use may in some respects propel the user into adulthood more quickly, but in doing so may prevent the learning of strategies for dealing with the demands of adult life. Thus, the drug-using young adult is less well equipped to succeed in their new adult roles. In this respect, the link between early adult marijuana use and marriage (but no other variables) is of interest. Here, two explanations are suggested by Brook *et al.* Taking on the responsibility of marriage may inhibit drug use, or having a spouse may offer the social support needed to abstain. However, there are several ways in which such interpretations may be criticised.

These conclusions ignore the possibility that troubled adolescents may be more likely to use marijuana and that, as a result of their adolescent difficulties, they may be less likely to become conventional adults. Alternatively, individuals with unconventional beliefs may respond both by using marijuana in adolescence and making unconventional life choices in adulthood. Furthermore, the study is biased in that it implies that conventional partnerships and living arrangements are representative of a more 'successful' transition to adulthood. This viewpoint might well be challenged some ten years after publication.

Other criticisms relate to procedural issues. The measurement of marijuana use was solely by self-report, so may therefore have been inaccurate. In recording only 'yes' or 'no' answers to questions about adult roles such as marriage or employment overlooks the extent to which that role was being fulfilled successfully. A young adult may be unhappily married or neglectful in their parental role, but such detail was not recorded.

Thinking critically: Evaluating explanations of drug misuse

In relation to the role of the reward system in dependence, we cannot truly separate operant conditioning and biological theories. Research is beginning to piece together the biological processes that are responsible for the effects of reinforcement. However, it is evident from the accumulation of evidence that both learning and biological factors are important to reward processes involved in drug use. As more is discovered about the neural processes involved in drug effects, so it becomes clear that there are direct links between specific neurotransmitters such as dopamine, associated receptors, particular brain areas such as the nucleus accumbens and the addictive properties of drugs. However, it is also clear that such explanations alone are not sufficient. If they were, then all users exposed to drugs would follow the same path to dependence and that is clearly not the case.

One cause of individual differences is, however, biological. Evidence suggests that genetic differences in predisposition to drug use exist. This means that for some people, drug use may be more initially attractive (for example, to high sensation seekers) or more compelling once taken (such as in the experience of withdrawal effects). At least some of this evidence, however, comes from animal studies from which generalisation to humans may not be valid.

Other individual differences may arise through exposure to different opportunities for learning. The presence or absence of external reinforcers, including vicarious reinforcement, will differ between individuals as will the presence and behaviour of role models. Family, peers, friends and celebrities can all act as models for drug use (or non-use). These factors may well be important, but separating their role in modelling behaviours from genetics, direct reinforcement and their influence on social norms is difficult.

Treating substance misuse

There is little doubt that drug use is dangerous, therefore dependent users need help. The study in Research Now illustrates just one profound negative effect of drug misuse.

One key finding from Wareing *et al.* (2000) is that past ecstasy users seem, in many ways, to be as severely affected as current users. This has important implications for health. However, such a conclusion depends on the honesty of the ex-users. It is possible that they were not truthful about having stopped their drug use. Furthermore, some of the significant differences that were identified, such as anxiety, ceased to be significant when the variables of health and other drug use were controlled for. The current and past users reported having taken drugs such as LSD and ampthetamine. These drugs, or combinations of drugs, could alternatively have been responsible for some of the cognitive changes observed.

Interactive angles

1. Describe two ethical issues raised by Wareing *et al.*'s research.

2. Explain how these two ethical issues were solved in Wareing *et al.*'s research.

Research now

Optional

Wareing, M., Fisk, J.E. & Murphy, P.N. (2000)

'Working memory deficits in current and previous users of MDMA ("ecstasy")'

British Journal of Psychology, 91: 181–8

Aims: To investigate the effects of long-term ecstasy use on memory, arousal and anxiety.

Procedure: 10 current, 10 past and 10 non-ecstasy users were found using snowball sampling. Non-users had never taken ecstasy, 'use' was defined as taking at least one tablet per month (although typical use was once or twice weekly). Past users had stopped using ecstasy at least six months before the study. Each group contained equal numbers of males and females, had a mean age of approximately 22 years and all groups performed equally on several tasks including word span, visual memory and verbal fluency. In addition to being given a self-report questionnaire on arousal and anxiety and being asked questions about physical health, participants were tested on cognitive functioning. These tests measured:

- **central executive functioning:** a random letter generation task in which participants had to produce a stream of consonants (not vowels) in non-alphabetical order, avoiding repetition and using each letter with a similar frequency. They were cued to produce a letter at 4, 2 or 1 second intervals.

- **state anxiety and arousal:** a measure of feelings about, and anxiety in, the experimental setting.

- **information processing speed and accuracy:** participants had to judge, at speed, whether two rows containing either 3, 6 or 9 letters were the same or different.

Advice was sought from 'Drugline' to ensure that the procedure was ethical and participants were given advice leaflets at the end of the study.

Results: The users all reported taking at least one other drug and were less healthy than non-users (significant at $p \le 0.05$). Both users and ex-users showed some cognitive impairment compared to the non-users, making more information processing errors. Users found the letter generation task very difficult and two past users found it so distressing that for ethical reasons they were not asked to complete the most difficult, 1-per-second, task (their data were excluded from the analysis of this task). At 1-per-second, the difference was significant at $p \le 0.01$, although the difference was not significant at the slower

rates. Non-users produced more letters, fewer vowels and repeated letters with a more even frequency. Differences in vowel production were significant at $p \le 0.05$ in the 1-per-second task and $p \le 0.01$ at the slower speeds. The difference between groups in terms of repetition of letters was only significant in the 1-per-second test (at $p \le 0.05$). In the information processing tasks, non-users were no faster, but produced fewer errors, although only significantly so for the longest lists (at $p \le 0.001$).

There were also differences in anxiety and users (both current and previous) were more anxious than non-users. The arousal scores of previous users were higher than the non-user controls, whereas those of current users were lower. The differences in cognitive ability persisted even when health, anxiety, arousal and other drug use were controlled for.

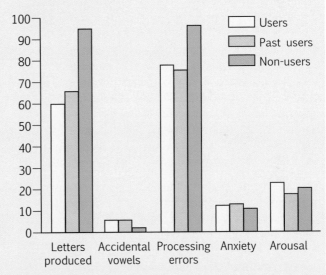

Figure 3.34 Relative measures of cognition and emotion in ecstasy users annd non-users.

Conclusion: Following weekend ecstasy use, users may experience a decline in arousal during the middle of the week. This may arise from the destruction of some serotonin pathways in the brain and abnormal growth in other areas in response to exposure to ecstasy.

In the sections that follow, we look at different ways to help people who have become dependent on drugs.

The biological approach to treating heroin dependence

Two strategies are typically combined in the biological treatment of opioid dependence: opioid detoxification and maintenance treatment. Opioid detoxification aims to detoxify dependent users quickly and safely, that is, to get the drug out of the user's body. This is done by administering long-acting opioid agonists in place of the misused drug. For example, heroin is commonly substituted with methadone chloride or L-alpha acetylmethadol (LAAM). Additional drugs (such as clonidine) can be used to limit the experience of withdrawal symptoms. Although such treatment achieves detoxification, relapse is frequent. This is probably related to the experience of craving.

The NICE (2007) guidelines make provision for the proper care of users seeking to become abstinent. When they are assessed, users should be provided with information and support so that they can give their informed consent to treatment. Opioid detoxification is closely monitored through a community-based programme. It normally lasts up to four weeks in an in-patient or residential setting. This is followed by up to 12 weeks in the community and up to six months of psychosocial support and contingency management. The advice includes details about alternative treatments, the duration and intensity of symptoms of withdrawal on opioid detoxification and how these can be managed (for example, the use of additional drugs to control agitation, nausea, insomnia, pain or diarrhoea), the loss of tolerance to opioid drugs after detoxification and the consequent risk of overdose and the importance of psychosocial as well as pharmacological interventions in order to maintain abstinence, treat other mental health problems and reduce the risk of adverse outcomes (including death).

The choice of medication for detoxification (for example, methadone or buprenorphine) is the user's, although if they are already receiving one of these two drugs as a maintenance dose, this should be used. An alternative is Lofexidine for those not already on methadone or buprenorphine. Rapid detoxification using an opioid antagonist (such as naltrexone) is not usually recommended (see below). When a user makes an informed choice to enter opioid detoxification, various assessments are made. The presence and severity of their opioid dependence and possible dependence and use of other substances is judged, for example, by analysis of urine or breath as well as through self-report and presence of clinical signs of withdrawal. Their history of drug and alcohol misuse and any treatment is recorded, as is their physical and mental health. Several factors affect an individual's suitability for opioid detoxification, such as risk of self-harm, loss of opioid tolerance, and misuse of other drugs and social and personal circumstances; these are also taken into account.

In addition to the biological treatment itself, the individual will also receive psychosocial support to help them to develop strategies to reduce the risk of relapse self-help groups (such as 12-step) and support groups (such as the Alliance). The treatment is also followed up with support for partners/families where appropriate and a contingency management programme. The latter includes the use of incentives (such as £2 vouchers) to reinforce a healthy lifestyle, for example, for drug-free urine tests. These are conducted three times weekly in the three weeks, twice weekly in the next three weeks and weekly thereafter. The vouchers, which increase in value with each continuous period of abstinence, can be exchanged for goods or services, or for privileges such as take-home methadone doses.

There are some situations in which detoxification is unlikely to be offered or requires caution. These include patients with medical conditions needing urgent treatment (as the drugs may interact) and those serving short prison sentences (as the programme needs prolonged supervision). Pregnant women may not be suitable for treatment as the foetus will be affected (although this can be done), nor are individuals with other physical or mental health problems or who misuse alcohol or other drugs necessarily suitable.

Finally, there are ethical issues involved in planning opioid detoxification. These include ensuring that the user has given their informed consent, that their confidentiality is respected and that the staff are competent to deliver the intervention.

Interactive angles

Read a recent NHS report on the use of drug therapy for drug dependence here:

http://www.nta.nhs.uk/publications/documents/nta_treat_drug_misuse_evidence_effectiveness_2006_rb5.pdf

1. Tabulate the evidence relating to two biological treatments.

2. Compare the effectiveness of the two treatments.

An alternative approach to detoxification is rapid anaesthesia-aided detoxification (RAAD). This treatment allows the patient to undergo complete detoxification using high doses of an antagonist. Since the patient is asleep or mildly anaesthetised, they avoid the conscious experience of the unpleasant symptoms of withdrawal. Clonidine and naloxone are administered together, the former to suppress withdrawal symptoms, the latter to achieve detoxification with the intention of reducing subsequent craving. The objective is therefore achieved in a matter of a few hours. However, this therapy is expensive, carries the risk of anaesthesia and still does not address the reasons for the initial drug dependence; as a consequence, it is not generally recommended by NICE.

The aim of maintenance treatment is to improve health by stabilising the user on a drug such as methadone. Thus a medically controlled, non-illicit opioid, which suppresses the symptoms of withdrawal but does not produce euphoria, is used in place of a more dangerous alternative. A different strategy is to use naloxone, an opioid antagonist. However, this produces withdrawal symptoms and is generally unsuccessful as a therapy.

One recent approach to therapy is to prescribe heroin itself. This is explored in the Research Now box below which looks at Blättler et al. (2002).

Research now

Compulsory

Blättler, R., Dobler-Mikola, A., Steffen, T. & Uchtenhagen, A. (2002)

'Decreasing intravenous cocaine use in opiate users treated with prescribed heroin'

Sozial und Praventimedizin, 47(1): 24–32

Aim: To investigate the benefits of giving maintenance doses of heroin to heroin users who also use cocaine.

Procedure: The study followed a group of heroin users in a naturalistic setting through at least 18 months on a treatment programme in six different clinics in Switzerland. The main sample consisted of 266 patients (98 female, 168 male) who had used heroin for 18 months or more, were aged at least 20 years, had made at least two previous unsuccessful attempts to treat their addiction and had given their informed consent. Potential participants were excluded if they were found dealing drugs in the treatment centre, selling their prescribed medication or mixing it with illicit drugs or were violent, although continued use of illicit substances itself was not a reason for exclusion. Participants were required to attend psychosocial therapy, such as counselling, and to receive health care. In addition, they were given maintenance doses of narcotics (all received heroin, some also received morphine or methadone). The mean dosage of heroin supplied was 479 mg daily and this was self-injected under staff supervision. Patients typically attended two or three times a day. Exact records of prescribed medication and drop-out from the programme were maintained. All participants were interviewed at intake and every six months thereafter, providing an initial and ongoing self-report of cocaine use. The interview included questions on drug use and symptoms. Urine tests for drug use were conducted on entry to the programme and randomly, without warning, approximately every other month.

Results: Only 16% of the sample reported no cocaine use in the six months prior to intake and gave a negative urine sample. Of the remainder, 90% reported injecting cocaine and 75% of the sample regularly injected drugs (such as heroin and cocaine). Alcohol was used by 33% of the sample and more than half also reported cannabis and illicit benzodiazepine use. They were therefore poly-drug users. The programme reduced both illicit heroin and cocaine use (see Figures 3.35 and 3.36). These differences were significant at $p \leq 0.001$. Since the cost of cocaine was stable throughout the 18 months, the reduction was likely to have been due to the programme rather than the factor of drug availability. The reduction in cocaine use was lower in individuals who had more frequent contacts with the drug scene at intake and those who had injected both heroin and cocaine prior to the programme. After the programme, continued cocaine use was related to a number of factors including more illegal income, prostitution, illicit heroin use, benzodiazepine use and contact with the drug scene (significant at $p \leq 0.001$).

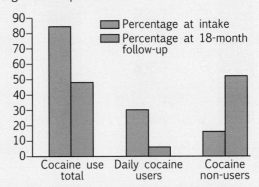

Figure 3.35 Cocaine use before and after treatment.

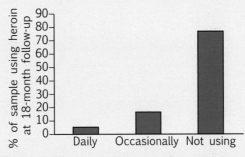

Figure 3.36 Illicit heroin use after treatment.

Conclusion: Heroin maintenance in a high-monitoring situation helps to reduce cocaine use. Where cocaine use persists, social factors such as illegal income and contact with the drug scene are important but it is unclear how these are associated.

One problem with studying drug use in humans by self-report is that they are affected by social desirability biases and tend to lie. However, in Blättler *et al.*'s (2002) study, only 2% of the participants who tested positive for cocaine use had self-reported as negative, which implies that they were being truthful. On the other hand, 24% self-reported as positive when their urine analysis was negative. This suggests that either they didn't understand the question, or they had been taking cocaine but longer ago than the test could detect. In either case, the self-reporting system is demonstrating a flaw. Another potential problem with this study was its longitudinal design. It is possible that those individuals most at risk are more likely to drop out of the programme. If so, this would appear to increase the success rate. After 18 months 71% of the patients were still in treatment, although the drop-out rate was only 11%, as some had moved to alternative treatments. The drop-out rate for cocaine users was higher than that of non-users, but this difference was not significant (see Figure 3.37). This suggests that the success of the programme for cocaine users was genuine and not a result of a selection bias in the sample.

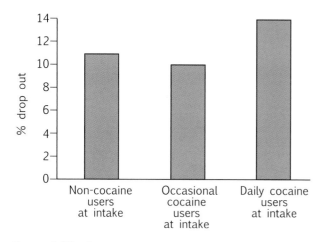

Figure 3.37 Cocaine users were not more likely to leave Blättler *et al.*'s study than non-users.

A final issue with the findings of this study relates to generalisability. The sample investigated were very specific – they were all heavily dependent poly-drug users. They were marginalised in society and had a variety of health and psychiatric problems. In these respects, the findings may not represent the value of such a programme with less severely disadvantaged individuals. Furthermore, the Swiss treatment programme is very unusual and is not typical of the resources for, or attitudes towards, drug rehabilitation elsewhere.

The learning approach: Aversion therapy

We have mentioned classical conditioning already in this chapter, so you will recall how the process works – by linking a new stimulus with one that naturally produces a particular response. In the case of aversion therapy, the existing

stimulus is an aversive one, that is, it produces an unpleasant response. This is linked with a behaviour, such as smoking or drinking alcohol in alcoholics, which is to be eliminated.

Prior to treatment, the unconditioned stimulus (UCS) produces an aversive unconditioned response (UCR). In the case of the treatment of alcoholics, these are an emetic drug such as Antabuse (the UCS) and vomiting (the UCR). During treatment, this unpleasant response becomes associated with the stimulus to be avoided; this is the conditioned stimulus (the CS). An association is built up, which causes the client's behaviour to change as the maladaptive habit (for example, drinking) becomes linked to the unpleasant conditioned response (the CR) (see Box 3.3).

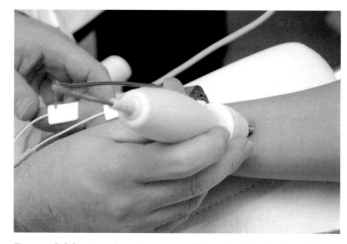

Figure 3.38 Aversion therapy pairing electric shocks with imagined opiate use produced a short-term reduction in craving but no long-term reduction in drug use (Houston & Milby, 1993).

Box 3.3

Aversion therapy

The drug Antabuse causes vomiting if combined with alcohol and, through classical conditioning, the response of drinking alcohol is removed:

UCS (Antabuse) $\longrightarrow$ UCR (vomiting)

UCS + NS (alcohol) $\longrightarrow$ UCR (unpleasant expectation accompanying vomiting)

CS (alcohol) $\longrightarrow$ CR (unpleasant expectation)

As the CR is aversive, the individual stops drinking alcohol.

Howard (2001) tested the effectiveness of aversion therapy with 82 alcoholic patients who were given a ten-day treatment programme. They were tested before and after the programme on how confident they were that they could avoid consuming alcohol in difficult situations where they would normally be tempted to drink. They were also checked to ensure that any effect of conditioning was specific to alcoholic drinks. After treatment, the patients were more confident that they would be able to resist drinking alcohol even in high-risk situations, showing that the conditioning had worked.

The aversive effect was, however, less strong in patients with a longer history of alcohol-associated nausea and more antisocial behaviour. For an alcoholic accustomed to vomiting, the conditioning process will be less aversive and therefore less effective. Howard *et al.* used pulse rate as an indicator of the level of aversion and found this to be specific to alcoholic beverages. This is an important finding, as one potential risk of this form of aversion therapy is that it could generalise to other drinks. In this case it clearly did not.

Aversion therapy clearly has other applications, such as in the treatment of smoking. One technique is to expose smokers to the aversive stimulus of their own exhaled smoke!

Figure 3.39 Rapid smoking is aversive.

Danaher (1977) tested the effect of a three-week aversive rapid smoking programme on 50 habitual smokers. This technique requires the smoker to inhale deeply and often until they feel ill – so they stop. He found that the treatment was effective for some participants, such as non-married treatment couples, but not for everyone. This study raises several issues. Firstly, one of ethics: the side effects of nausea, vomiting and dizziness are exceedingly unpleasant and potentially dangerous. Secondly, this therapy appears to be situation-dependent, suggesting that other more important factors affect cessation of smoking. Smith (1988) found that a commercial five-day smoke-aversion therapy 'Quick Puff' produced a 52% success rate with 832 clients. Interestingly, the best predictor of failure

was returning to a household with a smoker. This led to a 70.2% failure rate, supporting the idea that cessation is more dependent on social factors.

Not all evidence supports the success of aversion therapy for smoking. Curtiss *et al.* (1976) compared two treatment groups, one involving a discussion group and rapid smoking, the other only the discussion group. The participants were followed up for five months and, although smoking in both groups had declined, there was no significant benefit for the aversion therapy group. Two more recent studies present similar findings. Juliano *et al.* (2006) investigated the use of rapid smoking as a deterrent to relapse for smokers once they had quit (with the assistance of bupropion, a drug used to help reduce craving and withdrawal). They found that, although rapid smoking produced the typical aversive side effects and reduced the craving to smoke, it did not increase the likelihood of abstinence. In a meta-analysis of 25 studies, Hajek & Stead (2004) concluded that there was insufficient evidence of effectiveness to support the use of aversion therapy for smokers.

Token economy: a therapy using operant conditioning

The token economy approach to therapy employs operant conditioning. It uses positive reinforcement and a process called **shaping**. This is the rewarding of successive approximations to the desired behaviour. In the case of dependent users, this goal is to be drug-free, so increasing periods of abstinence are rewarded. Token economies can be used in an institutional setting or operated from outreach centres. The desired response is positively reinforced with 'tokens' such as cards, which are saved up and exchanged for primary reinforcers – things with real value, such as a CD. The tokens are **secondary reinforcers**, that is, they have reinforcing powers because they have been linked to a positive reinforcer by classical conditioning.

Olmstead *et al.* (2007) collected data from stimulant abusers undergoing treatment on token economy programmes at eight clinics; 415 participants abusing cocaine, amphetamine or methamphetamine were randomly assigned to 'usual care' or 'usual care plus abstinence-based incentives'. The latter group received positive reinforcers in the form of entries to a prize draw: they took chips from a fishbowl. Of the 500 chips, 250 said 'good job', 209 were for items worth about $1, 40 were for $20 prizes and there was one worth $100. The number of entries increased with the length of their drug-free period. Compared to the control group, the individuals with the potential to receive prize draw entries had significantly longer periods of abstinence. Although effective, the programme was costly.

Figure 3.40 Token economy programmes can help dependent drug users to stay clean.

Sindelar *et al.* (2007) demonstrated similar success using the same system with 120 cocaine abusers on a 12-week programme. When payouts were bigger ($240 rather than $80 payout), the participants provided a higher percentage of drug-free urine samples, stayed clean for longer and were more likely to complete the treatment programme. Even though the prizes were of higher value, the overall cost-effectiveness of the programme was better than when prizes were of a lower value.

Apart from cost-effectiveness, a token economy is also preferable to aversion therapy, as it is a more ethical way to modify behaviour because it is less distressing. However, token economies may lead to a dependency on the system, for example, drug users may expect to be rewarded simply for staying drug-free.

Drug abuse campaigns

Psychologists have a moral responsibility to use the knowledge they acquire to help people. One way in which health psychology contributes to this is by offering direction to and evaluation of health campaigns. Many health campaigns have tried to reduce the use of and harm done by drug taking, some more successfully than others. There are many challenges facing the developers of health

campaigns. For example, any anti-drugs campaign must effectively inform people about the dangers of drugs, for example, by making drug users look weak or undesirable. However, this has to be done with caution, otherwise the campaign risks alienating users themselves – the very people who are most at risk and in need of help. Another dilemma is the pitch of a campaign. If the main target is young people – in order to dissuade them from ever starting to use drugs – a campaign must be accessible and appealing to the younger generation. However, its resources must also be acceptable to that generation's parents, in order that they can encourage use of the resources and back up the messages of the campaign.

Finally, an important issue is how to present information honestly. Messages which are too 'parental', negative or over-the-top are unlikely to be believed. A balance needs to be struck between being realistic about the dangers of drugs without being either too positive, for example, through the use of humour, or too negative, for example, by using horrific material.

Talk to FRANK

'FRANK' is a brand name for the updated National Drugs Helpline; there is no single 'person' called Frank. This service provides a range of support about drugs including packs for schools, a website (www.talktofrank.com), a telephone service (available 24/7) and, most recently, a text-a-question facility to provide information about drug use. It is backed by an advertising campaign with an annual budget of several million pounds, which targets young people (and their parents). This uses TV, radio and printed promotional material including leaflets, posters and stickers. The idea is that people should see 'FRANK' as friendly and approachable so that they use the resources to seek out help.

Box 3.4

The four key aims of FRANK are:

1. to ensure that young people understand the risks and dangers of drugs and their use

2. to help young people know where to go for advice or help

3. to give parents the confidence and knowledge to talk to their children about drugs

4. to support professionals who work with young people, especially vulnerable groups.

The campaign aims to give realistic information to young people rather than just preaching about abstinence. When it was set up, focus groups recommended employing humour, but not in relation to very serious issues such as heroin use. It also aims to give parents the confidence to raise drug use issues with their children.

0800 77 66 00 talktofrank.com

Figure 3.41 The FRANK logo is well recognised by the target audience of young people and their parents.

The name 'Frank' was chosen as it sounded honest and straight-talking. Another advantage of a 'human' name is that it fits with the language of drug culture, such as calling cocaine 'Charlie'. Because 'Frank' sounds like an approachable person, it avoids resistance to 'institutions' and the problem of people not wanting to call a 'helpline'. By appearing neutral, confidential and non-judgmental, young people are more likely to ask FRANK things they wouldn't feel able to ask anyone else.

The TV advertisements which backed the launch of FRANK on 23 May 2002 were directed at young people so appeared in the breaks between programmes such as *Friends*, *Stars in their Eyes* and *Dawson's Creek*. Other ideas to make the marketing of FRANK highly targeted included having soap characters appearing in FRANK t-shirts, providing advice in teen magazines and putting up posters in club toilets and at music festivals.

In the week prior to the campaign launch, the service received 5,689 calls, an average of 813 a day. The week after the start of the advertising campaign, the service took 9,948 calls, an average of 1,421 a day. In the period April 2004 to April 2006 the FRANK helpline received 1.6 million calls (an average of over 2,000 a day) and directed over 45,000 young people to treatment services. To expand provision, a text service was added, allowing anyone to send a confidential question to a trained expert on 82111. Since its inception, the capacity for the helpline has been expanded tenfold – a clear indication that it is an improvement on the previous service.

The website has been similarly well used. In the two years to April 2006, the website had over 10 million hits including 500,000 hits on the treatment pages. 107,000 emails have also been answered. In 2008, FRANK's fifth year, the helpline had received 2 million calls and there had been 22 million visits to the website.

Theories of health behaviour, such as the health belief model (Hochbaum, 1958), suggest that, in order to make people engage in healthier behaviours, they need to be provided with information to change their beliefs. The information provided by the FRANK campaign certainly appears to have reached its target audience. By 2008, 89% of 11 to 21-year-olds recognised the FRANK adverts and 82% knew about the website (Mitchell, 2008). Importantly, this exposure to knowledge can affect beliefs. For example, young people who recognised a FRANK advert were more likely to believe that drugs were 'riskier' than those who did not recognise an advert (FRANK Review, April 2006).

One early criticism of the campaign was that it focused on the harm associated with drugs such as heroin and cocaine, apparently treating them more seriously than cannabis. This led to the assumption that children might infer that cannabis was therefore 'safe'. A recent television, radio and online campaign costing £2.2m has targeted cannabis use by young people. The television advert features 'Simon' smoking cannabis and the viewer is taken 'inside his head'. Initially he is seen experiencing the perceived positive effects of cannabis – feeling giggly and talkative and getting hungry. He then experiences negative effects such as paranoia, panic attacks and memory loss. According to theories such as the health belief model, health behaviours change as a result of increasing an individual's perception of the risks they face in contrast to the benefits they gain. By providing young people with information about the relatively high cost to health of taking drugs and the few and short-lived positive effects, such adverts aim to shift the balance in favour of resisting drug use by changing beliefs.

This campaign was well targeted, for example, appearing during the break in *Hollyoaks*, so is likely to have reached the intended audience. However, some critics have suggested that the recent cannabis campaign fails in FRANK's original ambition to avoid the 'parental' approach to drugs advice. For example, the animation implies that a single inhalation of cannabis will result in paranoia, panic attacks and vomiting. By taking such an extreme position, the campaign may make itself less credible. Indeed, the FRANK Review (April 2006) reports that the advertising campaign in 2005–06, which was less humorous and contained strong messages about drug use, whilst successful in providing information about the negative effects of drugs, also impacted negatively on the affinity young people felt for, and their trust of, FRANK. Nevertheless, by the end of the survey period, 30% of young people identified the FRANK phoneline as a source of information about drugs (compared to 31% trusting their mother). The website fared less well, but was considered by young people to be as likely a trusted source of information as school teachers at 22%.

Figure 3.42 Can anti-drugs campaigns be too hard hitting?

Another aim of the campaign was to provide realistic advice on reducing the harm done by drug use in young people. Studies such as Janis & Feshbach (1953) have demonstrated that strongly fear-evoking health messages are less effective than more moderate ones. The recent hard-hitting £1m TV and online FRANK advertising campaign about the dangers of cocaine use is highly evocative. It features 'Pablo', a drug mule dog, who died while being used to smuggle cocaine. In the advert, Pablo wakes from the dead and explores the risks and consequences of taking the drug.

The advert does contain some references to the risks for users – such as needing drugs and having to borrow money, violence and bleeding from the nose. In these respects, it should result in changes in health beliefs as the relative costs of drug use should be perceived to outweigh the possible benefits. However, it mainly focuses on the illegal drug trade (profits, violence and 'cutting' drugs). The video ends 'Finally, someone who made sense … visit talktofrank.com'. Some sources, such as the drugs charity Transform, question whether this will be effective in harm-reduction and indeed whether the video will make sense to young people.

No Smoking Day

A long-running national campaign to reduce smoking is the charity-run 'No Smoking Day'. This achieves consistently high levels of public awareness and participation, so has the potential to be a highly effective health intervention. Using local organisers and events, the day gains significant media coverage, expanding its sphere of influence.

In 2008, No Smoking Day was on Wednesday 12 March. The charity worked with both national and local organisations and set up 307 promotional events. In addition to these, resources included a website, text messaging, posters, leaflets, press articles, outdoor advertising and 'quit packs' which contained a leaflet, a sponsorship form, a window sticker, a badge and a wristband.

On No Smoking Day 2008 1.2 million smokers stopped smoking and 20% of smokers who were aware of No Smoking Day made an attempt to quit.

The campaign measures their success every few years. An evaluation of the 2004 campaign reported that 70% of all smokers were aware of No Smoking Day. Of those who attempted to quit, 11% were still not smoking more than three months later (Owen & Youdan, 2006). This relates to approximately 1.84 million smokers taking part in the day and 85,000 still abstaining after three months. These findings suggest that No Smoking Day is successful both in providing smokers with information and in helping them to quit.

Take the first step

No Smoking day

Wednesday
11 March 2009

Get help now
nosmokingday.org.uk
0800 169 0 169

Figure 3.43 No Smoking Day is a highly effective health intervention.

Over to you

Evidence in practice

Your task for this section of the course is to either produce summaries of two news articles or conduct a content analysis. In this section, we will guide you through examples of these tasks and give you examples to try for yourself. In order to summarise or analyse an article effectively, you need to be sure that you understand the content. Return to earlier parts of the chapter to help you where necessary. If you can, try to track down any original research that the article refers to, but be sure not to muddle up what is actually in the resource you are using and what you have found out as background material.

Scientists put price on addicts' treatment

Della Fok

yaledailynews.com, 11 October 2006 (http://www.yaledailynews.com/
articles/view/18333)

Yale scientists have put a price on incentive-based treatments for drugs abusers, helping to clarify the programs' costs and benefits.

Researchers from the Yale Department of Epidemiology and Public Health and the University of Connecticut Health Center found that it costs an additional $258 per patient to use prize-based incentives, which past research has shown can encourage patients to remain drug-free. The study, conducted by Yale research scientist Todd Olmstead and professor Jody Sindelar, along with University of Connecticut researcher Nancy Petry, was recently published in the September issue of Drug and Alcohol Dependence.

'Nobody knew how much more money this type of treatment cost in terms of the prizes themselves and the administrative costs,' Olmstead said. 'We wanted to shed light on the costs and cost effectiveness and to break down the barriers for wider implementations.'

The researchers gathered data from eight clinics serving a variety of patients across the country, focusing on treatment for addiction to cocaine, amphetamine and methamphetamine. The incentive method they explored was a supplemental program used alongside traditional treatment.

If the patients submitted drug-free urine samples, they earned chances to draw from a fishbowl with 500 chips, representing different levels of prizes. Out of 500 chips, 250 said 'Good job,' 209 were for small items worth about $1, 40 were for larger prizes worth $20, and one was for the jumbo prize worth $100. The longer the patients remained drug-free, the more draws they earned.

'The incentive is to have continuous days of abstinence, which encourages long periods of abstinence,' Sindelar said.

'This escalates the number of consecutive days and weeks patients stay clean, which mimics getting out of the habit.'

Petry, who designed the prize-based incentive technique, compared it to traditional behavior modification methods such as giving children allowances to encourage them to do a particular task more often.

Previous studies have proven that these types of treatment supplements are effective in helping substance abuse patients stay abstinent for longer periods of time, Olmstead said.

Although he said he wasn't surprised by the effectiveness of the method, he was surprised by the amount of money required for the administration. Including inventory, restocking and shopping for the items, the cost of the administration totaled almost as much as that of the prizes themselves.

'The next question is how to improve cost-effectiveness, streamline administration and improve efficiency,' Olmstead said.

While the researchers said it remains to be proven whether or not this strategy makes financial sense, they said they believe spending the extra $258 will cut back on some of the negative consequences of drug use, including crime and lost work days. The hope, they said, is that the results of their study will encourage more people to implement prize-based incentives in conjunction with traditional substance abuse treatment.

'Substance abuse treatment is becoming less punitive,' Petry said. 'It's becoming more of a positive experience, so the patients now like going to treatment because they get prizes and stay clean longer. It changes the atmosphere of the whole treatment.'

Exercise

Content analysis exercise

The author of this article is describing a token economy style treatment of people who misuse drugs. Your task is to carry out a content analysis of the article. You need to explore the language they are using and the psychological evidence they are employing to make their argument effective, then relate your conclusions to your understanding of drug use and its treatment.

1. Identify the categories of words that have been used, such as 'drug-free' and 'cost'. Some are positive, others negative. You might find ideas that relate to biological explanations or behaviourist ones.

2. Draw up a tally chart and record the frequency of each word, phrase or idea.

3. Looking at your chart, is the article mainly positive or negative about the system? What kinds of explanations are they using?

4. Write out an explanation of the psychological principles that underpin the article, showing how the author's views can be justified and suggesting ways that they may have 'glossed over' other important ideas.

5. Find another article about the treatment of drug misuse. Carry out the same procedure. Do the two articles use the same or different approaches to making their argument? Can you account for the ideas in your second article using the same psychological explanations as you used for the first?

REALlives

Key

You may be asked to describe one key issue from health psychology. You can choose this yourself from this chapter. Suitable examples include:

● How can drug misuse be treated?

● How can drug misuse be prevented?

● Are the media a cause of drug misuse?

● Are drug misusers born or made?

Make sure that for whatever you identify as your key issue, you can pose a question and draw on psychological theory and/or research to answer it.

Exercise

Summary exercise

1. Visit the following two websites:

   http://www.tdpf.org.uk/

   http://www.alcoholics-anonymous.org.uk/index.shtml

2. Summarise the ideas each organisation has about helping drug misusers which are related to psychological concepts.

3. You might want to explore other sources to discover more views about the organisations.

4. What conclusions are reached by each organisation?

5. What theory and/or empirical research might each organisation draw upon to make their argument?

6. What other factors might influence drug misuse that they don't consider?

Summary and conclusions

Health psychology can help us to understand the way drugs act at synapses, mimicking neurotransmitters and blocking or mimicking their effects, producing effects on cognition, behaviour and emotion. These include tolerance, physical and psychological dependence and, for different drugs, effects such as hallucinations or euphoria. In the absence of the drug, users suffer withdrawal symptoms, which are typically opposite to the drugs' effects, for example producing depression.

Drug use can be explained biologically through the effect's tolerance. The action of drugs on the brain's reward system explains why drug use is reinforcing. Genetic research has shown that some people inherit a greater predisposition to try or to become addicted to drugs. This could arise through personality differences, for example, people who are higher sensation seekers are more likely to try drugs (Stacy *et al.*, 1993).

Learning theories can also account for drug misuse as users initially find the effects positively reinforcing, then take the drug to avoid withdrawal. This can be explained by negative reinforcement. Social learning theory suggests that drug use may begin with people observing and imitating drug-taking models, such as friends (Morgan & Grube, 1991) and celebrities.

Research in both the biological and learning approaches uses animals. This has practical and ethical advantages and disadvantages compared to using human participants. Other research into drug effects uses brain scanning techniques, such as MRI and PET.

Heroin is an opiate which mimics the effect of the endorphin neurotransmitters. It causes initial euphoria and is a powerful analgesic. The user develops tolerance and becomes physically dependent. In the long term, heroin use is associated with an increased risk of mental illnesses, such as depression, and are at risk from overdoses.

Cocaine is a stimulant which acts on synapses using dopamine and is powerfully reinforcing causing tolerance and dependence. Cocaine initially raises self-esteem – the user feels euphoric, self-confident and energetic, but this is followed by a 'crash'. Long-term use results in an increased risk of psychotic disorders. Blättler et al. (2002) used heroin maintenance to help reduce cocaine misuse.

Marijuana is classified as a hallucinogen, acting on receptors for the cannabinoid neurotransmitters. It produces mild analgesia, sedation and appetite stimulation. Tolerance develops slowly. Long-term use, especially early in life, affects cognitive abilities such as memory and reaction time and can lead to an increased risk of schizophrenia, as well as social problems (Brook et al., 1999).

The FRANK campaign to reduce recreational drug use targets young people and their parents using a range of media. By making information accessible and acceptable, it can inform people about risks and provide a route to treatment. National No Smoking Day provides information and support for people trying to give up cigarettes and helps many people each year.

What do I know?

1. One misused drug is heroin.

   (a) Describe the mode of action of heroin and how this can lead to tolerance. [4]

   (b) Describe and evaluate **one** biological explanation of heroin dependence. [8]

2. Describe and evaluate Blättler et al.'s (2002) study into the use of heroin on prescription as an intervention to help dependent users. [12]

3. Stephen misuses drugs. He grew up living opposite some drug dealers. He lived in a rough part of town because his dad, who was an alcoholic, had lost his job so they had had to move. This was when Stephen was younger and he found the changes difficult as the staff at his new school seemed to think he was a problem from the outset.

   Drawing on your knowledge of psychology, suggest reasons why Stephen may have ended up being dependent on drugs himself. Evaluate the explanations you describe and explain at least one intervention that could help Stephen. [12]

4. The psychology of drug misuse can be difficult to study.

   (a) Outline **two** problems psychologists face when studying drug misuse. [2]

   (b) Describe **one** research method psychologists use in the study of drug misuse and explain how it helps to solve the difficulties that psychologists face in this area of research. [4]

   (c) Evaluate the method you have described in (b) in terms of its weaknesses. [4]

5. For the health psychology part of your course you will have studied a key issue, either by carrying out a content analysis, or by analysing written materials (producing a summary).

   (a) Identify the key issue you studied. [1]

   (b) Outline the findings from your content analysis or summary of this key issue. [2]

   (c) Draw conclusions about the key issue you identified in part (a) using:

   - your findings from your analysis
   - other evidence from health psychology. [6]

Chapter **4**

Sport psychology

What's ahead?

By the end of this chapter I should know about:

- know about what is meant by sport psychology
- outline factors affecting participation and performance in sport, including personality traits and developmental factors such as socialisation and/or reinforcement
- distinguish between intrinsic and extrinsic motivation
- describe and evaluate achievement motivation theory and one other theory of sporting motivation
- describe and evaluate the inverted-U hypothesis and one other explanation of the relationship between performance and arousal, anxiety and audience
- describe and evaluate two psychological techniques to improve sporting performance
- describe Boyd & Munroe's (2003) study of imagery in climbing and **one** of the following: Cottrell (1968), Koivula (1995) or Craft *et al.* (2003)
- know about one key issue of your choice from sport psychology
- know about **either** content analysis of an article **or** a summary of two sources provided in this chapter

In addition I should understand:

- the use of questionnaires including strengths and weaknesses
- correlational methods including their strengths and weaknesses
- quantitative and qualitative data

Where does sport psychology take us?

- What sort of person does sport?
- What motivates top athletes?
- Do audiences help or hinder performance?
- What causes performance catastrophes?
- Does setting goals help you score goals?

The European Federation of Sport Psychology (1996) has defined sport or sports psychology (as some prefer) as *'the study of the psychological basis, processes and effects of sport'*. The subject matter of sport psychology is broad, looking at questions such as why people choose particular sports, what psychological factors affect how successful someone is at sports and how we can use psychological strategies to improve sporting performance. Some American sport psychologists make a sharp distinction between academic sport psychology which looks at more theoretical issues – such as who chooses what sport – and applied sport psychology, which focuses purely on applying psychology to improve performance. However, most European sport psychologists do not make this distinction (Jarvis, 2006), and in this chapter we cover issues from both academic and applied sport psychology.

Factors affecting sporting participation and success

Personality traits

There have been many attempts to try and link personality traits (characteristics) to sporting behaviour. We can classify research into two categories: linking personality to **participation** in and choice of sport, and linking personality to **excellence** in sport. A study by Schurr *et al.* (1977) investigated both of these relationships. A sample of 1,596 male American university students were classified as athletes (defined as those representing the university in a sporting team) or non-athletes. Personality was assessed using a standard personality test, Raymond Cattell's 16PF (which stands for 16 personality factors, shown in Box 4.1). Athletes were compared to non-athletes on the 16 personality factors, and the relationship between each personality factor and choice of sport and sporting success were calculated. Overall athletes were less anxious, more self-sufficient and more objective. There were also differences between athletes opting for team and individual sports. Team players were more anxious, dependent and extrovert but less imaginative than individual athletes. No relationship emerged between any of the 16 personality factors and sporting success.

The Schurr *et al.* study remains of interest to sports psychologists because of the large sample size and the use of the 16PF, which yields interesting results because of the large number of personality variables it measures. However, there are problems with this and similar studies. The sample, consisting of young

adult American middle class males, was highly unrepresentative of sporting participants on a global level. Moreover, the factors that make someone participate and succeed in sport in the social setting of a university may be quite different from those operating under other circumstances. The definition of an athlete as someone participating in sport at university level has also been criticised for being too specific, giving us little information on the characteristics of those who take part in sports at both the more casual recreational level and the elite level (see Figure 4.1).

Box 4.1

Cattell's 16 personality factors

reserved ←→ outgoing
unintelligent ←→ intelligent
stable ←→ unstable
humble ←→ assertive
sober ←→ happy-go-lucky
expedient ←→ conscientious
shy ←→ adventurous
tough-minded ←→ tender-minded
trusting ←→ suspicious
practical ←→ imaginative
forthright ←→ shrewd
placid ←→ apprehensive
conservative ←→ experimenting
group-dependent ←→ self-sufficient
undisciplined ←→ controlled
relaxed ←→ tense

What's that?

- **Participation:** taking part in a sport
- **Excellence:** achieving high levels of skill and/or success in a sport

Figure 4.1 University athletes may not be representative of sporting participants.

Personality and participation in sport

Hans Eysenck (1952) suggested that personality can be understood by just two 'supertraits'. The first of these is **extroversion**, which describes the extent to which someone is lively, sociable and impulsive (an extrovert), or alternatively quiet and solitary (an introvert). The second trait is **neuroticism**, which describes the extent to which someone is emotionally stable and unflappable (a stable person) or emotionally unstable, moody and flappable (a neurotic). By looking at someone's extroversion and neuroticism we can classify them as one of four personality types or **temperaments**. These are shown in Figure 4.2.

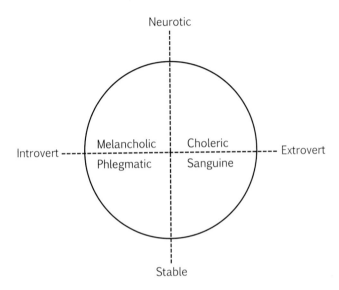

Figure 4.2 Eysenck's four personality types.

Eysenck *et al.* (1982) suggested that people high in psychoticism and extroversion are more likely to take up a sport than others. This is because sport can provide both the social and physical stimulation craved by extroverts, and because those high in psychoticism are suited to the competitiveness and assertiveness/aggression involved in sport. Some, though by no means all, research has supported Eysenck's position. Francis *et al.* (1998) compared Irish female students who participated in university hockey clubs with a control group of female students with no formal involvement in sport. The hockey players scored significantly higher in extroversion and psychoticism as measured by the EPQ. Although these results support Eysenck's view, we need to remember that university hockey players cannot be taken as representative of athletes as a whole. Hockey is a team sport in which players typically build a close-knit team identity, and the high levels of extroversion found in hockey players may reflect team players rather than athletes *per se*.

Figure 4.3 Hockey players are high in extroversion and psychoticism.

In a study of leisure activities, mood and personality in 275 adults, Hills & Argyle (1998) found that those who participated generally in competitive sport or exercise in general were higher in extroversion and psychoticism than others. This study has the advantage of including a wider range of participants than was typical of earlier studies, and further supports Eysenck's ideas. So far, however, no consistent picture has emerged of the relationship between extroversion and psychoticism and sporting participation.

A small body of research has also examined the relationship between neuroticism and participation in sport. Egloff & Gruhn (1996) compared 80 endurance athletes (distance runners and triathletes) with 73 non-athletes on extroversion and neuroticism. The athletes emerged as more extroverted and less neurotic than the control group. As well as providing information on neuroticism, this study is useful in identifying extroversion as a characteristic of individual as well as team sports.

Interactive angles

How would you describe your own personality in terms of traits like extroversion and neuroticism? What sports do you like? Does the relationship between your personality and choice of sport mirror the findings of sport psychology?

Personality and sporting success

Tutko & Ogilvie (1966) proposed that athletic performance could be explained in terms of personality traits. They suggested 11 traits associated with performance: aggression, 'coachability', conscientiousness, determination, drive, emotional control, guilt-proneness, leadership, mental toughness, self-confidence and trust. These were measured by a self-rating inventory called the **athletic motivation inventory** (AMI). It is generally agreed nowadays that the AMI had some serious flaws, both in the traits it identified (there is, for example, little evidence for leadership or coachability as stable traits) and in the items used to measure them. It is thus of little use in predicting performance.

Contemporary research using more widely accepted personality tests has provided some support for the idea that personality can impact on performance. Garland & Barry (1990) categorised 272 American university football players into different levels of skill and tested them with the 16PF. They found that four traits were significantly associated with skill: tough-mindedness, extroversion, group-dependence and emotional stability. Between them, these traits accounted for 29% of the variance in skill level. However, not all studies have found significant results. In a study by Feher et al. (1998) 67 rock-climbers were assessed on their skill level and given a battery of personality tests including the EPI. No personality characteristics were associated with rock-climbing skill.

Clearly, these two studies found very different results, but there are a number of possible factors that may have led to this. One obvious difference lies in the sport. Rock-climbing, although it involves co-operation, is not a team sport in the same way as American football, therefore we would expect extroversion and group-dependence to be less important. Rock-climbing is also less competitive than American football; hence we might expect tough-mindedness to be less of an issue. However, the two studies also used different personality tests and involved different populations, so we cannot assume that the nature of the sport was the principal reason for the different findings of the two studies. This is a good illustration of the difficulty in reaching hard and fast conclusions about personality and sport; two equally sound approaches to researching the issue can produce completely contradictory conclusions.

Figure 4.4 Success in rock-climbing is not associated with any personality traits.

114

Personality theories like Eysenck's and Cattell's are ambitious; they aim to explain *all* of human personality. Other theorists are more interested in highly specific aspects of personality. A lot of recent research has centred on mental toughness. Mental toughness involves the ability to cope with difficult circumstances. This requires a range of characteristics, for example coping with pressure of competition, bouncing back after failure, determination and resilience (Middleton et al., 2004). Box 4.2 shows items from a standard measure of mental toughness.

Box 4.2

Items from Goldberg's (1998) mental toughness questionnaire

(Answer T for True and F for False for each statement)

1. I frequently worry about mistakes. T F
2. I get really down on myself during performance when I mess up. T F
3. It's easy for me to let go of my mistakes. T F
4. If I start out badly, it's hard for me to turn my performance around. T F
5. I get distracted by what the coach thinks whenever I screw up. T F
6. I bounce back quickly from setbacks, bad breaks and mistakes. T F

There is evidence to suggest that mental toughness is important in performance. Crust & Clough (2005) assessed mental toughness in 41 male undergraduate athletes and tested them on how long they could hold a suspended weight. A moderate positive correlation between mental toughness and the time holding the weight was found ($r = 0.34$). Although single correlation statistics like this do not necessarily show a causal relationship, this finding does suggest mental toughness is helpful in performance.

Clough et al. (2002) have attempted to explain mental toughness as a set of coping skills that combine to make the individual *hardy*, that is, able to thrive under pressure. The concept of hardiness was developed in the field of health psychology by Kobasa (1979). Kobasa's aim was to explain why a minority of people do not appear to experience stress in circumstances that would be unhealthy for most of us. Clough and colleagues identified four characteristics underlying hardiness:

- **Control:** being able to keep emotions in check
- **Commitment:** taking an active role in events
- **Challenge:** a positive attitude to change
- **Confidence:** self-belief.

Support for the importance of hardiness comes from a study by Golby et al. (2003), in which 70 international rugby league players were assessed for mental toughness and hardiness using standard measures (the *Psychological Performance Inventory* and the *Personal Views Survey* respectively). Hardiness emerged as a significant factor affecting performance. At the time of writing, however, there is little consensus about how mental toughness should be defined and explained.

Development and sporting behaviour: Socialisation and reinforcement

The sort of personality traits we have looked at so far are believed to be largely genetic in nature. However, we cannot explain sporting participation or success by means of biology alone. Clearly, we have experiences that influence our attitudes to participation in sport and to competition. The general term used to describe the influence of other people on our social development is **socialisation**. One of the important mechanisms by which socialisation works is reinforcement.

Socialisation and sporting behaviour

The term socialisation describes the processes through which people acquire the rules of behaviour and the beliefs that form part of life in their society. Probably the most important influence on our socialisation is the family. **Primary socialisation** refers to socialisation within the family, especially by our parents. Other agents of socialisation include friends, peers, teachers, and in the case of athletes, coaches and team-mates. The influence of these others is known as **secondary socialisation**.

Figure 4.5 Watching sport with family members socialises children into sporting attitudes and behaviour.

Research suggests that primary socialisation is particularly important. The idea that families are a source of social influence on sporting behaviour is supported by a recent study by Jambor (1999). 165 parents of 5–10 year old children who did or did not participate in football were questioned on their beliefs and attitudes about sport. The parents of football players differed significantly from those of non-players, having more positive beliefs about sport, for example in terms of health benefits, and being more likely to take part in sport themselves. It seems that modelling

of sporting behaviour is thus one factor in children's participation, but that parental attitudes and beliefs also have an effect, independent of modelling (see Figure 4.5). It may be that family influences also moderate the effect of other variables such as gender. In a survey of 145 women (average age 21 years) Miller & Levy (1996) found that although women showed concern about being sufficiently 'feminine' if they participated in sport, this effect was sharply reduced if their mother was a sporting participant.

Socialisation also takes place at the level of wider culture. A culture is a set of beliefs and behaviours that characterises a group of people, for example a national or ethnic group. One way in which cultural beliefs affect our sporting development relates to our attitudes towards success and failure. Morgan *et al.* (1996) studied black, white and native American field and track athletes' perceptions about the influences on sporting success. Whereas the white athletes tended to see success as something unchangeable ('you've either got it or you haven't'), the black and native American athletes placed much more emphasis on effort, and saw success as something to be earned. This difference in attitudes may be important in sporting success – the more an athlete believes success is associated with hard work the more likely they are to train hard.

What's that?

- **Socialisation:** the social processes in which children take on the norms and beliefs of those around them
- **Gender:** the psychological aspects of sex, as distinct from the physiological aspects of being male or female

Another way we are socialised at the level of our wider culture is with regard to **gender**. Attitudes towards what is masculine and feminine are socialised and have important effects on sporting participation. Typically boys and girls are socialised into different patterns of behaviour. For example, girls are much more likely to be nagged at in childhood not to get dirty (Kremer & Scully, 1994). They also tend to have role models who maintain stereotypically feminine behaviour that does not normally involve wallowing in mud! Clearly, this is likely to lessen the chances of girls' involvement with any sport such as rugby and hockey that necessarily involve getting dirty. Guillet *et al.* (2000) tested whether gender identity affects sporting participation. They assessed 336 French schoolgirl handball players aged 13–15 for their femininity and androgyny (mix of traditionally masculine and feminine characteristics) and followed them up for three years. The more feminine and less androgynous they were at the start of the study the more likely the girls were to drop out from handball during the study. Another classic study by Nathalie Koivula looked at the extent to which gender and androgyny affected perceptions of sports as being masculine or feminine. We can examine this in detail in Classic Research.

Classic research

Optional

Koivula, N. (1995)

'Ratings of gender-appropriateness of sports participation: effects of gender-based schematic processing'

Sex Roles, 33: 543–57

Aim: To look at the difference between men and women and between androgynous and sex-typed individuals in their perceptions of sports as masculine or feminine.

Procedure: 104 men and 103 women took part in the study. They were assessed for androgyny using a standard psychometric test called the Bem Sex Role Inventory. Participants were also asked to rate a range of sports for gender-appropriateness, that is, how socially appropriate it was for men and for women to participate in that sport. Each sport was rated on a 1–7 scale where 1 = 'very appropriate for men, not at all for women' and 7 = 'very appropriate for women, not at all for men'. Sports rated on average between 1 and 3.5 were classed as masculine, those between 3.5 and 4.5 as neutral and those rated 4.5+ were rated as feminine. Thirty-seven sports including cycling, diving and tennis were classed as neutral; seven were classed as feminine, including ballet, aerobics and riding; 18 sports including football, rugby and boxing were classed as masculine.

Results: Men were more inclined than women to rate particular sports as highly inappropriate for one or other gender. More sex-typed individuals, particularly sex-typed men, were also more likely to rate sports as inappropriate for one or other gender than more androgynous individuals.

Male sex-typed participants rated sports most differently in terms of appropriateness for men and women. Their mean rating for women's participation in masculine sport was 2.2 as compared to 5.6 for feminine sport.

Conclusions: Men and sex-typed people are more likely to stereotype sports as masculine or feminine than women and androgynous individuals.

Figure 4.6 Highly feminine handball players are likely to drop out of this 'masculine' sport.

Interestingly, it seems that socialised attitudes to sport can also impact on performance. Chalabaev *et al.* (2009) looked at the relationship between girls' beliefs about the ability of girls to play football and their own performance. A sample of 102 French secondary school girls were questioned about their beliefs concerning boys' and girls' footballing abilities and their own ability. They were then observed playing football and performance was rated. Beliefs about the ability of boys and girls to play football predicted performance – those who believed that boys were always better footballers than girls played worse. Beliefs about their individual ability partly accounted for this relationship but not entirely – general views on gender and footballing ability still had an effect on performance when this was controlled for.

Reinforcement and sporting behaviour

Recall from your AS level the learning approach. To recap, reinforcement is said to take place whenever a behaviour has a pleasant result, increasing the chances that it will be repeated. Operant conditioning involves two sorts of reinforcement:

● Positive reinforcement takes place when something good, for example praise, money, sex, is added to the situation as a result of the behaviour.

● Negative reinforcement takes place when something bad such as pain or isolation is taken away as a result of the behaviour.

Social learning (Bandura, 1977) takes place when children imitate a model, usually an older same-sex model with high social status. A third form of reinforcement, called vicarious reinforcement, takes place when children see their model being rewarded for the modelled behaviour.

Reinforcement for participation and success in sporting activity can take place in a number of ways:

● Positive reinforcement happens whenever new and desirable things result from sporting behaviour, for example in the form of praise, trophies, certificates etc.

● Negative reinforcement happens whenever sporting participation or success leads to a reduction in something undesirable. For example, an isolated or bullied child might increase their social status through sport.

Vicarious reinforcement for sporting success takes place when spectating with family members. A child will hear athletes receiving praise from their co-spectators and perhaps see them collect trophies.

Figure 4.7 Seeing winners receiving trophies can be an example of vicarious reinforcement.

Strengths and weaknesses of the trait and developmental approaches

We have now looked at two very different approaches to understanding why individuals differ in their participation and success in sport. The trait approach focuses on largely genetic aspects of our personality such as extroversion, neuroticism and mental toughness. The great strength of the personality trait approach is that it lends itself to research. Traits are straightforward to measure using personality tests, and we can look easily at the statistical relationship between traits and participation or success in particular sports.

There are, however, some important limitations of this approach. There is no general agreement about what are the most important traits. Nor is there agreement about whether to look at specific traits like mental toughness or theories of personality like those of Eysenck and Cattell, which aim to understand the whole personality. Results of research have tended to be inconsistent, varying according to what sports, what populations and what personality measures are used. Trait researchers have not really succeeded in generating a set of rules for deciding who is likely to participate or succeed in sport. This in turn means that the approach has very limited practical applications.

The developmental approach is concerned with the influence of socialisation on sporting behaviour. This has different strengths and limitations. Although there is plenty of evidence to suggest that socialisation and reinforcement are important general influences on behaviour, it is quite hard to design studies to directly test their influence on sporting participation and success. On the other hand, the developmental approach has important practical applications. Through exposure to good role models and selective reinforcement parents, teachers and coaches can influence children's sporting participation and motivation to gain expertise.

Motivation and sport

When athletes are highly motivated 'they work hard in training and give 100% effort when competing' (Duda & Pensgard, 2002, p49). They also tend to respond better to difficulties, which can include a losing streak, injury or loss of confidence. It is important for all those who employ, coach or teach athletes to understand the ways in which their own behaviour can affect the motivation of the athlete.

Intrinsic and extrinsic motivation

An important distinction to make if we are to understand the range of motives underlying sporting participation and achievement is between intrinsic and extrinsic motivation. **Intrinsic motives** are those that come from within the individual. We might, for example, relish the physical sensations experienced in sport, and derive personal satisfaction from improving our performance. Competition provides us with excitement, and training with friends can be a happy social experience. What these factors have in common is the pleasure associated with sport.

What's that?

- **Intrinsic motivation:** motivation that comes from within the person, that is, the factors that make sport pleasurable
- **Extrinsic motivation:** motivation that comes from external rewards such as money and trophies

Extrinsic motives are the external rewards that we can gain from taking part and succeeding in sport. These include the obvious rewards such as trophies and lucrative prizes and contracts, but also less obvious but nonetheless powerful rewards such as social status and attractiveness. Research has strongly supported the importance of intrinsic motivation, both in the decision to participate in sport and in achieving a good performance. Studies to assess people's reasons for taking part in sport have tended to find that people report intrinsic rather than extrinsic motives. Ashford *et al.* (1993) interviewed 336 English adults (chosen on the basis of their use of a community sports centre) in order to ascertain why they participated in sports. Four intrinsic motivators emerged from their responses: physical well-being, psychological well-being, improvement of performance and assertive achievement (defined as achieving personal and competitive goals).

Because intrinsic factors are so important in sporting participation, a key aim of research has been to improve our understanding of what influences intrinsic motivation. Amorose & Horn (2001) assessed 72 American college athletes aged 17–19 on their intrinsic motivation at the beginning and end of their first year of inter-college level participation. They were questioned about the time put in on training, their coaching and whether they had sports scholarships. Neither scholarship status nor time had any impact on the extent to which the participants maintained their initial levels of intrinsic motivation. However, the behaviour of coaches had a profound impact. Those whose coaches spent more time in instruction and less time in *autocratic* behaviour (that is, throwing their weight about) tended to display significant increases in their intrinsic motivation during the year.

The additive principle

Clearly, most individuals are strongly influenced by intrinsic factors in their motivation to take part in sport and to try to achieve good performances. Common sense suggests that if we throw some extrinsic motivation into the equation as well then we will increase the athlete's total motivation. This is known as the **additive principle**, shown in the equation below.

$$\frac{\text{intrinsic}}{\text{motivation}} + \frac{\text{extrinsic}}{\text{motivation}} = \frac{\text{maximum}}{\text{motivation}}$$

There are numerous extrinsic rewards available to top-class athletes. As well as the high salaries paid to some professionals, there may be prize money and sponsorship money. Athletes also have high social status and are likely to be considered a good sexual 'catch'. Until the 1970s it was standard wisdom to provide athletes with extrinsic rewards in order to make use of the additive principle. However, it seems that in this case common sense is wrong, and introducing large material rewards undermines rather than enhances intrinsic motivation. In one study Sturman & Thibodeau (2001) tracked the performance of 33 American baseball professionals for two seasons before and two seasons after they signed lucrative new contracts. There was a sharp decline in performance as measured by batting average, number of home runs and so on, immediately following the new contract, and lasting for around one season. This suggests that the players' intrinsic motivation was undermined by their increase in salary.

Figure 4.8 Baseball performances typically decline when players achieve high salaries.

Achievement motivation theory

Although most people participate in sport and exercise for pleasure, when we consider sport at competition level we get into the realm of achievement, and we need to consider people's motives to achieve. According to McClelland *et al.* (1961) we can understand achievement motivation in terms of two factors: motivation to succeed and fear of failure. The motivation to succeed is understood in this theory to come from intrinsic motivation, that is, the pleasure derived from participating in sport (as discussed on page 117). Fear of failure is determined by our individual levels of competitive anxiety.

Whenever we enter a sporting situation we experience an **approach-avoidance conflict**. We want to approach the situation in order to enjoy taking part. At the same time, we also want to avoid it to escape the anxiety that taking part would produce. If the intrinsic motivation to take part in a sporting activity is greater than the anxiety we feel over the competitive situation, then we will be motivated to achieve highly in the event. This can be expressed as an equation:

$$\frac{\text{achievement}}{\text{motivation}} = \frac{\text{intrinsic}}{\text{motivation}} - \frac{\text{competitive}}{\text{anxiety}}$$

Individuals who are high in intrinsic motivation and low in anxiety are likely to be motivated to succeed at high levels. Those who are low in intrinsic motivation and high in anxiety are likely to experience considerable difficulty in competitive sport. Those who have moderate intrinsic motivation but high anxiety levels might enjoy sport but find it very difficult to compete at a high level where competitive anxiety is likely to be greater.

Figure 4.9 More pressurised high-level competition may reduce motivation for those high in competitive anxiety.

In later developments to the McClelland-Atkinson model, the role of extrinsic motivation was taken into account as well as intrinsic motivation and anxiety. Thus, if intrinsic motivation is low and anxiety high, it may still be possible to produce high levels of achievement motivation by introducing extrinsic motivation. In other words, if we don't particularly enjoy a sport and competition makes us anxious, we may still be motivated to succeed if success will give us a sufficiently attractive reward such as a trophy or prize money.

Evaluation

The principles that intrinsic motivation is important for success and that excessive anxiety can put us off competing are not controversial. Furthermore, the model is helpful in understanding why athletes respond differently to different levels of competition. However, there are serious limitations in the McClelland model. The main problem is that it cannot be used to predict successful performance. Research has found that those high in achievement motivation as calculated from intrinsic motivation and anxiety do not consistently do better in competition than those low in achievement motivation. A further problem is that the model does not take account of gender differences in achievement motivation. It seems that women may still fear to enter into competition even when intrinsic motivation is high and anxiety low.

Nicholls (1984) suggests that the term 'achievement' as used in the McClelland model is too vague, and that we need to distinguish between achievement of skill (mastery orientation) and achievement of tangible rewards (ego orientation). These appear to be related to intrinsic and extrinsic motivation. Zahariadis & Biddle (2000) assessed 412 children aged 11–16 about their reasons for taking part in sport. A clear relationship emerged between reasons and orientations. Task-oriented young people spoke of team spirit and skill development as their main reasons for taking part in sport, whereas those classified as ego-oriented were more concerned with extrinsic rewards such as their social status.

Self-efficacy theory

Bandura (1982) introduced the concept of self-efficacy to sports psychology. Self-efficacy is often confused with self-esteem, but actually the two concepts are quite distinct. Whereas self-esteem is the emotional experience of how we feel about ourselves, **self-efficacy** refers to our beliefs about our abilities. As well as being a cognitive rather than emotional phenomenon, self-efficacy differs further from self-esteem in being **situation-specific**. Whereas our self-esteem is fairly constant and generalises across quite different situations, we can have different self-efficacy in different situations. If we have good sporting self-efficacy we believe we are good at our sport and this generally has a positive impact on our motivation.

We get the information about our sporting abilities from several sources (Schunk, 1991). We draw on our past experiences of success and failure. We can be persuaded by other people. We also look at the self-efficacy of our peers. If other people of similar ability believe they can do something then it makes sense that we will also be able to. We also interpret our physiology. If, for example, we are in a relaxed state we might interpret this as meaning we can cope with the task at hand. On the other hand, if we are tense for whatever reason, we may interpret this as anxiety about being able to succeed, reducing our self-efficacy.

Evaluation

There is no suggestion that self-efficacy is a complete explanation of sporting motivation; however, it does appear to be one influence. Importantly, it is an influence that can be harnessed by coaches and teachers to improve motivation. In a classic demonstration of the impact of self-efficacy, Wells et al. (1993) randomly divided student participants into three groups and gave them weight-lifting tasks. In one condition the participants were given accurate feedback about how much they were lifting. In another condition they were misled into believing they were lifting heavier weights, and in the final condition they were misled into thinking they were lifting lighter weights. The three groups were then compared on how much they could lift, and the group who believed that they had lifted heavier weights than they really had were actually able to lift the most. This demonstrates both the power of self-efficacy and the ease with which a good coach can improve it, not necessarily by lying to athletes but by emphasising the positive aspects of their performance.

Figure 4.10 Weight-lifters given false feedback about how much they are lifting may be able to lift more next time.

There is also evidence that self-efficacy is associated with performance. Myers et al. (2004) examined the relationship between collective efficacy in women's ice hockey teams and team performance. Twelve teams were assessed for collective efficacy on the Saturdays of seven weekends in which they played on Friday and Saturday and correlated with scores on Friday and Saturday games. The efficacy scores were collected before the Saturday game so that their relationships to earlier and later games could be seen. Efficacy scores collected on Saturdays were strongly predictive of performance later that day (r = 0.56). There was a much weaker relationship performance the previous day. This suggests that performance had a modest effect on collective efficacy but that collective efficacy had a very powerful effect on performance.

Arousal, anxiety and performance

At the top level of sporting competition there is relatively little difference in skill, fitness or motivation. Perhaps the most important factor separating winners from losers at this level is the ability to cope with arousal and anxiety (Jones, 1991). Let us first distinguish between the terms 'arousal' and 'anxiety'. **Arousal** is our general level of physical and psychological activation. We are low in arousal when we are tired, bored

or sleeping, and we are high in arousal when we are excited, anxious or angry. High and low levels of arousal can thus both be positive or negative experiences. **Anxiety**, however, is a negative emotional state in which we experience high arousal accompanied by worrying.

There are important distinctions to make within anxiety. For example physiological (or somatic) anxiety – high arousal – is not the same as cognitive anxiety – worrying. Another distinction is between state and trait anxiety. State anxiety describes an athlete's current level of cognitive and physiological arousal and their self-confidence. Trait anxiety is their general tendency to be anxious as a function of their personality. This is closely related to Eysenck's idea of neuroticism. In a classic study Craft et al. (2003) carried out a meta-analysis of studies of the relationship between state anxiety and performance.

Classic research

Optional

Craft, L.L., Magyar, T.M., Becker, B.J. & Feltz, D.L. (2003)

'The relationship between the Competitive State Anxiety Inventory-2 and sports performance: a meta-analysis'

Journal of Sport & Exercise Psychology, 25: 44–65

Aim: To attempt to establish the overall relationship between the three dimensions of state anxiety and athletic performance in the light of previous inconsistent findings.

Procedure: 29 studies were selected for inclusion in the meta-analysis on the basis that they investigated the relationship between state anxiety (measured by the standard psychometric test, the Competitive State Anxiety Inventory-2 or CSAI-2) and sporting performance. These were mainly located by electronic searches of journals and conferences; however, an advert was also posted asking for unpublished studies. Each study was coded for a number of variables including the sport and the level of expertise of the participants. In total, results from 2,905 participants were included.

Results: Overall, relationships between state anxiety and performance were fairly weak. The variable with the strongest relationship with performance was self-confidence (r=0.36), compared to r=0.13 for cognitive anxiety and r=0.09 for physiological anxiety. The relationship between trait anxiety and performance was stronger in individual sports than team sports and weaker in elite athletes than those performing at club level.

Conclusion: Of the three dimensions of state anxiety only self-confidence is strongly correlated with performance. Strength of correlations is moderated by type of sport and level of performer.

how science works

Research Methods

...t two variables are said to be correlated when there is a measurable relationship between ...s of correlation representing the different sorts of relationship two variables can have. A positive ...ne variable increases, so does the other. When, on the other hand, as one variable increases the ...on is said to be negative. The easiest way to show correlations is using a scatterplot. Figure 4.11 ...representing a positive correlation and one a negative correlation. On a scatterplot each dot, ...participant. The stars are located level with the participant's score on each variable. The line of ...where it comes closest to most stars. The closer the stars are to the line of best fit the stronger

Much of sport psychology research makes use of correlations. For example, there is a lot of research looking at the relationship between personality variables and sporting success.

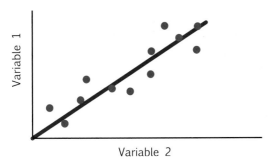

Figure 4.11a A positive correlation.

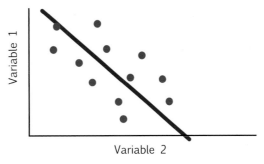

Figure 4.11b A negative correlation.

Evaluation

Correlations involve measuring two or more variables. The ways in which we measure these have a greater or lesser degree of reliability and validity, and they may raise ethical issues. Correlational research does not raise particular ethical issues – just those that depend on the measurement of the variables. As with any research it is important to consider issues of consent, deceit, privacy and harm. Personality tests, such as those used to assess people's extroversion and neuroticism, typically have quite good reliability (if we take them twice or split them in half and take the two halves separately the correlation between the two scores gives us a reliability figure, typically 0.7–0.8). We also need a measure of sporting performance for this type of study. This can come in the form of recent scores, such as number of games won, total points over a period of time or league position. *Validity* means the extent to which the figures used in this type of study represent what they are meant to. For example, is the most valid measure of a sprinter's performance their best time that season, their average time that season or some measure of their success in competition? Some correlational studies use several measures to ensure validity.

Correlations also raise validity issues when they are used as evidence for causal relationships. Crust & Clough (2005) assessed the correlation between mental toughness and time athletes were able to suspend a weight. However, although the obvious conclusion is that the mental toughness influenced the ability to hold the weight this conclusion lacks validity. It may be that athletes with good physical endurance develop greater mental toughness. Sometimes when we have a bit more information we can make cautious suggestions from correlational research about what might affect what. Myers *et al.* (2004) looked at correlations between team efficacy and performance before and after it was measured. Because there was a much stronger correlation between efficacy and *later* performance than earlier performance this suggests that efficacy influences performance rather than the reverse.

Audience effects

Explanations for the relationship between arousal, anxiety and performance need to be able to account for **audience effects**. Audience effects take place when being watched affects athletic performance. This may be a positive or negative effect. Past studies have found that the presence of an audience tends to improve performance in experts and make it worse in novices. Personality may also make a difference, with some studies showing that extroverts do better with an audience and introverts worse.

What's that?

- **Arousal:** the general level of physiological activation in the body

- **Anxiety:** a negative emotional state characterised by high arousal and worry

- **Audience effects:** positive or negative effects on performance resulting from being watched

Inverted-U hypothesis

The inverted-U hypothesis originated from Yerkes & Dodson (1908). The principle is that for every motor task we can carry out, there is an optimum level of physiological arousal. Performance is best at this level and drops off when arousal rises above or falls below it. This relationship is shown in Figure 4.12.

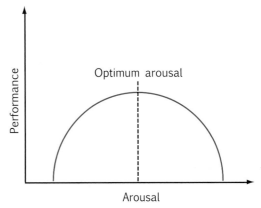

Figure 4.12 The inverted-U hypothesis.

The optimum level of arousal for a task depends on the complexity of the motor skills used to perform that task. For a complex task involving fine motor skill, such as placing a dart in the bull's-eye, low levels of arousal are preferable. For gross tasks such as weightlifting, the optimum arousal level is much higher.

Support for the inverted-U hypothesis comes from studies of athletes' perceptions of what factors affect performance. Thelwell & Maynard (2000) asked 198 county-level English cricketers (100 batsmen and 98 bowlers) what they considered to be the most important variables affecting their performance. Optimum level of arousal emerged in the top four factors affecting both batsmen and bowlers (the others were self-confidence, a pre-match routine and following a performance plan).

Figure 4.13 Cricketers report that too high or low arousal levels affect their game.

Understanding optimum levels of arousal has an important application in mental preparation for competition. Before a snooker or darts match players aim to achieve relatively low levels of arousal. This is the reason why darts players drink alcohol during competition and why beta blockers (drugs that control heart rate and blood pressure) are considered an unfair advantage in snooker. On the other hand, a sport involving gross motor skills and the application of power requires a process of 'psyching up' to raise arousal levels. Some athletes have rituals to help them do this, a classic example being the Maori display used by the New Zealand 'All-Blacks' prior to rugby matches.

The inverted-U hypothesis can partially explain audience effects. The presence of an audience raises arousal levels. If arousal is raised below or up to the optimum level, it will lead to an improved performance; however, if it goes up too high, above the optimum level, then performance will decline. This is a crude explanation for audience effects, however, because it does not take account of *why* the presence of other people should affect arousal.

An advantage of the inverted-U hypothesis is that it can explain why even world-class athletes make serious errors under conditions of high arousal – fine motor skills become unsupportable at high levels of pressure and arousal even in experts. However, the inverted-U hypothesis assumes that anxiety and arousal are the same. Most psychologists believe that this is not the case – anxiety is associated with arousal but also with particular cognitions and emotion. The emphasis in modern sports psychology is more on anxiety than arousal as a predictor of performance, for example in Fazey & Hardy's catastrophe model.

The catastrophe model

A problem with the inverted-U hypothesis is that it predicts that a small increase in arousal above the optimum will have only a small impact on performance. Fazey & Hardy (1988) pointed out that under some conditions a very small increase in arousal beyond the optimum level can lead to a **performance catastrophe**, that is, a massive fall-off in performance. According to Fazey & Hardy, the main factor affecting when performance catastrophes occur is cognitive anxiety. Catastrophes occur when levels of cognitive anxiety are high and not at other times. Figure 4.14 shows the relationship between arousal and performance under conditions of low and high cognitive anxiety.

a) Low cognitive anxiety

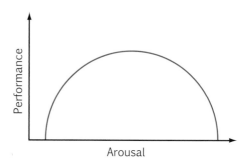

b) High cognitive anxiety

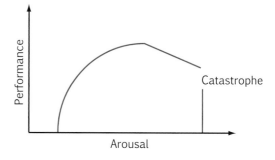

Figure 4.14 The relationship between arousal and performance under conditions of low and high cognitive anxiety.

According to Fazey & Hardy then, the inverted-U hypothesis is not worthless, but it only explains what happens under conditions of low cognitive anxiety. However, when cognitive anxiety is high then there comes a point just above the optimum level of arousal where performance drops off sharply, resulting in a performance catastrophe.

The catastrophe model provides a better explanation of audience effects than does the inverted-U hypothesis because it can explain why the audience might impact on anxiety. The effect of the audience becomes negative when it worries the performer, that is, when cognitive anxiety becomes too high. This explains why novices are negatively affected by audiences – they get more worried. In the experienced performer who does not worry about their audience physiological arousal increases without an increase in cognitive anxiety, improving performance.

The catastrophe model is hard to test directly, partly because cognitive anxiety is hard to assess during performance. However, there is evidence to suggest that athletes' best and worst performances occur when their cognitive anxiety is particularly high, and that under high cognitive anxiety performance drops off sharply when the optimum arousal level is exceeded. In a study by Hardy et al. (1994), eight expert crown green bowlers bowled three balls at a jack

on two consecutive days. On one day, prior to bowling they were given neutral instructions designed to create low cognitive anxiety and on the other day they were given a different set of 'threatening' instructions designed to create a state of high cognitive anxiety. To increase physiological arousal the participants were given shuttle-runs to perform and their heart rates were individually monitored. The relationship between arousal as measured by heart rate and performance could thus be measured in conjunction with low and high cognitive anxiety. Results supported the catastrophe model. In the low cognitive anxiety condition, the performance–arousal relationship showed a weak inverted-U. Under the high cognitive anxiety condition, however, performance was better, but dropped off sharply when arousal became too high. The results are shown in Figure 4.15.

It is important to note that, although high levels of cognitive anxiety are associated with performance catastrophes, they are also associated with the best performances. An important application of the catastrophe model and the research surrounding it is to show that cognitive anxiety can be a help as well as a hindrance to athletes (Hardy, 1996). Although studies like that of Hardy et al. (1994) do support the catastrophe model, they are few in number and can be criticised on the basis that the cognitive anxiety induced in artificial conditions is quite different to that experienced by athletes in competition (that is, they lack ecological validity). The difficulty in testing the catastrophe model more conclusively has proved frustrating to psychologists. Moreover the idea that high levels of cognitive anxiety can enhance performance remains controversial (Gill, 1992).

a) Low cognitive anxiety

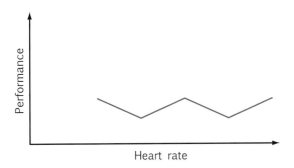

b) High cognitive anxiety

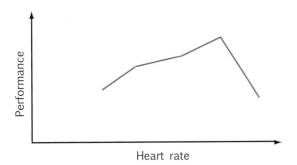

Figure 4.15 The relationship between arousal and bowls performance under conditions of low and high cognitive anxiety. (Adapted from Hardy et al., 1994.)

Figure 4.16 Deliberately worrying bowls players lacks ecological validity as well as raising ethical issues.

123

Quantitative and qualitative data

Recall from your AS-level that data can be qualitative or quantitative. 'Data' simply means information. Quantitative data comes in the form of numbers. Qualitative data is any information *not* in the form of numbers, for example verbal information such as notes from observers or interview transcripts. Almost all research in sport psychology is quantitative. All the studies in this chapter produce numerical information. This is probably for two main reasons. First, sport often yields performance data in numerical form. This might be anything from times to number of goals. We can look at this quantitative data in relation to psychological variables, which range from personality traits to arousal and anxiety. Much of the research in this chapter is correlational; this is not surprising when you consider how much of sport psychology is concerned with the relationships between these performance variables and psychological variables. A second reason why sport psychology is predominantly quantitative is that it has a clear aim – to improve performance. To know whether we have succeeded necessarily means looking at numbers.

In some situations, quantitative data can be crude and misleading, and can fail to capture the subtleties of what is being studied. Qualitative data comes into its own when we are interested in people's personal responses to a situation and when a study has political implications – this is notoriously hard to capture in the form of numbers. Sport psychology is not political, however, and although sport psychologists certainly care how athletes and spectators feel, they are usually interested in specific measurable variables like anxiety. These can be measured quantitatively. Qualitative data can be vague and fail to show key trends, and it is usually these that sport psychologists are interested in.

Psychological techniques for improving performance

This is very much applied sport psychology – the sort of thing you might find yourself doing with athletes if you ever work in sport psychology. Most top-level athletes are now influenced by some psychological techniques, although of course not all of these choose to work with a sport psychologist. These are the sort of techniques used on occasion by a good coach.

Goal-setting

Locke (1996) points out that having a large task to achieve can leave us overwhelmed, demotivated and anxious. However, the large daunting task can usually be broken down to a number of smaller and more specific goals. This can leave whatever we are trying to achieve less intimidating and more achievable. This process of goal-setting theory can be seen both as a technique for improving motivation and for handling anxiety.

Let us illustrate the process of goal-setting with an example. A hurdler might wish to improve their times in order to qualify for the county team next spring. However, this aim is hard to work towards because it is big, intimidating and hard to define. Using goal-setting the athlete should start by identifying one or two specific aspects of their technique to work on, each of which should make a difference to their overall times. They can set themselves small, manageable goals to aim for. For example, the hurdler might decide that they are quick off the blocks and competent at hurdles but their sprinting is letting them down. Based on this they could then set themselves the goal of cutting their 100m by 0.4 seconds by Christmas. A further goal could be to decrease their clearance distance from hurdles without reducing the percentage successfully jumped. Once these manageable goals have been achieved, the athlete should find that they are well on the way to achieving their overall goal.

Figure 4.17 Hurdlers can set themselves small, manageable goals in order to improve their performance.

There are two types of goal. The hurdler in the last paragraph has chosen to set a performance goal, that is, a goal to improve an aspect of their sporting performance. An alternative approach would be to set an outcome goal. This would be to succeed in competition as opposed to improving performance. Outcome goals can be useful provided they are achieved; however, winning is not normally entirely in the control of the athlete. If our hurdler were to set themselves an outcome goal of winning at a pre-season meet and improved their time during training, but was then beaten by a superior opponent, it would be demoralising. This shows how goal-setting has to be carefully thought out to be effective.

Evaluation

Research has generally supported the idea that goal-setting can be useful in improving sporting performance. However, there is disagreement about the best sort of goals to set. For example, should goals really be specific, or are more general ones better sometimes? Should goals be easy or difficult? Weinberg *et al.* (1987) tested the effect of goal-setting on sit-up performance and found no difference in the performance of participants given moderate or difficult goals and those told to 'do their best'. This seems to contradict the principle of specific goal-setting. However, most participants in the 'do your best' condition reported later that they had set themselves more specific goals. Therefore, success in this condition could be due to goal-setting.

Athletes and coaches report that goal-setting is seen as an important strategy. Weinberg *et al.* (2000) surveyed 328 Olympic athletes on their use of goal-setting, and found that all respondents used it and believed it to be useful. Interestingly athletes reported setting themselves three types of goal: performance and outcome, but also to have fun! This shows that these athletes considered it essential to maintain their intrinsic motivation. Weinberg *et al.* (2001) followed this study up by investigating coaches' views on goal-setting. Fourteen American high school coaches were interviewed and reported that they used goal-setting extensively. They reported that they used goals to provide structure and focus, and that goals needed be both long- and short-term and both negotiated with athletes and dictated by coaches.

Imagery techniques

Like goal-setting, imagery can be considered both a way of improving performance and managing anxiety. The golfer Jack Nicklaus once said that a good shot is 50% down to the golfer's mental image of the ideal shot. There are actually several ways of using imagery in sport. It can for example be used to aid relaxation and improve focus. An important distinction exists between **external imagery**, where the athlete pictures themselves from *outside* performing, and **internal imagery**, where they view themselves performing from *inside* their own body. Mental rehearsal is an example of an internal imagery technique. Mental rehearsal involves us imagining ourselves performing a technique. This does not necessarily involve imagery – we can mentally rehearse a squash serve without visualising a squash court around us. However, many athletes find that visualising themselves performing techniques in the competitive situation is particularly helpful.

Figure 4.18 Golfers make use of imagery to achieve accurate shots.

Mental rehearsal probably works for several reasons. The **psychoneuromuscular** theory emphasises the role of 'muscle memory'. When we form an image of ourselves performing a sporting technique, the nervous system and muscles react almost as if we were actually carrying out the technique. This means that imagery aids the process of learning sporting techniques. Mental rehearsal probably also works because it desensitises us to the anxiety of competitive situations. Exposure to stimuli that cause us anxiety – whether in real-life or in our imagination – is known to reduce the resulting anxiety. An example of this comes from Vealey & Walter (1993), who described the use of imagery by the Soviet Union team in the 1976 Olympic Games. The team were all provided with photographs of the various competition sites so that they could mentally rehearse themselves performing *at those sites*.

Figure 4.19 The Russian Olympic squad imagined themselves at the stadium before the 1976 Games.

Paivio (1986) classified imagery as serving a cognitive or motivational function and operating at a specific or a general level. Putting these together gives us four possible functions of imagery in sport. One of these, motivational-general, has since been subdivided so we are left with five functions (Hall, & Kerr 1998):

1. Cognitive-specific imagery is used to correct and plan specific skills; for example, a golfer might imagine carrying out a putt.

2. Cognitive-general imagery is used to learn less specific patterns of movement such as a dance routine or a football set-piece.

3. Motivational general-mastery imagery is used to imagine the individual coping well with a difficult situation, for example, keeping calm and focused after a bad referee's decision. This helps with self-confidence.

4. Motivational general-arousal imagery is used to control anxiety and arousal, calming nervousness or 'psyching up' according to the situation.

5. Motivation-specific imagery is used to maintain focus and motivation, for example, by imagining winning a competition.

Boyd & Munroe (2003) carried out a study comparing the use of these five types of imagery in climbers and track athletes. We can look at this in Classic Research.

Evaluation

It is very hard to evaluate retrospectively the success of imagery techniques in particular real-life instances like the 1976 Olympics. However, it is widely believed that this may have helped the Soviet team to be less affected by their new competitive environment. Certainly there are several studies that support the idea that mental rehearsal involving imagery is effective in enhancing performance. Grouios (1992) reviewed studies and concluded that mental rehearsal is more effective than no practice, although less effective than real-life practice. However, not everyone is equally able to make use of mental imagery. Expert performers and those with good mental imagery abilities make better use than novices and those with poorer imagery abilities. This means that imagery techniques are not the first choice for all athletes seeking to improve their performance. It also appears that athletes not skilled in mental imagery are not particularly disadvantaged. Gregg *et al.* (2005) measured imagery ability in 53 male and 47 female field and track athletes and looked for a correlation with best performance in the previous season's meetings. No correlation emerged, suggesting that the athletes low in imagery ability had effective alternative strategies.

Figure 4.20 Climbers and field-and-track athletes differ in their use of motivational but not cognitive imagery.

Classic research

Boyd, J. & Munroe, K.J. (2003)

'The use of imagery in climbing'

Athletic Insight, 5: 15–30

Compulsory

Aim: To compare novice and experienced climbers and to compare climbers and field-and-track athletes in their use of mental imagery to enhance performance.

Procedure: 38 field-and-track athletes (25 male, 13 female) took part in the study along with 48 climbers (28 male, 20 female). The mean age of both groups was in the early 20s (21.2 for field-and-track and 24.2 for climbers). Thirty climbers were classified as advanced and 18 as beginners. All participants were given a standard psychometric test called the Sport Imagery Questionnaire (SIQ) to complete. This has 30 statements with 7-point scales of agreement (strongly disagree–strongly agree). The SIQ is designed to measure the five types of imagery as identified by Hall & Kerr (1998). Some items in the SIQ are not appropriate for climbers so the climbers used a modified version.

Results: Climbers differed significantly from field-and-track athletes on three of the five types of imagery. Climbers used significantly less motivation-specific imagery (mean 2.95 vs 4.53) and significantly more motivation-general imagery (for motivation general-mastery 4.63 vs 5.54 and motivation general-arousal 4.26 vs 4.86). There were no significant differences between novice and advanced climbers.

Conclusion: Climbers did not vary in their use of imagery according to their experience. Nor did they differ from field-and-track athletes in their use of cognitive imagery. However, the climbers did differ from field-and-track athletes in their use of motivational imagery, using more motivation-general and less motivation-specific imagery.

how science works

Research Methods

Questionnaires

Recall from your AS-level that we can use questionnaires and interviews to gather information about what people think and feel. We also use these tools to find out about a person's psychological characteristics. Sport psychology uses questionnaires more often than interviews. More often than not questionnaires consist mostly of closed questions and give us quantitative data. Closed questions ask respondents to select a response from a set of options. This might be yes [ ] no [ ] or it might involve a Likert Scale – strongly agree [ ] agree [ ] don't know [ ] disagree [ ] strongly disagree [ ]. Some studies involve putting together a new questionnaire but often there is an existing questionnaire that we can use. For example, in this chapter we have come across the Sport Imagery Questionnaire (page 126) and the Mental Toughness Questionnaire (page 114). The advantage of using a standard questionnaire like these is that we probably know something about its reliability and validity. Remember that reliability is the consistency with which a measurement tool measures something. We know, for example, that the Sport Imagery Questionnaire has a reliability of between 0.7 and 0.9. This means that if you take it twice and see how close the two scores are or look for how closely your responses to each question correlate with others, you will see a correlation coefficient of between 0.7 and 0.9. Validity describes the extent to which it measures what we set out to measure. We can judge the validity of a questionnaire by seeing whether people scoring high or low on it differ in some relevant way. For example, we know that measures of mental toughness correlate with a coefficient of 0.4–0.5 with performance on endurance tasks. This validates the concept and measurement of mental toughness.

Questionnaires can raise ethical issues. The most basic ethical consideration in a study is to avoid harming or distressing participants. It is important when assessing someone with a questionnaire to be very clear what results show and do not show, and to feed this back very tactfully to participants. Someone might, for example, score low on mental toughness and we might distress them by saying so. Proper awareness of the limitations of the reliability and validity of the questionnaire will allow you to put someone's results in context. So will knowing how and when mental toughness is important – it may not be crucial for the person you are speaking to. For these reasons questionnaires that measure psychological variables should be used with caution.

Attributional retraining

Attribution is the mental process by which we decide why something happened, in other words what we attribute the event to. Self-attribution is the process in which we decide why we acted or performed as we did. One approach to improving motivation and performance is to challenge unhealthy attributions, in particular self-attributions.

Weiner (1974) produced a model of self-attribution based on two factors, whether an internal or external attribution is made, and whether this attribution is stable over time or rather varies from one situation to another. The relationship between attribution and stability is shown in Figure 4.20.

Attribution

	Internal	External
Stable	Ability	Task difficulty
Unstable	Effort	Luck

Figure 4.21 Weiner's model of attribution.

If we consistently succeed or fail, our attributions are likely to be stable. This means that we are likely to attribute the outcome to either our ability or the difficulty of the task. Because of self-serving bias, it is more likely that we will attribute success to ability and failure to task difficulty. If our results are less consistent we will probably attribute them to effort or luck. Again, self-serving bias means that we are likely to attribute success to effort and failure to bad luck.

Evaluation

There is evidence to show that attributions are associated with motivation. Foll et al. (2006) looked at the relationship between attributions and response to failure in 100 novice golfers undertaking a putting task. Generally those with unstable attributions (luck and effort) showed better persistence, suggesting these are healthy attributions. Weiner's model also gives us a starting point to work with athletes to correct athletes' attributions. We may wish to shift the attributions of a lazy athlete towards the unstable-internal position so that they realise more effort is needed. We may also wish to shift the attributions of a depressed athlete away from a stable-internal position, so that they cease to blame their lack of ability. This is examined further below when we look at the idea of learned helplessness. Altering an athlete's attributional state is called reattribution training, and is a form of cognitive therapy. An example of the use of attributional therapy comes from Orbach et al. (1999), who investigated the effectiveness of attribution training with 35 inexperienced tennis players. They were given false feedback over four training sessions, in order to lead them to attribute successes to internal factors. As hoped, the players changed their attributions in response to the feedback, and these changes led to improved self-esteem and performance.

Media watch

Evidence in practice

Your task for this section of the course is to either produce summaries of two news articles, or conduct a content analysis. In this section, we will guide you through examples of these tasks and give you examples to try for yourself. In order to summarise or analyse an article effectively, you need to be sure that you understand the content. Return to earlier parts of the chapter to help you where necessary. If you can, try to track down any original research that the article refers to but be sure not to muddle up what is actually in the resource you are using and what you have found out as background material.

Content analysis exercise

The writer(s) of this paper from the United Nations are discussing the relationship between gender and sport. Your task is to carry out a content analysis of the article with the aim of showing how the writer has used language to make their argument convincing. An extract is shown here. You can read the whole document on-line here, and you will probably wish to use a larger section for your content analysis: http://www.un.org/womenwatch/daw/public/Women%20and%20Sport.pdf.

Extract

Introduction

'Bicycling has done more to emancipate women than any one thing in the world'—Susan B. Anthony, suffragist, 1896.

Women's participation in sport has a long history. It is a history marked by division and discrimination but also one filled with major accomplishments by female athletes and important advances for gender equality and the empowerment of women and girls. Among the many remarkable achievements are those of Helene Madison of the United States of America, the first woman to swim the 100-yard freestyle in one minute at the 1932 Olympics; Maria-Teresa de Filippis of Italy, the first woman to compete in a European Grand Prix auto race in 1958; Nawal El Moutawakel of Morocco, the first woman from an Islamic nation to win an Olympic medal for the 400-metre hurdles at the 1984 Olympics; and Tegla Loroupe of Kenya, who in 1994 became the first African woman to win a major marathon. Women have taken up top leadership positions in sport, such as Presidents and Secretaries-General of National Olympic Committees. More and more women have also taken up employment opportunities in all areas of sport, including as coaches, managers, officials and sport journalists. These achievements were made in the face of numerous barriers based on gender discrimination. Women were often perceived as being too weak for sport, particularly endurance sports, such as marathons, weightlifting and cycling, and it was often argued in the past that sport was harmful to women's health, particularly their reproductive health.

In 1896, Baron Pierre de Coubertin, founder of the modern Olympics, stated: 'No matter how toughened a sportswoman may be, her organism is not cut out to sustain certain shocks.' Such stereotypes fuelled gender-based discrimination in physical education and in recreational and competitive sport, sporting organizations and sport media.

The benefits for women and girls of physical activity and sport.

Although many of the clinical trials and epidemiological studies in health research have excluded women, the data available suggest that women derive many health benefits from an active lifestyle. The health benefits of women's participation in physical activity and sport are now well established. Participation in sport and physical activity can prevent a myriad of noncommunicable diseases which account for over 60% of global deaths, 66% of which occur in developing countries. For girls, it can have a positive impact on childhood health, as well as reduce the risk of chronic diseases in later life. For older women, it can contribute to the prevention of cardiovascular diseases, which account for one third of deaths among women around the world and half of all deaths among women over 50 in developing countries. Physical activity also helps to reduce the effects of osteoporosis, which women have a higher risk of developing than men. Participation in physical activity aids in the prevention and/or treatment of other chronic and degenerative diseases associated with aging, such as type-2 diabetes, hypertension, arthritis, osteoporosis and cardiovascular abnormalities. It also helps in the management of weight and contributes to the formation and maintenance of healthy bones, muscles and joints. Physical activity can reduce the incidence of falls among older women.

1. Identify the uses of language you will be looking for in the article. You might for example look for words like 'health', named conditions and 'prevention' which flag up the physical benefits of sport.

2. Draw up a tally chart and record the frequency with which each of these key words are used.

3. Looking at your chart, what sort of word has the author used most to flag up health benefits of sport for women?

4. Get surfing and find another article on gender and sport. Carry out the same procedure. Do the two articles use the same or different approaches to making their argument?

Exercise

Summary exercise

1. Visit the following two websites:

    http://www.acton.org/commentary/commentary402.php

    http://www.slate.com/id/2082186

2. Summarise the points each article makes about the relationship between sporting participation and character development.

3. What conclusions are reached in each article?

4. How balanced is each?

5. What theory and/or research might each writer draw upon to make their arguments?

6. What other factors might influence each organisation (political, religious, commercial and so on)?

REALlives

Key

You may be asked to describe one key issue from sport psychology. You can choose this yourself using material from one or more parts of this chapter. Suitable examples include:

*   What factors might make someone a good coach?

*   What sort of person does sport?

*   What psychological factors might make an athlete well-suited for competitive sport?

*   What is the best way to handle anxiety in sport?

Make sure that for whatever you identify as your key issue you can pose a question and draw on psychological theory and/or research to answer it.

Summary and conclusions

Sport psychology is concerned with a number of issues, many of which have clear applications in improving performance. There is a large body of research into the relationship between personality and sporting behaviour. Studies using general measures of personality traits have shown only modest relationships, but narrow-band personality theories such as those looking at mental toughness in relation to performance show quite strong trends, particularly in relation to endurance sports. An alternative research tradition looks at the role of socialisation and reinforcement in sporting behaviour. Gender, culture and family interactions all contribute to children's attitudes to sport.

Motivation is closely related to sporting success. Intrinsic motivation is generally a more powerful factor than extrinsic motivation and adding extrinsic motivators often reduces rather than increases overall motivation. Achievement motivation has been thought of as the product of intrinsic motivation and competition anxiety. However, this model does not predict performance. A more useful theory of motivation involves self-efficacy. This is associated with performance and can be manipulated by coaches to improve performance. Many researchers have focused on the relationship between arousal, anxiety and performance. Overall, anxiety and arousal have only a small impact on performance; however, the relationships are different for different sports and for different types of anxiety. The catastrophe model shows how high levels of cognitive anxiety can trigger performance catastrophes – complete collapses in performance. Sports involving fine motor skills are particularly badly affected by high levels of arousal or physiological anxiety.

There are a range of techniques to improve performance based on the idea of regulating motivation, anxiety, expertise or a combination of these. Goal-setting is one effective technique in which athletes break down large aims, which are anxiety-provoking and demotivating, into smaller, more manageable goals. Mental imagery can be used in a number of ways to enhance performance. Cognitive imagery is used to directly work on technique whilst motivational imagery is used to regulate anxiety and motivation. Attributional retraining aims to change the ways in which athletes think about their performance.

What do I know?

1. (a) Explain what is meant by sport psychology. [3]

   (b) Outline **one** way in which sport psychologists have tried to enhance sporting performance. [5]

2. (a) Outline the use of correlations in sport psychology research. [5]

   (b) Evaluate the usefulness of correlations. [5]

3. Outline and evaluate research into the relationship between personality and sporting participation and performance. [12]

4. (a) Explain what is meant by intrinsic motivation. [3]

   (b) Outline achievement motivation theory. [5]

   (c) Evaluate one other theory of motivation. [5]

5. (a) Outline Craft et al.'s study of imagery in climbing. [6]

   (b) Evaluate imagery techniques in sport psychology. [5]

Chapter 5 Clinical psychology

What's ahead?

By the end of this chapter I should know about:

- what clinical psychology is
- the statistical and social norms definitions of psychological abnormality, including strengths and weaknesses
- psychiatric diagnosis with particular regard to the reliability and validity of, and cultural issues raised by, the *DSM* system
- the features and symptoms of schizophrenia
- two explanations for schizophrenia, one biological and one other, for example cognitive or psychodynamic theory, including their strengths and weaknesses
- two treatments for schizophrenia, for example drugs, CBT or psychodynamic psychotherapy, including their strengths and weaknesses
- the features and symptoms of one other disorder, for example unipolar depression or phobias
- two explanations for the disorder you have chosen, including their strengths and weaknesses
- two treatments for your chosen second disorder
- Rosenhan's study of psychiatric diagnosis and one of the following: Goldstein (1988), Lewine *et al.* (1990), Brown *et al.* (1986), or Cook & Mineka (1989)
- one key issue from clinical psychology, displayed in a leaflet

In addition I should understand:

- techniques from biological and/or psychological treatments, for example, drugs, free association
- at least one treatment from each approach: social, cognitive, psychodynamic, biological and learning theory
- the use of twin studies, animal studies and case studies in research into schizophrenia
- issues of reliability and validity in clinical psychology
- the distinction between primary and secondary data

Where does clinical psychology take us?

- When is behaviour abnormal?
- Are we any good at diagnosing mental disorder?
- Is mental disorder all in the genes?
- Can poor parenting lead to mental health problems?
- Drugs or psychological treatments?
- Is ECT effective and is it safe?

Clinical psychology is the branch of applied psychology that deals with understanding and treating mental disorder. In this chapter we are concerned with understanding how we can define behaviour as abnormal and how abnormal behaviour is classified and diagnosed as mental disorder. We will also look in detail at how schizophrenia and one other mental disorder of your choice are diagnosed, explained and treated. These explanations and treatments are based on the five approaches you studied at AS level.

Defining abnormality

We have probably all at some point looked at someone's behaviour and thought 'that's not normal'. What we mean by this is that the person's behaviour is outside the range of what we see as typical of people with good mental health. Individually and as a society, we make decisions to declare some people to be mentally disordered or 'abnormal'.

As we will see in this chapter, there are several ways in which we can define an individual's mind and behaviour as abnormal. These matter for two reasons. First, there is a philosophical and ethical issue; at what point do we draw a line and say that someone is abnormal rather than simply unusual, eccentric or rebellious? When is it fair to call one person abnormal and another normal? Second, when we diagnose mental disorder we need some consistent and, as far as possible, objective ways to assess people and decide whether they qualify as abnormal. The following are some of the ways that have been used to define abnormality.

Statistical abnormality

The most literal way of defining something as abnormal is according to how often it occurs. According to this definition, anything that occurs relatively rarely can be thought of as 'abnormal'. This approach is most useful when dealing with human characteristics that can be reliably measured, for example, intelligence, anxiety and depression. We know that in any measurable human characteristic, the majority of people's scores will cluster around the average, and that as we move away from this average fewer and fewer people will attain that score. This is called the *normal distribution*. We can look at the normal distribution of IQ (intelligence quotient) in Figure 5.1.

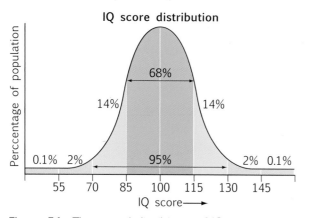

Figure 5.1 The normal distribution of IQ scores.

The average IQ according to tests on a cross section of the population is set at 100. The 85 and 115 scores are set as those between which 65% of people will fall and the 70 and 130 scores are set as those between which 95% of people will fall. If someone scores below 70, they fall in the bottom 2% of the population. This means that they meet one of the three criteria for diagnosis of **mental retardation** (the other two being onset of the low IQ before 18 years and the inability of the individual to meet the standards of their cultural group in communication, self-care, social skills, work, health or safety).

The limitations of the statistical infrequency approach to defining abnormality are obvious and serious. IQ scores of 130+ are just as infrequent as those of below 70, but we wouldn't consider calling someone abnormal or giving them a diagnosis just because they were very bright! Neither would there be any advantage to giving someone a diagnosis of retardation based on their IQ score if they were living a happy and fulfilled life. Statistical infrequency *on its own* is thus not a sufficient criterion for defining behaviour as abnormal, although statistical measures, for example of IQ, depression or anxiety, may form part of the process of diagnosis.

Deviation from social norms

A social norm is a behaviour or belief that most people stick to within a society. When someone simply follows the social norms of their culture it is very hard to use their behaviour to make judgements about them. However, when someone defies social norms it attracts our attention and provides us with the sort of information we can use to make judgements. We probably all therefore tend to notice and be a bit wary of people whose behaviour does not conform to social norms. In some cases where behaviour runs counter to the social norm but is clearly harmless, we might think of people as eccentric or rebellious rather than abnormal. However, there are cases where behaviour runs counter to the moral values shared by whole societies. In these cases we can use deviation from social norms as a basis for defining someone as abnormal. An example is in the diagnosis of **antisocial personality disorder**. People with a diagnosis of antisocial personality are commonly known as psychopaths. The psychopath is impulsive, aggressive and irresponsible. One of the defining symptoms of antisocial personality disorder is 'failure to conform to social norms with respect to lawful behaviours as indicated by repeatedly performing acts that are grounds for arrest' (from the *Diagnostic and Statistical Manual of Mental Disorders-IV-TR*; American Psychiatric Association, 2000).

We would probably all agree that psychopaths are abnormal on the basis that they defy some important social norms. Other diagnoses, like paedophilia (sexual attraction to children) and zoophilia (sexual attraction to animals), are also based largely on the social unacceptability of the individual's behaviour. However, although deviation from social norms is important in defining some mental disorders, it can lead to two problems.

Personal liberty and social control

First, focusing on the ways in which an individual chooses to deviate from social norms can lead to severely restricting their freedom of choice. Table 5.1 shows some examples of real diagnoses that were given to people in the past because their behaviour defied social norms.

Table 5.1 Historical diagnoses made on the basis of deviation from social norms

Condition	Symptoms
Drapetomania	Slaves showed an irrational desire to escape from their owners
Nymphomania	Middle class women were attracted to working class men
Moral insanity	Women inherited money and irrationally wished to keep it
Unmarried motherhood	Unmarried women became pregnant
Homosexuality	Sexual attraction to members of the same sex

Figure 5.2 Escaping slaves were once regarded as abnormal.

It is probably no coincidence that all these diagnoses have been aimed at groups that have always experienced discrimination. In these cases the main motivation for applying labels of mental disorder was probably a desire to maintain **social control** over women, black people and gay people. For example, by being able to get women diagnosed with nymphomania or moral insanity (with the co-operation of white, middle class male doctors), nineteenth century men were able to maintain strict control over women's economic and sexual lives. It is probably also no coincidence that standard treatments for most of the five 'conditions'

in Table 5.1 included what we would now call cruel and unusual punishment. The diagnoses in Table 5.1 all appear absurd in twenty-first century Britain, but only because social norms have changed so much. As recently as the 1970s, gay men were given a psychiatric diagnosis and 'treated' by means of painful electric shocks. Even more recently in the 1990s, audits of patient records revealed women who were still kept in psychiatric hospitals because they had had children out of wedlock some decades earlier.

Cultural variations in social norms

Social norms are culturally specific. They differ therefore between any two groups with a different culture, including different ethnic, regional and socio-economic groups, and different generations within the same community. This can cause huge problems when a mental health professional from one cultural group assesses someone from another. This is probably why in the UK Black and Irish people are significantly more likely than others to receive a diagnosis of mental disorder (Littlewood & Lipsedge, 1997). Littlewood & Lipsedge (1997) illustrate this problem with the case of Calvin.

> ### Box 5.1
>
> ## The case of Calvin
>
> Calvin was a Jamaican man. A post office clerk had accused Calvin of cashing a stolen postal order (it was not in fact stolen). An argument resulted and the police were called. Calvin was arrested. A prison psychiatrist assessed him for possible mental health problems. The following is an extract from his report:
>
> *'This man belongs to Rastafarian – a mystical Jamaican cult, the members of which think they are God-like. The man has ringlet hair, a straggly goatee beard and a type of turban. He appears eccentric in his appearance and very vague in answering questions. He is an irritable character and has got arrogant behaviour.'*

This nightmarish case illustrates the difficulty a psychiatrist can have in assessing someone with a different cultural background. Calvin's appearance was described as eccentric, although for a Rastafarian it was entirely normal. Calvin is also described as 'irritable' – if either of us had just popped out to cash a postal order and been called a thief, arrested and found ourselves being assessed by a psychiatrist, we'd be absolutely livid! Having never experienced this kind of discrimination, the psychiatrist clearly had difficulty appreciating this.

Figure 5.3 Members of groups with distinctive appearances are still at increased risk of being labelled as abnormal.

Classification and diagnosis of mental disorder

We begin this section with an explanation of what classification and diagnosis are and a brief account of how they operate in the mental health system.

Classification

Classification of mental disorder involves taking sets of symptoms and putting them into categories. For example, symptoms of depressed mood, feeling hopeless, having low self-esteem, eating too much or little, sleeping too much or little and having difficulty in concentration often occur together. We can therefore say that someone showing these symptoms has a particular disorder. We can go on to classify that disorder as part of a wider class of disorders. Table 5.2 shows the 14 major classes of mental disorder identified by the *Diagnostic and Statistical Manual of Mental Disorders (DSM)*, one of the major systems for classification and diagnosis.

Table 5.2 The major categories of mental disorder according to *DSM-IV-TR*

1	Disorders usually first diagnosed in infancy, childhood or adolescence
2	Delirium, dementia, amnesic and other cognitive disorders
3	Substance-related disorders
4	Schizophrenia and other psychotic disorders
5	Mood disorders
6	Anxiety disorders
7	Somatoform disorders
8	Factitious disorders
9	Dissociative disorders
10	Sexual and gender identity disorders
11	Eating disorders
12	Sleep disorders
13	Impulse control disorders
14	Adjustment disorders

In fact, our set of above symptoms are those used to diagnose *dysthymia*, a form of depression. Looking at the 14 classes of mental disorder in Table 5.2, you can probably guess that dysthymia is classified as a mood disorder.

What's that?

- **Classification:** categorising groups of symptoms into mental disorders and those disorders into classes of disorder
- **Diagnosis:** the process of deciding what if any mental disorder a patient is suffering based on their symptoms

Diagnosis

Once we have sets of abnormal symptoms classified into disorders we can diagnose individuals according to their symptoms. Diagnosis involves assessing a patient's symptoms and deciding whether they meet the criteria for one or more mental disorders. Typically a diagnosis requires that a certain number of symptoms are present for a particular period of time. It may also require the *non-presence* of factors that are known to produce similar symptoms. For example, to return to our example of dysthymia, diagnosis requires that depressed mood and two other symptoms are present for two years (or one year in children), and that the symptoms are not the result of medication or a medical condition.

Systems for classification and diagnosis

There are several systems with which we can classify abnormal patterns of thinking, behaviour and emotion into mental disorders. These systems are highly detailed; they both classify abnormality into many different disorders and they give guidelines on how to diagnose them, in some cases including standard interview questions to help make the diagnosis. The two most widely used systems of classification and diagnosis are the *DSM*, produced by the American Psychiatric Association, and the International Classification of the Causes of Disease & Death, produced by the World Health Organisation. The original *DSM* was published in 1952. Since 2000 it is in its fourth edition with text revisions (that is, revisions to the wording rather than the disorders). This is usually shortened to *DSM-IV-TR*.

The idea behind classification and diagnosis

In this chapter we will look quite critically at the success with which mental health professionals diagnose and treat particular mental disorders. Given the limitations of our success in this area, it is perhaps worth explaining at the outset just why most professionals believe it is worth classifying and diagnosing. The major reason to classify mental disorder is so that we can provide individuals with a diagnosis. The major reason to give people a diagnosis is so that we can target appropriate treatments and services towards them.

There are also spin-off benefits to classifying and diagnosing mental disorder. First, patients and their families may be able to take a degree of comfort in understanding that their symptoms can be understood and to some extent treated. Second, researchers have something solid to work with in order to better understand the origins of, and effective treatment for, sets of symptoms. For example, once we have the classification of dysthymia and a procedure for diagnosing it, we can take a group of people with dysthymia and test the effectiveness of a range of treatments. Without the classification of dysthymia it would be much harder to establish what sort of treatments are likely to be helpful for people with these symptoms.

Reliability and validity

For a system like *DSM-IV-TR* or ICD-10 to work effectively it should be capable of accurately diagnosing individuals. However, we meet a logical problem here; when we talk about accuracy in many situations we make the assumption that there is an absolute value to compare against. A watch is accurate if it keeps approximately the same time as our most accurate clocks. When it comes to diagnosis, however, there is no 'most accurate clock' to compare diagnostic systems against. We therefore cannot measure true accuracy and we must rely on two approximations of accuracy. These are **reliability** and **validity**.

Reliability

Reliability means consistency. A system can be said to be *reliable* if people using it consistently arrive at the same diagnoses. One way of seeing how reliable a diagnosis is, is by testing whether different clinicians agree on the same diagnosis for the same patient. Technically this is called **inter-rater reliability**. Another way of assessing reliability is to assess the same patients two or more times and see whether they consistently receive the same diagnosis. This is called **test–retest reliability**. Test–retest reliability is the most common way of judging the consistency of diagnosis. Reliability is often presented numerically. If you're not a lover of maths try not to be too put off; there is a simple explanation in Box 5.2.

Pontizovsky *et al.* (2006) looked at the agreement between diagnosis on admission and on release for the 998 patients admitted to Israeli psychiatric hospitals in 2003 suffering from depression and related mood disorders and 1,013 with schizophrenia and related psychotic disorders. Diagnosis was by means of the ICD system. The PPV for the mood disorders group was 94.2%, that is, 94.2% of patients had the same diagnosis when released from hospital as they had when admitted. The Kappa figure, which represents the statistical relationship between diagnosis on admission and diagnosis on release, was 0.68. For psychotic patients the PPV was 83.8%, that is, 83.8% of patients had the same diagnosis when released from hospital as they had when admitted. The Kappa figure, which represents the statistical relationship between diagnosis on admission and diagnosis on release, was 0.62. This study shows reasonably good reliability for ICD diagnosis.

A study by Nicholls *et al.* (2000) shows that neither ICD-10 nor *DSM-IV* demonstrates good inter-rater reliability for the diagnosis of eating disorders in children. Eighty-one patients aged 7–16 years with some eating problem were classified using ICD-10, *DSM-IV* and a system developed especially for children by Great Ormond Street Hospital. Over 50% of the children could not be diagnosed according to *DSM* criteria. Reliability was 0.64 (that is, 64% agreement between raters), but this figure was inflated by the fact that most raters agreed that they couldn't make a diagnosis. Using ICD-10 criteria there was 0.36 reliability (36% agreement between raters). The Great Ormond Street system emerged as far superior, having a reliability of 0.88 (88% agreement between raters).

What's that?

- **Reliability:** the consistency with which a measure of a psychological variable like mental disorder identifies the same thing
- **Validity:** the extent to which a measure of a psychological variable measures what it sets out to measure

Box 5.2

Making sense of reliability figures

Reliability is calculated mathematically and presented as a figure, usually either a percentage or a number between 0 and 1. You will come across two common measures of reliability; both measure test–retest reliability:

1. **The PPV** (positive predictive value): this is simply the proportion of people that keep the same diagnosis over time. It is usually expressed as a percentage. If depression

has a PPV of 80, this means that 80% of people with a diagnosis of depression received a subsequent diagnosis of depression when re-assessed.

2. **Cohen's Kappa:** this is a slightly more complex statistic. It is the correlation between the results of two rounds of diagnosis in a group of patients. Like all correlation coefficients, it is a number between 0 and 1. A kappa of 1 would indicate complete agreement in two rounds of diagnosis of the same patients, that is, excellent reliability. A kappa of 0 would indicate no agreement and very poor reliability.

Validity

A way of measuring a psychological variable can be called valid if it successfully measures what it sets out to measure. A diagnostic system is *valid* if the diagnosis successfully identifies a condition. But what does 'successful' mean here? Actually, we can answer this in several ways and hence there are several ways of defining validity. It could be that our system identifies a condition that will respond a particular way to a treatment. This is known as **predictive validity**. It may be that our diagnosis agrees with a diagnosis made a different way. This is known as **criterion validity**. We can also step back and be a bit more philosophical; **construct validity** is the extent to which a category of mental disorder really exists. This might be called into question if symptoms are very similar to those of another condition or if two conditions regularly occur together. Allardyce *et al.* (2007) question the construct validity of schizophrenia for three reasons:

1. Although delusions and hallucinations are bizarre experiences, actually they occur fairly commonly amongst the general population. There is thus no clear cut-off point beyond which we can say someone is suffering schizophrenia.

2. Schizophrenia has a range of symptoms that occur in different combinations, thus individual patients with the diagnosis may appear very different from one another. Meanwhile, there is overlap between the symptoms of schizophrenia and those of other serious mental disorders. This means that one patient with a diagnosis of schizophrenia may appear more similar to someone with a different diagnosis (or none) than to another person with the same diagnosis.

3. It is unclear whether patients suffering predominantly from negative symptoms have the same condition as those suffering mostly positive symptoms.

The criterion validity of the diagnosis of some disorders is moderately good. Sanchez-Villegas *et al.* (2008) administered the standard interview from *DSM-IV-TR* to 62 participants with a current diagnosis of depression and 42 without any diagnosis: 42 of the 62 (68%) who had been previously diagnosed with depression were correctly identified as depressed; 34 of the 42 (81%) without a previous diagnosis were confirmed as not depressed. Of course, we need to be careful about interpreting these results. It may be that previously depressed patients were doing better or just having a 'good day' when Sanchez-Villegas' team failed to diagnose them. Similarly, the 19% who were identified by *DSM-IV-TR* criteria as depressed and who had not had a previous diagnosis might simply have never been picked up previously. This shows us just how difficult validity is to establish. A classic study by David Rosenhan tested the validity of the diagnosis of schizophrenia by looking at how easily psychiatrists could be fooled by means of faking a single symptom.

Classic research

Compulsory

Rosenhan, D.L. (1973)

'On being sane in insane places'

Science, 179: 250–8

Aim: To tell how well psychiatrists could distinguish real patients with schizophrenia from pseudopatients, who faked a single symptom. This provided a measure of the validity of the DSM-II system for diagnosis.

Procedure: Rosenhan himself and seven volunteers, five of whom were doctors or psychologists (a total of three women and five men), arrived at a range of hospitals (12 in total) reporting a single symptom, hearing voices saying 'empty', 'hollow' and 'thud'. Once admitted, they then acted normally, co-operating with staff and seeking to be released as soon as possible. When asked they reported no further symptoms. The pseudopatients recorded the responses of doctors and nurses when they spoke to them. In a follow-up procedure staff at another hospital were informed that one or more pseudopatients would present over the next three months. Staff at this hospital rated all new patients on a 1–10 scale for how likely each new admission was to be a pseudopatient. In fact, no pseudopatients approached them in this time; the idea was to see how many real patients were misidentified.

Results: All eight pseudopatients were admitted to hospitals. The average stay was 19 days (the range being 7–52 days). In every case they were released with a diagnosis of schizophrenia in remission. In 30% of the cases, real patients made comments to the effect that the pseudopatients had nothing wrong with them. However, in no case did doctors or nurses notice that there was nothing wrong. This is perhaps unsurprising as 71% of doctors and 88% of nurses completely ignored the pseudopatients when they tried to speak to them. In the follow-up study, 193 genuine patients presented themselves over three months. In 41 of these cases at least one member of staff was confident that they were a pseudopatient.

Conclusions: The study revealed two major weaknesses in the psychiatric system of the time. Firstly, the environment has a major impact on the process of diagnosis, and in the hospital environment staff could not tell the mentally disordered from the mentally healthy. Secondly, once labelled with a condition like schizophrenia, patients find it very difficult to escape the label and be judged as 'normal'.

Schizophrenia

Around 1% of the population suffer from schizophrenia. It is equally common in men and women, although symptoms typically begin at a younger age in men. Schizophrenia is more common in lower socio-economic groups and in urban rather than rural areas. The symptoms of schizophrenia can interfere severely with everyday tasks, to the extent that a number of people with schizophrenia end up homeless.

It is commonly believed that the long-term prospects for someone with a diagnosis of schizophrenia are very poor. Actually, whilst that was once true, tremendous advances have been made in treating schizophrenia and nowadays prospects are much better. In a recent review Hopper *et al.* (2007) concluded that more than half of patients become free of symptoms and go on to lead a normal life. There is some evidence to suggest that men often suffer more serious symptoms than women. This was investigated in a classic study by Goldstein (1988).

Clinical characteristics

Unlike the other disorders in this chapter, depression and phobia, schizophrenia does not have a single defining characteristic. It is instead a cluster of symptoms, some of which appear at first glance to be unrelated to others. If you have no personal or professional experience of mental disorder and you call to mind your perception of what 'madness' looks like it is probably something close to schizophrenia. Box 5.3 shows the symptoms required for diagnosis according to *DSM-IV*.

Figure 5.4 People with schizophrenia sometimes struggle with day to day living to the extent of becoming homeless.

Positive and negative symptoms

Some psychiatrists and psychologists make a distinction between positive and negative symptoms of schizophrenia. Positive symptoms are unusual experiences such as hallucinations and delusions. Hallucinations are distortions to perception. These are most often auditory in nature, for example, patients often report hearing voices. Delusions (or paranoia) are irrational beliefs, for example that the patient is someone else or is being controlled by someone else. These are called 'positive' symptoms because they are in addition to our everyday experience. Negative symptoms, on the other hand, involve the loss of normal functioning, for example, reduced emotional responsiveness and reduced richness of speech.

Classic research
Optional

Goldstein, J.M. (1988)

'Gender differences in the course of schizophrenia'

American Journal of Psychiatry, 145: 684–9

Aim: To compare the course of schizophrenia in men and women for the first ten years of the condition, in particular with regard to hospitalisation.

Procedure: 90 patients took part in the study, 32 women and 58 men. Most were receiving treatment at a private psychiatric hospital in New York. All were hospitalised with a diagnosis of schizophrenia for the first or second time at the start of the study. The diagnosis was confirmed by two independent psychiatrists. The mean age of participants was 24 years. The majority were white and middle class. The course of schizophrenia was measured by number of hospitalisations and length of hospitalisations over a ten-year period. Patients were also assessed retrospectively for their functioning during childhood and adolescence.

Results: Men were hospitalised an average of 2.24 times over ten years as opposed to 1.12 times for women. The mean number of days spent in hospital was 417.83 for men and 205.81 for women. Both these differences were significant at the $p < 0.05$ level. Differences were sharper in the first five years of the disorder. There was a strong association between level of functioning in childhood and adolescence and the course of the condition. This was typically worse for males than females and statistically this accounted for 50% of the difference in the course of schizophrenia for men and women.

Conclusion: Men with schizophrenia are typically admitted more times to hospital and spend more time there than women. This appears to be related to worse functioning before the onset of schizophrenia in men.

Diagnostic criteria for schizophrenia

A two characteristic symptoms for at least one month

Characteristic symptoms must include:

1. delusions

2. hallucinations

3. disorganised speech

4. grossly disorganised or catatonic behaviour

5. negative symptoms (for example, affective flattening)

or one characteristic symptom if delusions are bizarre or hallucinations consist of a voice keeping up a running commentary on the person's behaviour or thoughts, or two or more voices conversing with each other

B social/occupational functioning below levels prior to onset

C continuous signs of the disturbance for at least six months

D no major changes in mood (depression or elation)

E no evidence of organic factors (for example, drugs) or medical conditions

F if there is history of a developmental disorder (for example, Autism), prominent delusions or hallucinations must be present for a month.

Interactive angles

1. Explain how both positive and negative symptoms of schizophrenia might make it so hard to go about everyday tasks such as shopping and working.

2. It is very difficult for anyone not suffering from schizophrenia to appreciate the experience. However, there is a video here that attempts to recreate the perceptual distortions of schizophrenia: http://www.schizophrenia.com/sznews/archives/005976.html. Consider how difficult everyday living would be with this sort of visual and auditory experience.

3. You can read highly critical perspectives on the diagnosis of schizophrenia here: http://www.asylumonline.net/. At first reading how impressed are you with this critical approach?

Explanations for schizophrenia

There are believed to be a number of factors underlying schizophrenia, including both the biological and psychological. With the rapid developments in our understanding of genetics and brain functioning over the last decade, the emphasis in recent research has been on biological factors. However, although it seems certain that schizophrenia has some biological basis, there is also evidence suggesting that psychological factors can also be important.

Biological explanations
Genetic vulnerability

It has long been observed that schizophrenia tends to run in families. However, this is only circumstantial evidence for a genetic link because families share an environment as well as genes. There is, however, strong evidence for a genetic element to schizophrenia from family studies. Family studies look at the degree of genetic similarity between different relatives and the likelihood of their sharing schizophrenia. For example we share 100% of our genes with an identical twin, 50% with a parent etc. Gottesman (1991) combined results of 40 European studies to examine whether genetic similarity to a patient with schizophrenia was associated with risk of developing it. The greater the genetic similarity of relatives, the more likely they were to both have a diagnosis of schizophrenia. For an identical twin of a patient suffering schizophrenia the risk was 48%, whilst for a non-identical twin this was 17%. For a child of one parent with a diagnosis the risk was 6%; if both parents had a diagnosis this rose to 46%. Percentage risks are shown in Figure 5.6. This suggests that schizophrenia is partly genetic in origin. However, the risks were nowhere near as high as we would expect if the condition were entirely genetic.

Figure 5.5 If this man has schizophrenia there is around a 5% probability that his grandson will go on to develop it.

Interestingly, genetic factors may still be important in schizophrenia when there is no family history of the condition. This may occur because of mutation. Mutations are changes to genes, resulting from copying errors during cell division or exposure to radiation, poison or viruses. Xu et al. (2008) examined the genetic make-up of 1,077 people including 152 with schizophrenia and their parents; 10% of the patients but only 2% of a control group had a mutation that distinguished their DNA from that of their parents. This suggests that around 10% of cases of schizophrenia with no family history can be explained by mutation. The

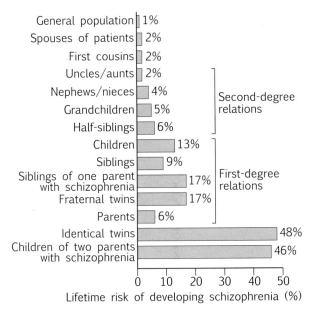

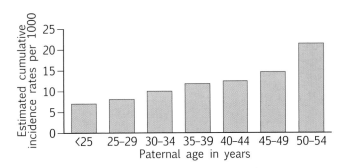

Figure 5.7 Paternal age and the risk of developing schizophrenia. (Adapted from Brown *et al*, 2002.)

Figure 5.6 Risks of developing schizophrenia. (From Gottesman, 1991.)

risk of mutation increases with parental age. Brown *et al*. (2002) showed that the risk of a child going on to develop schizophrenia increases with the age of their father when they were conceived. Results are shown in Figure 5.7.

There is thus strong support from family and mutation studies for the idea that genes are involved in the development of schizophrenia. However, there are only fairly small statistical relationships between variations in particular genes and the development of schizophrenia. This suggests that either several genes are involved, or that genes work in conjunction with particular environmental conditions to make some individuals particularly vulnerable to schizophrenia.

Another line of research suggesting that schizophrenia has a genetic basis looks at gender differences. Male and female brains develop differently as a result of genetic differences and it may be possible to link these differences to schizophrenia. We can look at one study that attempts to do this in Classic Research.

Classic research

Optional

Lewine, R.R.J., Gulley, L.R., Risch, C., Jewart, R. & Houpt, J.L. (1990)

'Sexual dimorphism, brain morphology and schizophrenia'

Schizophrenia Bulletin, 16: 195–203

Aim: To compare male and female brains with and without schizophrenia to see whether schizophrenia may be explained by sex differences in the brain.

Procedure: 27 male and four female patients with a diagnosis of schizophrenia were recruited through requests to professionals working with them arranged by a social worker. A control group of 16 males and 12 females were recruited through newspaper adverts and personal requests to acquaintances. Most of the patient group were taking antipsychotic drugs; none of the control group were taking any medication with psychological effects. MRI scans were conducted on all 59 participants, looking in particular at the corpus callosum, the area of the brain that connects the left and right hemispheres. Each scan was classified as positive if it showed any abnormality and negative if it did not.

Results: Nine of the 27 male participants in the schizophrenia group (33%) had significant abnormalities to their brain structure as indicated by the MRI. In particular, they had a small or distinctively (bulbous) shaped corpus callosum (56% of males, 33% of females). None of the females in this group had such brain abnormalities. In the control group, men were more likely than women to have the bulbous corpus callosum but less likely than females (12% vs 45%) to have a small corpus callosum. Males with schizophrenia were the most likely group to have an abnormal corpus callosum.

Conclusion: Size and shape of the corpus callosum were associated with both schizophrenia and sex differences in the normal brain. The fact that males with schizophrenia had the most unusual corpus callosum suggests that schizophrenia may be related to the male brain.

Biochemical factors

Several chemical processes appear to work somewhat differently in the brains of people with schizophrenia. In particular, it has been believed for some decades that a neurotransmitter called dopamine (or DA) may be involved. Specifically, dopamine is present in higher levels in the brain and this leads to the symptoms of schizophrenia. Evidence for this *dopamine hypothesis* comes mainly from studies of drugs, in particular amphetamines (speed), which are dopamine agonists (that is, they prevent the breakdown of dopamine and so lead to an increase in levels). When amphetamines are given in large quantities they lead to delusions and hallucinations similar to those in schizophrenia. When they are given to patients suffering from schizophrenia their symptoms get worse (see Figure 5.8).

Figure 5.8 A dopamine molecule. High levels of dopamine may be linked to the symptoms of schizophrenia.

Evidence for the dopamine hypothesis is mixed. There is certainly evidence to suggest that dopamine levels are higher in the brains of people with schizophrenia. In one study Lindstroem et al. (1999) radioactively labelled a chemical called L-DOPA, which is used by the brain to produce dopamine. They administered the L-DOPA to ten untreated patients with schizophrenia and a control group of ten people with no

diagnosis. Using a brain scanning technique called PET scanning, they were able to trace what happened to the L-DOPA. The L-DOPA was taken up more quickly in the patients with schizophrenia, suggesting that they were producing more dopamine than the control group.

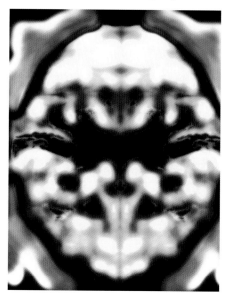

Figure 5.9 PET scans like this show that chemicals needed to produce dopamine are used more quickly by the brains of people with schizophrenia.

There are problems, however, with the dopamine hypothesis, at least in its original form. Raised dopamine levels only explain the positive symptoms of schizophrenia. Negative symptoms are not neatly explained – in fact, we would expect negative symptoms to be associated with low rather than high levels of dopamine. Moreover, some drugs that are known to be dopamine agonists do not induce the symptoms of schizophrenia (Depatie & Lal, 2001). Clearly then, there is more to schizophrenia than simply raised dopamine levels.

 how science works Research Methods

Animal studies and schizophrenia

It may seem slightly odd to research schizophrenia using animals, when, as far as we know, schizophrenia is unique to humans. However, our hormonal and nervous systems, which are important for many psychological characteristics, are very similar. We have the same endocrine glands that release the same hormones. We have the same basic brain structure: mammals such as rats and humans all have a hind-, mid- and fore-brain. We can reasonably assume, therefore, that the biological processes determining our development and ongoing functioning are the same. Wood et al. (1998) successfully used animals to model aspects of mental illness by manipulating brain function and behaviour. They bred rats with a genetic variation believed to be associated with schizophrenia in humans. The rats were

apathetic and socially withdrawn – these are symptoms of schizophrenia. This study supports the role of genes in schizophrenia.

This is an example of an experiment that casts light on schizophrenia, but could not be carried out on humans for practical and ethical reasons. However, there are serious limitations to this sort of animal research. There are important ways in which the nervous systems of humans and rats differ, most obviously in the size of different parts of the brain. In humans, the cortex (outer layer) is very much larger relative to our size than any other animal. So, whilst in some respects generalisation from animals to humans is highly credible, in other ways it is not.

Psychological explanations of schizophrenia
The cognitive model

A number of cognitive factors have been proposed to explain schizophrenia. Frith (1992) set out to explain the symptoms of schizophrenia in terms of difficulties in information processing. Specifically Frith was interested in difficulties in two cognitive abilities:

- **Metarepresentation** is the ability to reflect on our thoughts, behaviour and experience. It is the mental ability that allows us self-awareness of our own intentions and goals. It also allows us to interpret the actions of others. Problems in our metarepresentation would seriously disrupt our ability to recognise one's own actions and thoughts as being carried out by 'me' rather than someone else.

- **Central control** is the ability to suppress our automatic responses to stimuli while we perform actions that reflect our wishes or intentions.

Positive symptoms of schizophrenia such as delusions and hallucinations can be neatly explained by metarepresentation problems. Many patients, for example, report hearing voices. Frith suggests that the failure of metarepresentation means that the patient is unable to distinguish speech heard externally from a thought generated in their own mind. They therefore think something and cannot tell accurately whether they or someone else said it. The common delusion of thought insertion, in which the patient believes their thoughts come from someone else, can be explained in exactly the same way. Another common delusion, that of being persecuted, could also be neatly explained by metarepresentation failure because we require metarepresentation to make judgements about other people's intentions.

Figure 5.10 It is hard to trust without a fully functioning metarepresentation system.

What's that?

- **Willed behaviour:** behaviour initiated in order to satisfy an intention or motive

- **Stimulus-driven behaviour:** behaviour produced in response to a change in the environment

- **Clanging:** a pattern of speech common in schizophrenia, in which sentences are interrupted as the patient fixes on words and identifies other words associated with it

Frith (1992) also explained negative symptoms in terms of problems with central control. According to Frith all behaviour is either **willed** or **stimulus-driven**. In other words we either choose to carry out an action because we have an internally generated wish to do it, or we do it in response to an external stimulus. Whenever we want to achieve something, we suppress the brain systems responsible for stimulus-driven behaviour and activate those responsible for willed behaviour. The disorganised thinking and behaviour that characterise schizophrenia result from a failure to regulate willed and stimulus-driven behaviour. For example, speech in schizophrenia sometimes includes '**clanging**', in which the patient takes one word in a sentence and drifts from the sentence into words associated (for example, by rhyming) with that word. For example the sentence 'the boy went to school' might be clanged to 'the boy toy went to school scam scum'. According to Frith's model the rhyming word 'toy' and the alliterations 'scam' and 'scum' are driven by the stimulus words 'boy' and 'school'. They are spoken because of the failure to suppress stimulus-driven behaviour.

There is supporting evidence for Frith's model. Bental et al. (1991) carried out a study where participants either read out category words (for example, plants beginning with the letter C) or think of category items themselves. One group had a diagnosis of schizophrenia, whilst a control group had no diagnosis. A week later they were given a list of words and asked to identify which words they had read, which were new and which they had thought of themselves. The schizophrenia group did significantly worse, suggesting that they struggled to distinguish between words they had come up with themselves and those they heard. This supports Frith's idea that people with schizophrenia have metarepresentation problems; presumably participants with normal metarepresentation would be able to spot which words they had thought of themselves.

Interactive angles

You should not attempt any research with people suffering any psychological condition. You are not qualified and your teacher is probably not qualified to supervise you. However, you can investigate metarepresentation. Try Bental's procedure for yourself. How hard is it to remember after a week which words you thought of?

The psychodynamic model

The basic assumption of the psychodynamic model is that our adult characteristics, including psychopathology, are rooted in our childhood experiences. Of particular importance are the quality of our early relationships and early traumatic experiences. There are several theories within the psychodynamic model seeking to explain the development of schizophrenia. What they have in common is the belief that early experience can drastically affect the way the developing child perceives and interacts with the world.

One influential theory comes from Melanie Klein and Wilfred Bion. Klein (1946) and Bion (1967) proposed that all children go through a stage in the first few months of life characterised by feelings of persecution and omnipotence (being all-powerful). Klein and Bion called this the paranoid–schizoid position. A poor relationship with the primary carer in this critical period can prevent the child growing out of their sense of being omnipotent and persecuted. Bion (1967) described such individuals as having a 'schizophrenic core of personality'. Those with a schizophrenic core are likely as an adult to respond to stress by reverting to their early mental state characterised by feelings of paranoia and omnipotence – classic symptoms of schizophrenia.

Figure 5.11 According to Fromm-Reichmann, cold domineering mothers can cause schizophrenia.

Another influential psychodynamic explanation for schizophrenia came from Fromm-Reichmann (1948). Based on the stories her patients told her about their childhoods, she suggested the existence of a particular type of parent, the **schizophrenogenic mother**. The word 'schizophrenogenic' literally means 'generating schizophrenia'. The schizophrenogenic mother is cold and controlling and creates a family climate characterised by tension and secrecy.

Interactive angles

Mothers with schizophrenia are more likely than fathers to have children who go on to develop the condition themselves. This has sometimes been taken as support for the schizophrenogenic mother hypothesis. Suggest an alternative explanation for this statistic. Hint: if you are struggling, look back to the first paragraph on schizophrenia (page 139).

There is ample evidence to suggest links between early experience and later development of schizophrenia. This should not strike us as odd; remember (page 141) that even identical twins do not usually share schizophrenia, so we would expect some aspects of the environment to be associated with the condition. In particular, childhood neglect and abuse increase the risk of developing schizophrenia. In a major Scandinavian review, Read *et al*. (2005) looked at studies linking adult schizophrenia to physical and sexual abuse in childhood published between 1984 and 2005. They found that schizophrenia was the most likely mental disorder to be associated with child abuse. The actual percentages of adult patients who reported child abuse varied according to the population and the method of measuring abuse but averaged at 68.8% for women and 59.1% for men.

Interactive angles

Many studies linking adult psychopathology to childhood experience are retrospective, that is, they ask patients about their childhood experiences after their symptoms have started. Why is this a dodgy method for investigating schizophrenia?

There is thus evidence suggesting that early family relations may be important in explaining some cases of schizophrenia (although bear in mind the limitations of retrospectively gathered data). It may be that some of the environmental influence on schizophrenia is due to family interactions in childhood. However, almost no contemporary psychologists believe that schizophrenia is the direct result of upbringing alone. The evidence for genetic influence is simply too strong. Moreover, studies like that of Read *et al*. (2005) only support the psychodynamic principle that early experience impacts on later mental health; they do not directly support the details of particular theories like those of Bion or Fromm-Reichmann.

It is important for ethical reasons to be cautious and sensitive in how we respond to research linking schizophrenia to child abuse. On one hand it seems likely that, in conjunction with genetic vulnerability, child abuse increases the risk of developing schizophrenia. On the other hand, most patients have probably not been abused, and there is a real risk of blaming families without good reason when people develop schizophrenia. Given the stress associated with caring for a relative with a serious mental disorder, this is the last thing families of sufferers need.

Figure 5.12 Families can suffer extra stress if they feel blamed for schizophrenia.

The social model

Actually a number of social psychologists have applied social-psychological ideas to understanding schizophrenia; there isn't a single agreed social explanation for mental disorder in general, or schizophrenia in particular. Social psychology emphasises the role of the social situation on behaviour, in contrast to other approaches that explain behaviour with reference to the nature of the individual. One important aspect of the social environment associated with schizophrenia is urban living.

Schizophrenia is much more commonly diagnosed in urban than rural areas. This has been confirmed in a number of studies carried out in the Western world (Freeman, 1994). It has been suggested that urban living in some way causes schizophrenia (the social causation hypothesis). This may be due to stress resulting from high population density and turnover, high levels of unemployment, poor housing, anonymity and low socio-economic status – these factors are associated with inner cities. The stress of city-living may trigger the onset of schizophrenia in individuals who are already vulnerable as a result of their genes or early experiences. Alternatively, it may be that individuals who have schizophrenia are more likely to end up in cities (the social drift hypothesis).

There is evidence to support the idea that people who develop schizophrenia are born in cities rather than moving there. Castle *et al.* (1993) compared the birthplace of patients with a diagnosis of schizophrenia in Camberwell, South London with that of a control group who had no history of schizophrenia or related problems. A similar proportion of the two groups had been born in and around Camberwell. This supports the social causation hypothesis. However, it may be that it is not the *social* aspects of urban life that lead to the development of schizophrenia. Birth complications and flu, both of which are statistically associated with schizophrenia, are more common in cities and it may that it is these biological factors that lead to higher rates of schizophrenia.

how science works

Research Methods

Using twin studies to study schizophrenia

Twin studies

Identical or monozygotic twins (MZs) share 100% of their genes. Fraternal twins or dizygotic twins (DZs) only share 50% of their genetic material. These facts give us the basis for two types of twin study. One design of twin study involves comparing the similarity of MZs and of DZs who have been reared together, so have experienced a similar environment. If genes control the characteristic being studied then MZs, who share all their genes, should be more similar than DZs. Gottesman (1991) conducted a study of this type (see page 141). He found that for an identical twin of a patient suffering schizophrenia the risk was 48%, whilst for a non-identical twin this was 17%.

If genetic factors are important in determining a characteristic, then the score for one twin will be close to that of the other. So, if one twin has a low score, the other one will have a low score too – similarly with high scores. This would give us a positive correlation. This pattern is represented by a single value, between 0 and 1, called the correlation coefficient. The closer it is to 1, the more similar the twins would be. This expresses the probability that both twins will share a characteristic and is referred to as the concordance rate.

Another way to investigate the effects of genes is to compare the similarity of identical twins who have grown up in the same family or in different environments. If those who have grown up together are more alike than those who grew up apart, this would support role of the environment. Conversely, if the twins are alike despite being reared apart, this supports the importance of genes.

Biological treatments for schizophrenia

By convention the first line of treatment for schizophrenia is biological. Antipsychotic drugs are the usual treatment, although other biological treatments like ECT and psychological treatments like CBT may also be used.

Antipsychotics

The standard treatment for schizophrenia involves the use of antipsychotic drugs. Antipsychotics can be divided into traditional and newer, or first and second generation, drugs. The first antipsychotics were the phenothiazines, including chlorpromazine. These work by blocking the receptors in synapses that absorb dopamine. Effectively they reduce the action of dopamine. Second-generation antipsychotics such as clozapine have fewer side effects. Each drug in this class is quite distinct in its chemistry and in some cases we have no idea how they act on the brain to reduce psychotic symptoms (see Figure 5.13).

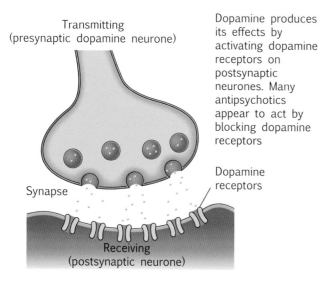

Transmitting (presynaptic dopamine neurone)

Dopamine produces its effects by activating dopamine receptors on postsynaptic neurones. Many antipsychotics appear to act by blocking dopamine receptors

Synapse

Dopamine receptors

Receiving (postsynaptic neurone)

Figure 5.13 The mechanism of traditional antipsychotics. We do not know how some newer antipsychotics work.

Antipsychotics can be taken in tablet or syrup form. For patients at high risk of failing to take their drugs regularly, injections are available. Some people can take a course of antipsychotics and stop without their symptoms returning. Others require antipsychotics for life in order to avoid suffering the symptoms of schizophrenia.

Evaluation of antipsychotics

There is strong evidence to suggest that antipsychotic drugs are effective at reducing the symptoms of schizophrenia. There are, however, controversies over their use. Many patients suffer relapses, either through failing to take their medication or in spite of doing so. There are also potentially serious side effects. Key aims of the second generation antipsychotics were to reduce side effects and prevent relapse. A number of studies have compared these in

What's that?

- **Neuroleptic malignant syndrome:** a rare complication of antipsychotic drugs. Serious neurological problem. Can be fatal or lead to permanent brain damage
- **Tardive dyskinesia:** neurological damage from antipsychotic drugs, leading to uncontrollable limb and facial movement

first and second generation antipsychotics. For example, Schooler *et al.* (2005) randomly allocated 555 patients in their first episode of schizophrenia to either treatment with haloperidol, a first generation antipsychotic, or risperidone, a second generation drug. In both groups, 75% of patients had a reduction in symptoms. However, there were fewer side-effects in the risperidone group and 42% of patients had relapses as opposed to 55% in the haloperidol group.

Antipsychotics are thus reasonably effective. However, there has been concern over their appropriateness due to their side effects. Common side effects include constipation and weight gain. In a minority of cases there can be more serious damage to the nervous system. In 0.05% of patients antipsychotics can lead to **neuroleptic malignant syndrome**. This is a serious neurological condition, the symptoms of which include nausea, high blood pressure, confusion, coma and death. Up to 10% of cases lead to serious long-term neurological problems (Adityanji & Kaizad, 2005).

Figure 5.14 Involuntary facial movements are a disabling feature of tardive dyskinesia.

Neuroleptic malignant syndrome is extreme and unusual; however, more common is **tardive dyskinesia**, repetitive involuntary movements of the face and limbs. These risks are lower where second generation antipsychotics are used, and the **National Institute for Clinical Excellence** (NICE, 2002) recommends second generation antipsychotics as the most appropriate treatment for schizophrenia.

Interactive angles

Figure 5.14 gives an idea of the facial distortions that characterise tardive dyskinesia. You can see this rather more vividly on video. www.youtube.com contains several films of tardive dyskinesia. Consider how these symptoms might interfere with everyday social interaction.

Psychological treatments for schizophrenia

Cognitive behavioural therapy

We introduced cognitive behavioural therapies or CBT in AS level. In this section we are specifically concerned with the use of CBT to treat schizophrenia. CBT is now the most commonly used form of psychological therapy, in particular amongst clinical psychologists. It usually takes place once a week or fortnight for between five and 20 sessions. CBT involves helping patients identify irrational and unhelpful thoughts and trying to change them. This may involve drawing diagrams for patients to show them the links between their thinking, behaviour and emotions.

CBT cannot completely eliminate the symptoms of schizophrenia, but it can make patients much better able to cope with them. According to Turkington *et al.* (2004) the purpose of CBT for schizophrenia is to help patients make sense of how their environment, including delusions and hallucinations, impacts on their feelings and behaviour. Understanding where symptoms originate can be crucial for some patients. If, for example, a patient hears voices and believes they are demons they will naturally be very afraid. Offering a range of psychological explanations for the existence of hallucinations and delusions can help reduce this anxiety. An example of this sort of dialogue can be seen in Box 5.4.

Box 5.4

An extract from a session of CBT with a patient with schizophrenia. From Turkington *et al.* (2004)

Paranoid patient: The Mafia are observing me to decide how to kill me.

Therapist: You are obviously very frightened ... there must be a good reason for this.

Paranoid patient: Do you think it's the Mafia?

Therapist: It's a possibility, but there could be other explanations. How do you know that it's the Mafia?

Paranoid patient: Who else would persecute someone like this?

Therapist: Well, for us to find out together, we need to examine the evidence, although it might feel frightening to do this. I will help you to look into this a bit more.

Figure 5.15 CBT for schizophrenia involves helping the patient identify rational explanations for their delusions and hallucinations.

CBT can also help normalise the experience of schizophrenia. Patients may, for example, benefit from hearing about how common hallucinations and delusions are amongst people without a diagnosis. CBT may also focus on the patient's beliefs about schizophrenia itself. Therapists may share the results of recent studies showing good long-term prospects for sufferers.

A case study of CBT for schizophrenia

Bradshaw (1998) recorded the case of Carol, a 26-year-old white American female from a conservative Christian family. She had suffered from schizophrenia for seven years. She experienced voices making negative comments and she made comments herself like 'I'm no good' and 'I'll always be this way'. For the first three months the therapist focused on gaining trust and rapport with Carol, allowing her to decide

Case studies in the study of schizophrenia

Psychiatrists, clinical psychologists and other mental health professionals frequently record case studies. An example is the case of Carol (Bradshaw, 1998). The purpose of case studies is to illustrate conditions like schizophrenia and give a detailed account of the experience of having and treating the condition. This is useful in educating people about the condition. Cases like Carol's bring schizophrenia to life much more vividly than lists of symptoms and diagnostic procedures. Cases like Carol's also illustrate one way in which schizophrenia can be treated and are therefore very valuable in the training of therapists.

Case studies are thus useful as long as we bear in mind their purpose. Where the case study method is very limited is in its status as *evidence*. A single well-recorded case study provides some evidence that a phenomenon *can* be true. The case of Carol thus suggests that CBT *can* be effective for treating schizophrenia. However, it is limited even as evidence for this modest claim because we have no way of knowing what would have become of Carol if she had *not* had CBT. Even if we take it that Carol was helped by CBT we cannot take the case as evidence that CBT is generally helpful for schizophrenia, because we have no idea how typical a patient Carol is. In other words, we cannot generalise from a single case study to the whole population.

the length of sessions, which ran from 15 minutes to an hour. For the next two months, therapy underwent a 'socialisation phase'. The emphasis here was on getting the patient used to CBT and the cognitive understanding of her symptoms. For the next year therapy focused on increasing Carol's activity levels. She was set goals and encouraged to rediscover her hobbies prior to developing schizophrenia. The therapist also taught Carol stress management techniques. The following 16 months of therapy focused on dealing with stressful situations and recognising and challenging negative cognitions like 'I'm no good'. At this point, Carol resumed socialising once a week and began volunteer work. The end-phase of therapy focused on Carol's anxiety about relapsing. At the end of therapy and one year later Carol was greatly improved on measures of symptoms and social functioning. She was able to return to education and paid work, and at four-year follow-up she had no re-admission to hospital.

Evaluation of CBT for schizophrenia

There is a reasonable body of evidence to support the effectiveness of CBT in the treatment of schizophrenia. Pilling *et al.* (2002) reviewed eight random control trials that varied in how and for how long CBT was delivered and how outcome was measured. Overall CBT came out as superior to standard care, in particular in long-term outcomes. Whereas patients in standard care tend to lose some of the benefits of treatment when it finishes, CBT patients maintain their gains over longer periods. Even studies that have not supported the initial effectiveness of CBT have supported this long-term benefit (Rathod & Turkington, 2005).

NICE (2002) suggest that CBT is an appropriate treatment for schizophrenia and should be made available to patients. CBT may be particularly appropriate for new patients. Morrison *et al.* (2004) administered six months of CBT to patients showing early signs of schizophrenia. Twelve months later, significantly

fewer had a full diagnosis than was the case in a control group. CBT may also be particularly appropriate for patients at high risk of not taking medication. Turkington *et al.* (2002) found that CBT was effective in increasing patients' insight into their psychopathology and their awareness of the importance of taking medication. There was, however, a downside; with insight into how serious a condition patients were suffering came increased depression.

Psychodynamic therapies

Psychodynamic therapies originated with the work of Freud. The original form, classical psychoanalysis, is very intensive, taking place four to five times per week and lasting for several years. Psychoanalytic psychotherapy is slightly less intensive and long term, typically one to three times per week for one to five years. Traditionally, patients in psychoanalysis lie on a couch, and patient and analyst do not face each other. Nowadays, particularly in psychotherapy as opposed to psychoanalysis, patient and therapist are more likely to face each other on comfortable chairs.

To a psychodynamic therapist the symptoms of schizophrenia, like those of other mental disorders, are rooted in early relationships. One aim of therapy for schizophrenia is to give patients insight into these links between symptoms and early life. For example Benedetti (1987) proposed that our sense of self develops in childhood through relationships with others. Failed early relationships can lead to a poor sense of self, which can explain why people with schizophrenia have poor metarepresentation and find it hard to distinguish between their own thoughts and external sights and sounds. At the same time, the therapist offers themselves as a model substitute relationship, providing a kind of substitute parenting that in turn allows the patient to undergo normal personality development and become fully aware of the distinction between themselves and others.

Techniques of psychodynamic therapy

A basic principle in psychodynamic therapy is to allow patients to *free-associate*. This means to speak without direction, saying whatever comes into their mind. The idea behind free association is that if we stop consciously trying to think about something and let our mind wander it will soon turn to what is really bothering us. Freud and later psychodynamic therapists have found that patients in therapy frequently return to childhood events and early relationships when allowed to free-associate. This fits in with psychodynamic theory, which sees a lot of adult problems as rooted in these early events. Free association is useful in a couple of ways. First, it can lead the patient to describe painful events and feelings, and get 'it off their chest' (the technical term for this is catharsis). Second, free association can lead patients to identify early events as important. The therapist can then make a link between these events and what is happening currently for the patient, for example their symptoms.

Another psychodynamic technique is dream analysis. Many, though not all, patients in psychodynamic therapy bring significant dreams to their therapist for analysis. Psychodynamic therapists are informed by a range of theories and different theories suggest interpreting dreams in different ways. Freud believed that many dreams represent wishes, which are partially satisfied by the dream. However, in a process called dreamwork the thing we are wishing for is transformed into something else, so that the dream is not too exciting and we can carry on sleeping. A therapist might thus interpret a dream as being about something we wish for, with something in the dream representing the wish. A patient might for example dream of being aggressive to an older man and woman. This might be interpreted as representing the wish to express anger towards their parents.

Evaluation of psychodynamic therapies for schizophrenia

The theoretical basis for treating schizophrenia psychodynamically is weak, with many competing theories of the origins of the condition and hence different aims for treatment. Furthermore, even Freud questioned whether psychoanalysis would ever be capable of tackling schizophrenia. However, in spite of these problems, there is actually quite good evidence for the effectiveness of psychodynamic therapies for schizophrenia. Gottdiener & Haslam (2002) carried out a meta-analysis of studies into psychodynamic therapies, CBT and assorted supportive therapies. CBT and psychodynamic therapies emerged as equally effective, with 67% of patients improving significantly as opposed to 34% of untreated controls. Controversially, this meta-analysis suggests that psychodynamic therapies are effective without accompanying antipsychotic medication.

Gottdiener (2006) argues that the evidence supporting psychodynamic treatment is strong enough to see it as generally appropriate for use with schizophrenia. This is, however, controversial, both because of the weak theoretical basis for therapies and because of the relatively small body of supporting evidence. NICE guidelines for the treatment of schizophrenia (2002) comment that it is appropriate to make use of psychodynamic principles to understand the experience of patients within their family but do not mention the use of psychodynamic therapies.

Community care: a social approach to treating schizophrenia

Traditionally patients with schizophrenia stayed in psychiatric hospitals. However, the conditions in such hospitals were often poor, and there was an emphasis on keeping patients contained,

rather than on a serious attempt to treat them with a view to their rehabilitation. In the 1970s and 1980s the emphasis in treatment changed. Older, larger institutions were shut down and a variety of community-based care programmes established. In theory, this freed up money for smaller numbers of patients to receive better quality in-patient care, but in the UK this was not effectively done until relatively recently. The majority of patients with schizophrenia, who do not need to be hospitalised most of the time, could receive care and support in the community. In Britain this care involved the following elements:

- sheltered accommodation with 24-hour care
- work and employment opportunities in sheltered social firms and co-operative businesses
- specialist mental health outreach teams to provide long-term social support and care
- in-patient hospital care when required. (Department of Health, 1997)

Figure 5.16 Traditional psychiatric hospitals were often large forbidding buildings.

Living in the community is demanding and, although most patients prefer it, their symptoms can make it hard to cope with day-to-day stresses. Patients living in the community can still be treated in a hospital setting if their schizophrenia worsens. There are places available in psychiatric wards on a short-term basis, where patients can stay until their condition improves. Sheltered accommodation is then available for those who are not well enough to live by themselves, or with their family, when released from hospital.

Evaluation of community care

Outcome research has shown that community care has the potential to enhance quality of life and perhaps reduce symptoms for patients with schizophrenia. Trauer *et al.* (2001) assessed the effectiveness of American sheltered accommodation; 125 patients moved from a psychiatric hospital to community units, sheltered accommodation for up to 20 patients. Patients were assessed a month before and a month after leaving hospital and one year later for symptoms, personal functioning, quality of life and for where they wanted to live. After one year there was little change in the severity of symptoms; however, the quality of life for patients was significantly better. Patients much preferred this sort of supported community living. Another study by Leff (1997) showed that patients suffering from schizophrenia who were housed in long-term sheltered accommodation showed much lower levels of symptom severity (especially negative symptoms) than hospitalised patients.

There is little doubt that for many patients community care is ideal. The major problem is that community care tends to be underfunded. It seems that it is often too tempting for the authorities to hang on to the money that is saved by closing psychiatric hospitals rather than spend it on proper community care. In Britain, Margaret Thatcher's government saved £2,000 million by closing psychiatric hospitals between 1985 and 1991 alone; however, none of this money was reinvested in community care (Shepherd, 1998).

Unipolar depression

Depression is a relatively common mental disorder. Estimates vary but up to 10% of us are likely to be depressed at any one time and perhaps 20% of us will suffer depression during our lifetime. Women are at least twice as likely to suffer it than men, and lower socio-economic groups are more vulnerable than higher groups. Many of the most severe cases begin in adolescence. The defining symptom of depression is disruption to our mood. Technically this type of disorder is classified in *DSM-IV-TR* as a mood disorder. The *DSM* system recognises a number of different mood disorders, each of which has a distinct set of clinical characteristics.

Depression researchers often follow up people before they develop depression in order to get a clear idea of what factors make people vulnerable. Because women are more likely than men and lower socio-economic groups are more vulnerable than higher, this sort of study has tended to focus on working class women. A classic example is a study by Brown *et al.* (1986), who looked at the role of self-esteem and social support in vulnerability to depression.

Classic research

Optional

Brown, G.W., Andrews, B., Harris, T., Adler, Z. & Bridge, L. (1986)

'Social support, self-esteem and depression'

Psychological Medicine, 16: 813–31

Aim: To test whether self-esteem and social support affected the likelihood of suffering depression in the year following a stressful life event.

Procedure: The design was prospective. Participants were 400 women, mostly working class, all with children living at home and a husband or partner who worked in a manual occupation. All were from Islington, North London. They were recruited through their GPs and interviewed. The initial interview assessed mental health, self-esteem and social support using a range of standard interview schedules. A year later 353 of the participants consented to be re-interviewed. These second interviews re-assessed the same variables and in addition looked for major stressful life events that had taken place in the previous year. This was done using a standard interview called the Life Events and Difficulties Schedule (LEDS). Social support was re-assessed with particular regard to the support received during stressful life events in the previous year (this is called crisis support). Fifty participants who had shown signs of depression in the first interview were not included in the analysis, as the researchers were interested in new cases of depression.

Results: 91% of the participants (29 of 32) who experienced depression during the year between the two interviews had experienced a severely stressful life event, as compared to 23% of women who did not suffer depression. This difference was significant at the $p < 0.01$ level. Low self-esteem did not make the women more vulnerable to depression unless there was a stressful life event, but it did make depression more likely where such a life event took place. General level of social support assessed at the first interview was not associated with depression; however, in those who suffered a stressful life event, women who received good crisis support from husband or partner were less likely to suffer depression.

Conclusion: Both low self-esteem and lack of social support make it more likely that stressful life events will lead to depression. However, there was no evidence from this study that either factor led to depression in the absence of stressful life events.

Clinical characteristics of depression

Because we all vary in our moods and feel 'down' sometimes, it is important to have a clear cut-off point where ordinary variation in mood ends and clinical depression begins. This is achieved by requiring that a certain number of symptoms are present for a certain length of time. All the major systems of classification and diagnosis distinguish between two types of unipolar depression: major depressive disorder and dysthymia.

Major depressive disorder

The distinguishing feature of major depression is that it is cyclical; in other words symptoms come and go. When present, symptoms can be very severe and typically last from four to six months, although in exceptional cases over a year. Over the course of a case, the average patient with major depressive disorder is depressed 27.5% of the time (Thornicroft & Sartorius, 1993). The criteria for diagnosis of a major depressive episode according to the *DSM-IV-TR* are shown in Box 5.5.

Figure 5.17 Some of the most severe cases of depression begin in the teens.

Box 5.5

Diagnostic criteria for a major depressive episode

A Five (or more) of the following symptoms have been present during the same two-week period and represent a change from previous functioning; at least one of the symptoms is either
1. depressed mood or
2. loss of interest or pleasure.
Note: do not include symptoms that are clearly due to a general medical condition, or mood-incongruent delusions or hallucinations.
1. Depressed mood most of the day, nearly every day, as indicated by either subjective report (eg, feels sad or empty) or observation made by others (eg, appears tearful). Note: in children and adolescents, can be irritable mood.
2. Markedly diminished interest or pleasure in all, or almost all, activities most of the day, nearly every day (as indicated by either subjective account or observation made by others).
3. Significant weight loss when not dieting or weight gain (eg, a change of more than 5% of body weight in a month), or decrease or increase in appetite nearly every day. Note: in children, consider failure to make expected weight gains.
4. Insomnia or hypersomnia nearly every day.
5. Psychomotor agitation or retardation nearly every day (observable by others, not merely subjective feelings of restlessness or being slowed down).
6. Fatigue or loss of energy nearly every day.
7. Feelings of worthlessness or excessive or inappropriate guilt (which may be delusional) nearly every day (not merely self-reproach or guilt about being sick).
8. Diminished ability to think or concentrate, or indecisiveness, nearly every day (either by subjective account or as observed by others).
9. Recurrent thoughts of death (not just fear of dying), recurrent suicidal ideation without a specific plan, or a suicide attempt or a specific plan for committing suicide.
B The symptoms do not meet criteria for a Mixed Episode.
C The symptoms cause clinically significant distress or impairment in social, occupational, or other important areas of functioning.
D The symptoms are not due to the direct physiological effects of a substance (eg, a drug of abuse, a medication) or a general medical condition (eg, hypothyroidism).
E The symptoms are not better accounted for by bereavement, ie, after the loss of a loved one, the symptoms persist for longer than two months or are characterised by marked functional impairment, morbid preoccupation with worthlessness, suicidal ideation, psychotic symptoms, or psychomotor retardation.

Dysthymia

Whilst major depression involves severe symptoms but also breaks, dysthymia is characterised by constant although usually less severe symptoms. Depression must last for longer than two years for a formal diagnosis, although treatment can begin earlier. Diagnostic criteria for dysthymia according to the *DSM-IV-TR* are shown in Box 5.6.

Box 5.6

Diagnostic criteria for dysthymic disorder

A Depressed mood for most of the day, for more days than not, as indicated either by subjective account or observation by others, for at least two years. Note: in children and adolescents, mood can be irritable and duration must be at least one year.

B Presence, while depressed, of two (or more) of the following:
  1. poor appetite or overeating
  2. insomnia or hypersomnia
  3. low energy or fatigue
  4. low self-esteem
  5. poor concentration or difficulty making decisions
  6. feelings of hopelessness.

C During the two-year period (one year for children or adolescents) of the disturbance, the person has never been without the symptoms in criteria A and B for more than two months at a time.

D No Major Depressive Episode has been present during the first two years of the disturbance (one year for children and adolescents), ie, the disturbance is not better accounted for by chronic Major Depressive Disorder, or Major Depressive Disorder in Partial Remission.
  Note: there may have been a previous Major Depressive Episode provided there was a full remission (no significant signs or symptoms for two months) before development of the Dysthymic Disorder. In addition, after the initial two years (one year in children or adolescents) of Dysthymic Disorder, there may be superimposed episodes of Major Depressive Disorder, in which case both diagnoses may be given when the criteria are met for a Major Depressive Episode.

E There has never been a Manic Episode, a Mixed Episode, or a Hypomanic Episode, and criteria have never been met for Cyclothymic Disorder.

F The disturbance does not occur exclusively during the course of a chronic Psychotic Disorder, such as Schizophrenia or Delusional Disorder.

G The symptoms are not due to the direct physiological effects of a substance (eg, a drug of abuse, a medication) or a general medical condition (eg, hypothyroidism).

H The symptoms cause clinically significant distress or impairment in social, occupational, or other important areas of functioning.

Interactive angles

You can look at the standard interview questions for diagnosing depression according to *DSM-IV-TR* here: http://cpmcnet.columbia.edu/dept/scid/revisions/pdf/module_a.pdf. You'll get an idea of how complex it would be to carry out such an interview.

Biological explanations for depression

Historically depression has been something of a battlefield between those who see it as a biological condition and those who see it as psychological. In fact, there is strong evidence for the role of both biological and psychological factors.

Interactive angles

Hammen (1997) has suggested four reasons why we might think depression is biological in origin:

- some symptoms are biological, for example, disruption to sleep and appetite

- depression is more common in some families than others

- antidepressant drugs reduce symptoms of depression

- some medical conditions lead to depression.

How strong are these arguments? Suggest a counter-argument to each.

Genetic vulnerability to depression

Children of depressed parents are much more likely than their peers to suffer depression themselves. However, this is just circumstantial evidence for a genetic link. Recall from your AS level the difference between genotype and phenotype. Our genotype is our genetic make-up, whilst our phenotype is our characteristics, which are a product of both our genes and environment. Families provide much of our environment as well as our genotype, and it may be this family environment that leads depression to run in families.

Figure 5.18 If one of these identical twins develops depression there is a high probability that the other will also do so.

That said, there is stronger evidence from twin studies to show that there is some genetic element to depression. In one study McGuffin *et al.* (1996) studied 214 pairs of twins, of whom one or both was being treated for major depressive disorder. Of the identical twins, 46% shared major depressive disorder; 20% of fraternal twins shared major depression. This greater sharing of depression in identical as opposed to fraternal twins suggests some genetic influence on major depression.

In recent years the emphasis in genetics research has shifted somewhat. Rather than just looking at whether there appears to be a genetic influence on variables like depression, modern research looks in particular at the influence of particular genes and how those genes may interact with the environment, together influencing symptoms. Researchers have been particularly interested in the serotonin transporter gene, which is responsible for producing serotonin in the brain. This gene comes in three forms, varying in the length of its two strands: long-long, long-short and short-short. It is believed that the short form leads to inefficient serotonin production. Wilhelm *et al.* (2006) recruited 165 participants from an Australian teacher-training programme and followed them up for 25 years. Every five years the teachers were interviewed about positive and negative life events (such as bereavement, unemployment and marital break up) and assessed for major depression using several standard interviews. By the end of the study, 149 participants were still alive, well and contactable. Of these, 127 consented to have genetic material taken by blood test or mouth swab. The associations between major depression, life events and serotonin transporter gene type were calculated; 53 of the 127 participants who completed the research (42%) were diagnosed with major depression at some point during the 25 years. Negative life events were strongly associated with major depression, with 68% of those suffering depression reporting at least one major negative event prior to becoming depressed. Variations in the serotonin transporter gene alone were *not* associated with depression; however, where there were negative life events *and* the short-short form of the gene, participants were particularly vulnerable to depression. This suggested that variations in the serotonin transporter gene do not directly lead to major depression. Instead they appear to affect the individual's response to negative life events. People with the short-short version of the gene appear to be the most sensitive to negative life events.

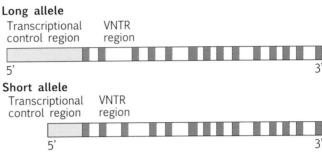

Figure 5.19 The long and short forms of the serotonin transporter gene.

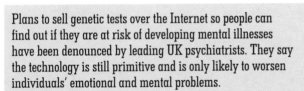

Internet gene tests provoke alarm

Robin Mckie, Science Editor

The Observer, 3 February 2008

Plans to sell genetic tests over the Internet so people can find out if they are at risk of developing mental illnesses have been denounced by leading UK psychiatrists. They say the technology is still primitive and is only likely to worsen individuals' emotional and mental problems.

The tests, which biotechnology companies will begin selling in a few months, will allow people to find out, by sending off a spittle sample, if they possess gene variants that increase their chances of suffering bipolar depression or schizophrenia. The information will help both patients and doctors, it is claimed.

But scientists argue that selling these tests on the Internet is dangerous. The technology is still in its infancy and cannot yet help make helpful diagnoses. 'These tests will only worry, confuse and mislead the public and patients,' said psychiatrist Professor Nick Craddock, of Cardiff University. 'There is a long way to go before we have genetic tests that may be helpful to patients. Using tests at the moment is only likely to cause harm.'

But the usefulness of such tests was disputed by Dr Cathryn Lewis, also of the Institute of Psychiatry. 'The general risk of developing bipolar depression is around 1 per cent. If you possess the worst set of gene variants, then your risk rises to 3 per cent. That means you are three times more likely than average to get bipolar depression. That may seem worrying but it is still a very low risk. It is still 97 per cent likely that you won't get depression. People are not likely to realise that, however.'

Another test, to be marketed by NeuroMark, first in the USA and later this year in Europe, is based on genes that predispose people to react badly to stress. If a person inherits this gene section from both parents, he or she has an increased chance of suffering from severe depression after stressful situations. 'About 20 per cent of people have this combination,' said Kim Bechthold, chief executive of the biotechnology company. 'It is useful information to know.'

1. What gene do you think the tests might identify in relation to depression?

2. Given that the risk of depression is still small even when the genetic test identifies the target gene, are tests like this a good idea?

Biochemical factors in depression

It is widely believed that a group of neurotransmitters called the **monoamines**, which include noradrenaline, dopamine and serotonin, exist in lower levels in the brains of depressed patients. This belief is based primarily on the action of antidepressant drugs, each of which increase the levels of one or more monoamines and ease the symptoms of depression. Some newer antidepressants such as Reboxetine work by increasing the action of noradrenaline. It thus appears that noradrenaline also has a role in depression.

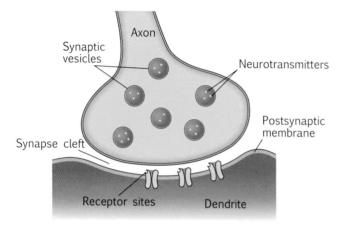

Figure 5.20 A synapse like those crossed by noradrenaline and serotonin. Depression appears to be associated with reduced levels of these neurotransmitters.

What's that?

- **Monoamines:** a group of neurotransmitters including serotonin and noradrenaline, which are believed to help regulate mood
- **Cerebrospinal fluid:** salty fluid that surrounds the brain and spinal cord

There is further evidence for a role for the monoamines in depression from metabolite studies. Typically, patients suffering depression show lower levels of a chemical called 5-H1AA (which is formed when serotonin is broken down) in **cerebrospinal fluid** as compared to non-depressed people. This suggests that depressed people have lower serotonin levels (McNeal & Cimbolic, 1986). An additional source of evidence for the role of noradrenaline comes from post-mortem studies showing either lower levels of noradrenaline in the dead brain or abnormalities in the locus coeruleus, an area of the brain that produces noradrenaline. Klimek *et al.* (1997) compared the locus coeruleus of 15 dead patients with major depression with that of 15 non-depressed people and found significant differences in structure. Studies like this suggest that depression may result from abnormality in brain structure which affects the production of neurotransmitters.

It is clear then that depression is *associated with* abnormal monoamine levels. Be a little wary, though, about assuming that there a simple relationship between brain chemistry and symptoms. Common sense suggests that brain chemistry affects symptoms rather than the reverse; however, this is not necessarily the case. It could well be that psychological factors affect both biochemistry and symptoms of depression.

Interactive angles

Before you read the next section, if depression may be the result of abnormal brain chemistry, what sort of treatment does this suggest may be effective?

Psychological explanations for depression

Recall your AS level when we looked at psychological models of abnormality, including psychodynamic, behavioural and cognitive approaches. All of these can be applied to explaining and treating depression. Particularly important are the cognitive and psychodynamic models.

The cognitive model of depression

In modern applied psychology the cognitive model is the dominant one for explaining and treating depression. The cognitive model owes a lot to the work of Aaron Beck. Beck (1976) saw depression as the result of patterns of negative thinking. He identified three types of negative thinking that are particularly common in people suffering from depression:

- negative automatic thinking
- selective attention to the negative
- negative self-schemas.

Let us explain each of these a little, starting with negative automatic thinking. The *cognitive triad* of negative automatic thoughts consists of a negative view of the self, a negative view of the world and a negative view of the future. The cognitive triad is shown in Figure 5.21.

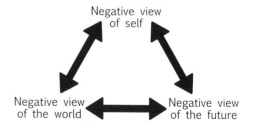

Figure 5.21 Beck's cognitive triad.

Beck's second form of negative thinking involves attending to the negative aspects of a situation and ignoring the positive aspects. This causes us to overestimate the 'downside' of any situation and reach the most negative possible conclusions. To most people half a glass of drink is half full. A depressed person will typically see it as half empty instead.

Figure 5.22 A depressed person is likely to see a half-full glass as half empty.

The third form of negative thinking identified by Beck involves *negative self-schemas*. Our self-schema contains all our information about ourselves, including beliefs, feelings and so on. We acquire this negative set of beliefs about ourselves through criticism from our parents. When we meet a new situation, we interpret it using any relevant schemas including our self-schema. If our beliefs about and feelings toward ourselves are negative, then so will be any interpretation we make about ourselves in a new situation. Say, for example, we meet someone we fancy and they are nice to us. If our self-schema contains the information that we are unattractive and unlovable, then we will not interpret the person being nice to us as meaning they fancy us. We might think instead that they feel sorry for us.

There is plenty of evidence to support a role for cognitive vulnerability in understanding depression. Studies have, for example, shown that depressed people selectively attend to negative stimuli. Koster *et al.* (2005) examined the role of attention to negative stimuli in depression; 15 depressed and 15 matched non-depressed students were identified and given a selective attention task. They were presented with positive (for example, successful, powerful), negative (for example, loser, failure) or neutral words (for example, crane, paper) for 1.5 seconds each

on a computer screen. Half a second after each word they saw a square on either the left or right of the screen. Their task was to press q if the square was on the left and 5 if it was on the right. How long they took to identify the location of the square was a measure of their attention to the words. The longer they took to locate the square, the harder they found it to disengage their attention from the word. The depressed participants took an average of 12 milliseconds to disengage from words like 'loser', whereas the non-depressed group took only two ms. This shows that depressed people do attend to negative stimuli as Beck suggested.

Interactive angles

Although the results of the Koster *et al.* study are impressive support for Beck's theory of depression, the study was carried out in artificial conditions and used a procedure quite far removed from people's everyday experiences. Design a study to test whether depressed people selectively attend to negative aspects of a situation in real life surroundings.

Figure 5.23 Depressed people find it hard to look away from words like 'loser' on a computer screen.

Mezulis *et al.* (2006) examined the origins of cognitive vulnerability. Recall that Beck believed that negative thinking was acquired from parental criticism. They followed up 289 American children from infancy to 11 years. Cognitive style, life events and parenting style were measured by standard questionnaires. In addition, 120 of the children were filmed receiving feedback on a task from parents. As we would expect if Beck were correct about the origins of depression, negative cognitive style was strongly associated with maternal anger during the feedback task in conjunction with negative life events in childhood. Interestingly, paternal behaviour was not associated with negative cognitive style.

The psychodynamic model of depression

Freud (1917) believed that many cases of depression were due to 'constitutional' factors. He was writing before we had a modern understanding of genetics, but essentially he meant that some people are genetically very vulnerable to depression. However, Freud suggested that at least some cases of depression could be linked to childhood experiences of loss or rejection in the family. He saw adult depression as a type of delayed mourning for this childhood loss. Freud emphasised the role of anger in both adult mourning and depression. The child's anger at being separated from or rejected by their loved-one is not easily expressed at the time, so it is repressed. Freud's theory covers the physical symptoms of depression as well the psychological. Lack of energy is caused by the amount of energy needed to keep anger repressed. Appetite suffers because eating is associated with nurture from the lost childhood figure. Their loss affects the ability to accept nurture and so to enjoy food.

Figure 5.24 Children who lose parents may be more vulnerable to depression.

Although Freud was writing before much of our current understanding of depression was developed, there are important strengths to his approach in that it links depression to both loss and anger (Champion, 2000). Modern cognitive theories of cognitive vulnerability can equally well explain the link with loss experiences, but perhaps not that with anger. Although it is methodologically difficult to directly test Freud's explanation for depression, there is support for the idea of a strong link between depression and unexpressed anger. For example, when Swaffer & Hollin (2001) gave 100 young offenders questionnaires to assess anger and health, it emerged that those who suppressed their anger had a significantly greater risk of developing depression.

It is interesting to look at some aspects of modern studies of cognitive vulnerability in the light of psychodynamic theory. Note for example the Mezulis *et al.* study (page 155). Maternal but not paternal parenting was associated with later risk of depression. This is more neatly understood from a psychodynamic perspective, because the mother is usually the primary carer and has a more emotionally intense relationship with the child. We would thus expect rejecting behaviour by the mother to have more emotional impact than that by the father.

Biological treatments for depression

Depression can be treated biologically using drugs and/or electroconvulsive therapy. We have already considered these at AS level, so many of the following details should look familiar.

Antidepressant drugs

Traditionally, most people approaching their GP with symptoms of depression have been prescribed antidepressant drugs. There are a number of different antidepressant drugs and these work in slightly different ways. Generally though, antidepressants work by raising the levels of monoamine neurotransmitters in the brain. Monoamine oxidase inhibitors (MAOIs) prevent the breakdown of serotonin, noradrenaline and dopamine, so that levels of all three monoamines build up. Tricyclics prevent serotonin and noradrenaline being reabsorbed after it has crossed a synapse, again increasing their levels. Although these now old-fashioned antidepressants are effective in reducing symptoms, because they interfere with a number of neurotransmitters they can have serious side effects. Tricyclics, for example, can cause drowsiness, dry mouth and constipation.

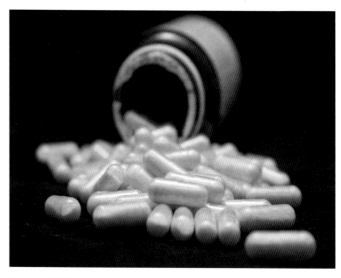

Figure 5.25 Antidepressant drugs are reasonably effective but many psychologists feel they are overused.

Newer antidepressants tend to work on one monoamine only. Selective serotonin reuptake inhibitors (SSRIs) such as Prozac and Seroxat stop serotonin being reabsorbed and broken down after it has crossed a synapse and noradrenaline reuptake inhibitors (NRIs) do the same with noradrenaline. It is important to have a number of antidepressants available because individuals patients vary quite a lot in how they respond to each drug, both in terms of effects on their symptoms and side effects. Different people also show variations in their symptoms and this can influence the choice of drug. NRIs, for example, may be particularly useful for motivating patients whose depression has left them very inactive.

Evaluation of antidepressants

The standard procedure for testing the effectiveness of drugs is the random control trial with a placebo condition. A random control trial is an experimental procedure in which participants are randomly divided into two groups (or more than two if more than one treatment is being tested). One group is given the treatment and the other a placebo. In the case of drugs, this is an inactive chemical. Arroll et al. (2005) reviewed random control trials with placebo conditions that investigated the effectiveness of antidepressants prescribed by GPs. Ten studies were found that compared tricyclics with placebos, three comparing SSRIs with placebos and two comparing both with placebos. Overall, 56–60% of patients treated with antidepressants improved as opposed to 42–47% of people given the placebo. SSRIs took longer to work but had fewer side effects. This study suggests that both tricyclics and SSRIs are moderately effective when prescribed by GPs.

There is some debate about when antidepressants are an appropriate treatment. The problem is that there are alternative treatments that may be more effective. Pinquart et al. (2006) reviewed studies of antidepressants and psychological therapies used to treat depression. They concluded that psychological therapies were overall more effective. Drugs are, however, cheaper and can be provided immediately, whereas there is usually a waiting list for psychological therapies. In an ideal world, these would not be considerations and drugs would be used less often and psychological therapies more often. Many psychologists feel strongly that in spite of the cost more psychological therapy should be made available to patients, and that we should

rely less on cheap and easy drug treatment. Antidepressants are perhaps most appropriate when patients just want their symptoms relieved as quickly as possible and have no interest in psychological treatments.

Clinicians also need to consider the appropriateness of different types of antidepressant in different circumstances. Gender is an issue here; women suffer more side effects than men from tricyclic antidepressants, so the latter are perhaps more appropriate for men. Women generally tolerate MAOIs well; however, these are highly toxic drugs so they are perhaps not appropriate when the patient is considered to be at high risk of suicide (National Institute for Clinical Excellence, 2004).

Electroconvulsive therapy (ECT)

ECT is an alternative medical procedure for treating depression. The procedure involves administering an electric shock for a fraction of a second to the head, inducing a seizure similar to that experienced in epilepsy. This seizure generally lasts between 15 and 60 seconds. In most cases the shock is bilateral, that is, given to both sides of the head. This is generally considered to be more effective than unilateral ECT (given to one side of the head), although also more likely to lead to side effects. In a typical course of treatment, ECT is repeated between six and 12 times, usually two to three times per week.

ECT has a dodgy reputation, largely a result of its early use when the shock was relatively large and given without anaesthetic or muscle relaxants. The resulting fits sometimes resulted in broken bones and occasionally burns to the brain. Modern ECT involves small shocks given for short periods (typically 800 milliamps for 1 second), given under anaesthetic and using drugs like succinylcholine to paralyse muscles and so prevent broken bones.

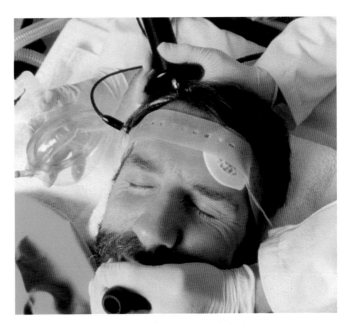

Figure 5.26 ECT.

Evaluation of ECT

Eranti *et al.* (2007) evaluated the effectiveness of ECT; 46 patients with major depression were randomly allocated to either ECT or a control condition in which they were exposed to powerful magnetic fields, which are also believed to benefit depressed patients. Depression was assessed immediately, after one month and after six months using standard depression scales; 59% of the ECT patients went into remission, experiencing no symptoms immediately after treatment and at one-month follow-up. Only 17% of the control group experienced similar remission. However, at six months follow-up most of the patients were suffering major depression again. This suggests that ECT is effective in the short-term but not the long-term. This pattern of good short-term gains but poor long-term effectiveness is typical of ECT research.

There are ethical issues to consider in the use of ECT. One concerns side effects. The major side effect is memory loss. This is usually temporary and a single treatment does not result in serious memory impairment. However, memory problems are cumulative, that is, they get worse over a course of treatment. Lisanby *et al.* (2000) randomly assigned 55 patients with major depression to either bilateral or unilateral ECT conditions. A standard memory test called the Personal & Impersonal Memory Test was administered before and in the week after ECT and two months later. A control group without ECT were also assessed for memory. In the week after ECT the patients forgot significant personal (relating to their own lives) and impersonal memories (of events not directly connected to themselves). At two months follow-up they had recovered most but not all personal memories. Generally memory loss is not permanent, but neither is the remission from the symptoms of depression.

What's that?

● **NICE:** the National Institute for Health and Clinical Excellence. A publicly funded body attached to the NHS that is responsible for recommending safe and effective treatments for all physical and mental health problems based on research findings

So when is ECT an appropriate treatment? The National Institute for Clinical Excellence (2003) suggests that ECT is appropriate when other treatments have failed, or if the patient's depression is considered to be life-threatening. NICE also note that the risks associated with ECT are worse for children, adolescents, older people and pregnant women, and that particular care should be taken when choosing ECT for patients in any of these categories.

Psychological treatments for depression

Cognitive-behavioural therapies (CBT)

We introduced cognitive-behavioural therapies or CBT in your AS level. In this section, we are specifically concerned with the use of CBT to treat depression. CBT is now the most commonly used form of psychological therapy, in particular amongst clinical psychologists. It usually takes place once a week or fortnight for between five and 20 sessions. CBT involves helping patients identify irrational and unhelpful thoughts and trying to change them. This may involve drawing diagrams for patients to show them the links between their thinking, behaviour and emotions. The rationale of CBT is that our thoughts affect our feelings and behaviour, so by changing our thoughts we can make ourselves feel better. Some forms of CBT also focus on directly encouraging changes to behaviour.

Figure 5.27 In CBT therapists may use diagrams to show patients the links between their thinking, behaviour and emotions.

According to the British Association for Behavioural & Cognitive-behavioural therapies (BABCP) (2002) the aims of CBT in treating depression are as follows:

● to re-establish previous levels of activity
● to re-establish a social life
● to challenge patterns of negative thinking
● to learn to spot the early signs of recurring depression.

Therapy is collaborative; the therapist and patient will agree on what the patient wants to change. The therapist may then ask the patient to express their negative beliefs, for example, in relation to their social life. A depressed patient might believe that there is no point in going out as they won't enjoy it. The therapist might respond to this by vigorous argument to convince the patient that they will in fact enjoy going out. They might also employ reality testing in which the patient might be encouraged to go out and record in a diary that they enjoyed it.

Evaluation of CBT for depression

There is an impressive body of research supporting its effectiveness. Butler *et al.* (2006) reviewed studies of CBT and found 16 published meta-analyses, each of which included the results of several smaller studies. Based on this very large body of evidence, they concluded that CBT was very effective for treating depression. The Royal College of Psychiatrists and the National Institute for Clinical Excellence (NICE) recommend CBT as the most effective psychological treatment for moderate and severe depression.

Although CBT is strongly supported by research and is increasingly dominating clinical psychology, there are some grounds for caution. Holmes (2002) has identified a number of limitations of the evidence to support such whole-hearted support for CBT.

● The single largest study into effective treatments for depression (carried out by the National Institute for Mental Health, 1994) showed that CBT was less effective than antidepressant drugs and other psychological therapies.

● There is insufficient evidence for the long-term effectiveness of CBT (or other treatments).

● The evidence for the effectiveness of CBT comes mainly from trials of highly selected patients with only depression and no additional symptoms. There is much less evidence of effectiveness in real patient populations where the majority have more complex problems.

Interactive angles

You can read Holmes' paper in full and the responses of various pro-CBT commentators here: http://www.bmj.com/cgi/reprint/324/7332/288. CBT practitioners can certainly cite a large volume of research in support of CBT but Holmes concludes that this simply makes them superior at marketing. Where do you stand in this debate?

Holmes' critique aside, the majority of current commentators recommend CBT as the most appropriate first line of psychological treatment for depression. There is considerable evidence for its effectiveness and little evidence of side effects. However, not all patients benefit from CBT, and NICE (2004) recommend psychodynamic therapies for more complex cases of depression.

Psychodynamic therapies

Psychodynamic therapies originated with the work of Freud. The original form, classical psychoanalysis, is very intensive, taking place four to five times per week and lasting for several years. Psychoanalytic psychotherapy is slightly less intensive and long term, typically one to three times per week for one to five years. Traditionally, patients in psychoanalysis lie on a couch, and patient and analyst do not face each other. Nowadays, particularly in psychotherapy as opposed to psychoanalysis, patient and therapist are more likely to face each other on comfortable chairs.

Figure 5.28 Traditionally patients in psychoanalysis lie on a couch.

In psychoanalysis or psychoanalytic psychotherapy there is no attempt to teach the patient more constructive patterns of thinking or behaviour. Instead the emphasis is on exploring the patient's past and linking it to their current symptoms. Early experiences of loss or rejection are particularly important in depression so these in particular may be explored. The patient may vividly recall these experiences (this is called **abreaction**) and 'discharge' the associated emotion (this is called **catharsis**). They may thus become very angry or upset. Often these negative emotions can become **transferred** on to the therapist, who can be treated as if they were the absent or rejecting parent. The therapist can feed this back to the patient, who can thus gain insight into the way they transfer their anger on to other people. From a psychodynamic perspective the relationship difficulties often associated with depression are often the result of transferring anger from early losses. In the more modern brief dynamic therapy (BDT), rather than wait for negative emotions to be transferred on to the therapist, patients are educated about the links between their current functioning and past experiences.

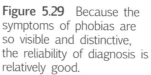

What's that?

- **Abreaction:** recalling and re-experiencing painful memories
- **Catharsis:** Discharge of accumulated emotion
- **Transference:** transferring emotions from one relationship to another, for example, from patient to therapist

Evaluation of psychodynamic therapies for depression

There is a much smaller body of research into the effectiveness of psychodynamic therapies than for CBT. This reflects the fact that many more CBT practitioners are psychologists and therefore trained researchers. That said, the research that does exist is highly supportive of psychodynamic therapies for depression. Leichsenring *et al.* (2004) reviewed random control trials of BDT for specific disorders and found three studies of depression. On the basis of these studies they concluded that BDT is as effective as CBT for treating depression.

Publicly funded psychodynamic therapies are controversial because of the relatively small body of evidence supporting their effectiveness and because some varieties are so expensive. NICE (2004) recommends BDT as appropriate for complex cases where patients suffer a range of symptoms alongside depression. Psychodynamic therapies may also be appropriate where patients are aware of childhood events and have a strong desire to explore them. Psychodynamic therapies are probably inappropriate in cases of depression where patients are primarily seeking quick relief for their symptoms.

Phobias

Rather like depression, anxiety disorders are extensions of the very normal experience of anxiety. A certain amount of anxiety is good for us in many situations. It can boost exam performance, for example, and make us more alert in dangerous situations. However, extreme anxiety can be disabling. Estimates vary but probably between 15 and 20% of the population suffer some form of pathological anxiety. Phobias are the most common form of anxiety. They involve an irrational anxiety directed towards a particular object or situation.

Clinical characteristics of phobias

Phobias come in different forms. Best known are the specific phobias. These involve fear of a single stimulus, such as spiders or snakes. Around 13% of us experience a specific phobia at some time. Most phobias begin in childhood and their intensity usually declines throughout adulthood. The criteria for a diagnosis of a simple phobia in the *DSM-IV* system are shown in Box 5.7.

There are other forms of phobia. Social phobias are related to other people. Common examples include fear of public speaking and using public toilets. Some anxiety before social situations is quite common, reported by about 40% of the population. It becomes a clinical condition in around 2% of people when it interferes with their daily lives. Agoraphobia is the fear of public places, occurring in 2–3% of people. It differs from the other anxiety disorders in appearing rather later, typically in the mid-20s.

Figure 5.29 Because the symptoms of phobias are so visible and distinctive, the reliability of diagnosis is relatively good.

Interactive angles

Ever wondered how many different phobias there are? Go to http://phobialist.com/. You may be surprised!

Biological explanations for phobias

Genetic vulnerability

It seems unlikely that a single gene or a particular set of genes directly cause phobias. However, it does seem likely that some people are more vulnerable than others to acquiring anxiety conditions because of the inherited characteristics of their nervous system. For example, twin studies suggest that phobias are more likely to be shared by identical than non-identical twins. In one study Skre *et al.* (2000) compared the frequency of sharing phobia in 23 pairs of identical twins and 38 pairs of same-sex non-identical twins. The identical twins were significantly more likely to share a diagnosis of phobia (particularly specific phobias) than non-identical twins. Looking more broadly at the role of genetic vulnerability in anxiety disorders, Hetterna *et al.* (2001) reviewed the results of twin and family studies concerned with a range of anxiety problems including generalised anxiety, panic disorder, phobias and OCD. Overall, family members of a patient with an anxiety disorder were four to six times as likely as others to develop an anxiety condition themselves.

Diagnostic criteria for a simple phobia

A Marked and persistent fear that is excessive or unreasonable, cued by the presence or anticipation of a specific object or situation (eg, flying, heights, animals, receiving an injection, seeing blood).

B Exposure to the phobic stimulus almost invariably provokes an immediate anxiety response, which may take the form of a situationally bound or situationally predisposed Panic Attack. Note: in children, the anxiety may be expressed by crying, tantrums, freezing, or clinging.

C The person recognises that the fear is excessive or unreasonable. Note: in children, this feature may be absent.

D The phobic situation(s) is avoided or else is endured with intense anxiety or distress.

E The avoidance, anxious anticipation, or distress in the feared situation(s) interferes significantly with the person's normal routine, occupational (or academic) functioning, or social activities or relationships, or there is marked distress about having the phobia.

F In individuals under age 18 years, the duration is at least six months.

G The anxiety, Panic Attacks, or phobic avoidance associated with the specific object or situation are not better accounted for by another mental disorder, such as Obsessive-Compulsive Disorder (eg, fear of dirt in someone with an obsession about contamination), Post-traumatic Stress Disorder (eg, avoidance of stimuli associated with a severe stressor), Separation Anxiety Disorder (eg, avoidance of school), Social Phobia (eg, avoidance of social situations because of fear of embarrassment), Panic Disorder with Agoraphobia, or Agoraphobia Without History of Panic Disorder.

Specify type:

- Animal type
- Natural environment type (eg, heights, storms, water)
- Blood-injection-injury type
- Situational type (eg, airplanes, elevators, enclosed places)
- Other type (eg, phobic avoidance of situations that may lead to choking, vomiting, or contracting an illness; in children, avoidance of loud sounds or costumed characters).

Interactive angles

Just because a disorder is shared by family members, to what does this indicate that it is genetic in origin? What other factors apart from genes are shared within families?

Biochemical factors in phobias

Few if any professionals believe that anxiety disorders are entirely the result of abnormal chemical levels. However, they may play an important role in individual vulnerability to and symptoms of anxiety problems. We know, for example, that the normal experience of anxiety is regulated in the brain by an amino acid called GABA. GABA operates a feedback loop, helping arousal levels to return to normal after a fright. It is possible that some people have a problem with their GABA system and so cannot control their anxiety as easily.

The serotonin system can also be linked to phobias. Studies, for example Stein *et al.* (1998), show that the symptoms of social phobia are reduced by SSRIs and other antidepressants, suggesting a role for serotonin. Specific phobias are normally treated psychologically rather than with drugs; however, Benjamin *et al.* (2000) tested the antidepressant paroxetine on patients suffering specific phobias and found that symptoms were sharply reduced in 60% of patients as opposed to 20% of a control group. This suggests that the symptoms of specific phobias are serotonin related. This does not mean that phobias are acquired simply as a result of low serotonin levels; however, low serotonin levels may make some people more vulnerable than others or they may be important in the experience of phobic anxiety.

Psychological explanations for phobias

Behavioural (learning) theory

Although behavioural theory is one of the older approaches to psychology it is still important in explaining anxiety disorders. You may recall hearing about classical conditioning and phobias at AS level, in particular the case of Little Albert. Recall that classical conditioning takes place when we come to associate something that initially does not produce any response (a neutral stimulus) with something that already produces a response (like anxiety). We now need to consider another type of learning. Operant conditioning takes place when we learn to repeat a behaviour if it has a good consequence and not repeat it if it has a bad result.

Avoidance conditioning

The simplest idea about how people can learn anxiety disorders is the *avoidance-conditioning model*, based on classical conditioning. In avoidance conditioning the phobic-stimulus-to-be is paired with another stimulus that already leads to anxiety. What was a neutral stimulus becomes a conditioned stimulus. This is almost certainly how some specific phobias are learnt. The classic study of avoidance conditioning was the case of Little Albert. Early behaviourists Watson & Rayner (1920) paired the neutral stimulus of a white rat with the unconditioned stimulus of a loud noise to make the rat a conditioned stimulus producing a fear response. This study is described in detail in *Exploring Psychology for AS-level*.

The avoidance-conditioning model can also be applied to social phobias. One of the most common social phobias concerns public toilets. A common experience is paruresis – not being able to urinate because of the presence of others. Someone who experiences paruresis once and suffers the resulting anxiety may become conditioned to avoid the situation of being in a public toilet. If other people notice and laugh this can be intensified – being laughed at is an unconditioned stimulus and if it is paired with public toilets then toilets will produce the same anxiety response as laughter.

Figure 5.30 Public toilets can produce anxiety responses in sufferers of social phobias.

Avoidance learning is a well documented phenomenon. However, what is not clear is how commonly it takes place or how many cases of phobia it can account for. Menzies (1996) surveyed patients on the origins of their phobias and the majority cited other reasons. Also, we can develop phobias of things we have never had experiences with (such as snakes). Presumably we cannot have a classical conditioning experience without directly encountering the stimulus.

Operant conditioning

Recall operant conditioning from your AS level. It is a form of learning in which we repeat behaviours that are rewarded and do not repeat behaviours that have a bad consequence. Although classical conditioning remains an important explanation for acquiring phobias, operant conditioning may be important in keeping them going. Every time we persuade someone else to put a spider out for us, or manage to get out of a social situation that provokes anxiety, our anxiety levels go down. This reduction of anxiety rewards or *reinforces* the avoidance behaviour. When we reinforce a behaviour we increase the likelihood of it being repeated, and so the phobic response continues.

Social learning

Classical conditioning explains neatly how we acquire phobias of objects and situations with which we have had bad experiences. However, sometimes we can develop phobias of things we have never encountered. One explanation for this is social learning; it seems that we can learn phobic behaviour by observing in others (called models) and imitating it. However, it also seems that we acquire some phobias much more easily than others this way. This was demonstrated in a classic study by Cook & Mineka (1989), using rhesus monkeys.

Cognitive theory

A problem with learning theory as an explanation for phobias is that it doesn't explain why some people are more prone to acquiring anxiety problems than others. This can be

explained from a cognitive perspective. The cognitive process of visual attention appears to work somewhat differently in people prone to acquire phobias. Eysenck (1992) proposed that anxiety disorders are caused or at least maintained by a form of *attentional bias*. Phobic patients tend to focus their attention more on threatening stimuli than do the rest of us.

Kindt & Brosschot (1997) tested for attentional bias in arachnophobic patients using the Stroop task. In the Stroop procedure, participants have to name the ink colour of each word in a multicoloured word-list. The time taken to name the ink colours of whole lists or individual items is recorded. If people take a particularly long time to name the ink colour of particular words, this shows that they could not disengage their attention from that word, and thus shows cognitive bias. In this study, arachnophobics took significantly longer to name the ink colours for spider-related words and pictures. This showed that arachnophobia is associated with cognitive bias.

Another cognitive factor is the sort of beliefs people have about phobic stimuli. In an experimental procedure Armfield (2007) manipulated people's beliefs about the danger, predictability and controllability of a spider before asking them to imagine putting their hand in an aquarium with a spider. All the beliefs affected how afraid of spiders the participants were; high levels of danger, unpredictability and uncontrollability were associated with spider phobia.

Drug treatments for phobias

Various types of drugs can be used to reduce anxiety. Severe anxiety can be treated in the short-term by benzodiazepines such as diazepam (Valium). These work by increasing the effectiveness of the GABA system. Benzodiazepines are quite effective at tackling the symptoms of anxiety; however, they are addictive and when patients stop taking them after some time they often experience a sharp rise in anxiety. In the 1960s and 70s benzodiazepines were commonly prescribed long-term for anxiety problems, but it is now generally agreed that this was a serious error, leaving large numbers of people addicted and suffering further anxiety problems when they tried to stop their medication.

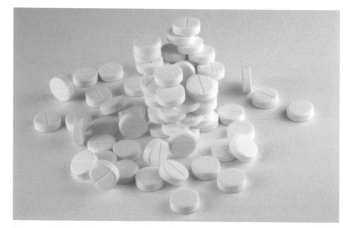

Figure 5.31 Some people with social phobias respond best to drugs.

Cook, M. & Mineka, S. (1989)

'Observational conditioning of fear to fear-relevant versus fear-irrelevant stimuli in rhesus monkeys'

Journal of Abnormal Psychology, 98: 448–59

Aim: To test whether monkeys can acquire fear responses by imitation of other monkeys and to see whether they are more likely to learn fear of dangerous objects than non-dangerous ones.

Procedure: Two laboratory experiments were run. In the first, 22 lab-reared rhesus monkeys aged 4–11 years observed a 32-year-old wild-reared monkey who had a fear of snakes. The observer monkeys watched a videotape of the model responding with fear to a snake. They also watched a video in which the fear response was spliced with footage of flowers so that it appeared that the model was afraid of the flowers. In the second experiment, the procedure was repeated with 20 lab-reared rhesus monkeys. This time the model was lab-reared and had been taught to fear crocodiles. In one condition, the observers watched footage of the model reacting with fear to a crocodile or the

fear response spliced with a toy rabbit so that the model appeared to be afraid of the toy. Fear in the observers was then assessed by the time taken to reach for food in the presence of the fear stimulus (toy snake, toy crocodile, flowers or toy rabbit).

Results: In both experiments the times taken to reach for food increased after watching the videotape when the fear stimulus was dangerous, that is, the snake or crocodile (for example, it increased from nine to 27 seconds in the presence of a toy snake after watching the video). It did not increase when the fear stimulus was not dangerous – as in the case of the flowers or toy rabbit.

Conclusion: Fear responses can be acquired by social learning, but only to objects that are potentially dangerous.

An alternative class of anti-anxiety drugs is beta-blockers. These counter the action of neurochemicals like adrenaline and noradrenaline that increase the body's arousal levels. This means that they tackle the rises in blood pressure and heart rate associated with anxiety and so are effective in reducing its physical symptoms. Recently attention has turned to the use of antidepressants to treat anxiety. These work by preventing the breakdown of serotonin and so causing its levels to build up in the brain. Antidepressants are currently the most common biological treatment for social phobias (see Figure 5.31).

Evaluation of drug treatments for anxiety

Biological treatments can be effective in reducing the symptoms of anxiety disorders. We have already looked at studies by Stein *et al.* (1998) and Benjamin *et al.* (2000), showing that antidepressants are effective in the treatment of social and specific phobias. The appropriateness of biological treatments for anxiety disorders is a more complex question. Antidepressants have side effects. In the Hammad (2007) review it was concluded that antidepressants led to a small but detectable increase in suicidal thinking. For specific phobias it is well established that psychological therapies are very effective treatments that do not have the side effects biological treatments do. It is thus very questionable whether drug treatments should ever be used. OCD and social phobias can be treated with psychological therapies, but people vary as to which sort of treatment works best for them. It is therefore important to have a range of treatments available.

Psychological treatments for anxiety disorders
Systematic desensitisation

Systematic desensitisation is a behavioural therapy based on the principles of classical conditioning. The aim of systematic desensitisation is to unlearn conditioned responses like phobias. Modern desensitisation depends on the idea that we cannot be relaxed and afraid at the same time – by definition fear involves a high level of physical arousal. If we can stay relaxed in the presence of the thing we fear we will no longer fear it. Patients learn in desensitisation that they can remain relaxed in the presence of the thing they fear. Relaxation can be achieved by hypnosis or meditation, or by anxiolytic drugs like Valium. The patient is then exposed to the thing they fear, working through an anxiety hierarchy. This starts with a form of exposure they feel reasonably comfortable with and building up to the one they most fear. An arachnophobic patient may

Figure 5.32 We can learn to tolerate frightening things if we work up to them.

thus start by being exposed to a small picture of a spider and end up with a Venezuelan tarantula on their face. Once the patient successfully remains relaxed with this sort of intense exposure to the object of their phobia, they will have learnt not to fear it (see Figure 5.32).

Evaluation of desensitisation

There is plenty of evidence to support the idea that desensitisation helps reduce phobic anxiety. Brosnan & Thorpe (2006) used a ten-week desensitisation programme to help 16 technophobic students (who were afraid of computers) on an information technology course. As compared to a control group who had no desensitisation, their anxiety levels were significantly lower at the end of the course. Desensitisation has also been applied to social phobia, but with more mixed results. Duff *et al.* (2007) treated students on a public speaking course with either systematic desensitisation, no treatment or a mixed programme of treatments. Although anxiety about public speaking declined throughout the course there was no advantage to having formal therapy of either type. The participants' anxiety declined with experience anyway.

The appropriateness of systematic desensitisation depends on the trade-off between effectiveness and ethical acceptability. Desensitisation is fairly effective and involves only minimal distress for patients. However, there is a more effective but far more brutal alternative treatment available. In flooding, patients are exposed immediately to an extreme form of the thing they fear. This is more effective than desensitisation and can work in a single session. However, it is traumatic and many patients leave rather than complete the session.

Cognitive-behavioural therapy

CBT is now the most commonly used form of psychological therapy, in particular amongst clinical psychologists. It usually takes place once a week or fortnight for between five and 20 sessions. CBT involves helping patients identify irrational and unhelpful thoughts and trying to change them. This may involve drawing diagrams for patients to show them the links between their thinking, behaviour and emotions. The rationale of CBT is that our thoughts affect our feelings and behaviour, so by changing our thoughts we can make ourselves feel better. Some forms of CBT also focus on directly encouraging changes to behaviour.

The aim of CBT in treating anxiety is to challenge and help patients overcome the cognitions that are involved in their symptoms. To treat a spider phobia for example a cognitive-behavioural therapist might first explore exactly what beliefs the patient has about spiders. They might then challenge these beliefs by argument. They might also set the patient reality-testing tasks like confronting a spider and showing themselves that they could touch it without harm. The patient might be encouraged to record successful encounters with spiders in a diary so they could be reminded afterwards if they felt negative about their progress.

Evaluation of CBT for anxiety

There is considerable support for CBT as an effective treatment for anxiety disorders. For example, Butler *et al.* (2006) reviewed meta-analytic studies of CBT and concluded that it was effective for a range of anxiety disorders including social phobias. Gould *et al.* (1997) compared the effectiveness of CBT versus drugs for social phobia by putting studies of each into a meta-analysis. They concluded based on this that CBT was significantly more effective. A fascinating recent study suggests that CBT has significant effects on brain functioning. Paquette *et al.* (2003) scanned the brains of 12 arachnophobic patients when exposed to spiders and found increased activity in three key areas of the brain. They were scanned again following CBT and it was found that all three regions were functioning normally.

> ## What's that?
>
> - **Random control trial:** a procedure in which patients are randomly allocated to a treatment or control condition and the outcomes compared
> - **Secondary data:** information taken from studies that have been carried out already by other people

CBT is not associated with the same ethical issues as drugs as it has no biochemical side effects. Nor does it raise the same issues as do behavioural treatments like desensitisation, as it does not lead to the same degree of distress. Therefore, for social phobias and OCD, CBT can be seen as an appropriate first line of treatment. For specific phobias exposure therapies are probably at least as effective and can be quicker. There have been more fundamental objections to CBT however. Holmes (2002) points out that there are relatively few long-term studies of CBT's effectiveness and that most studies have involved highly selected patients with single symptoms or very simple sets of symptoms. They may not generalise well to most real-life settings where patients present with complex sets of symptoms.

Summary and conclusions

There are several ways in which we can define behaviour as abnormal. For example, we say that statistically unusual behaviour or behaviour that deviates from social norms is abnormal. Both these definitions play a role in psychiatric assessment and diagnosis but neither is adequate on its own. By convention we classify abnormal behaviour and experience into a set of mental disorders and try to diagnose the individual who is behaving abnormally. Diagnosis raises issues of reliability and validity. It can also cause problems when one culture imposes its ideas about normal behaviour on another.

Schizophrenia is one of the most serious mental disorders. It is widely though not universally agreed to be biological in origin, though with important

You may be asked to describe one key issue from clinical psychology. You can choose this yourself from this chapter. Suitable examples include:

- How reliable and valid is psychiatric diagnosis?

- Is schizophrenia a biological condition?

- Is there still a place for psychodynamic therapy in the mental health system?

- Is CBT all it's cracked up to be?

Make sure that for whatever you identify as your key issue, you can pose a question and draw on secondary research to answer it. Secondary data is information taken from existing studies, as opposed to primary data, which is information collected specifically for the purpose of a study. An example of a study using secondary data is Gottesman's study of the genetic basis of schizophrenia. The best sources of secondary data are review articles and meta-analyses. Technically, information from textbooks and websites is tertiary data, but that's being a bit picky. For purposes of this exercise you are looking for reviews, but it's fine to obtain summaries of those reviews from textbooks or websites.

Whatever issue you choose, look first for information you can use from this chapter. Then look on-line for more information. Try to find some statistics but nothing that you can't easily explain to someone who has not studied psychology. www.pubmed.gov and http://scholar.google.co.uk are good tools for searching for psychological studies. Also try organisations with websites aiming to improve awareness of mental health issues.

When you have enough information, your task is to put together a leaflet explaining the issue for the non-expert. You can see some examples what good leaflets look like here: http://www.darlington.gov.uk/Health/AdultServices/Leaflets.htm#General and http://www.rethink.org/dualdiagnosis/pdfs/Leaflet.pdf. Google for more examples using search terms 'mental health' and 'leaflet'. Make sure you are clear about the following when you put your leaflet together:

- You are clear who your target audience is, and why you chose them. You might, for example, choose children as your audience because children with older family members with schizophrenia have little access to appropriate information. A leaflet for children will have simpler information and more visual aids than one aimed at General Practitioners.

- You are clear what strategies you are using to put the information across, for example, pictures, diagrams, statistics, and why these might be appropriate for your target audience.

- When your leaflet is complete, evaluate its strengths and weaknesses.

psychological features. Schizophrenia is associated with particular genetic make-up and abnormal neurochemical functioning. Psychological models including those from cognitive and psychodynamic perspectives are useful in understanding the experience of schizophrenia and possibly environmental factors that can make people more vulnerable to it. Schizophrenia is most commonly treated by means of antipsychotic drugs. Sometimes ECT or psychological therapies may also be used.

You need to know about one other disorder as well as schizophrenia. We have offered a choice of unipolar depression and phobias. These are both relatively common problems – up to 20% of us will suffer one of these during our lives. Depression can be explained biologically with reference to genes and/or neurochemistry. However, although it has traditionally been treated using drugs, modern research suggests that psychological therapies may often be more effective. Phobias are usually explained psychologically. Learning theory provides good explanations for how phobias are acquired and maintained, whilst cognitive theory shows why some people are more vulnerable to acquiring them than others. Treatment is generally by means of psychological therapies.

What's that?

1. (a) Outline the social norms definition of abnormality. [4]

   (b) Evaluate the social norms definition of abnormality. [6]

2. (a) Describe the main symptoms and/or features of schizophrenia. [5]

   (b) Evaluate **one** explanation for schizophrenia. [5]

3. Describe and evaluate Rosenhan's study of psychiatric diagnosis. [12]

4. (a) Identify **one** key issue from clinical psychology. [2]

   (b) Discuss the issue you identified in (a). [8]

5. You have studied **one** disorder other than schizophrenia. Identify your chosen disorder.

   (a) Describe **one** way in which this disorder can be treated. [5]

   (b) Evaluate the treatment you described in (a). [5]

Where does psychology take us?

- Can therapy implant false memories?
- How important are hospital family rooms?
- Is culture important in understanding schizophrenia?
- Do antipsychotic drugs work on animals?

What's ahead?

By the end of this chapter I should know about:

- two contributions to society of each of the approaches to psychology (social, cognitive, biological, psychodynamic and learning)
- one contribution to society from two applications from criminal psychology, child psychology, health psychology and sport psychology
- one contribution to society from clinical psychology
- five ethical guidelines for psychological research relating to human participants
- five ethical principles relating to non-human animals in psychological research
- ethical issues in psychological research in relation to both humans and non-human animals
- two studies in terms of their ethical issues
- the strengths and weaknesses of the following research methods and be able to describe and evaluate one study using each method:
  - laboratory experiment
  - field experiment
  - natural experiment
  - observation
  - questionnaire
  - interview
  - content analysis
  - correlational analysis
  - case study
- how to plan a study from a given context, including: the aim, hypotheses, design, procedure, ethical considerations and analysis of results including choice of statistical test
- how to evaluate studies with reference to the research method and suggest improvements
- a key issue relevant to today's society from each psychological approach, from two applications and from clinical psychology and be able to explain it using concepts, theories and research and including reference to methodological and ethical issues
- the issue of ethnocentrism in psychological research and its effects
- what makes a subject a 'science' and the extent to which psychology is, and whether it should aim to be, a science
- how to compare the five approaches and the extent to which their content and methods are scientific
- the use of psychological knowledge for social control and be able to assess the ethical and practical implications of such control
- the role of nature and nurture in psychology, considering both content and methods from the approaches and applications and consider the extent to which they place differing emphasis on nature and nurture

In addition I should understand:

- how to apply my knowledge of psychology to new situations such as studies and key issues using psychological concepts, theories and research from the approaches and applications

How do the approaches to psychology contribute to society?

In your study of psychology at AS you will have explored at least one key issue in each approach. These are ways in which the different psychological perspectives have made a contribution to psychology. In some of the approaches there were also specific examples of applications in the content that you learned, such as therapies using learning theory. In this section we will look at some of the possible applications of each approach. You will find some ideas that you have not encountered before, but you should be able to use your understanding of the approach to see how the psychological concepts have been used to contribute to society.

It is important that psychological knowledge is put to good use. The British Psychological Society identifies as one of its primary aims a responsibility to use psychology for the public good. Clearly, there are many ways in which psychology can make contributions of public benefit, but it is also worth acknowledging that, in order for this to be possible, people must believe in and trust the body of psychological knowledge. This is one, though perhaps not the most important, reason why psychologists should conduct their research ethically. If they fail to do so, their findings, and any potential benefits for society that result from them, are less likely to be recognised and accepted by the public.

Figure 6.1 How can psychology be used for the public good?

Contributions of the social approach to society

The social approach to psychology is about the way that people affect one another. Since the role of society and culture are central to this approach, there are clear applications to society.

Understanding the maltreatment of prisoners

The horrors of war show us many unpleasant things about human behaviour. 'Man's inhumanity to man' often appears incomprehensible. Social psychology has offered some insights into the reasons for such behaviours as the systematic degradation of prisoners by guards in both war and peacetime. Human rights abuses at the Abu Ghraib prison illustrate this issue, with American soldiers subjecting Iraqi detainees to mock executions and other forms of ritual humiliation and physical torture. Reports from soldiers at the prison describe the instructions they received to treat the prisoners harshly to 'break them down' for interrogation.

When the soldiers faced court appearances for their conduct, their defence lawyers said that they were not bad people but that their misconduct was a product of the situation. Interpreting the situation using Milgram's (1974) agency theory, the soldiers were acting agentically. Orders from their senior officers, that is, from authority figures within their society, were to make the prisoners stressed and ready to talk. In the agentic state, the soldiers would have been able to resist the moral strain produced by knowing that what they were doing was wrong so were able to follow the commands. If they had been in the autonomous state they would have felt responsible for their actions so would not have been able to override their conscience and commit the atrocities. In the agentic state, in contrast, the responsibility was passed on to their commanding officers.

The soldiers were following orders, as Milgram's (1963) participants had done, because they felt that the situation demanded that they obeyed rather than acting independently. Also like Milgram's participants, a small number of individuals did behave autonomously, such as the soldier who ultimately made the world aware of the abuse of prisoners by revealing photographs.

In Milgram's studies, the more legitimate an authority figure appeared the greater the obedience to authority. When the status of their location was higher (a university rather than a run down office block) and their dress suggested they were more important (a lab coat or not), participants were more likely to obey. For the soldiers, the setting indicated the need to behave agentically – they were in the midst of military conflict – and the orders were given by legitimate sources – military intelligence investigators and civilian interrogators. This would have made their obedience more likely. However, there was no evidence that the commands included orders to abuse prisoners to the extent that became apparent. Some other explanation is therefore also required.

In addition to the effects of agency, social identity theory (Tajfel & Turner, 1979) is also important in this situation. The US soldiers were the 'in-group', the Iraqi prisoners the 'out-group'. Strong social identification reinforced by the soldiers' uniforms and regimented behaviour would have reinforced the social norm of behaving in a particular way, ie abusing prisoners. That identification alone is sufficient to affect behaviour was demonstrated by Tajfel (1970) in his study of boys awarding points to others apparently in their group. In the situation of military conflict the out-group would be clearly seen as rivals, thus increasing the probability of violence against them, as shown by Sherif *et al.* (1961) in the 'Robber's cave' study when the Eagles and Rattlers were encouraged to compete for prizes and tension between them increased.

Figure 6.2 Although Haney *et al.* (1973) concluded from their mock prison study that destructive behaviour by guards is inevitable, Reicher & Haslam (2006) showed that prisoners can also rebel.

Understanding prejudice and reducing discrimination

Another area of human behaviour that social psychology has helped us to understand is prejudice. Using social identity theory (Tajfel & Turner, 1979), it is possible to explain why members of different social groups can develop the resentment and hatred which leads to inter-group conflict. In 2007 Sophie Lancaster and her boyfriend were brutally attacked by a group of teenage boys. Sophie went to her boyfriend's aid as they kicked his head when he was already unconscious. They then set upon her and she died of her injuries. Why? Apparently because they were Goths.

Figure 6.3 Social identity theory can explain how prejudice arises and offers ways to reduce it.

According to social identity theory (SIT), such violence arises because our social judgements and behaviour are based on three processes. First, we use social categorisation to place people into groups based on stereotyped beliefs. This decision is made using characteristics such as gender, skin colour or accent – in the case of the Goths by their dress and make-up. Social identification causes the individual to adopt the attitudes and behaviours of the group to which they belong themselves, that is, they *identify* with their own group. This serves to distinguish group members from non-members and, as Sherif *et al.* (1961) showed in the 'Robber's cave' study, belonging to a group matters. Groups can then be evaluated against one another – social comparison. This judgement is biased – the out-group is devalued and the self-esteem of the individual's own group is raised. It is this need to boost the in-group at the cost of the out-group which leads to discrimination (as Tajfel (1970) demonstrated in his laboratory study and Levine *et al.* (2005) showed with football fans) and, in some cases, to violence.

An understanding of the processes indicated by SIT provides possible routes for the reduction of prejudice. Collective action aims to raise the self-esteem of the out-group, thus boosting their social status. It includes activities such as rallies and other public demonstrations to build up recognition of minority or oppressed social groups. For example, political activism by suffragettes enabled women to gain social identity and obtain legal status such as the right to vote. Similarly, campaigning by gay-rights groups such as Stonewall led to the wider social acceptance of gay people, legal protection in the work place and the right to civil partnerships. In an experimental situation, Reicher & Haslam (2006) showed that the low-status prisoners ultimately acted collectively against the unfair regime imposed by the guards. This changed the prison regime and the prisoners had higher identity scores than the guards throughout the rest of the study.

Prejudice can also be tackled by reducing social categorisation, identification and comparison. In order to achieve this, the stereotypes on which the process is founded must be broken down and opportunities provided to help build up a unified identity. For example, in reducing prejudice between racial groups it is important that people:

- get to know members of the other group as individuals so that they can recognise similarities with themselves (to reduce social categorisation)
- work together towards a shared goal (to reduce social identification)
- have equal status (to reduce social comparison).

Strategies based on social co-operation aim to achieve this. For example, in the 'Robber's cave' study, Sherif *et al.* (1961) showed that getting the Eagles and Rattlers to work together to repair the water supply reduced competition and discrimination.

Whilst much evidence suggests that SIT is an adequate and useful explanation of prejudice, there are some problems with the theory. For example, even when conflicting groups spend time together so ought to be able to get to know one another as individuals, this does not always lead to a reduction in prejudice, such as desegregation of schools in America initially increasing racial prejudice. Of course, evidence such as this is historical and more recent studies suggest that, at least in some cases, contact does reduce prejudice. Bowen & Bourgeois (2001) found that students in university accommodation who were on the same corridor

as gay people were less homophobic. SIT can explain the reduction of prejudice is achieved by such contact because involvement with members of the out group helps to break down the sort of overt barriers that lead to clear separate identities. For example, in the Bowen & Bougeois example contact does not simply lead to acceptance – 'now I've got to know him/her, I can see they're okay' – but a shifting of identities – 'they're gay but they're *our* gay!'

Media watch

Calamity captain's court martial culpability cancelled

On 22nd June 1893 Vice Admiral Tryon ordered his fleet of ten battleships to perform a complex manoeuvre only 1,200 yards apart – too close for vessels of that size.

Vice Admiral Tryon ordered the ships to form two matching columns then turn in towards the other column – giving a breathtaking spectacle to the crowd assembled on the Tripoli shore as each ship came close to its pair – too close.

Tryon's three senior officers knew this was a potentially disastrous plan but their protest was ignored. The staff commander suggested increasing the distance to the Admiral, who appeared to agree, but later Tryon reiterated his original instruction. The staff commander passed a note to another officer to check that he really meant 1,200 yards. They began to signal to the ships, by flag, to perform the turns as Tryon had commanded.

The first pair of ships, HMS Camperdown and HMS Victoria, began to follow the orders given by flag. Victoria's Flag Captain, recognising the danger, questioned the Vice Admiral's order and sent a warning. He was ignored. Rather than taking evasive action, he continued on the collision course. The Victoria began turning and he asked three more times for permission to reverse or turn away. The Admiral eventually said to turn. However, the Flag Captain, acting on his own initiative, ordered the ship to reverse but it was too late.

HMS Camperdown rammed Victoria and, since the ships were armed with steel rams designed for sinking enemy ships, tore a gaping hole in her. HMS Victoria sank in under 13 minutes, losing all 358 crew who stood to attention on the listing deck before the order to abandon ship was given.

Figure 6.4 HMS Victoria.

The court did not fully accept Vice Admiral Tryon's admission of responsibility, instead identifying Vice Admiral Markham, Tryon's second in command, and the captain of the Camperdown, as partly to blame because of their willingness to obey and follow order that they knew would almost certainly lead to catastrophe.

1. Use your understanding of social psychology to discuss this news report.

Interactive angles

Apply concepts from the social approach to explain how it has contributed to society in one of the following contexts:

- understanding genocide
- understanding blind obedience by pilots
- understanding football violence.

Contributions of the cognitive approach to society

The cognitive approach to psychology is about the internal workings of the mind and the way we process information. Since our memories are so important to everyday functioning – both making them work well and dealing with problems that arise when they don't – there are clear applications of the cognitive approach to society.

Eyewitnesses and how psychology can help to improve their accuracy

Work by Bartlett, Loftus and many other researchers has shown us that memory is reconstructive. This means that a witness to a crime does not store a perfect record of what they have seen, but reassembles their account when they recall it and, as a consequence, their testimony can be affected by information they have received after seeing the crime. This post-event information can cause the memory to be distorted. Bartlett (1932) showed how an individual's understanding of a story was vital to being able to reproduce it accurately. This occurs because we need a schema to interpret and store information appropriately. If a witness applies schemas inappropriately to crime scene information, perhaps because they have a bias based on a stereotype, they are unlikely to recall accurately. This is supported by studies such as Wynn & Logie (1998) who found that, in the absence of a schema, recall was not reconstructed and Carli (1999) who showed that believing a story ended in a rape caused people to remember events differently than if they were not given an ending.

In addition, eyewitnesses may not always have a good view of events, distorting their memory further (Yuille & Cutshall, 1985). Their recall may be impaired by trying to remember details without the benefit of state cues, perhaps because they are no longer frightened, or context cues because they are no longer at the crime scene. Various experimental studies of memory and forgetting rather than eyewitnesses have shown the effects of cue dependency such as Godden & Baddeley's (1975) study of divers.

Theories of memory can also help us to understand the problems faced by eyewitnesses. According to the multi-store model (Atkinson & Shiffrin, 1968), if they fail to pay attention to events, the memory may never be rehearsed in short-term memory, so will quickly be forgotten. This is likely if they are unaware that they are witnessing a crime. The levels of processing theory (Craik & Lockhart, 1972) suggests that witnesses would need to deeply process information about the scene in order to remember it well. This is also unlikely as the very things that witnesses need to remember, such as what people or objects looked like, are very superficial so are only likely to be processed structurally.

Psychologists, however, can offer some ways to improve the accuracy of witnesses' recall. Studies such as Loftus & Palmer (1974) showed how leading questions can worsen the effects of reconstruction. To avoid this happening, police interviewers should use only direct questions and allow witnesses enough time to complete their answer before asking the next question. These are important techniques in cognitive interviewing. In this approach, the witness is also encouraged to think about the scene in different ways to try to provide cues that will help them to access more details. Of course, the best way to provide both context and state cues is crime scene reconstruction, allowing the witness to re-experience not just the location, but some of the events and perhaps some of the feelings they had at the time. If this is not possible, state and context dependent memories can be enhanced by asking questions such as 'how did you feel then?' and asking them to imagine the scene. This produces a significant increase in the number of correct facts recalled, although some additional errors are also made.

Improving your study technique

Since you are reading this chapter, you are probably quite close to finishing your A level, so will be thinking about effective ways to revise. The final chapter of the book is devoted to helping you with this, but we can also consider the psychology behind some of the techniques.

At AS you will have learned about the levels of processing theory (Craik & Lockhart, 1972). This suggests that deeper processing, using phonemic (sound-based) or better still semantic (meaning-based) processing, will result in better recall than shallow (structural) processing. Rote learning and simply re-reading your notes is a very superficial, 'shallow' way to revise. In line with laboratory experiments of memory based on learning word lists and other tasks lacking in mundane realism, Jarvis (2006) found a relationship between study habits and performance at AS. The more inclined students were to use deep learning techniques, the better they did at AS. Of course, findings such as this have the disadvantage of being correlational, so we can't draw causal conclusions. It might be that students who use deep learning strategies are simply cleverer, or make more effort to do their homework during the course.

Box 6.1 Using phonemic processing

What makes gender?

Bio says genes make us women or men,
through our hormones and the SDN.
Freud says no, it's mum and dad,
the Oedipus complex is a passing fad.
The learning approach looks at who we copy,
stick to same-sex models or folk get stroppy.

However, levels of processing theory (LoP) does offer some useful ideas in terms of maximising recall. Using phonemic processing is better than shallow processing, so learning rhymes or singing songs that provide psychological information will help (see Box 6.1). Even better than that is semantic processing. This is really about making yourself think. The harder you have to work cognitively, the greater the by-product of memory according to LoP. Semantic processing can include doing things like working out the links between concepts, expressing ideas in your own words and summarising details by extracting the important points. Try the tasks in Box 6.2 and decide which ones involve the shallowest and which the deepest processing.

You may have learned about the multi-store model (Atkinson & Shiffrin, 1968) at AS. This can also guide good study habits. Since we only remember seven plus or minus two items in short-term memory at one time, we should limit the number of new ideas we try to absorb. It's better to spend a little while on one idea than to keep glancing at lots of different things – they will just be displaced. In order to transfer information to long-term memory we need to rehearse it, so we have to repeat tasks to make things 'sink in'. It is useful to tackle the same information in a range of different ways, perhaps reading it first, then saying it out loud or summarising it before trying to answer questions.

Interactive angles

Apply concepts from the cognitive approach to explain how it has contributed to society in one of the following contexts:

- understanding the effects of amnesia
- understanding how schemas distort memory
- understanding how cue dependency can elicit fears.

Box 6.2

Deep and shallow processing tasks: which are which?

1. What are the similarities and differences between the biological and cognitive approaches?

2. Which of these are ideas from the social approach?
   - prejudice
   - agentic state
   - Oedipus complex
   - obedience
   - neurotransmitters

3. In how many different approaches might you encounter each of these ideas?
   - displacement
   - stereotyping
   - schemas
   - models
   - repression

4. List the key studies from AS.

Media watch

Victim who made false rape claims gets £20,000 payout

Katrina Fairlie falsely accused her father of raping her as a child. She also claimed that she had been abused by 17 other men, including two politicians.

These accusations were made as a result of memories that were uncovered during therapy sessions with psychiatrist Dr Alex Yellowlees. Ms Fairlie had received five months of psychotherapy, during which she described other scenes such as watching her father murder a six-year-old girl with an iron bar.

After operations to remove her gall bladder and appendix, Ms Fairlie, aged 25 at the time, was admitted to hospital with severe abdominal pains. However, she was referred to a psychiatric unit because doctors decided that the pain was

psychosomatic — that she was imagining it. To help her, she received a form of Recovered Memory Therapy (RMT), which was supposed to unlock painful memories that the patient had blocked out of their conscious mind. It has since been discredited by the Royal College of Physicians.

The police dropped their investigations of the case against Mr Fairlie and others when Katrina later withdrew all her allegations. Nevertheless, the unfounded allegations had wrecked Mr Fairlie's reputation and his close relationship with his daughter.

Ms Fairlie subsequently brought charges of negligence against the NHS trust, which had failed in its duty of care because it had not checked the likely truth of her statements

— which ultimately caused so much distress to her and her family.

She won a £20,000 payout in an out-of-court settlement, although the NHS trust did not admit liability. Nevertheless, it has allowed her to make public the trauma caused to the family, who are now united in a bid to stop it happening to others. Mr Fairlie, in support of his daughter, cited that the British False Memory Society is aware of more than 1,400 cases like his daughter's.

1. How could false memories such as described above be explained using cognitive concepts such as repression, cue dependency and reconstructive memory?

Contributions of the psychodynamic approach to society

The psychodynamic approach to psychology is about our unconscious processes and the way that they can affect us. The ideas in psychodynamic psychology can help us to understand why people often appear to be irrational as such actions can be explained in terms of unconscious motivation. This approach has an important application to society in understanding and helping people with mental health problems, but is also useful in other aspects of society, such as helping people to understand themselves.

Psychotherapy and understanding mental health problems

Through concepts such as defence mechanisms and the effects of early childhood relationships, the psychodynamic approach can explain how some mental illnesses arise. For example, Massie & Szajnberg (2002) found associations between adult mental health and both traumatic childhood events and the quality of parental relationships.

There are now many different therapies based on the psychodynamic approach, one of the oldest being psychoanalysis. This is an intensive, long-term therapy. It uses techniques such as dream interpretation and free association to allow the analyst to interpret the patient's current symptoms in terms of their history. By finding such links, the analyst can explore unconscious issues that may be causing the symptoms of mental illness, such as repressed feelings of guilt or anger or childhood fears.

If traumatic early experiences are identified, these can be explored in therapy sessions to allow the patient to re-experience them and work them through in the safety of the therapy session – that is, to experience catharsis. Similarly, therapy sessions may reveal the use of defence mechanisms and help individuals to see how they are protecting themselves and perhaps causing problems. For example, denial may lead to the avoidance of problems and a failure to confront real issues.

One important early experience which can affect adulthood is the nature of our relationships with others. If they are poor, this may be reflected in our adult relationships too, making us less effective. Through transference, the patient can express the feelings towards someone which they have carried from childhood by playing them out in their relationship with the therapist. In their feedback to the patient, the therapist can help the patient to understand the roots of their relationship problems and where they are going wrong.

Figure 6.5 Working through our childhood issues can help our relationships in adulthood.

Evidence suggests that psychodynamic therapies are effective. You may recall from AS the review by Bachrach et al. (1991) which found between 60 and 90% improvement in patients following psychoanalysis. More recent studies, such as Leichsenring & Leibing (2007), have come to similar conclusions using a much more tightly controlled and therefore valid sampling method.

Psychodynamic techniques are not only useful for people with mental illnesses, but can be employed to enable people to function more effectively. For example, understanding early relationship problems and resolving them can help people to enjoy better adult relationships, both in the home and at work. By exposing and working through fears, people can become more confident and effective. Imagine a person who employs defence mechanisms such as projection. They may be argumentative and critical – not the best way to make friends or get on with the neighbours!

There are also possible problems with psychodynamic therapies. Apart from being very expensive and demanding in terms of time, it can have negative effects. An understanding of one's unconscious motives, such as the need for dependency, can lead to relationship breakdown. For example, if a patient begins to understand that they don't have to be dependent they can begin to cope on their own. Another potential problem is the focus of the therapy on our childhood. It may be more effective to look to the future than to dwell on the past. Finally, at AS you may have explored the problems associated with recovered memories. Whilst an extreme case, such problems can arise in some instances of psychodynamic therapy and it can be difficult to distinguish real recovered memories from false ones.

Interactive angles

Apply concepts from the psychodynamic approach to explain how it has contributed to society in one of the following contexts:

● understanding homophobia

● understanding the purpose and meaning of dreams

● understanding how unconscious motives can affect behaviour such as shopping.

Contributions of the biological approach to society

Biological research has shown us how neurotransmitters act at synapses. Leading on from that, researchers have explored the roles of different neurotransmitters and the way synapses can respond to drug molecules in place of neurotransmitters. This has led to benefits in terms of the treatment of mental illnesses. If you have studied health psychology, you will also know about advances in the treatment of people with drug dependencies, which would be an alternative topic for the contribution of the biological approach to society (see page 100).

Drugs and mental illnesses

In the biological approach at AS, and in your studies of clinical psychology at A2, you will have explored the use of drugs in the treatment of schizophrenia and other mental illnesses such as depression and obsessive-compulsive disorder (OCD). The examples below can be found in *Angles on Psychology for AS*. A meta-analysis conducted by Adams *et al.* (2005) found chlorpromazine to be effective in 48% of patients with schizophrenia. One of the possible causes of schizophrenia, based on the biological approach, is that the individual has too much dopamine in certain brain areas. Chlorpromazine acts by blocking the access of dopamine to the receptors on the post-synaptic membrane, therefore reducing its effect. This reduces the positive symptoms of schizophrenia.

A similar pattern is seen in the treatment of depression. Here one biological explanation is a lack of the neurotransmitter serotonin. One route for drug therapy is to artificially increase the efficacy of existing serotonin. This can be done by slowing down the recycling of the neurotransmitter into the pre-synaptic membrane. A group of drugs called the selective serotonin reuptake inhibitors (SSRIs) do exactly this. Trivedi *et al.* (2006) found that the SSRI Citilopram produced a 47% reduction in symptoms of depression over a 14-week treatment period. A related drug, Escitilopram, is used to treat the symptoms of OCD as well as depression. Although it is effective, as with many other drugs, part of the patients' response is the result of a placebo effect. Fineberg *et al.* (2007) found that of a group of 320 patients with OCD who were known to respond to Escitilopram, only 52% relapsed when treated with just a placebo (compared to 23% of the drug group). Although the placebo is clearly less effective than the drug itself, it did prevent almost half of the control group from relapsing. This suggests that the efficacy of drug treatment relies on more than just the direct effect of the drug on the target neurotransmitter. However, studies such as Fineberg *et al.*'s are highly controlled, using random allocation of participants to control and drug groups and double-blind procedures. This raises the validity and reliability of the findings.

Another problem is that such drugs are often developed using animal research. For example Rung *et al.* (2005a,b) used drugs to induce and reverse schizophrenia-like symptoms in rats. They produced symptoms such as social withdrawal and changes in motor activity. Although this enabled them to ascertain that the drug therapy could reverse the symptoms, such results may not generalise to schizophrenia in humans. The symptoms induced may not have the same causal processes so the treatment may not be effective for the actual disorder and, even if the biochemical model is accurate, the findings from animal studies may not reflect the changes in cognition or behaviour experienced by people. This is particularly important in investigating treatments for disorders such as depression and schizophrenia in which many of the symptoms are cognitive or affective rather than behavioural – these are much harder to investigate effectively using animal models.

Interactive angles

Apply concepts from the biological approach to explain how it has contributed to society in one of the following contexts:

● understanding the causes of sleep disorders

● understanding how to treat disorders such as Parkinson's disease using gene therapy

● understanding the limitations of gender reassignment.

Anti-fat pill fiasco

The wonder drug for obesity has turned nasty. Acomplia, a prescription drug used to help obese people to lose weight, has been withdrawn.

Acomplia, also known by the name of its active ingredient rimonabant, works on the same brain circuits that give people the munchies when they smoke marijuana. It blocks the action of natural chemicals that attach to cannabinoid receptors – slots in the membranes of brain cells that are there to receive stimulation from our body's own cannabis-like molecules.

It turns out that Acomplia nearly doubles the likelihood of developing a psychiatric disorder such as anxiety, depression, a sleep disorder or becoming aggressive. It also increases the risk of suicide with five cases being reported in trials worldwide in the three months June to August 2008. Only one person in any placebo group committed suicide. The drug seems to be less effective in treating overweight people and has greater risks than clinical trials suggested. Basically, it's safer to be fat than sorry.

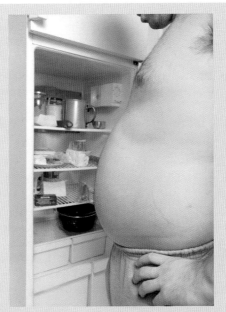

Figure 6.6 Is it safe to prescribe drugs that affect cannabinoid receptors?

1. **Use your understanding of biological psychology to discuss this news report.**

Contributions of the learning approach to society: behaviourism

The learning approach to psychology is about the ways in which behaviour can be changed, for example by stimuli and consequences in the environment. This leads to useful applications to society in terms of being able to deliberately change people's behaviour and to exploring ways to limit the potential for damage caused by exposure to inappropriate models.

Behaviour therapy and behaviour modification

Learning theories have led to ways to help people by changing their behaviour. Classical conditioning underlies behaviour therapies such as systematic desensitisation and aversion therapy. Systematic desensitisation is used to help to reduce phobias and works by pairing a calm state with increasingly fearsome objects in a stepped procedure. In Chapter 5 you learned about the use of systematic desensitisation with technophobes. They were less anxious about computers after a 10-week course than control participants (Brosnan & Thorpe, 2006). However, it isn't always effective as Duff et al. (2007) found – see page 164. People with an anxiety about public speaking did improve over the course, but so did those who did not receive treatment. One explanation for this is that confronting the fear directly, as happens in flooding, is just as effective if much less ethical.

Aversion therapy aims to reduce undesirable behaviours, such as drinking alcohol in alcoholics. It works by associating an unpleasant (aversive) unconditioned stimulus with the to-be-removed behaviour; for example, using an emetic drug which causes the individual to vomit on consuming alcoholic drinks. Howard (2001) found that the level of aversion caused by this therapy was very specific to alcoholic drinks so was a safe way to treat people with alcoholism.

The procedure has been used to treat other problems such as inappropriate sexual arousal in sex offenders (Weinrott *et al.*, 1997) and self-harming in children (Duker & Seys, 2000). Whilst these are examples of use which clearly benefit society, other examples have been less justifiable, for example historical (and modern) attempts to 'cure' homosexuality.

Behaviour modification techniques, including token economies, are based on operant conditioning. The token economy has been used in many different settings including schools, mental hospitals and prisons. The aim is to reinforce desirable behaviours such as hard work or socialisation. Secondary reinforcers or 'tokens' are given out by staff immediately the individual engages in the desired behaviour. These are saved up and exchanged for primary reinforcers such as CDs, luxury foods or outings. It can be used to shape behaviour, gradually reinforcing closer and closer approximations to the behaviour to be acquired. In this way, new behaviours can be learned.

In mental hospitals, token economies are not necessarily used to reduce symptoms, but to encourage rehabilitation. For example, Paul & Lentz (1977) found that the technique successfully increased self-care and pro-social behaviour. Although Paul & Lentz found that over 97% of patients who had previously been unsuitable for discharge from a state hospital setting were able to live in the community within two years of the programme. However, in many instances the learning does not generalise beyond the institutional setting as the new responses extinguish in the absence of external rewards. There are also ethical issues with the use of token economies.

Limiting the effects of violence in the media

Considerable evidence demonstrates a link between exposure to violence in the media and aggressive behaviour. Laboratory experiments such as Bandura's and other studies including natural experiments (Williams, 1985) and correlational analyses (Eron *et al.*, 1972) have found that exposure to violence on television is linked to later aggressive behaviour and to criminality. Such findings can be explained by social learning theory. Models displaying aggressive behaviour are observed and imitated. This is especially likely when they are the same gender, likeable and powerful. One problem with characters on television, in video games and in the public eye is that they are indeed highly effective models. A cartoon character, for example, may be funny and celebrities wield considerable power. These models are even more likely to be imitated if their behaviour is seen to reap rewards – this is vicarious reinforcement. Again, many role models are seen to receive positive reinforcement: cartoon characters and baddies in films 'win' and celebrities earn huge salaries. These factors present a problem for parents and authorities concerned about the effect of models on behaviour, especially of children.

Media watch

Nervous of the news? Take a token

Professors Joel Goldberg and M Weisenberg of Bar-Ilan University, Israel, have helped a boy overcome his fear of newspapers. The nine year old boy, known only as 'E', developed the phobia over a four-year period. Becoming ever more frightened, E's life was eventually governed by avoiding the risk of seeing a newspaper.

Goldberg and Weisenberg developed a scheme to reduce his fear that his parents used in the home. The treatment involved giving E a reward each time he coped with something related to newspapers. Oddly, the rewards weren't even worth having, just a token he could save up to get a real treat. Even though he was combating his fear for no instant gain, it made a difference.

Figure 6.7 Coping with your worst fear could be as strange as holding a broadsheet.

1. Use your understanding of the learning approach to psychology to discuss this news report.

Of course, not all evidence demonstrates such a link. For example Charlton *et al.* (2000), in a natural experiment on the effects of introducing transmitted television, found it had no negative effect on behaviour. These children were, however, exceptional in their initial behaviour and in the control exerted by their community. In general, evidence suggests that there is a need for social controls. These are implemented through measures such as the 9:00pm watershed, before which television programme content is restricted, and through certification. All films and video games are required to carry an indication of their suitability for different age groups on the basis of their content.

Interactive angles

Apply concepts from the learning approach to explain how it has contributed to society in one of the following contexts:

● understanding why gambling is so compelling

● understanding why sexism in the media matters.

How do the applications to psychology contribute to society?

The applications of psychology which you have learned about in your A2 studies are directly relevant to society. Each area uses theories and studies to explore the ways in which the topic has been used in the real world and the extent to which this has been effective. Some of these are extensions of the applications we have seen in the AS approaches. Use your understanding of psychological concepts to tackle some of the interactive angles questions posed above.

Contributions of criminological psychology to society

Criminological psychology makes contributions to society at many stages of the criminal justice process. When suspects are being identified, ideas about leading questions and reconstructive memory can help to ensure that the best possible information is retrieved by eyewitnesses. You may also have considered the role psychology plays in identifying perpetrators of crime using offender profiling or importance of psychological theory in conducting fair trials.

Figure 6.8 How does society benefit from the use of psychological techniques with offenders?

Once convicted of a crime, attempts may be made to reduce the likelihood of recidivism in offenders, using such techniques as anger management or token economies. You may also have explored the extent to which controlling the diet of prisoners helps to reduce antisocial behaviour.

Media watch

'I thought Paul was a success story': Paul is dead. Aycliffe, Durham, is home to some of Britain's most disturbed children. But can it help them?

Ann McFerran

The Independent, 14 December 1992 [edited]

Tony McCaffrey does not remember clearly all the children who have passed through his care. But he has never forgotten Paul. 'He was epileptic and diabetic, devious and violent. I learnt my whole job from that boy.'

Like other children who are sent to Aycliffe, the Durham centre that houses some of Britain's most disturbed children,

Paul's background was one of violence and family break-up. He had defeated the efforts of many other care agencies. 'At its simplest level, our job was to make him responsible for his own life,' says Mr McCaffrey, who ran Franklin House at Aycliffe. Paul once attempted to stab this gently spoken master; he also frequently faked diabetic comas.

When Michael Whyte went to Durham in 1977 to make Aycliffe, his acclaimed ITV documentary, the cameras watched Mr McCaffrey struggle with his task. At Franklin House, the basis of corrective behaviour was a system of rewards and punishments. 'Good' behaviour was rewarded with tokens called 'Franklins'; 'bad' behaviour, which was seen as 'attention-seeking', was ignored and later punished by fines of tokens. If a child misbehaved — frequently a temper tantrum, or in Paul's case, not eating his food — the other children were paid tokens to ignore his bad behaviour. Despite many hiccups, Paul's behaviour gradually seemed to improve.

Mr McCaffrey, who developed the token economy system, says: 'I realised you can't see behaviour in a vacuum. It became obvious to me that who gave the token mattered most. A token from me, the boss, really counted. Tokens from a care worker, whom the kids had nicknamed 'Robot', were tossed back at him. It was the relationship that mattered.'

Last winter, when Polly Bide set out to make a film about what had happened to the seven children featured in Mr Whyte's original documentary, Paul was the only one she was unable to trace. He died eight years ago, when he was 22, having failed to take his insulin. His body lay for two months in his council flat. 'Ironically, we thought he was one of our success stories,' Mr McCaffrey said when he learnt of Paul's fate.

What now emerges from the histories of the other six children is a bleak picture of persistent criminality, failure to cope and victimisation. Every one of the men has spent some time in prison. Two are living in Salvation Army hostels. Janice, the only woman interviewed, who endured a home life of horrendous abuse, has spent most of her adult life drugged, in mental institutions. 'I can't relate to anyone,' she says. 'I'd like to have children, but I can't because of what's been done to me.'

The unavoidable conclusion is an indictment of how our society treats its most damaged young people. Incredible as it seems today, Aycliffe in the Seventies overlooked the effects of possible sexual abuse. In retrospect, the token economy seems a totally inadequate response to such disturbed children.

David's violent temper tantrums, for example, appeared to be contained by the token economy. He collected a record 5,000 tokens, and was awarded an expensive racing bike by Aycliffe's boss, Masud Hoghughi. But in the outside world rewards for good behaviour do not exist. Since he left Aycliffe, David has been jailed countless times, usually for violent behaviour. 'We didn't touch what was bothering him,' Mr McCaffrey says. 'We barely scratched the surface.'

Eddie, who frequently had uncontrollable rages in which he destroyed his few precious possessions, now lives a vagrant existence, unable to hold down a job. There is no evidence from the 1992 film that the patterns of damaged behaviour that marred these children's lives has been helped by Aycliffe's treatment: the roots of their disturbance have not been touched and they cannot cope with life outside institutions.

In the 1977 film, Mr Hoghughi, who has been at Aycliffe for 25 years, chillingly diagnosed 'a new disorder in children which has no precedent: children who are increasingly murderous and persistently suicidal in an ever-increasing spiral'.

Watching Aycliffe's Children, which is shown on Channel 4's Cutting Edge tonight, depressed him. 'We did the best we could and it wasn't enough.' But he says: 'If you were to bring cameras into Aycliffe today, you would see an even greater range of bizarre and disturbed behaviour. The children now are coming out with the most incredible horror stories of sexual and physical abuse.' Today, Aycliffe's children include an 11-year-old girl who killed a baby; a 16-year-old boy who tried to gas his family; and an 11-year-old girl with a frightening history of sexual and physical abuse, criminality, aggression and continual running away. 'These children are sophisticated failures when they arrive at Aycliffe,' Mr Hoghughi says.

The token economy still exists at Aycliffe, but today Mr Hoghughi also uses other methods, including a unit run by a cognitive therapist for children with severe aggression problems. 'I would try anything, even voodoo, if I thought it worked,' he says.

'But part of the tragedy is that here we are with all our faults — trailblazers, at the cutting edge of what is done for these children. In a sense, Aycliffe is the pathology laboratory of the nation: unless we identify the diseased processes of our society, we may never help.'

1. How was the original token economy used at Aycliffe?

2. How successful was it?

3. What are suggested as causes of violent and criminal behaviour?

Another way in which the criminological approach can contribute to society is by identifying the causes of criminal behaviour. As described on page 6, recognising the role that social learning plays in the acquisition of aggressive behaviours enables society to respond to reduce the risks. Similarly, the effect of labelling and stereotyping can guide strategies for the rehabilitation of offenders. For example, Ageton & Elliott (1974) found that boys displaying delinquent behaviour who experienced police and court proceedings had lower self-esteem and more delinquent self-concepts. This could lead to even more antisocial behaviour suggesting that a 'light-touch' treatment of youth offenders may have merits in order for them to avoid developing a criminal label. The same self-fulfilling prophecy argument can be applied to the questionable value of making offenders under community orders wear fluorescent jackets demonstrating their criminal tendencies.

Interactive angles

1. Explain how society can benefit through the use of anger management programmes with violent offenders.

2. An understanding of the biological causes of criminality is unlikely to lead to direct treatments. However, recognising that some individuals may be predisposed to aggressive behaviour may be of benefit to society. Consider the potential advantages and disadvantages of possible interventions.

Contributions of child psychology to society

Child psychology can help society to provide the best opportunities for children to grow into happy, capable, well-balanced adults and to limit the effects of damage to their development when it arises.

One of the important contributions from child psychology is an understanding of the role of attachments in children's development. Bowlby's ideas about the central role of the care-giver indicates some of the characteristics of good parenting and has enabled child psychologists to explain the effects of deprivation and privation.

Bowlby (1957, 1969) identified the role of sensitive responsiveness. A mother who responds to the infant's social releasers early in their development helps the child to form an attachment. It is therefore important for the main carer to be present most of the time, attentive to the child and responsive to them. This is vital because the formation of a strong attachment helps the child to feel secure and to develop successfully in both social and cognitive domains.

For example, Banse (2004) found that adults who had been securely attached as children were more satisfied with their marital relationships in adulthood. Conversely, negative effects are associated with insecure attachments. In a sample of males, Smallbone & Dadds (2000) showed that insecure attachment was linked to aggression and antisocial behaviour.

The effects of attachment appear to be progressive, with a child's early experiences affecting their own behaviour as a parent. A child who internalises a working model of others as attentive, loving and reliable will enter future relationships with this expectation. A neglected or abused child, in contrast, may seek out or display these behaviours themselves in adulthood. Such risks are illustrated by the findings of Bailey *et al.* (2007) who studied teenage mothers and their babies. The teenagers with insecure attachments to their own parents were likely to have insecurely attached babies themselves. These findings have implications for society in terms of supporting young mothers and those experiencing difficulties in forming attachments to their children.

Short-term separation, such as when a parent or child needs hospital treatment, can be distressing for the child. Robertson & Bowlby (1952) illustrated how a child's deteriorating emotional state during a short hospital stay can damage the bond with a main carer, with protest leading to despair and detachment. Whilst many factors affect the stability of attachments, such as the seriousness of the condition, society has changed the way children and their parents are viewed in hospitals. Visiting is much less restricted and parents can sometimes sleep in the hospital in order to provide emotional support for their children.

Media watch

Keeping families of sick children together

RMHC – Ronald McDonald House Charities – is an independent charity which aims to provide free 'home away from home' accommodation in hospitals, enabling families to stay close to their child and maintain a degree of normal family life.

The charity has achieved a lot in the last 20 years. Twelve Ronald McDonald Houses have been built which, along with 29 sets of Ronald McDonald Family Rooms, provide over 350 bedrooms every single night of the year.

Figure 6.9 The first RMH at Guy's and St Thomas' in London.

However, there is still a great deal to do. Many families still have to sleep on camp beds or in their cars in order to be close to their children, and RMHC is determined to help as many of these as possible.

The first Ronald McDonald House in the UK opened in June 1990. Eighteen families can be accommodated in comfortable family rooms with the use of self-catering kitchens, sitting rooms, laundry facilities, playroom and a peaceful garden. Most of the families that stay at the House have children receiving treatment at The Evelina Children's Hospital at Guy's.

1. Using your understanding of child psychology, explain why having Ronald McDonald accommodation in hospitals is so important.

Long-term separation, such as from family reordering, is associated with developmental problems including lower educational attainment and behavioural problems (Richards, 1995). However, it is unclear whether this is due to the reordering itself or the problems many families encounter – such as parental discord – and their consequences for the children. For example, Cockett & Tripp (1994) found that children of reordered families experienced problems such as lower self-image, school success and health than children with intact families. An important finding for society was that so few children had been prepared for the separation of their parents and few had regular contact with the absent parent. These findings show that child psychology can identify ways to help children who experience long-term separation by keeping them informed about what is happening and supporting their need to see absent parents to whom they are attached.

Interactive angles

1. Many members of modern society rely on daycare for their children. Imagine that you are a daycare provider.

   (a) Some concerns have been raised about the negative effects of daycare on children. Explain why society should be concerned.

   (b) In defence of your daycare facility, what arguments would you offer to counter these claims?

Contributions of health psychology to society

Health psychology aims to promote healthy behaviour and to enable people to benefit from psychological interventions to improve health care and overcome health problems. For example, by investigating the risks to health and cognitive function posed by drug-taking, psychological research is able to inform users about the dangers of drug misuse. Furthermore, an understanding of the mechanisms of addiction helps us to guide the development of strategies to reduce addictive behaviours. These strategies contribute to the health and safety of people in society.

Health campaigns to reduce drug use

As the saying goes, 'prevention is better than cure'. If we can help people to avoid becoming dependent on drugs, they will be healthier and society will benefit from reduced health-care costs. In order to achieve this, campaigns aim to reduce drug use by providing knowledge about harm.

Health campaigns such as 'Talk to FRANK' provide information about drug use to give young people sufficient knowledge to allow them to make reasoned decisions about drug use. In order that the messages are effective, they must be accurate, believable and not too frightening. Surveys investigating use of and attitudes to FRANK suggest that it has been largely successful in these aims. Mitchell (2008) found that around four fifths of young people recognised the FRANK adverts and knew about the website so knew how to access health information relating to drugs. Furthermore, the messages appeared to have done more than just make them aware of where to seek information. Those individuals who did recognise an advert also believed that drug taking was more risky than individuals who did not recognise an advert (FRANK Review, April 2006). Realisation of the ambition of FRANK to be more acceptable to young people by avoiding being 'parental' was perhaps less successful with almost the same percentages trusting the FRANK phoneline as their mother (about 30%) and trusting the website as trusting their teachers (22%). Nevertheless, FRANK has been accessed by a huge number of individuals and is much better used than its predecessor. In this respect, it is a highly effective health intervention.

Helping drug misusers with behavioural interventions

Even when people have been given, and understand, information about the damage that drugs can do, they carry on taking them. Many smokers know the risks they are taking but smoke anyway. In these instances, behavioural interventions may be more helpful than health campaigns. Two learning theories, classical and operant conditioning, can offer ways to help people to change their behaviour.

In aversion therapy, the principles of classical conditioning aim to link the addictive behaviour to an unpleasant effect – such as vomiting. As the two stimuli are repeatedly paired so the individual comes to associate the unpleasant effect with their drug use, hence it becomes less appealing. This technique has been successful with both smokers (for example, using a rapid-smoking technique; Danaher, 1977) and with alcoholics (using the drug Antabuse; Howard, 2001).

Figure 6.10 How does society benefit from the psychological treatment of alcoholics?

Aversion therapy can be problematic, for example alcoholics can avoid taking their medication in order to drink and rapid smoking in itself carries dangers. Long-term drinkers and smokers with other smokers in their household were less likely to benefit from such programmes. In terms of helping people to quit, this means that other strategies also need to be offered if a range of people are to benefit.

Token economies employ operant conditioning, positively reinforcing individuals for maintaining appropriate behaviours, such as staying drug-free. Again, this has been successful in reducing addictive behaviours. A series of studies using a prize draw reward system like a token economy has found that abstinence could be maintained in stimulant abusers (Olmstead et al., 2007) and cocaine users (Sindelar et al., 2007).

The prize draw systems were even more effective when the prizes were bigger and although this meant the financial outlay was greater, the scheme was in fact run more economically. Furthermore, using a reinforcing system is more ethical than using aversive stimuli so in this sense token economy programmes are more ethical than ones using aversion.

In neither of these interventions, however, is any attempt made to identify or treat the initial cause of the addictive behaviour. This means that there is a risk that, given a similar set of predisposing circumstances, individuals could resume their habit. Until we can offer a fuller understanding of the causes of addictive behaviour such that the potential for relapse can be reduced, even after a long period of abstinence individuals may continue to be at risk.

Contributions of sport psychology to society

Sport is healthy for everyone and a route to career success for a few. In both of these domains, psychology can help to promote access to sport and success within a sport.

Widening participation in sport

Different things motivate different people to participate in and strive at a particular sport. Because girls and boys grow up differently, they often have different attitudes to sport. Think about women in boxing or boys in ballet. Koivula (1995) found in an investigation into the expectations of men and women about the suitability of different sports for each gender that women, and to a greater extent men, did hold stereotyped views. Furthermore, these attitudes affect later behaviour. Guillet et al. (2000) found that more feminine girls were less likely to carry on playing handball as they grew older.

Figure 6.11 The plot of the film *Billy Elliot* involves a boy who, even though he knows 'ballet is for girls', does it anyway. Why is this so unusual?

In order to counteract these stereotypes, psychologists can draw on learning theory. As Chalabaev et al. (2009) found that girls who believed that girls were less good at football than boys did indeed play worse, learning theory can be

181

used to promote more positive attitudes and correspondingly better performance. Operant conditioning, for example using positive reinforcers, such as ongoing praise and badges to mark success, should increase the amount of effort or practice an individual puts in. The role played by a parent, PE teacher or coach is therefore vitally important. Vicarious reinforcement matters too, especially when the model is seen to have similarities to the individual, such as being the same gender.

Of course, all of these are extrinsic motivators which, whilst easier to manipulate, are less effective than intrinsic motivators. A good coach, however, may even be able to raise intrinsic motivation. Wells *et al.* (1993) demonstrated how leading weightlifters to believe they were lifting more than they actually were helped them to actually do so. This self-efficacy is vital to success. An athlete therefore needs to be positively reinforced in order to have good self-belief.

In the zone: not too wound up, not too relaxed

One way to maximise performance of sportsmen and women is to use the idea of the optimum level of arousal. This is important in the mental preparation leading up to a competition. Depending on the nature of the sport, success may rely on being calm, such as in precision tasks like snooker, or raising arousal to improve power, such as in rugby. The difference arises because the optimum level of arousal differs with the complexity of the task with fine motor skills requiring lower levels and gross motor tasks needing much higher levels. A good trainer would therefore calm a snooker or darts player down but would psych a weightlifter or rugby team up. It is also important to understand audience effects as they too contribute to arousal.

Figure 6.12 How might the pre-event tactics of a coach differ for an archer and a shot-putter?

Contributions of clinical psychology to society

Clinical psychology has clearly contributed to society by developing a range of different therapies for mental illnesses. By helping people to overcome their symptoms, these interventions improve the quality of life for the affected individuals. There are also potential gains for their family, friends and for wider society. Clearly such benefits depend on being able to diagnose accurately in order to treat effectively, so indirectly the benefits to society accrue from the validity and reliability of diagnostic systems. In terms of cultural biases it is beneficial to society that diagnosis is accurate and consistent. Furthermore, where clear and avoidable risk factors have been identified in psychological research these are of benefit to society. For example, recognising the effect stress has on vulnerable individuals is important in ensuring that employers do not make unreasonable demands of their employees.

Figure 6.13 Why is the maintenance of a healthy work–life balance in society's interest?

Drug therapies

The treatment of many mental illnesses relies on the use of drugs. For schizophrenia antipsychotic drugs are used, including chlorpromazine (a first generation phenothiazine) and clozapine (a second generation antipsychotic). The older drugs had more side effects (such as weight gain and tardive dyskinesia) and were less effective. However, any drug is only effective if taken and patients may suffer relapses if they fail to do so (although they may relapse even when they do).

Since the symptoms of schizophrenia can be so impairing for the individual, it is very important to be able to offer effective treatment. In a comparison of two drugs, Schooler *et al.*

(1995) found that both produced a reduction of symptoms in 75% of patients, but the group treated with a second generation antipsychotic experienced fewer side effects and fewer patients relapsed.

Depression is also treated with drugs which again have changed over time resulting in a wide variety of medication currently in use including monoamine oxidase inhibitors (MAOIs), tricyclics and selective serotonin reuptake inhibitors (SSRIs). Since each of these works in a different way, they provide a variety of treatment options for different individuals and their use depends on both symptoms and side effects.

In a review of random control trials with placebo conditions, Arroll et al. (2005) found that 56–60% of patients taking antidepressants improved compared to 42–47% of those receiving a placebo. SSRIs took longer to work than tricyclics but had fewer side effects. Drug interventions treat symptoms rather than necessarily tackling the cause of a mental illness. In this respect some other courses of action, such as psychological therapies, may be more appropriate in some situations.

Cognitive behavioural therapy

Cognitive behavioural therapy (CBT) is a widely used psychological therapy. As it helps patients to identify irrational and unhelpful thoughts and try to change them it can be

of use in disorders such as schizophrenia, depression and obsessive-compulsive disorder.

In addition to helping individuals with schizophrenia to understand their symptoms, it can also normalise their experience – for example, recognising that hallucinations and delusions are also experienced by people without a diagnosis. Bradshaw (1998) reported the successful use of CBT with schizophrenia in a young woman, improving her understanding of her symptoms, socialisation, activity level and stress management. After a year of therapy her symptoms were so much reduced that she returned to education and paid work. After four years she still had not relapsed. Reviews of more cases of schizophrenia have also supported the success of CBT, especially in the long term (for example, Pilling et al., 2002).

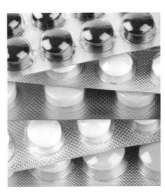

Figure 6.14 Which is best?

Media watch

Failing to hear the voices

We've all done it – shot past the dirty looking bag-carrying person engaged in an irate conversation with nobody.

Hallucinations, especially auditory ones, are symptoms of schizophrenia and, thanks to modern drugs, can be well controlled. The cognitive symptoms are even more debilitating – and don't even get a mention on DSM, the American system for deciding what's wrong with mentally ill patients.

The new solution of brain training might improve things. It aims to help affected individuals to learn to plan and

remember using a special computer game. Researchers have used it in labs and the Brain Gym patients were better after two-and-a-half hours a week over ten weeks than ones playing ordinary computer games.

Bruce Wexler at Yale University hopes to show that the Brain Gym will help people with schizophrenia to hold down a job – but will it work in real life? It's a whole different ball game from making a difference in a laboratory test.

1. The next edition of DSM, due out in 2012, should include cognitive symptoms in the diagnostic criteria for schizophrenia. As DSM-IV-TR stands, it does not. How does this affect its credibility?

2. To what extent can the success of Bruce Wexler's research be predicted from the previous studies?

CBT is also used to treat depression. It aims to re-establish a social life and activity, to challenge negative thinking and to help the individual to recognise signs of relapse. Evidence such as Butler *et al.* (2006) suggests that CBT is a highly effective treatment for depression. However, Holmes (2002) identified some issues such as that it is less effective in treating depression than drugs and less effective in patients with multiple problems and also that few studies had evaluated its effectiveness in the long term. It is important, therefore, that research continues to explore the relative efficacy of different treatments.

Interactive angles

Compare two of the following mental health interventions:

- ECT
- community care
- psychodynamic therapy.

Ethics in psychological research

You will already have encountered ethical issues and how to solve them both at AS and in earlier chapters. Here we will recap the range of ethical dilemmas that psychologists face and how they can deal with them effectively. For the examination, you will need to be able to describe five guidelines relating to humans and five relating to non-human animals. You also need to be able to describe and evaluate ethical issues in psychological research in relation to both humans and non-human animals, which could require you to consider unfamiliar material. Finally, you need to know two studies in detail which you can describe and evaluate in terms of ethical issues.

Ethical guidelines for psychological research with human participants

To help psychologists to deal with ethical issues arising in research and professional practice, the British Psychological Society (BPS) regularly updates its ethical guidelines. Since psychologists are concerned with people's welfare, it is important that these guidelines are followed. They are summarised in Box 6.3. When research is conducted at institutions such as universities, the planned study must be approved by an ethical committee. This ensures that these guidelines are being followed. Whilst the primary concern is for the welfare of individuals, another issue is the perception of psychology in society. Participants who are deceived or distressed may not want to participate again, may portray psychology in a poor light to others, and are unlikely or trust the findings of psychological research. These are all outcomes we would want to avoid.

Box 6.3

British Psychological Society (2006) Code of Ethics in summary

1. **Introduction:** the public need to have confidence in psychology, so the way that researchers treat participants is important as it affects public perception of all psychologists.

2. **General:** psychologists must always consider the ethical implications of their research. Foreseeable threats to the well-being, dignity, health and values of participants should be eliminated. They should only conduct research in areas where they are competent.

3. **Consent:** researchers must take reasonable steps to obtain *real* consent from participants. Real consent can only be given by participants who fully understand what they are agreeing to. Researchers should not use payment or their position of power over participants to persuade them to consent to activities.

4. **Deception:** deceiving participants should be avoided whenever possible. Participants should be told about the aim of the investigation as soon as possible. Deception should not be used when it is likely that participants will object or become distressed when debriefed.

5. **Debriefing:** whenever participants are aware that they have taken part in a study they should be given a full explanation of the research as soon as possible. Researchers should also ensure that the participants' experiences were not distressing and that they leave the study in at least as positive a mood as they entered it.

6. **Withdrawal:** participants should be made aware of their right to withdraw from a study at any point and that payment does not affect this right. When debriefed, participants have the right to withdraw their data.

7. **Confidentiality:** unless agreed with participants in advance, their individual results and any personal information about them should be completely confidential.

8. **Protection:** participants should be protected from physical and psychological harm, including stress. They should not be exposed to any more risk than they would encounter in their usual lifestyle.

9. **Observation:** observational studies risk invading privacy. If participants are unaware they are being observed, this should only be done in places and situations where they would expect people to watch them.

10. **Advice:** if a researcher sees signs of a physical or psychological problem that the participant is unaware of, but which might be a threat, they should inform them about it. Where participants seek professional advice the researcher should be cautious.

11. **Colleagues:** if colleagues are seen to break any of these principles, it is important to tell them and to try to persuade them to alter their conduct.

Interactive angles

In your AS you studied the classic research of Stanley Milgram (1965) on obedience.

1. Identify each of the ethical issues raised in this study and explain why these steps were necessary in order to achieve the aims.

2. Describe the steps that Milgram took to minimise the harm caused to participants (that is, the 'teacher').

3. Outline a study that illustrates an alternative way to investigate obedience that raises fewer ethical issues. Explain the relative advantages and disadvantages of this approach compared to Milgram's method.

Designing and conducting ethical research

Competence

When a psychologist plans a piece of research they should intend to work within the level of their own competence. This means that they should only attempt to do things for which they are sufficiently well trained and experienced and should update their training. This will enable them to foresee possible threats to the well-being, dignity, health and values of participants and thus to ensure that their work is designed and conducted ethically. If issues arise that challenge their professional ability they should seek the help of more experienced colleagues.

One component of competence is to limit the techniques used to those in which the researcher is qualified and/or experienced. For example, the use of therapeutic techniques such as cognitive-behavioural therapy, administering drugs and making diagnoses of mental illnesses all require specific training and experience. University and medical facility ethical committees consider competence when they approve research proposals. For example, the work by Blättler et al. (2002) was approved by an ethical committee at the Swiss Academy of Medical Sciences and the medical therapy was monitored by a safety assurance group (see page 101).

Interactive angles

If you studied health psychology, consider why Blättler et al.'s study in particular required such careful monitoring of competence.

Consent

It is often important in experiments to hide the aims from participants in order to reduce demand characteristics. However, potential participants also have the right to know what is going to happen so they can give their *informed consent*. These two opposing needs mean that it may be hard to get genuine consent. Ideally, researchers should obtain full and informed consent from participants by giving them sufficient information about the procedure to decide whether they want to participate. Payment, or the researcher's position of authority, should not be used to coerce participants into giving consent.

However, in some situations the researcher cannot ask for consent. This is often (but not always) the case in naturalistic observations and field experiments and in laboratory experiments where deception is used (see below). In these situations, a researcher can attempt to decide whether participants in the sample would be likely to object by asking other people. Using a group of people similar to those who will become participants, the researcher can ask whether they would find the study acceptable if they were involved. This is called *presumptive consent* because it allows the researcher to *presume* that the actual participants would also be happy to participate.

In Yuille & Cutshall's (1985) study of eyewitness testimony, informed consent was sought from 20 witnesses to a real shooting (see page 24). Seven of these chose not to participate, that is, given enough information they opted against joining the sample. Two of the witnesses had moved away from the area and another five did not want to be participants in the study. One of these was the victim.

Figure 6.15 Providing sufficient information about the study is ethically important. If you were the victim of a violent crime wouldn't you want to have enough information to decide whether to relive the experience for research?

In studies of children, particular care must be taken. In a school or playgroup, consent from the institution as well as the guardians is essential. Children themselves should be asked for their consent if they are aware that they are being watched and should also have the right to withdraw. Researchers need to be mindful that children may express their desire to leave a study in different ways from adults, such as by not wanting to join in or walking away. It is important that such indicators are recognised and responded to.

Interactive angles

If you studied criminal psychology, consider why Krackow & Lynn (2003) required informed consent from the parents of the children (page 197).

Deception

Whilst it is ethically ideal to allow participants to give fully informed, real consent, sometimes this is counterproductive to the aims of the research. Imagine if Milgram had said 'This is a study about obedience, I'm interested in seeing how far you will obey me when I asked you to potentially, though not really, hurt, or perhaps kill, another person'. It just wouldn't have 'worked' as the participants would have known that the situation involved neither legitimate authority nor actual harm to the 'learner'. The study would not, therefore, have been a valid test of the effect of the situation on obedience. So, in a small number of cases, deception is essential but it should be avoided whenever possible. Furthermore, it should not be used if the participants are likely to object to what has happened to them or to become distressed when they find out. Remember, Milgram's study was done over 40 years ago. If deception is used, participants should be told the aim of the investigation as soon as possible.

Rosenhan (1973) investigated the behaviour of hospital staff towards patients who had a diagnosis of schizophrenia based on pretend symptoms (see page 138). In this study deception was necessary in order to achieve the aims as the staff had to be unaware of the real role of the pseudopatients.

Debriefing of participants

It is important to debrief participants for many reasons. They should be informed of the purpose of the research and the intended outcomes as well as correcting any misunderstandings. This is important as the feelings of participants towards psychology as a whole can affect their trust in the findings of research and the potential success of applications. The public face of psychology needs to ensure that participants feel positively about their experience.

If participants have been negatively affected by a study, for example, if it has caused unforeseen harm or discomfort, the researcher has a responsibility to return them to their previous condition. Whilst this is one of the reasons for debriefing participants it should not be used in place of designing an ethical study.

Right to withdraw

Participants have the right to leave a study at any time if they wish. This is their right to withdraw and it must be observed, even if this means data are lost. Whilst participants can be

offered incentives to join a study, these cannot be taken back if they leave – so they do not feel compelled to continue. Nor should researchers use their position of authority to encourage participants to continue beyond the point where they want to stop. In practice, this means that researchers must make the right to withdraw explicit to participants and be prepared to relinquish data if a participant chooses to withdraw. So if, in a repeated measures design, a participant leaves between the first and second testing, their data from the first condition cannot be used.

Wilhelm *et al.* (2006) investigated life events, genetics and depression (see page 153). They obtained informed consent for the collection of both psychological and physiological data. The participants were followed up every five years. At the 20 year point, 149 of the original 165 participants remained. Some could not be located or had died and four exercised their right to withdraw. This is an example of a longitudinal study where attrition over time means the sample shrinks. Although this is problematic for the researchers, they must not pressurise participants to continue especially as over time this may become more onerous (for example, if they move away).

Protection from harm

Studies have the potential to cause participants psychological harm (for example, distress) or physical harm (for example, engaging in risky behaviours such as taking drugs). In these situations, participants have the right to be protected and should not be exposed to any greater risk than they would be in their normal life. If participants have been negatively affected by a study the debrief can be used to return them to their previous condition but this is *not* an alternative to designing an ethical study. It is therefore important to consider all the ways in which a study could cause distress and to minimise them.

For example, Eranti *et al.* (2007) evaluated the effectiveness of ECT, and a therapy using a magnetic field (rTMS), for depression (see pages 188, 196 & 205). They excluded possible participants from the study for their own safety if they had metallic implants or foreign bodies. This ensured the participants were protected from physical harm in relation to exposure to magnetic fields. The same precaution is taken with any participant in studies using MRI, such as Lewine *et al.* (1990), since the scanner uses a very powerful magnetic field.

Figure 6.16 Potential participants for studies using MRI scanners are asked about metal objects inside their bodies (such as pacemakers or shrapnel) in order to protect them from physical harm as the scanner contains a powerful magnet.

Turkington et al. (2002) investigated the effectiveness of different treatments for schizophrenia (see page 147). To satisfy the right of participants to be protected from psychological harm, all were offered CBT as part of the experiment or immediately following this they were part of the control group. This ensured that the control group was not disadvantaged by having not received the therapy.

Interactive angles

Rosenhan (1973) investigated the behaviour of hospital staff towards patients who had a diagnosis of schizophrenia based on pretend symptoms.

1. Identify the ethical issues raised in this study and explain why these steps were necessary in order to achieve the aims.

2. Describe the steps that were taken to minimise the harm caused to participants (ie the hospital staff) and to the confederates (the pseudopatients).

3. Outline an alternative way to investigate the aim that would have raised fewer ethical issues. Explain the relative advantages and disadvantages of this approach compared to Rosenhan's method.

Confidentiality

Figure 6.17 Privacy and confidentiality should still be maintained even when consent cannot be obtained.

In general, a participant's personal information, including their data, should be kept confidential. It should not be disclosed by the researchers, should be stored securely and when the findings are published individuals (or contributing institutions such as schools or hospitals) should not be identifiable.

Participants' identities can be protected by allocating each person a number and using this to identify them. In experiments with an independent groups design this helps to keep a record of which condition each participant was in. In repeated measures designs participant numbers are used for pairing up an individual's scores in each condition.

Interactive angles

How did Morgan & Grube (1991) (page 95) ensure the confidentiality of their participants' data?

When completing a test or questionnaire in a laboratory situation, participants should be given an individual space in order to ensure the confidentiality of their data.

The only exceptions to this general principle are that personally identifiable information can be communicated when the individual gives their prior informed consent to do so or, in exceptional circumstances, when the safety or interests of the individual or others may be at risk.

Interactive angles

Plan a study to investigate whether people with depression are less likely to find positive words in anagrams than negative ones. Include in your design variables that you will control and steps you will take to make sure that the study is ethical.

Which words would a person with depression find?

frae	acres
dandes	idm
rathet	veil
spedres	orels
gwonr	brad

Answers on next page

Observations and privacy

Any study which asks for personal information or observes people risks invading privacy. In a questionnaire for example a researcher should make clear to participants their right to ignore questions they do not want to answer, thus protecting their privacy.

In observations, people should only be watched in situations where they would expect to be on public display. When conducting a case study, including those of larger groups such as institutions, confidentiality is still important and identities must be hidden. For example, the identities of schools or hospitals should be concealed. When observing children, particular caution is necessary. Children should not be observed in public places and never without the consent of their guardians.

Interactive angles

Klimek *et al.* (1997) (page 154) interviewed the next-of-kin of suicide victims (and of control participants) whose bodies were to be used in an investigation on brain abnormalities and depression.

Koster *et al.* (2005) (page 155) tested depressed and non-depressed participants using lists of words which included the following: Worthless Loser Failure Inferior Rejected Lonely Desperate Useless Vulnerable Incompetent Unwanted Hopeless Lost.

What special ethical care would need to be taken in these instances?

Answers to anagrams on page 187:

frae	fear	fare
acres	scare	cares/races
dandes	sadden	sanded
idm	dim	mid
rathet	threat	hatter
veil	vile/evil	live
spedres	depress	pressed
orels	loser	roles
gwonr	wrong	grown
brad	drab	bard

Interactive angles

1. Use the Research Now box to evaluate Omoaregba *et al.*'s study in terms of ethical issues.

2. Eranti *et al.* (2007) invited participants who had been referred for ECT for depression by a psychiatrist and were at least 18 years old to join their study. Possible participants were excluded if they had a history of seizures, were unable to give informed consent or refused to do so. Patients received their usual medical care and medications during the study and the study was approved by local ethical committees. Potential participants received a complete description of the study, written informed consent was obtained and the patients were not blind to their allocated treatment. Participants were asked about side effects (such as scalp discomfort or hearing loss). Five patients in the rTMS group terminated treatment early because they felt they were not improving, and one patient could not attend a session. All but one agreed to being assessed following treatment.

   Describe the ethical issues raised in this study and explain how they were dealt with.

Research now

Omoaregba, J.O., James, B.O. & Eze, G.O. (2009)

'Schizophrenia spectrum disorders in a Nigerian family: 4 case reports'

Cases Journal, 2: 14

Aim: To investigate a family with four members affected by a schizophrenia spectrum disorder and to observe how cultural beliefs affect and hinder management of the condition.

Method: Four sisters with schizophrenia spectrum disorders from one Nigerian family of Ibo tribal origin were investigated (Miss P, Miss X, Mrs Q and Mrs Y). They had all been previously diagnosed and had responded, if only marginally, to drug treatments. Two women also received psychotherapy to resolve psychosocial problems. Written consent was obtained from each of the women for the publication of detailed information about their health and their family. They were interviewed to investigate their own interpretations of their symptoms and to look for evidence of a family history of schizophrenia-like symptoms. The women's other siblings and mother, and Mrs Q's husband, were also interviewed.

Results: All the women experienced symptoms of schizophrenia such as delusions and/or hallucinations. Many of these were interpreted by the patients as religious (for example, Miss P believed that she must stay pure and isolated as she was the wife of Jesus Christ and Mrs Y heard voices telling her to 'fulfil her calling as a priestess'). Miss P refused to take her medication, believing it to be poisoned. Mrs Q was reported to be irritable and unhappy and refused to accept that she was ill. The mother refused to allow Mrs Y home if she continued to be a priestess because she believed the daughter's consultations and prayers attracted evil spirits which could harm them. Through the family therapy (and without divulging the reason) Mrs Y was encouraged to live away from the family home and was happy to do so, as it enabled her to continue her work as a diviner. No history of schizophrenia in the parents was identified, although an older sister had also been affected. During the interview Mrs Y was unco-operative. Mrs Y was also agitated during the interview, with poor attention and concentration.

Conclusion: Western models of mental illness are not necessarily accepted in developing cultures and there are corresponding limitations to contemporary treatment so interventions need to be evaluated in terms of their cultural relevance. In this instance the efficacy of drug and family therapy was affected by the beliefs of the patients and their family.

Using non-human animals in psychological research

There are several reasons for using animals in psychological research and we need to bear these in mind when considering ethical arguments relating to their use. Driscoll & Bateson (1988) identified four reasons for using animals:

- to understand natural principles – animals provide convenient models for processes such as learning
- some procedures cannot be carried out ethically on humans – for example, isolation, lesioning
- animals are especially good examples of some phenomena – for example, communication in birds
- animals are interesting in their own right – for example, bat sonar or whale song.

Ethical principles for psychological research with non-human animals

From 1876, animals used in scientific experiments in Britain have been protected by the Cruelty to Animals Act. With regard to experimentation, this has been replaced by the Animals (Scientific Procedures) Act (1986) which ensures that any research requires a project licence covering:

- **procedures:** the degree of *animal suffering* is weighed up against the *certainty of medical benefit*
- **animals:** their breeding, supply, daily care and veterinary treatment are monitored
- **premises:** these are checked by inspectors.

Figure 6.18 Animals in experiments are protected by law.

In order to help psychologists to fulfil these requirements, the British Psychological Society provides guidelines to assist researchers in planning their research.

Interactive angles

In your AS you may have studied the classic research of Pickens & Thompson (1968) on the effects of drugs on learning in rats.

1. Identify each of the ethical issues raised in this study and explain why these steps were necessary in order to achieve the aims.

2. Describe the steps that Pickens & Thompson took to minimise the harm caused to the animals.

3. Outline a study that illustrates an alternative way to investigate the effects of drugs that raises fewer ethical issues. Explain the relative advantages and disadvantages of this approach compared to Pickens & Thompson's method.

BPS Guidelines for the Use of Animals in Research (1985)

These guidelines aim to minimise the discomfort caused to living animals in experiments. They expect researchers to seek veterinary advice when unsure and to consider:

- **ethics and legislation:** if animals are confined, harmed, stressed or in pain, suffering should be minimised. Researchers should ensure that the means justify the ends and that replacing animal experiments with other alternatives have been considered (such as videos from previous studies or computer simulations) and should work within the law.

- **species:** the chosen species should be the ones least likely to suffer pain or distress. Factors such as whether the animals were bred in captivity, their previous experience of experimentation and the sentience of the species should be considered.

- **number of animals:** only the minimum number of animals required that will produce valid and reliable results should be used. To achieve this appropriate pilot studies, reliable measures of behaviour, good experimental design and appropriate choice of statistical tests are essential.

- **procedures:** in experiments causing death, disease, injury, physiological or psychological distress or discomfort researchers should, if possible, use a design which enhances rather than impoverishes the animals' experience (eg contrasting early enrichment on development compared to normal rather than early deprivation) or consider using naturally occurring instances (eg where stress arises naturally in the animal's environment or life time). Researchers conducting such experiments must hold and comply with a Home Office licence, eg in the provision of proper daily care for the animals, having appropriate veterinary attention and being able to justify any costs to the animals and the scientific benefit of the work.

- **reward, deprivation and aversive stimulation:** in planning deprivation studies researchers should consider the normal feeding or drinking patterns of the animals and their needs (for example, carnivores eat less frequently than herbivores, young animals need more continuous access to food and water). Highly preferred food should be considered as an alternative to deprivation (eg for reinforcement in learning studies). Alternatives to aversive stimuli and deprivation should be used where possible.

- **isolation and crowding:** caging conditions should depend on the social behaviour of the animals (for example, isolation will be more distressing for social species than solitary ones). Overcrowding can cause distress and aggression (therefore also physical harm). The level of stress experienced by individuals should also be considered (eg the animal's age, sex, and status: is it dominant?).

- **aggression and predation:** damage caused to an experimental animal by another animal is still the responsibility of the researcher and deliberately causing such harm should be avoided, eg by using natural rather than staged encounters or models rather than live animals. Where real encounters are used the number should be minimised, barriers and escape routes should be available and there should be a predefined level at which any encounter is stopped.

- **wild animals:** disturbance to free-living animals should be minimised. The influence of observing, marking or tracking, capturing and releasing animals should be considered in terms of the survival and reproduction of the species being studied and the effect on the wider ecosystem.

- **anaesthesia and euthanasia:** animals should be protected from pain, eg relating to surgery, and killed if suffering enduring pain.

- **suppliers:** all captive-bred animals should be obtained from reputable (eg Home Office registered) suppliers. The Association for the Study of Animal Behaviour additionally provides guidelines on the (very unusual) use of wild-caught animals. These are used only in studies on conservation.

- **housing and care:** between tests, animals should be housed with enough space to move freely and with sufficient food and water for its health and well being – this refers to both its biological and ecological needs (it does not require, however, that the artificial environment is recreated, just that those aspects of the natural environment important to welfare and survival are included, such as appropriate warmth, room for exercise or somewhere to hide). Cage cleaning should be a compromise between achieving cleanliness and avoiding stress. The same balance should be achieved with regard to human contact – we may for example be seen as conspecifics or predators. Social companions and a source of cognitive stimulation should be available where appropriate.

Think back to some of the non-human animal research you have learned about in earlier chapters, studies such as Lorenz's studies of hatchling birds (page 40). The animals imprinted on Lorenz rather than their mother and he may not have been as effective at keeping them safe or allowing them to learn what to eat as another bird would have been. Certainly it affected their ability to mate when they reached adulthood. In these respects, even a study which did not overtly cause distress to the animals had the potential to harm them in the long term.

Many other studies we have explored, such as those in the chapter on health, were distressing to the animal subjects or invasive. Especially in these cases, a researcher needs to consider whether the ends justify the means; in other words, is the animal suffering caused by such experiments outweighed by the benefits to humans? For some, the answer is necessarily 'no' because they hold the view that animals should not be put at the service of mankind. Another perspective looks at whether the overall gain is sufficiently valuable. This can be expressed using Bateson's (1986) 'cube'. When the certainty of benefit is high, the research is good, and when the suffering is low, the research is worthwhile. For example, research on drugs often uses animals. Sim-Selley & Martin (2002) used mice to demonstrate that there was a physiological basis to the development of dependence on cannabis and Klein *et al.* (2008) demonstrated a genetic link to the experience of withdrawal symptoms from heroin use in mice. Such studies necessarily induce pain and suffering to the animal subjects but the researchers can justify this on the basis of the usefulness of the findings. One factor that affects the usefulness of these findings is the extent to which dependence and withdrawal symptoms are similar in mice and humans. Certainly the withdrawal symptoms seen in mice – such as jumping – are rather different from those exhibited by people. We will consider this issue in the next section.

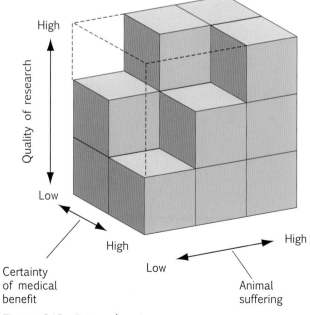

Figure 6.19 Bateson's cube.

In your AS you will have studied the classic research of Pavlov and Skinner on learning in animals.

1. Using these studies as examples, illustrate some of the ethical issues raised in research with non-human animals.

2. Explain why each of the aspects of the procedure you have identified were necessary in order to achieve the aims.

3. Consider the study in the Research Now box in terms of its ethical strengths and weaknesses.

Research
now

Broberg, B.V., Glenthøj, B.Y., Dias, R., Larsen, D.B. & Olsen, C.K. (2009)

'Reversal of cognitive deficits by an ampakine (CX516) and sertindole in two animal models of schizophrenia-sub-chronic and early postnatal PCP treatment in attentional set-shifting'

Psychopharmacology, April 24 [epub ahead of print]

Aim: To investigate the treatment of cognitive impairments in schizophrenia using animal models.

Method: Rats were injected with the hallucinogenic drug phencyclidine (PCP) either for a week as adults or soon after birth. A control group were later injected with saline. As adults they later received an injection of either the second generation antipsychotic sertindole or an ampakine drug, CX516. These were expected to reverse cognitive deficits. To test this, the ability of the adult rats to shift attention was measured by judging how well they could switch between different learned discrimination tasks in which they had to dig for food.

Results: The detrimental effects of early and late administration of PCP treatment were significantly reduced by both sertindole and CX516.

Conclusion: PCP can be used to produce an animal model of cognitive deficits related to schizophrenia and to provide evidence for interventions that could improve these problems by observing changes in ability on a learning test requiring a task change.

Generalising from non-human animals to humans

In addition to ethical issues, researchers need to consider the extent to which they can generalise the findings of work based on animals to humans.

You will recall from your AS that much of what we know about the effect of hormones on the development of sex differences stemmed from early research on non-human animals. And even now animals are providing us with sources of information that we could not gain through experimentation on humans. For example, in investigating the role of genes in behaviours or mental illnesses, studies using animals (for example, deliberate mutations) provide more rigorous evidence than twin and adoption studies in humans.

You may remember a study conducted by Dominguez-Salazar et al. (2002) from your AS. They investigated receptors for male hormones by treating pregnant female rats in different ways. The offspring born then had their ovaries or testes removed and some received hormone replacements. Their findings showed that hormone levels around birth are important in determining later sexual behaviours of both male and female rats. Whilst this research was highly scientific and it clearly would not have been ethical to conduct on humans, the extent to which the findings are relevant to human sexual development is questionable.

On one hand, we should be able to generalise from animals such as rats to humans because we have a shared evolutionary history so have similar hormonal and nervous systems. These are important in the determination of physiological and psychological characteristics such as receptors to which drugs attach and sexual development so it seems likely that we function in similar ways. For example, studies such as Wood et al. (1998) have successfully used animals to model aspects of mental illness by manipulating brain function and behaviour (see page 142).

There are also important ways in which humans and animals differ, such as in sexual behaviour and our capacity to learn. The human brain is also much larger relative to our size than other animals. The cortex (outer layer) is very much larger than any other animal. One consequence of this difference is that we are much more receptive to the effects of our environment, for example learning more quickly and in a greater variety of different ways. These factors reduce the credibility of animal studies.

Practical issues in animal research

There are many ways in which experimenting on animals is easier than on humans. For example, they are small and cheap to keep, so it is easy to use lots of animals and use them for replications, thus improving the reliability of findings. Many small species such as rats and mice reproduce quickly, so whole life cycles can readily be observed. Importantly, greater control can be achieved in animal research than with humans. For example, an animal's diet, social companions, sleep and reproduction can all be controlled. Finally, experimental procedures can be conducted on animals that could not be performed with humans, such as organ removal and hormone injections.

Interactive angles

1. Look back through the topics you have studied for A2. Find examples of each of the following studies in which:

    *   animals suffer greater or lesser degrees or pain or distress

    *   there are examples of at least five of the ethical issues in Box 6.2

    *   you can justify the animals' suffering as the aim of the study was to achieve a reduction in human suffering

    *   there is evidence that the results would not generalise to humans.

2. Find any two studies from your AS or A2 and evaluate them in detail in terms of ethical issues.

Research methods

With the exception of how to conduct a content analysis, you learned everything you now need to know about research methods during your AS studies. However, you will need to refresh your memory to be able to apply the ideas to examples from A2 and be more detailed, precise and critical in your thinking about research methods for your Unit 4 exam. This section will remind you of the details and help you to use the ideas in the applications. Table 6.1 summarises the methods you need to know.

When designing a study you need to consider several important steps. You should:

*   decide on the aim and, if appropriate, develop null and alternative hypotheses

*   select the most appropriate research method

*   identify and operationalise the variables

*   make design decisions (for example, the experimental design, population and sampling technique, materials, the need for a pilot study)

*   suggest suitable controls

*   plan a procedure

*   ensure the plan is ethically sound

*   decide how the results will be analysed (including the statistical test if appropriate).

Similar considerations are important when evaluating studies. Here, questions to ask are:

*   Was the most appropriate research method used?

*   Could better controls have been used (for example, in experimental studies)?

*   Were the variables fully operationalised?

*   Was the experimental design, sampling technique or procedure appropriate?

*   Was the study conducted ethically?

Such questions raise issues of reliability and validity. Reliability refers to how consistent something is. If a psychological test or measure is reliable it will always produce the same results in the same situation. Laboratory experiments are likely to be reliable because they are highly controlled so the situation can be reproduced exactly; in field experiments this is less likely to be so. When we repeat – or replicate – a study we expect to get the same results. If so, it is reliable. Reliability can be improved by controlling extraneous variables (such as participant and situational variables), using standardised instructions and using operational definitions (which are agreed when there is more than one researcher).

Validity is the extent to which a technique is capable of achieving the intended purpose. For example, if a score on an experimental task is a valid indicator of the DV it measures the variable under scrutiny rather than varying because of the influence of demand characteristics, fatigue or the effect of the experimenter. Ecological validity is the extent to which findings from one environmental setting generalise to other settings. One important example of this is whether results from laboratory experiments apply outside the laboratory, that is, whether they generalise to 'real life'. Ecological validity also includes the extent to which an experimental task is representative of the real world; this is its mundane realism. This takes into account factors such as whether the task required of participants is a plausible one or if the stimuli used are things that they might genuinely encounter. So, findings from experiments that are realistic representations of the real world and which are likely to generalise to other settings have high ecological validity.

Like reliability, validity assesses not only experimental procedures but tools such as tests, questionnaires and behavioural categories in observations. Validity can be improved by using controls and blind or double blind procedures and taking a larger or wider sample so that it is more representative of the target population. These help to reduce experimenter effects and demand characteristics. The effect of individual differences can be reduced by randomisation or counterbalancing in repeated measures designs and by random allocation of participants to conditions in independent groups designs. In experiments a

Table 6.1 Research methods and when to use them

Research method	Description of the method	When is the method used?
Laboratory experiment	A true experiment, conducted in an artificial environment, in which the experimenter manipulates an IV and measures the consequent changes in a DV whilst carefully controlling extraneous variables. Participants are allocated to conditions by the experimenter.	When looking for differences, comparisons or cause and effect relationships. It must be possible to actively change the levels of the IV and record the DV accurately. It is important that the behaviour is likely to be relatively unaffected by a contrived environment.
Field experiment	A true experiment in which the researcher manipulates an IV and measures a DV in the natural setting of the participants. Participants are allocated to conditions by the experimenter.	When looking for differences, comparisons or cause and effect relationships. It must be possible to actively change the levels of the IV and record the DV accurately. It is preferable when it is likely that behaviour could be affected by a contrived environment.
Natural experiment	A study in which an experimenter makes use of an existing change or difference in situations to provide levels of an IV and then measures the DV in each condition. Participants cannot be allocated to conditions so it is not a true experiment.	When looking for differences or comparisons between variables that cannot be artificially controlled or manipulated.
Correlational analysis	A technique used to investigate a link between two measured variables.	When looking for relationships between variables. Can be used when it is unethical or impractical to artificially control or manipulate variables. There must be two variables that can be measured.
Observation	A technique in which the researcher watches and records the behaviour of participants. This can be either in a situation that has been set up by the researcher (controlled observation) or in their own environment, for example, in the normal place for the activity being observed (naturalistic observation). The participants may or may not be aware of the presence of the observer (and the observer may or may not be a member of the group or activity being observed).	Controlled observations are used to record behaviours that require an artificial situation, eg when they are unlikely to arise spontaneously. If behaviours are unlikely to be observable in an artificial situation, for example, are only likely to arise in real-life settings and/or social situations, naturalistic observations are used. The recording units must be observable behaviours rather than inferred states but may be variables that cannot be measured by asking questions.
Questionnaire	A self-report method used to obtain data by asking participants to provide information about themselves using written questions.	When aiming to collect data about opinions or attitudes from a large sample and when the questions to be asked are largely straightforward and the same for every participant. Also if face-to-face contact might reduce the response rate or honesty.
Interview	A self-report method used to obtain data by asking participants to provide information about themselves by replying verbally to questions asked by an interviewer.	When aiming to collect data from individuals using questions which may require explanation or when the questions may need to vary between participants.
Case study	A method which focuses on a single instance – eg one person or one family or institution – which is explored in detail. Other methods are used to gain a range of information, for example, observations, questionnaires and interviews. A history of the participant is obtained and this is related to their subsequent development.	When varied, detailed data is required from one participant, especially if they are a rare or particularly interesting case. The aim of a case study may be to report on, investigate or help someone so the outcomes are also varied.
Content analysis	A method of indirect observation which assesses the themes and concepts expressed in communication media such as transcribed speech or the printed word. It can produce qualitative or quantitative data.	When researchers are interested in the overt and hidden meanings and messages present in communication. It can provide a way to compare historical and current trends, eg in gender stereotypes.

balance must be sought between improvements achieved by using more controls (which increase validity) and making the situation or task more realistic (so that ecological validity and hence generalisability is increased).

Figure 6.20 Improving validity is a balance between controls and mundane realism. Highly controlled tasks are often less realistic.

Experiments

The most commonly used method is the experiment. In a true experiment an independent variable (IV) is manipulated and consequent changes in a dependent variable (DV) are measured in order to establish a cause and effect relationship. This is possible because the researcher actively allocates participants to conditions or manipulates the situation to create different conditions. True experiments include laboratory experiments (in contrived situations) and field experiments (conducted in the participants' normal surroundings for the activity being tested). If the IV will change during the experiment, but this is not under the control of the researcher, then it is a natural experiment – that is one in which the researcher does not control the IV or allocate participants to conditions. It does not, necessarily, have to be conducted in the participants' 'natural' environment although this is likely to be so. The only thing which is natural is the changing of the experimental conditions. This method tends to be used when it is unethical or impractical to manipulate the IV.

Different experimental designs may be used in which participants are allocated to levels of the IV in different ways. These include:

● *independent groups design* – different groups of participants are used for each level of the IV

● *repeated measures design* – each participant performs in every level of the IV

● *matched pairs design* – participants are arranged into pairs, each pair is similar in ways that are important to the study and the members of each pair perform in the two different levels of the IV.

You will have encountered studies using these designs, for example Lindstroem *et al.* (1999) (page 142) conducted an experiment using an independent groups design, comparing

people with schizophrenia to a control group who did not have a diagnosis of schizophrenia. Brain scans showed that the schizophrenics produced more dopamine. Clearly the participants could not have been randomly allocated to the 'affected' and 'unaffected' groups, so there was no choice. However, sometimes an independent groups design is preferred to reduce the effects of demand characteristics or order effects.

Another advantage of an independent groups design is that it is possible for all conditions to be tested simultaneously (although this is not always desirable or possible). Imagine a field experiment comparing attention in recovered-depressives and never-depressed participants which relies on a particular social context such as a staged distraction. As there may be many variables that *could* affect attention, it might be better to have all the participants, from both levels of the IV, together.

Interactive angles

1. In the example of a comparison between recovered-depressives and never-depressed participants what possible variables could affect attention?

2. If an experimenter wanted to compare attention in a real-life situation for people with depression who were undergoing treatment and those who were untreated, why might it be better to conduct a laboratory experiment than a field experiment?

Figure 6.21 A repeated measures design runs the risk of a fatigue effect.

Sometimes a repeated measures design is preferable as it overcomes the problems presented by individual differences. If there are different participants in each level of the IV, any differences found between these conditions could be due to the people rather than the variable being manipulated. In a repeated measures design each individual acts as their own 'baseline'. Any differences between their performance in each level of the IV should be due to the experimenter's manipulation. However, there is a problem here. It is possible that differences may arise because an individual experiences the same (or similar) tasks more than once, ie the risk of order effects.

Order effects cannot be avoided in a repeated measures design but their influence can be cancelled out using **counterbalancing**. Let's say participants will get bored and perform worse the second time they do a task. All we need to do is ensure that, for half the participants, the 'second' task is one level of the IV and, for the remaining participants, it is the other level of the IV. This will even out the influence of being the 'first' task in the experiment compared to the second. Consider a researcher who wants to test memory for familiar and unfamiliar lists of words in people with schizophrenia. The participants might improve as they get practised at the task or used to the experimental setting. Alternatively, their performance might decline on the second task as the words from the first list become muddled with those from the second. Using counterbalancing, the experimenter could have some participants recalling the familiar list followed by the unfamiliar one, and others performing these two conditions in the opposite order.

Ideally, researchers would like to avoid the problems of both individual differences and order effects. This is, to an extent, possible with a matched-pairs design. To set up a study using matched-pairs the researcher decides on the important ways in which participants could differ. Consider a study about eating disorders that is investigating the influence of a big meal on body image. What design would be best? In repeated measures the aim would be obvious so demand characteristics would be a problem. Using two groups of participants, one who ate a large meal and one who did not, an independent groups design would be possible but variables other than the meal size could influence the individuals. Age, gender, educational level or socioeconomic group could all affect vulnerability to eating disorders. In a matched-pairs design, participants are identified who share important characteristics so that one of each similar pair can be placed into each level of the IV. So, in this case, if two 25-year-old female students from the same socio-economic group were found, one would be allocated to each group. As you can imagine, this procedure is very time consuming and is not without risk – it relies on the assumption that the criteria being used for matching are those which are most important – and this may not be the case. Nevertheless, once established, the two matched groups have all the advantages of an independent group design.

The statistical significance of experimental data can be analysed using inferential tests. The choice of test depends on the experimental design and the level of measurement of the data. At AS you learned about two inferential tests for use with data from experiments, both used with independent groups designs (there are other tests which are used in studies with repeated measures designs). The chi-squared test is used with nominal data, that is, when the results are in named groups. The Mann Whitney test is used with ordinal, interval or ratio data.

Interactive angles

1. Consider the study on the effects of drugs conducted by Lubman *et al.* (2000). They used matched-pairs design to compare the reaction time of 16 opiate addicts and 16 control participants. Each addict was age-matched to a control participant. They found that the addicts had an attentional bias for drug-related cues.

   Evaluate this study with reference to the research method and design.

2. Find an example of a study using a repeated measures design. Explain why this was preferable in their study.

What's that?

- **experimenter effects:** any unwitting influence a researcher has on the participants. These include experimenter bias and the effects of researchers in non-experimental investigations such as in interviews
- **demand characteristics:** aspects of an experimental setting that accidentally tell the participants the aim of the study. They can cause the participants' behaviour to change. They can be reduced by deception and using an independent groups design

Laboratory experiment

A laboratory environment offers high levels of control over the situation, accurate measurement of the DV and the potential to use specific apparatus. For example:

- presenting stimuli at a fixed distance or for a specific length of time can only practically be achieved in laboratory conditions
- timing participants' reactions requires precision that can only be achieved in the lab
- using a brain scanner requires a laboratory.

A laboratory experiment is therefore chosen when practicality or the need for experimental rigour exceeds the importance of reducing **experimenter effects** and **demand characteristics**. When, however, it is more important that the participant is responding without the influence of an artificial setting, or may even be unaware that they are participating in an experiment at all, a field experiment would be chosen if this were possible.

Koster *et al.* (2005) conducted a laboratory experiment. They found that depressed people were slower to move their attention away from negative words than non-depressed people, supporting the cognitive explanation of depression. Although there may be disadvantages to a laboratory experiment in this instance, such as severely depressed people being less likely to volunteer for laboratory studies, biasing the sample, there are also advantages. It is possible to use apparatus such as computers to measure attention and to rigorously control variables to ensure that only differences in the participants' mental health could influence their performance.

Klimek *et al.* (1997) investigated brains of depressed and non-depressed individuals after death. They used a **single blind** procedure so the experimenters assessing the brain samples were unaware of which participant group each individual belonged to. Schooler *et al.* (2005) used a **double blind** procedure. In a test of drug treatments for schizophrenia, the patients themselves did not know which drug they were receiving (risperidone or haloperidol) and neither did the researchers assessing their mental health.

If a researcher conducts a laboratory experiment they have the advantages of rigorous control over the situation and their participants. They can control precisely the nature and presentation of stimuli, sources of distraction and the order of conditions. However, they also have some hurdles. Demand characteristics can be a risk as they indicate to the participants the aims of the study which, in turn, affects the participants' behaviour. Clearly, this should be avoided. A researcher can minimise the effects of demand characteristics by disguising the purpose of the experiment, for example by using 'filler' questions between the critical ones in a questionnaire. Such distractions make it harder for the participants to correctly guess the experimental aims. Alternatively, participants can be deliberately deceived about the aims. This is likely to be effective but also raises ethical issues.

Another risk in laboratory studies is that of experimenter effects, for example the distortions that arise because the experimenter responds differently to participants in the different levels of the IV. This response may be unconscious but can subtly alter responses creating or hiding patterns in the results. Imagine a researcher looking for differences between participants with and without an eating disorder who acts in a kindlier way to the participants with mental health problems. This might make them feel more confident or positive about completing the experimental task so they try harder or persist for longer. Any differences

in the results could be caused by experimenter bias so would be erroneous. Experimenter effects can be reduced using controls such as standardised instructions and blind procedures.

Field experiment

A field experiment, like a laboratory experiment, is a true experiment with an IV manipulated by the experimenter and a DV which is measured. The experiment, however, is conducted in the normal surroundings of the participants for the activity being investigated. This would include looking at play in children in a school playground, responses to authority in the work environment or the recall of witnesses to a staged crime in the street.

Figure 6.22 Field experiments are less highly controlled than laboratory experiments.

Krackow & Lynn (2003) conducted a field experiment investigating the accuracy of children's testimonies with regard to being touched by an adult (see page 28). The experimenters controlled the independent variables, which were whether the children were touched or not and whether they were asked direct or 'tagged' questions (for example, 'Amy touched your bottom, didn't she?'). The opportunity for touching (on the hands, arms, calves or feet) was set up in a game of Twister with which children played with an experimenter. As the moves were predetermined, the experimenter was able to treat every child in the same way, raising the reliability of the study. It also made it possible for the non-touch group to have an identical experience except for the touching, improving the validity of the study by controlling for potential extraneous variables such as how exciting the game was. As being touched (or not) during a game of Twister is a normal event for children, the situation was natural for the task. As the parents (and their children) were recruited largely from paediatricians' offices and preschools, they would have been used to playing games indoors so the researchers' laboratory would, in fact, have seemed like a normal environment in which to play.

The main advantage of a field experiment over a laboratory one is that the participants are unaffected by the influence of being in a strange place. This can also help to reduce the influence of demand characteristics, especially if the participants are unaware that they are in an experiment (although this is not always the case). Here are two examples of possible field experiments. Imagine a workplace is interested in the criminal behaviour of its employees. They manipulate an IV of level of supervision, having more senior members of staff around for one month, and fewer for the next. The number of items inexplicably missing from the stationery store is recorded in each case. A field experiment in sport psychology could investigate the influence of goal-setting on performance. School children could be told that they would be set targets in PE lessons for one month as part of an experiment, then teaching would revert to normal the next month. Measures of effort and achievement could be rated by the teachers. These would both be field experiments although the degree of awareness of the participants is different.

Compared to a laboratory experiment, control of variables is more difficult in field experiments. Consider the example of the level of theft of stationery. Other factors could affect the amount that employees stole, such as the number of items in the store, the number of employees present and factors such as whether they were feeling positive towards the company. In the second situation, there were uncontrolled variables such as whether the children had been worked hard in other lessons, had played sport outside school or the weather! With many extraneous variables that cannot be controlled, such experiments may lack validity, as it is difficult to be sure whether any changes that do occur have definitely been caused by the IV.

Interactive angles

1. Identify one field experiment which you know well and evaluate it. Suggest how the method could have been improved.

2. The management of a local hospital is concerned about the level of depressive symptoms seen in their medical staff. They want to investigate whether these symptoms are due to changing shifts too often. Design a field experiment to test this. Your answer should state the aim, hypotheses, design, procedure, ethical considerations and how you would analyse the results including choice of statistical test. Justify your decisions, such as the experimental design you would use.

Natural experiment

A natural experiment differs from a true experiment because the experimenter does not set up the levels of the IV. Natural experiments make use of natural, ie not artificially produced, changes or differences in circumstances to provide the experimental conditions. They can be conducted in laboratory or field settings. Researchers use natural experiments when it would be impractical or unethical to generate the conditions necessary for the different levels of the IV. For example, if we wanted to investigate the effects of maternal deprivation in humans we could not randomly allocate babies to deprived and non-deprived conditions.

Figure 6.23 Charlton *et al.* (2000) conducted a natural experiment to test the effect of television on children's behaviour.

If you studied criminal psychology you may have read about Charlton *et al.* (2000) (page 9). This was a naturalistic experiment on the children in an isolated community on St Helena Island. The DV was the level of aggression displayed by children in the playground. The two levels of the IV were before and after the introduction of satellite TV enabling the researchers to investigate its effect on behaviour. The two levels of the IV were 'natural' because they were not controlled by the experimenters, not because TV is in any way natural. In child psychology, Belsky & Rovine (1988) used a natural experiment to investigate the formation of attachments in children in relation to whether the mother worked outside the home. Clearly it would not have been ethical or practical to randomly allocate babies to different conditions of parental employment, or hours spent in daycare.

Where natural experiments are conducted in the field, they have the benefit that the participants are in their usual environment so their behaviour is more likely to be representative of real life. Since the participants are not actively allocated to conditions, it is more possible that the existence of the experiment can be hidden from them. This reduces the risk of demand characteristics affecting behaviour. Of course, because participants are not randomly allocated to different levels of the IV it is difficult to distinguish the effects of any existing differences between groups of participants and those differences that are due to the experiment. For example, if we were to investigate the effects of daycare on children's socialisation it would not be possible for experimenters to allocate children to receive daycare or not – this would be a decision made by the parents. The problem here is that there may be other, extraneous variables that also affect socialisation that could obscure the effect of the IV. For example parents who choose to put their children in daycare might also have few relatives living locally – reducing the children's other experiences

of socialisation – or might have jobs that rely on their own strong social skills giving their children a genetic advantage in terms of socialisation. In either case, these effects could invalidate the findings of a natural experiment. If the children in the daycare group had poor social skills, it might be due to a lack of nearby relatives rather than the daycare. If their social skills were better they wouldn't know if this was due to the daycare or whether it was influence by inheritance.

Observation

Observations allow researchers to record actual responses – what people (or animals) do – rather than what they think or say they would do. In this sense, it is a direct and valid method. Observations are also useful if participants, for example, babies, are unable to follow instructions or give verbal responses. Clearly the only way to gain information about infants' attachment from the infants themselves is to watch them.

Figure 6.24 The dangers of participant observation.

Observational techniques may be used as a research method in their own right or as a means to measure the DV in an experiment. In either case, records may be taken in the form of a checklist, with each occurrence of a behaviour being tallied. This is called event sampling. Alternatively, records may be taken at fixed time intervals such as every ten seconds. The events may also be recorded so that a more detailed analysis can be performed at a later date.

If you have studied child psychology you will have read about Koluchova (1972, 1991) who studied the development of twin boys who had been isolated from other people for most of their lives (page 54). Some of Koluchova's work included participant observation in which Koluchova engaged with the boys in activities in order to find out about their skills and understanding. This was a participant observation because she was involved with the participants in the activities she was observing. An alternative would have been to use a non-participant observation in which the observer is not included within the activities being studied, for example, when the behaviours are observed through a one-way screen (as in Bandura's experiments; see page 7) or using a video recorder.

Interactive angles

1. If you were a researcher trying to answer each of these questions, which would you choose – a lab, field or natural experiment – and which design would you use?

   - Do depressed and non-depressed people respond differently to compliments?

   - Are eating disorders more prevalent in a school population after a tragedy such as a mass shooting?

   - Do drug users behave in more risky ways in their everyday life than non-drug users?

   - Does watching a physically violent TV programme lead to immediate increases in verbally aggressive behaviour?

   - Are people who have been in daycare as children more or less friendly as adults?

2. Identify one natural experiment which you know well and evaluate it. Suggest how the method could have been improved.

3. A researcher believes that high stress levels will lead to a greater incidence of depression. It would clearly be unethical to deliberately increase stress with the intention of inducing depression. Design a natural experiment to their idea. State the aim, hypotheses, design, procedure, ethical considerations and how you would analyse the results including choice of statistical test. Justify your decisions, such as the experimental design you would use.

Table 6.2 Strengths and weaknesses of the experimental method

Experimental method	Strengths	Weaknesses
Laboratory experiments	Good control of extraneous variables Causal relationships can be determined Strict procedures allow them to be replicated so researchers can be more confident about their findings.	The artificial situation may make participants' behaviour unrepresentative Participants may respond to demand characteristics and alter their behaviour Investigator effects may lead to biased results.
Field experiments	As participants are in their normal situation their behaviour is likely to be representative Participants may be unaware that they are in a study so demand characteristics are less problematic than in laboratory experiments Control of the IV means that causal relationships can be investigated.	Control over extraneous variables is more difficult than in a laboratory so the researcher cannot be certain that changes in the DV have been caused by changes in the IV Fewer controls so more difficult to replicate than laboratory experiments If participants are unaware that they are in a study, this raises ethical issues.
Natural experiments	They can be used to study real-world issues If participants are in their normal situation their behaviour is likely to be representative If participants are unaware that they are in a study demand characteristics will be less problematic Enables researchers to investigate variables that could not practically or ethically be manipulated.	They are only possible when naturally occurring differences arise Control over extraneous variables is more difficult than in a laboratory experiment As the researcher is not manipulating the IV they can be less sure of the cause of changes in the DV, ie a causal relationship cannot be established They generally cannot be replicated.

In a covert observation the participants do not know that they are being watched, in contrast to an overt observation where they are aware, at least to an extent. Clearly covert observations raise practical issues as the observer has to be hidden, eg by observing from far away or disguising their role. There are also ethical problems as the participants cannot give informed consent and if they work out the observer's role this can cause distress.

Observations may be useful if the behaviour being investigated might be strongly affected by participants' expectations or beliefs. For example, we are more likely to obtain representative information about carers' responses to an infant's persistent crying by seeing how parents behave than by asking them. This is simply because people might not know how they would respond or might choose to lie because they want to give a socially desirable impression. However, this advantage may be lost if they are aware that they are being observed.

Non-participant observations are easier to conduct as the observer can concentrate exclusively on the behaviours of interest. This would be more difficult in a participant observation as focusing on one individual or behaviour might draw attention to the role of the observer within the social group. It is also easier for the observer to remain objective if they are non-participant, that is, to avoid becoming biased by their own personal viewpoint. In contrast, a participant observer may benefit from precisely the opposite – by becoming involved in the social situation they may gain greater insight into the participants' feelings or motives than a non-participant observer. Covert observation is especially important in situations where the participants may change their behaviour to conform to what they think the researcher wants to see or what is socially acceptable. For example, a carer may respond more quickly to a child's needs because they know they are being observed.

Figure 6.25
Rosenhan (1973) conducted a covert observation of the reactions of hospital staff to pseudopatients who initially reported hearing voices. Each pseudopatient was a participant observer and described the behaviours of doctors and nurses towards them, which was mainly to ignore them.

Interactive angles

1. Ainsworth & Wittig (1969) used the Strange Situation to simulate real-life events so that they could classify infants' attachment types. Were they participant or non-participant observers? Were they overt or covert?

2. Curtiss (1977) (page 53) studied Genie, a child who has suffered severe privation. One of the ways in which Curtiss observed Genie's development was to play with her. What kind of observational technique is this?

3. Charlton *et al.* (2000) (page 9) conducted naturalistic observations as part of their experiment on the effect of television on aggression in children. A researcher in the playground had a video recorder on view. Recording began when the children stopped taking any notice of the camera operator. The recordings were then scored by pairs of observers watching together. Why did they use these procedures?

Figure 6.26 Mezulis *et al.* (2006) (page 155) used a controlled observation to support the cognitive model of depression. They recorded children at home doing a maths task on a lap-top and their mother's reaction when the child received negative computerised feedback.

Observations may be either naturalistic, where the participants are watched in their normal environment without input from the researcher, or controlled – in situations which have been artificially contrived. A naturalistic observation allows the observer to gain information about the normal behaviour of the individuals in real life. For example Ainsworth (1967) (page 44) observed children in their own homes interacting with their carers and strangers. She followed this with a set of controlled observations called the 'Strange Situation'. This technique enables researchers to observe the same situations repeatedly without having to wait for them to happen spontaneously. This would be very time-consuming and each event would potentially be slightly different. If we wanted to observe infants' responses to particular behaviours by their carers (such as smiling at them or ignoring them) this would be much quicker and systematic in a controlled observation than a naturalistic one.

Naturalistic observations are highly representative of real behaviour because they are records of the way people behave in actual situations. However, they are harder to control and may present more ethical issues than controlled observations as participants are less likely to be aware that they are being observed.

Interactive angles

1. Observations are commonly used in child psychology. Why do you think this is the case?

2. Look back at these observations if you studied child psychology:

   ● Lorenz (1935) (page 40) observed the way that hatchlings follow their mothers. Is this a naturalistic or controlled observation?

   ● He went on to show that birds would imprint on him, but only if he was crouching down when they first encountered him! (See Lorenz, 1952.) What kind of observation was this?

   ● Fuertes *et al.* (2006) (page 47) observed maternal sensitivity and attachment. Were these measured using naturalistic or controlled observations?

   ● Brazleton *et al.* (1975) (page 41) observed mothers and babies turn-taking during interactions. They then asked the mothers to ignore the babies' signals and observed whether this caused distress. Which aspects of this observation were naturalistic and which were controlled?

   ● Bailey *et al.* (2007) (page 41) used controlled observations to measure maternal sensitivity in teenage mothers and the attachment behaviours of their babies. What advantages are there of this technique over naturalistic observations?

Figure 6.27 Lorenz observed imprinting.

Initially, an observer may conduct a non-focused observation, recording all the behaviours they see. This is useful at first to indicate the range so that the researcher can decide which behaviours will be the focus of observations. These behavioural categories must be operationalised, that is, clearly defined. This is particularly important when there is more than one observer as it is essential that they record the same information when observing the same events. The behavioural categories must be observable rather than inferred states. For example, behaviours such as cowering or crying can be observed but 'being afraid' cannot. This appears to be a disadvantage of observations but it can also be seen as a strength – observations can be highly objective. Since all that is being recorded is directly observable behaviour there is no need for interpretation and especially when the observer is covert and non-participant.

Interactive angles

Donovan *et al.* (2007) (page 47) conducted naturalistic observations of free play between mothers and their infants at 24 months. Suggest two behavioural categories that could be observed that would indicate the quality of the interactions between the toddlers and their mothers.

Another weakness of the observational method arises when more than one observer is used. It is difficult to ensure that they are each making the same record when they see the same behaviours. This issue is called inter-observer reliability. This can be improved by agreeing operational definitions and by practising recording data together.

Table 6.3 Strengths and weaknesses of observational techniques

Strengths	Weaknesses
In naturalistic settings and with covert observers behaviour is likely to be highly representative of real life unlike questionnaires or interviews in which people may report different behaviours than they would actually do.	Participant observers may be biased if they become involved in the social situation they are observing.
	If multiple observers are used, inter-observer reliability may be low.
The technique allows for data collection from participants who are unable to contribute to interviews, questionnaires or experimental testing.	Ethical issues arise when participants are unaware that they are being observed.
Observational techniques can be used to collect data when manipulation of a situation would be unethical or impractical.	It is harder to control extraneous variables, even in a controlled observation, than in a laboratory experiment.

Interactive angles

1. Identify one observation which you know well and evaluate it. Suggest how the method could have been improved.

2. A psychiatric ward wishes to investigate whether patients copy the bizarre behaviours they see in each other. Design an observation to test this. Your answer should state the aim, hypotheses, design, procedure, ethical considerations and how you would analyse the results including, if appropriate, your choice of statistical test. Justify your decisions, such as whether the observation is controlled or naturalistic and the role of the observer.

Self-report techniques

Self-report techniques are so called because the participant is reporting to the researcher their beliefs, thoughts or feelings about themselves rather than these being recorded directly. These methods include questionnaires and interviews. In both techniques the researcher presents the participant with questions. In a questionnaire, these are on paper (or on a computer) and the participant fills them in. In an interview the questions are asked by the interviewer, usually face to face or by telephone. The methods share some basic question types although there are some differences too. As participants are in the company of a researcher in an interview but not in a questionnaire, they may be more likely to be truthful about socially sensitive issues in a questionnaire. However, face-to-face, an interviewer can respond to the answers a participant gives, making it a more flexible method and more likely to gain useful, detailed information when this is difficult to obtain.

Figure 6.28 If people are likely to clam up under the scrutiny of an interviewer, a questionnaire is a better choice.

Open and closed questions

Both open and closed questions can be used in either questionnaires or interviews. A closed question gives the participant little choice and often requires just one of a small number of alternative answers. In a questionnaire, these may be presented as boxes to cross or tick. For example:

Do you frequently find that you forget things you have deliberately tried to remember? yes [ ] no [ ]

Which of the following memory aids do you use?

(Tick all that apply)   [ ]

   lists   [ ]

   notes to yourself   [ ]

   repeating things over and over again [ ]

   tying a knot in your handkerchief [ ]

What is your main occupation?

Figure 6.29 Interviews tend to be more flexible than questionnaires as they can be unstructured.

One advantage of using closed questions is that the results they generate are easy to analyse because they are simple numbers. For example, we could ask a group of mothers and fathers whether they cuddled, smacked and played with their children using a yes/no format. This would allow us to say that x% of mothers and x% of fathers reported particular parenting behaviours. Results that are numerical are called quantitative data.

Banse (2004) used a questionnaire called the 'Relationship Assessment Scale' to assess marital satisfaction and found

that insecurely attached individuals were less satisfied in their partnerships (see page 48). The questionnaire included closed questions such as:

1. How well does your partner meet your needs?

A	B	C	D	E
Poorly		Average		Extremely well

2. How much do you love your partner?

A	B	C	D	E
Not much		Average		Very much

3. How often do you wish you hadn't gotten into this relationship?

A	B	C	D	E
Never		Average		Very often

Note that in the last question the responses are reversed – the 'good' answer is on the left, not the right.

An open question does not require a fixed response and should, instead, elicit an extended answer if the participant has one to offer. For example, the open question 'How do you express your affection to your child?' will supply much more information than ticking boxes about cuddling or play. Unlike the numbers produced by closed questions, the results generated by open questions are qualitative, that is, they are detailed and descriptive. This data is more difficult to analyse, the aim being to look for common themes across different participants' responses. For example, if carers from different cultures were interviewed about their child care strategies and similar themes emerged this would suggest that cultural differences were small. If different themes could be identified it would suggest that cultural differences in parenting styles were greater.

Figure 6.30 Swaffer & Hollin (2001) (page 156) used a questionnaire to assess anger in young offenders. Those who suppressed their anger were more likely to suffer depression, supporting the psychodynamic model.

Both qualitative and quantitative data can be collected using either questionnaires or interviews. In practice, researchers mainly use questionnaires to gather specific, quantitative information and interviews to gather more in-depth, qualitative data.

Questionnaires

In a questionnaire the questions are generally strictly ordered, so it is 'structured'. It is possible, especially using computers, to tailor the questions somewhat to each participant (for example, when a questionnaire says 'Leave out this section if...'). However, in general questionnaires are necessarily more structured than interviews.

A greater variety of closed questions can be used in a questionnaire than an interview as in written form it is possible to offer a variety of choices for responses. One form of forced-choice question used in questionnaires is the Likert scale, used to elicit opinions. It allows the participant to offer one of a range of responses:

Questions like this can be used to find out people's views, for example in relation to day care. Participants would indicate their response on the scale above to statements such as:

- I think that day care is good for children.
- I believe that a child should spend his or her early years with the mother.
- It is wrong to separate children from their parents during the working day.
- All parents ought to have the opportunity for a fulfilling working life.
- I feel that my child benefits from spending time with other children.
- Families need quality time together.

When Likert scales are used it is important to 'reverse' some statements so that the 'positive' or socially acceptable response is not always at the same side of the page.

Interactive angles

Fuertes *et al.* (2006) (page 47) found out about each infant's temperament by giving the mothers a questionnaire. Consider what advantage there might have been to avoiding assessing temperament by observation. Devise about five questions that could have been used by Fuertes *et al.* to investigate infant temperament.

Other kinds of questions that generate quantitative data can be used in questionnaires, for example the semantic differential. This is designed to elicit people's feelings about a topic or situation. For example in relation to an eyewitness the following questions could be posed:

Does the prospect of giving a statement in court make you feel:

powerful	weak
confident	doubtful
tense	calm
sad	excited

Again, it is important to ensure that some of the scales have the positive emotion on the left, others on the right.

Questionnaires often end with an invitation that reads 'Please tell us anything else you would like to about this topic'. This is an open question which allows the researchers to collect some qualitative data. However, this is likely to be much less effective than the qualitative research conducted through interviewing as, in the absence of prompts from the interviewer, the participant may give very little information.

Interactive angles

1. Identify one study that you know well which uses a questionnaire and evaluate it. Suggest how the method could have been improved.

2. Staff responsible for organising care in the community for patients with mental health problems are interested to know how well the patients' families believe they have coped with the transition from institutional to independent living. Design a questionnaire to investigate this. In addition to the questionnaire, you should include a specific aim, hypotheses, procedure, ethical considerations and how you would analyse the results including, if appropriate, your choice of statistical test. Justify your decisions, such as the types of questions you would use.

Interviews

The interview as a research method uses questions spoken by the interviewer to the participant. These may be structured, but can be much less so than a questionnaire. In an unstructured interview new questions can be incorporated in response to the participant's answers, which cannot be done in a questionnaire. This makes interviews particularly useful for gaining in-depth information about individuals and for new topics of investigation. The advantage in both cases is that if new themes arise that have not been encountered before, these can be thoroughly explored. In such situations a questionnaire would be unable to delve further. For example, a questionnaire or structured interview about a child's attachment may ask the carer 'Does the child display resistant behaviours?', followed by another saying 'If yes, indicate which of the following' with a list such as 'turning face away, avoiding being held, moving away'. The answers are fairly limited, whereas an unstructured interview could pursue lines such as when the child resists, what the carer is doing prior to the behaviour, how the carer responds and so on. This would give a much fuller picture of the carer–infant relationship.

Structured interviews generally employ closed questions that are asked in the same order. These are the kinds of interviews you may have encountered in surveys being conducted outside supermarkets or in town centres. Everyone is treated in the same way and numerical data is generated, ie the findings are quantitative. In semi-structured and unstructured interviews more open questions are used. These generate detailed, descriptive responses, that is, qualitative data. These are the type of interview you probably have with your doctor. This generally begins with 'How are you feeling?'. The questions that follow depend on the symptoms the patient describes. The qualitative data produced by questionnaires and structured interviews is relatively easy to analyse because it is numerical. The findings of unstructured interviews in contrast are qualitative. There may be a great deal of

information in the form of continuous speech. This has to be analysed by identifying themes, that is, ideas within the respondent's comments that can be classified or interpreted. This is much more difficult and time consuming. It is also potentially open to investigator bias as the interviewer's beliefs about the findings in general or particular participants may bias the way they extract or interpret information.

Wilhelm *et al.* (2006) interviewed trainee teachers every five years for 25 years (page 153). The participants were asked about positive and negative life events and assessed for depression with standard interviews. The results showed that negative life events were strongly associated with major depression.

There are some potential problems with interviews as a research method. Compared to questionnaires, people may be less likely to be honest. Imagine how a respondent in a questionnaire study compared to an interview study might feel towards questions about punishing their child. There is likely to be a greater effect of social desirability when the respondent is face-to-face with the investigator. Conversely, participants in questionnaire studies may develop a different sort of response bias, one in which they tend to always give

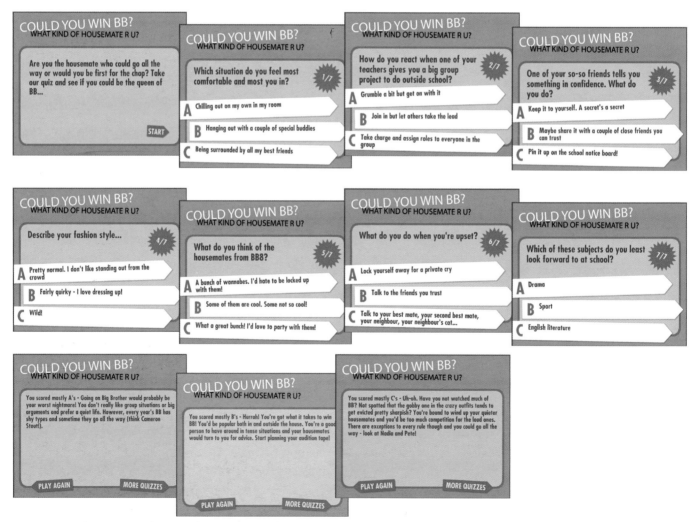

Figure 6.31 A structured questionnaire using closed questions.

the same kind of answer. Have you ever done a quiz in a magazine that asks you questions with answers 'a', 'b' or 'c'? After a few responses you have decided which 'type' you are and this will colour the way you answer the rest of the quiz. Have a go at the quiz in Figure 6.31.

Participating in a questionnaire or interview study requires time and effort from participants and a willingness to divulge things about themselves. Especially when some of the questions might invade their privacy or bring back painful memories, some people would be reluctant to participate. Think about participants asked about losing a parent when they were young, or those in studies about crimes or disasters. This means that the people who do volunteer are probably not very representative of the whole population. In a questionnaire study the participants also have to return the completed questionnaire. Even when they are provided with a postage-paid envelope, many potential participants do not return the questionnaire. This adds an additional bias to the sample.

Interactive angles

1. Eranti *et al.* (2007) (pages 188 and 196) used many different ways to assess patients following ECT for depression. These included the Hamilton Depression Rating Scale (a structured interview), questionnaires including the Beck Depression Inventory and visual analogue mood scales. In a questionnaire to assess any side effects from treatment, patients were asked five questions: 'Have you had trouble recalling people's names?' 'Have you felt confused or disoriented?' 'Have you had any memory problems?' 'Have you had trouble concentrating?' and 'Have you had trouble holding in your memory new things you have learned?'

   - Why do you think they used both interviews and questionnaires to assess the effectiveness of the treatment?

   - Were the questions about side effects open or closed?

   - Suggest two more questions they could have asked to reveal possible effects on memory.

Visual-analogue scales for mood are like semantic differentials, they consist of a line with opposing mood descriptions at either end along which the participant makes a mark. The position of the mark along the line is then measured.

   - Will this generate quantitative or qualitative data?

   - Draw two possible visual-analogue scales that could have been used to assess mood in this study.

2. Wilhelm *et al.* (2006) (page 153) interviewed participants every five years about positive and negative life events such as bereavement and unemployment. Why do you think they chose an interview rather than a questionnaire to assess these life events?

3. Harrison & Ungerer (2002) (page 64) used an interview to find out about mothers' working lives and their attitudes to work. This was then related to their children's attachment type. Why do you think they chose to use an interview rather than a questionnaire to assess this variable?

Table 6.4 Strengths and weaknesses of self-report techniques

	Strengths	Weaknesses
Questionnaires	They are relatively easy to administer and can be sent or emailed to participants making them time and cost-efficient	Response biases such as tending to always answer 'no' or always tick the box on the left can lead to biased results if the questionnaire is not well designed
	Respondent may be more truthful than in an interview as they are not face-to-face with someone, especially if their answers are personal	Limited because, unlike unstructured interviews, there is no flexibility to allow for collection of useful but unexpected data as new questions cannot be added.
	Data is relatively easy to analyse as it is quantitative.	
Interviews	Structured interview data is relatively easy to analyse as it is quantitative	Structured interviews are limited by fixed questions
	Semi- or unstructured interviews enable the researcher to gain specific and detailed information from the respondent that may be missed in structured techniques.	Investigator bias may be a problem as the expectations of the interviewer can alter the way they ask questions so unconsciously affecting the respondents' answers or can affect the way their responses are interpreted.
Both questionnaires and interviews	Structured questionnaires and interviews can be easily repeated allowing researchers to generate more data or check their findings	Participants may be affected by biases such as social desirability and may be influenced by leading questions
	They can be used to generate quantitative or qualitative data.	As only some people are willing to fill in questionnaires or be interviewed, the participants may not be representative of the majority of the population.

Interactive angles

1. Identify one study that you know well which uses an interview and evaluate it. Suggest how the method could have been improved.

2. A therapist has seen many clients with phobias lately. She is interested by a pattern which suggests that there may be a link between their fears and those of members of their families. Design an interview to investigate this. In addition to the interview plan, you should include a specific aim, hypotheses, procedure, ethical considerations and how you would analyse the results including, if appropriate, your choice of statistical test. Justify your decisions, such as whether the interview is structured and the types of questions you would use.

Content analysis

A content analysis is an indirect way of investigating the meanings and messages in a variety of forms of communication. It can be used to analyse speech (for example, using transcripts of interviews) and media sources such as television, magazines, web pages and books. It is possible to use the technique to produce either qualitative or quantitative data depending on the way the material is assessed.

Figure 6.32 Content analysis can be used to find out how topics of interest to psychologists, such as gender stereotypes, are presented in the media.

The researcher begins by familiarising themselves with the range of ideas that are expressed in the data. To produce in-depth qualitative data, concepts or themes of interest are identified so that the data can be organised within these themes preserving the diversity of the findings. This is different from purely putting the data into simple categories. Importantly, it can retain unusual but significant examples of responses. Imagine a researcher exploring transcripts of a psychoanalyst analysing his patient's dreams. Their comments might include:

- I dream that I am swimming against an incoming tide
- Sometimes the water drains away leaving an empty shoreline

- At the end of a dream I sometimes feel relieved that I've succeeded at something
- Then realise it's just because everyone else has disappeared
- A clock will appear and I keep looking at it getting faster and faster
- I dreamt that I hid in a corner while everyone else was voting
- Then I got up and threw all the ballot boxes away
- I often dream about reading, usually I close the book and put it away

Some themes might include:

conflict

- winning (feeling of success)
- losing (clock getting faster, swimming against incoming tide)
- avoiding conflict (hiding in a corner)

completion

- incidental (water draining away, other people disappearing)
- deliberate (throwing the boxes away, closing the book)

This qualitative analysis is more than just listing examples within themes. The researcher may identify comments which demonstrate each particular theme clearly as well as retaining examples which are uncommon. If a patient said 'most dreams end with me shutting a door in someone's face' and few others mentioned this, it could become an important theme, even though it would be the only instance. This illustrates the capacity of qualitative data over quantitative data to preserve unique findings, rather than obscuring them by averaging.

Data from a content analysis can also be quantitative. Here, too, it is important to operationalise categories but these are used to count up the number of examples falling into each one. For example, in an analysis of the content of children's television programmes, a researcher might look for instances of gender stereotyped or gender neutral behaviours. These categories would need to be clearly defined and the definitions agreed between all raters assessing the material to improve reliability.

Interactive angles

You may remember from your AS a study about clip art (Milburn et al., 2001). They analysed the visual images in standard computer clip art packages and found that they were stereotyped, more often showing males than females as active and non-nurturing. Suggest how 'active' and 'nurturing' might have been operationalised. Look through a clip art package and find an image that fits into each category.

Figure 6.33 Are these clip art images stereotyped?

Table 6.5 Strengths and weaknesses of content analyses

Strengths	Weaknesses
content analyses have high ecological validity as they are based on real sources of information, for example, current TV programmes or newspapers, so indicate the nature of the media to which we are genuinely exposed.

Media sources are 'permanent' so can be retained and used for comparison and replication to improve reliability.

As documents are archived it is a cheap way to conduct a longitudinal study as there is no 'waiting time'. | Causal judgements cannot be drawn from content analyses. Media sources could be either reflecting or causing differences in the social world.

Researchers may be biased, lowering their objectivity, for example, in the way that they implement the categories reducing the validity of the findings.

Inter-rater reliability may be low if raters do not apply definitions for categories in the same way.

The findings of content analyses are generally culture-dependent as the interpretation of written or spoken content is likely to be affected by language and culture. |

Whether qualitative or quantitative data are being collected, the researcher needs to decide how they will sample the available material. In a study based on a small number of interviews, all may be analysed. If media sources are being used, strategies for selecting editions of newspapers or TV channels and times must be decided. Such design decisions may be made to ensure a wide spread, for example, looking at four randomly chosen newspapers on each week and weekend day in order to provide a range. Alternatively, the choice may be deliberately narrow, for example, children's TV programmes between 3:30pm and 6:00pm that fall adjacent to an advertising slot.

You may remember from your AS a content analysis of children's books which showed that, although male and female characters were approximately equally represented, the males tended to be more aggressive and competitive but less emotionally expressive than the females (Evans & Davies, 2000). Using content analysis in such studies is useful as the source of data (in this case books) is permanent so it is possible to look at changes over time, for example, to investigate whether books are less stereotyped now than they were. However, even if a changing pattern is detected, a content analysis, unlike an experiment, cannot lead to causal conclusions. Just because we find that books are less stereotyped does not allow us to decide what has caused this change. Haninger & Thompson (2004) analysed the content of computer games for teenagers (page 11). They found that 98% of the games required the player to be violent. They also looked for whether they showed victim's blood (42%), required the player to cause injury (90%) or to kill (69%).

Interactive angles

1. Identify one content analysis that you know well and evaluate it. Suggest how the method could have been improved.

2. Managers at a psychiatric practice are concerned that interviews may be culturally biased. Design a content analysis to investigate this. In addition to operationalising the categories you would use and defining the sample, you should include a specific aim, hypotheses, procedure, ethical considerations and how you would analyse the results including, if appropriate, your choice of statistical test. Justify your decisions, such as the categories you would use and whether you would try to obtain qualitative or quantitative data or both.

Correlational studies

A correlational study looks for relationships between two variables. Both variables must exist over a range and it must be possible to measure them numerically. This means that the participants' scores cannot just be in named categories, they must be on a scale which is, or can be converted to, numbers, ie measured on an ordinal, interval or ratio level of measurement. The findings of a correlational analysis can be described in two ways, by the direction and the strength of the link. In a positive correlation both variables increase in the same direction, that is, higher scores on one variable correspond with higher scores on the other. When two variables are negatively correlated higher scores on one variable correspond with low scores on the other. There may alternatively be no relationship at all between two variables (called a zero correlation). The Spearman test is used to decide the statistical significance of a correlation.

Interactive angles

Rutter & the English & Romanian Adoptees Study Team (1998) studied Romanian orphans and found that the younger they were adopted, the more successfully they developed once adopted (page 55).

Ahnert *et al.* (2004) investigated the effects of day care and found that, for children in day care, there was no link between socio-economic status and security of attachment. For children who did not have day care, those from families of higher economic status were more securely attached (page 65).

From the studies above, identify three situations: a positive correlation, a negative correlation and a zero correlation.

Figure 6.34 A correlation can be used to demonstrate the extent of similarity between identical twin pairs compared to non-identical pairs.

A researcher is likely to choose to conduct a correlational study when the variables they are investigating cannot be manipulated for practical or ethical reasons. Consider variables such as the length of time a person has had schizophrenia, the depth of an individual's depression, the severity of the parenting strategies used with a child or the number of negative life events an individual has experienced.

A correlational design is also used when the similarity between individuals is being assessed, such as in a twin study. For example, McGuffin *et al.* (1996) found a stronger positive correlation for major depression between identical twin pairs than non-identical pairs (page 152). A similar pattern was found by Gottesman (1991) in relation to schizophrenia (page 140).

Another occasion when correlations are used is to assess reliability. If participants are assessed on the same variable twice, the two sets of scores should correlate. This means the measures are consistent or reliable. For example, Pontizovsky *et al.* (2006) (page 134) assessed the relationship between diagnosis on admission to hospital and release in depressed patients. They obtained a Kappa value of 0.62, a fairly strong correlation.

We cannot say from one correlation that an increase in one variable has *caused* an increase (or decrease) in the other. This is because it is possible that the changes in both variables could have been caused by some other factor. Suppose we measure the two variables, severity of phobia and level of depression, and find they are positively correlated. It might be tempting to say that being depressed is responsible for the phobia, but we cannot be sure of this. It is possible that having a phobia causes depression or that both of these factors depend on another variable such as negative childhood experiences. All we can conclude is that the two factors we have measured vary together, not that there is a causal relationship between them. If we want to make judgements about causality, we need to conduct an experiment where we can be sure that it is the manipulation of one variable that is responsible for the changes in the other. Of course, if we conduct a correlational analysis and find there is no link between two variables then we can conclude that there is *no* causal relationship.

Interactive angles

Why do you think the following studies were conducted as correlations rather than any other design?

● McGuffin *et al.* (1996) found a stronger correlation for depression in monozygotic than dizygotic twins (page 152)

● Eron *et al.* (1972) found a positive correlation between the level of TV violence seen by children and their aggressiveness (page 8)

● Eron & Huesmann (1986) found that the more violence boys watched as children, the more likely they were to be violent criminals in adulthood (page 8). What is the direction of this correlation?

● Williams (1981) reported that TV viewing patterns in children in 'Notel' and their aggressiveness were not correlated (page 8).

There are some other advantages to correlational analyses. If a variable can neither be actively changed nor exists in different forms it is not possible to use it as an IV in an experiment. The correlational method allows us to study variables such as intelligence or aspects of personality that cannot be manipulated. Furthermore, because there is no need to manipulate the variables, only measure them, correlational studies can also be used when it would be impractical or unethical to artificially create changes. For example, in investigating the effects of different phobias or exposure to violent television. This is an important reason why researchers use correlational techniques.

Table 6.6 Strengths and weaknesses of correlational analysis

Strengths	Weaknesses
A correlational study can be conducted on variables which can be measured but not manipulated, that is, when experimentation would be impractical or unethical.

A correlation can demonstrate the presence or absence of a relationship so is useful for indicating areas for subsequent experimental research. | A single correlational analysis cannot indicate whether a relationship is causal so when a relationship is found this may be due to one of the measured variables or alternatively another, unknown, variable may be responsible.

Correlational analysis can only be used with variables that can be measured on a scale. |

Interactive angles

1. Identify one correlational study that you know well and evaluate it. Suggest how the method could have been improved.

2. A practice nurse in a health centre has noticed that many of the people coming in for help with drug misuse rarely stay at one address for long. She wants to investigate whether the severity of their drug use is related to this problem. Design a correlational study to investigate this. You should include a specific aim, hypotheses, procedure, ethical considerations and how you would analyse the results including your choice of statistical test. Explain the relationship the nurse might expect to find and explain what conclusions could be drawn from such a relationship.

Case studies

Case studies differ from other methods used by psychologists in several ways. Firstly, they focus on a single instance – usually one person although it is sometimes a family or an institution. This is explored in detail, often employing other methods in order to gain a range of information. For example, a case study of an infant might include observations, giving the parents questionnaires and interviewing them. Secondly, there are several reasons for conducting case studies. In general, experiments and other methods are used to gather evidence – they are planned with the aim of discovering new information. In contrast, case studies are typically conducted as a consequence of an event or situation that has already happened and may aim to either find things out or help the individual. This will affect the methods used within the case study.

Another factor affecting the choice of methods is the theoretical perspective taken by the researcher. Consider a psychodynamic theorist helping a patient with depression, versus a biological or cognitive psychologist investigating unusual brain patterns in a person with auditory hallucinations. The former is likely to use interviews, perhaps aiming to build up a relationship with the client that allows catharsis and transference to occur. The latter would use more objective techniques, perhaps conducting a single-participant experiment using a brain scanner.

Case studies can provide useful tests of ideas that could not be investigated using experimental methods, such as investigations of people with brain damage – which could not be experimentally induced. In such case studies, the context in which information is gained is a real one. This means that the findings are likely to be representative, at least of the one individual's experience, because the situation includes all the complex interactions that exist in real life. For example, in a case study of a victim's recall of a crime many more variables could be considered than would be explored in a single experiment that might test just leading questions or the role of anxiety. In real life, many other factors such as prior experiences of crimes as a witness or victim, the extent of injuries or the familiarity of the perpetrator could be important. Only in a case study would it be possible to explore these variables together.

Bradshaw (1998) reports a detailed account of a case study of a patient with schizophrenia. After gaining the patient's trust, the therapist was able to employ CBT to improve the patient's understanding of her symptoms, activity levels and ability to manage stress and avoid relapses. Although this instance was both useful for the patient and as a subsequent illustration for training other therapists, it could not provide evidence for the success of CBT in general as the patient may not have been typical.

The obvious advantage of the case study method is the depth and detail of the data collected. By using several different techniques, a researcher can produce a large amount of information about the case and can explore those findings that seem most interesting or useful in more depth. By using several techniques the researcher can also be more sure about the value of their findings. For example, in a case study of a child who has experienced privation, indicators from tests, interviews and observations might all suggest the same problems with language, attachment or cognition. Similarly, a case study of a dependent drug user might use tests to assess the effect of drug use on their memory, interviews with the family to find out about factors which may have led to their dependence and observations to see what problems their addiction presents in everyday life. When researchers use several techniques to check their findings, this is called triangulation. So although case studies are not a traditionally 'scientific' approach to research, the findings can be validated.

Figure 6.35 Case studies use many different techniques. Curtiss (1977) gained some information from Genie through her drawings.

Interactive angles

Here are some examples of case studies:

● the women with schizophrenia studied by Omoaregba *et al.* (2009) (page 188)

● Koluchova (1972, 1991) and the Czech twins and Curtiss (1977) and Genie (from child psychology; page 53).

● From your AS you may also recall Forde & Humphreys (2002) who studied an amnesic, FK, whose errors showed that STM can use semantic as well as auditory code and the case of the amnesic HM whose STM was unaffected but LTM was severely impaired (Milner & Scoville, 1957).

For each of these, decide why the researchers conducted a case study and explain the different techniques they used.

One disadvantage of case studies is that they are impossible to replicate because no two cases are the same. As they cannot be repeated, it is both impossible for researchers to replicate the data collection themselves to be sure that the results are correct and difficult for any findings to be checked by others. Another consequence of the uniqueness of a case study means that we cannot generalise the findings to other people. There are also potential problems with conducting a case study. As a researcher would usually spend many hours interviewing their participant, they are likely to get to know them well. On one hand, this is good as the individual will learn to trust them and may reveal more about themselves. However, the researcher's relationship with the participant

is also likely to make them biased and subjective. Another source of bias is the researcher's psychological beliefs. If the researcher has a particular view, they are likely to find examples to match and interpret evidence to fit in with their thinking, making them less objective. The setting itself makes these factors more of a problem than they would be in an experimental setting as variables cannot be controlled. For example, interviews are likely to be unstructured and observations participant and disclosed. These situations mean there is more opportunity for uncontrolled variables to affect both the participant and the investigator.

Table 6.7 Strengths and weaknesses of case studies

Strengths	Weaknesses
Case studies provide rich, in-depth data that provide more detailed information than can be obtained through methods such as experimentation.	Each case study is a unique investigation of a single situation or individual so the findings cannot be generalised to others.
Rare cases offer opportunities to study situations that could not – ethically or practically – be artificially contrived.	The evidence obtained from an individual that relates to the past may be hard to verify.
The realistic context of an individual's life or other unique instance allows for the investigation of the complex interaction of many factors.	When an investigator studies an individual in depth they may get to know them well and begin to lose objectivity.
Using many different sources of information from a range of techniques allows researchers to verify findings and be more certain about them.	In a case study, variables cannot be controlled so the method cannot be used to investigate causal relationships.
	The theoretical perspective of the investigator may cause them to interpret their findings in a biased way.

Psychology in today's society: the key issues

Key issues are current problems or questions in today's society. In the first two sections of this chapter, on pages 168–184, we explored a range of key issues from the approaches and applications. These included:

● blind obedience to authority (social approach)

● eyewitness reliability (cognitive approach)

● effectiveness of psychotherapy (psychodynamic approach)

● the use of drugs for mental illness (biological approach)

● the effects of media violence (learning approach)

● the effectiveness of token economies with offenders (criminal)

- the importance of family rooms in hospitals (child)
- the treatment of drug abuse with behavioural techniques (health)
- widening participation in sport (sport)
- drug therapies for mental illness (clinical).

Figure 6.36 The reliability of eyewitness memory is a key issue.

The concepts, theories and studies from each psychological approach or application can be used to understand these issues as you have seen in earlier chapters. Each of the approaches, and to an extent the applications, tend to favour one or more of the research methods discussed in the previous section (pages 192–210). For example, psychodynamic psychology uses more case studies than any other approach. Cognitive and biological psychology, in contrast, use mainly laboratory experiments. The applications of health psychology and to an extent clinical psychology place greater emphasis on animal research than the other applications. You can use these strengths and weaknesses of the research methods to help you to evaluate the research you use to explain a key issue. The research in different approaches and applications also tend to raise different ethical issues. For example, health and biological psychology raise the most ethical issues in relation to research using animals.

means that their view is determined by their cultural group. This leads to overestimating the importance and worth of members of their own group and underestimating the importance and worth of people who are not in their group. This idea will be familiar to you from your understanding of social identity theory from your AS. Consider the attitudes and behaviour of the participants in minimal groups studies (for example, Tajfel, 1970) or in Sherif et al.'s (1961) 'Robber's Cave' experiment. The participants in each case discriminated against members of the 'other' group, devaluing them and acting preferentially towards members of their own group. This prejudice leads to cultural bias, such as assumptions that the cultural norms of one's own society are 'normal' everywhere or are in some way 'better' than alternatives in other cultures.

In psychology, having an ethnocentric perspective means that researchers tend to focus on investigating phenomena and taking samples of participants exclusively from their own ethnic group. Indeed in many experiments attempts to reduce participant variables lead to actively avoiding or ignoring individual diversity in order to produce 'average' results that can be applied to 'everyone'. Thus from narrow samples (typically of white, American, middle class male students) conclusions are drawn that are believed to apply to 'people in general'. However, generalising the findings beyond the population from which they were obtained is invalid if the variable in question is not a universal one. Since the environment is clearly important in the development of so many psychological characteristics, this is likely to be the case. Smith & Bond (1993) analysed the research presented in a range of introductory psychology textbooks. They found that the work that was reported came almost exclusively from the USA and Europe yet the findings or theories are assumed to be relevant to humans worldwide on the basis that fundamental psychological processes are unaffected by culture. This, however, is a misassumption based on an ethnocentric bias.

Interactive angles

Decide on one key issue from each approach, one from the clinical application and one from each of the other two applications you have studied. In each case, describe and explain the issue using concepts, theories and research. Include reference to methodological and ethical issues in your discussion.

Debates in psychology
Ethnocentrism in psychology

Ethnocentrism refers to the tendency of people in general, and in this case researchers in psychology, to conceptualise the world exclusively from their own perspective. This

Interactive angles

Brown et al. (1986) (page 150) investigated social support, self-esteem and depression. Their sample included only working class women with a child under 18 living at home, a spouse or partner in a manual job, who were aged between 18 and 50 years and of European or Caribbean origin. In their discussion, the researchers ask the question 'What, then, do these results suggest about the role of social support in the development of depression?' Although they express some reservations, they conclude 'It appears that confiding alone is not enough; it also has to be associated with active emotional support from the person [providing support]'.

Is this representing a universal conclusion and to what extent is it justified on the basis of the sample?

The ethnocentrism demonstrated in research leads to two problems in psychology. Firstly, there is a lack of balance in research, with most being conducted on American and European samples. Secondly, the ideas based on this research may be inappropriately applied to different cultural groups because the researchers find it difficult to recognise or understand the differing experiences and behaviours of people from groups which differ from their own. That there are important cultural differences is supported by evidence that you have encountered. For example, in sport psychology Morgan *et al.* (1996) compared black, white and native American athletes' perceptions of sporting success. The white athletes had a 'you've either got it or you haven't' attitude, whereas the black and native American athletes placed much more emphasis on effort.

In clinical psychology we described the case of Calvin, an example illustrating the problems of ethnocentrism in diagnosis. This is an issue because cultural differences in social norms lead to misdiagnosis when psychiatrists from one cultural group assess patients from another. The UK black and Irish people are significantly more likely than others to receive a diagnosis of mental disorder. Littlewood & Lipsedge (1997) suggest that this is why black and Irish people in the UK are more likely than other groups to be diagnosed with a mental disorder.

Interactive angles

Goldstein (1988) describes the sample in her study of gender differences in schizophrenia based on data from patients at a New York City hospital as 97% 'non-Hispanic white'. She concludes that 'the determinants of gender differences occur during the premorbid period and are manifest early in the development of the disorder'.

Cultural differences are known to exist in attitudes to the diagnosis of schizophrenia. For example, Cinnirella & Loewenthal (1999) found that Britons of different ethnic groups had differing beliefs about the stigmatisation associated with the disorder. There are also cultural differences in the rates of diagnosis, for example Keith *et al.* (1991) report that 2.1% of African-Americans are diagnosed with schizophrenia; only 1.4% of white Americans receive the same diagnosis. To what extent is Goldstein's global conclusion valid?

In child psychology you may have learned about Van Ijzendoorn & Kroonenberg's study. The differences they found between cultures in terms of attachment types may be explained in a number of different ways. For example, attachment may mean different things to different cultures; what in Britain and America might be negatively interpreted as avoidant behaviour by an infant could be a positive sign of independence in Germany. Alternatively, apparent cultural

variations in attachment may arise because the Strange Situation that was developed in the USA is not appropriate for all cultures. For example, Japanese mothers tend to rush straight to the child in the reuniting stage which can lead to children being falsely labelled as type C.

Figure 6.37 Do cultural differences in attachment make generalisations invalid?

Cross-cultural research can be approached in two different ways. An 'etic' approach makes the assumption that there are universals in human behaviour and that cultural influences may or may not produce variations upon these. Etic approaches therefore look for similarities by studying many different cultures, generally from the perspective of an 'outsider'. One problem here is that in order to investigate a phenomenon in another culture, researchers use the same tools (for example, tests) that they have in their own culture – this is an 'imposed etic'. It carries the assumption that the tool is equally valid yet we know from examples like the Strange Situation that this may not always be so. The 'emic' approach, in contrast, investigates cultural uniqueness. Such studies focus on individual cultures and are typically studied from the perspective of an 'insider'. The ultimate aims of these two approaches are different. Findings from research using an etic approach are used to draw conclusions that can be generalised across cultures (although they may not be valid). Findings from research using an emic approach on the other hand are applied only to the culture from which they were derived.

Some research actively attempts to overcome the problems of ethnocentrism. For example, Omoaregba *et al.*'s (2009) case studies of Nigerian women with schizophrenia (see page 188) investigated the extent to which the cultural beliefs of the patients and their therapists were in conflict. Although differences in perspectives were acknowledged, the close contact possible in a case study gave the researchers insight into the viewpoints of the patients. This is rarely possible in experimental work where contact is limited or in most studies in which the sample is composed of a narrow demographic range.

Using examples from one application, describe one or more issues of ethnocentrism and explain the effects this may have and how any problems that arise could be overcome.

Psychology as a science

What is a science?

Science is about 'knowing' rather than just 'believing'. This leads to two ideas: that scientific knowledge is somehow different from non-scientific information and that it is obtained through a different, ie 'scientific', process. This process, called the **scientific method**, is important and, confusingly, can again mean two things. 'Scientific *methods*' are ways of collecting data, like experiments for example. The 'scientific *method*' is the process of making an observation and developing an explanation for it which is tested and refined (see Figure 6.38).

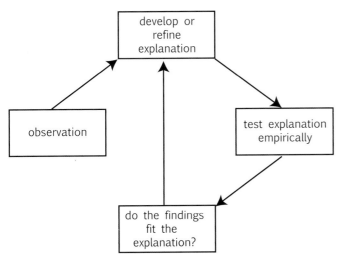

Figure 6.38 The scientific method.

The body of information built up using the scientific method constitutes science in the sense of scientific knowledge. We will explore each of these meanings, and some related ideas, in a little more detail.

Subjectivity, objectivity and replicability

For science to be based on knowledge, rather than belief, evidence is needed. What makes evidence 'scientific'? One important consideration is whether the evidence is objective, that is, whether it has been obtained without reference to the observer. To increase objectivity in their research, psychologists use standardised instructions, operational definitions of variables they are observing and physical measures of performance such as reaction time. These ensure that the researcher is not affecting the outcome of the study. If a researcher knows which condition of an experiment a participant is in they may respond to them in a particular way. This could influence the outcome of the study.

A personally biased perspective is described as being subjective. For example, an interviewer may be affected by a participant's emotions. If this biases their choice of questions or their interpretation they are being subjective.

When a study can be repeated in exactly the same way, it is replicable. This matters as scientific evidence needs to be consistent. If the investigation produces the same results when replicated it is likely to be valid and reliable (see page 192).

The scientific process: Popper and Kuhn

Although many philosophers of science have influenced the development and understanding of the scientific method, Karl Popper (Figure 6.39) and Thomas Kuhn (Figure 6.40) are especially important. Popper was concerned with the difference between whether a theory was scientific and whether it was true. He suggested that science involves proposing explanations and testing them against experience, that is, by observation and experiment. These methods are described as **empirical** because they are based on experiences with the world. They allow scientists to move from observations and experiments to theories by **inductive** generalisations. However, Popper was concerned that the scientific theories developed must make *specific* predictions; when tested they must risk being contradicted. It must be possible to show that they are wrong – this is called **falsifiability**. So, according to Popper, what separates science from non-science is not the ability to verify but to falsify. Scientists propose explanations, test them and reject those which are disproved and can then tentatively accept those which are not – although we cannot be certain that they will not be falsified in the future so science cannot establish truths.

Figure 6.39 Sir Karl Popper.

Figure 6.40
Thomas Kuhn.

Interactive angles

Table 6.8 demonstrates the application of scientific criteria to a study from your AS course. Select a study from your A2 course. To what extent do you think the study you have chosen counts as 'scientific'?

Kuhn suggested that science 'cycles' with new sets of beliefs about science replacing old ones. The sets of beliefs – or the **paradigm** – are the underpinning assumptions of a scientific approach. The paradigm is used to explain and predict the world but also defines the way in which research is conducted. As progress is made, and theories are improved and applied, new evidence ultimately results in the old paradigm being replaced. This is called a *paradigm shift* or 'scientific revolution'. Not only do the beliefs (or theories) change but the standards and measures, that is, the methods, change too. In Kuhn's view, this means that science does not result in progress, merely change. He concludes that science is what the scientific community accepts as scientific. This is one reason for the importance of peer review – to maintain scientific credibility.

Constructing a theory and hypothesis testing

A theory is developed in order to explain observation about a phenomenon in the world, such as the behaviours or beliefs exhibited in a particular situation. An effective theory should be able to account for the range of possible responses which occur and to predict which response will arise under a specified set of circumstances. Think back to the topic of memory you studied at AS. A useful theory of memory should be able to explain what will be remembered and what will not be. It should also be able to predict sets of circumstances which will cause us to remember or will cause us to forget.

Table 6.8 An experiment on eyewitness testimony: is it science?

What characterises a science?	Loftus & Palmer (1974)
isolating a single variable and measuring it to see what happens, that is, science focuses on objective measures.	They studied EWT by deliberately manipulating verbs (*contacted, bumped, hit, collided, smashed*) and measured the participants' estimates of speed.
Generating a hypothesis which is testable.	They predicted that changing a single word in the question would cause estimates of speed to change.
Employing controls so that changes in the variable being measured should only occur because of the researcher's manipulation as it is isolated from other features of the situation.	They controlled the setting (a laboratory) and stimuli (that is, the crash scenes on film) and changed only the verb to be sure that differences in estimates of speed were due to the leading questions.
The intention to falsify rather than confirm hypotheses.	Similar estimates for all verbs would have falsified the hypothesis. Also, as the study was well controlled it could be replicated so the findings could be refuted.
The development of general laws from the evidence of rigorous studies.	This study and others like it formed the basis of ideas about reconstructive memory; the findings support the common assumptions that memory is not a static structure but a fluid process.
Having a single paradigm – a common set of general laws or principles that are used to explain and predict the world and which define the way that research is conducted.	The findings support the cognitive paradigm – that information flows through a system and is processed along the way (so it is open to change).

Interactive angles

Theories help us to predict. Name a theory of memory and use it to imagine a situation which would cause a person to remember a piece of information. Now imagine a situation which would cause the person to forget a piece of information.

If you recall Popper from page 213, you can see why we need to test hypotheses. Firstly, they make predictions. When the variables are operationally defined, those predictions are very specific. When we state an alternative hypothesis, we are accepting that it could be falsified – the evidence we find might show that the alternative hypothesis is wrong. This is why we need a null hypothesis – it states the conclusion we must draw if the evidence fails to confirm the alternative hypothesis. Sometimes it is obvious that our alternative hypothesis is incorrect. For example, if we predict that people will concentrate better when they have eaten than when they are hungry, but we find that hungry people concentrate the best. However, deciding which hypothesis to accept is not always that easy, which is why we use statistical tests.

When the evidence we find fails to confirm our alternative hypothesis we assume that it is false. However, this may be a misassumption. A failure to confirm our prediction may be due to other factors, such as errors in the procedure or bias in the sample. If this is the case, a theory may be rejected for the wrong reasons. By using falsification, we may discard or change a theory unnecessarily.

Interactive angles

If you learned about the working memory model at AS, explain how evidence supporting this theory falsified the simple view of short-term memory proposed by the multi-store model.

Empirical methods

As we explained on page 213, empirical evidence comes from our observations and experiments. Some philosophers of science argue that we can never experience the world as it really is. Nevertheless, we should aspire to do so. This means using direct observation and recording of data. However, making direct observations can, in itself, be problematic.

We can make data collection more objective by introducing controls and limiting or removing the human element from the process of recording results. The Skinner box (see page 89) automatically counts the frequency of an animal's responses so there can be no subjective influence on the scoring of a 'bar press', unlike there might be if a person were keeping count. This would be an example of observer bias – and is avoided altogether by using electronic recording.

In order to investigate the world 'as it really is', we need to limit the influence of people in research. To this end, researchers use strategies such as standardised instructions and blind procedures. These help to ensure that the findings are the consequence of the variables being investigated and not the result of investigator effects or demand characteristics.

Human observers are used in many studies, for example in recording the responses of a child in the 'Strange Situation' (see page 44). In this instance, the accuracy of observations can be improved by using operational definitions for the various possible responses (such as showing fear). This helps to ensure that the records of one observer are consistent over time and are similar to those of other observers watching the same behaviours, that is, they show good inter-observer reliability.

The development of general laws or principles

According to Kuhn (see page 214) a science has a single paradigm – shared assumptions that are used to explain and predict the world and which define the way that research is conducted. Central to any paradigm, therefore, should be a unified set of general laws or principles. Whether psychology has such a unifying thread is open to debate.

If you think back to your AS and to applications such as clinical, you will have noticed that psychology encompasses a number of perspectives. Each is different in its underlying principles and, correspondingly, in its methods. For example, biological explanations rely on general principles about the function of neurones and genes. The psychodynamic approach in contrast is based on ideas about the unconscious mind and the effect of early experiences. Both can be applied to the same phenomena, such as explaining mental illness, but in different ways. This suggests that psychology has not yet reached the stage of a true science as it does not have a single paradigm, but has several simultaneously. This is reflected in the use of different research methods. Biological and cognitive psychologists use laboratory experiments as their predominant methods, whereas psychodynamic psychologists use case studies.

Within each of the psychological perspectives, however, there are general laws and principles. To an extent, the major paradigm has shifted over time. Early psychologists used a method called 'introspection' – they obtained evidence by studying their own conscious experience. This was replaced by more objective experimentation, for example by behaviourists who focused on observable responses, in learning experiments using Skinner boxes. The general laws for behaviourists were based on relationships between stimuli and responses, such as in operant conditioning. The paradigm for the cognitive psychologists who followed them returned to the study of events that could not be directly observed, but this time using more rigorous methods such as experiments to test the way information is processed. In these changes you can see how Kuhn's idea of science being cyclical applies to psychology.

Psychology and social control

There are a number of situations in which psychological knowledge and techniques are used to alter or control people's behaviour. Some are relatively uncontroversial because we agree that certain behaviours need controlling, others raise issues of personal freedom. Social control is the term given to the regulation of people's behaviour for social purposes.

The different theoretical approaches to psychology have led to different techniques of social control. From the biological approach we have developed ways to alter the functioning of the brain, for example using drugs. The psychodynamic approach gives us more subtle techniques with which to manipulate people's behaviour, via the unconscious mind. Through the learning approach we can use a different kind of unconscious process to manipulate behavioural responses. Each of these techniques raises ethical and practical issues of concern to psychologists.

Drug therapies and social control

Evidence suggests that many drug therapies are effective at reducing symptoms. Their use is still, however, somewhat controversial. Many patients suffer relapses, either through failing to take their medication or in spite of doing so, and many drugs can have serious side effects (see page 30). These include weight gain and more serious tardive dyskinesia for antipsychotics and the potential for violent behaviour and increased risk of suicide in the early weeks of taking some antidepressants.

For patients in institutions, the reasons for administering the drugs may be in part governed by the convenience of the staff rather than the benefit of the patients. For patients being treated by their GP, prescribing medication may be an 'easy option' when alternative treatments may be more effective. For example, in the treatment of depression psychological

therapies are more effective than drugs for many patients. Drugs are cheaper and instant – there may be long waiting lists for other therapies.

Token economies and social control

Token economies use operant conditioning techniques (see page 30). This involves responding to desirable behaviour by recording points, which can be saved up and swapped later for a tangible reward. This is used in prisons, schools and psychiatric hospitals. In psychiatric settings token economies can be used to rehabilitate long-term patients who need to pick up socially desirable habits again in order to fit back into society on leaving a hospital. In prisons, they can be used to improve social behaviour of offenders. There is a problem with this, however, in that every professional involved in recording points has a degree of power to determine what habits or behaviours are 'desirable'. Patients or inmates could thus potentially be conditioned to be clean-shaven, religious and so on, perhaps against their will. This illustrates the power of individuals and small institutions to exert social control over people.

In comparison to giving patients in a mental institution drugs which is very easy for staff, running a token economy programme is more demanding in practical terms. Staff have to be constantly watchful for good behaviours so that they can reward them immediately. They also have to ensure that they are consistent in their reinforcement, between staff members, between patients or offenders and over time.

Figure 6.41 We are being controlled by operant conditioning when we use loyalty cards.

There are clearly social control issues even when token economies are used with entirely humanitarian aims. Much more controversial is their use to control customer behaviour for reasons of profit. This is exactly what happens to us when we use supermarket 'reward' or 'loyalty' cards. Reward cards are electronic token economies in which we receive points for spending money in a particular store. These points accumulate and allow the customer to claim a later reward. Supermarkets are keen to allow us to benefit from this because it gives them control over us – we are reinforced every time we shop there and so are more likely to do so in the future. Reward cards also allow supermarkets to push sales of particular products of which they have an excess or which attract a higher than usual profit margin by means of offering bonus points when we purchase them.

Classical conditioning techniques and social control

By the systematic use of classical conditioning our responses to particular stimuli can be tightly controlled. We can, for example, condition a paedophile to respond to children with fear rather than sexual arousal by pairing images of children with painful electric shocks (an example of aversion therapy – see page 102). Given social attitudes to child abuse this might seem to many of us to be perfectly reasonable, especially as the procedure is performed with the offender's consent and alongside supportive counselling. What may surprise you, however, is that this painful and humiliating 'treatment' was used less than 30 years ago to 'cure' gay people, homosexuality being classed as a mental disorder under the DSM system until 1980. It is only because social attitudes towards the gay community have changed so much in recent years that we would now consider this to be barbaric, and an example of excessive social control. Clearly then aversion therapy is open to abuse; however, we can't now uninvent it, and it has legitimate uses. What we can do is keep in mind that it is a very powerful technique and be careful how and when we use it.

Interactive angles

If you studied health psychology, return to the topic and look for evidence of the specific arguments for and against the use of aversion therapy.

Another therapeutic technique using classical conditioning is systematic desensitisation used in the treatment of phobias (see page 163). As we cannot be relaxed and afraid at the same time, if we can stay relaxed in the presence of the thing we fear we will learn not to fear it. While maintaining a relaxed state (with the help of the therapist and, if necessary, drugs, hypnosis or meditation) the patient works up a hierarchy starting with exposure to a mildly fearsome situation and working up to the thing they most fear. This is fairly effective and only minimally distressing. However, it is less effective

than flooding, a technique which exposes the patient immediately to an extreme form of the thing they fear. If their fear eventually subsides (rather than them abandoning the session) this desensitisation can work. However, it is traumatic and many patients do not complete the session so are likely to be even more frightened. Whilst patients enter into these techniques voluntarily, social pressure to do so may mean that they feel obliged to do so, for example if their phobia is interfering with their work commitments.

Figure 6.42 By linking products to sex, advertisers make products seem attractive.

Classical conditioning can also be used to make us respond favourably towards products, and this is used to its full effect in advertising. At the start of an advertising campaign the product is a neutral stimulus but if we regularly see an advertisement in which it is paired with an unconditioned stimulus such as a sexy image, it becomes a conditioned stimulus and elicits the same response. For example a well-known bitter from the Manchester area was paired with the beautiful and scantily dressed Melanie Sykes. In classical conditioning terms, she was an unconditioned stimulus and the beer became a conditioned stimulus, literally making it sexy! This is perhaps an amusing and very harmless example of classical conditioning as social control, but such is the power of conditioning in adverts that it is illegal to advertise harmful products such as tobacco.

The influence of the practitioner in therapy and their role in social control

Psychological therapies include cognitive behavioural therapy (CBT) and various psychodynamic therapies. Evidence suggests that CBT is effective for patients with schizophrenia, depression and anxiety disorders, even producing good long-term outcomes. For people with schizophrenia NICE recommend CBT as particularly appropriate for new patients and those at high risk of not taking medication. However, CBT provides such patients with an insight into the seriousness of their condition and this can lead to depression.

CBT is also recommended by NICE as the most effective psychological treatment for moderate and severe depression. Again, however, there is need for caution as some evidence suggests that CBT is less effective than drugs and other psychological therapies and there are few studies of long-term effectiveness. It is also inappropriate for complex cases of depression for whom psychodynamic therapies are more appropriate.

In general, CBT does not raise the same ethical issues as drugs as it has no biochemical side effects. Nor are there the problems of distress associated with behavioural treatments like desensitisation. In this respect its use is more ethically acceptable. However, the therapist is still able to exert control over the individual's behaviour through the tasks and challenges they set, thus there is the potential for unscrupulous use. Of course, the same ethical guidelines that apply to researchers in psychology also apply to practitioners, so they should be qualified, supervised and acting with the benefit of the client in mind.

Psychodynamic treatments for schizophrenia are moderately successful – in spite of a lack of theoretical underpinning and Freud's own doubts. Some evidence suggests that psychodynamic therapies are effective without accompanying antipsychotic medication which has the potential to encourage patients and their clinicians to cease the use of drugs, which could be detrimental. Brief dynamic therapy has been shown to be useful in depression, especially in complex cases where there are other symptoms.

In general, psychodynamic therapies have the potential for misuse as a therapist may be able to implant false memories (see page 172). Although such situations do arise it is unlikely that this could be used in any systematic way for social control. Another objection to psychodynamic therapies is their cost. As the treatments are highly regarded, individuals and the health service may be pressured into paying for psychodynamic therapies which are typically intensive so very costly. In this sense social control is exerted for profit.

The nature–nurture debate

You should recall from AS that the nature–nurture debate is concerned with the extent to which human psychological characteristics are the product of our genes (nature) and of our environment (nurture). In its classic form the nature–nurture debate is concerned with individual differences in our psychological characteristics, for example the determination of our gender identity or the presence of mental disorder. The role of genes and environment in the development of individual differences can be investigated using methods such as twin studies, adoption studies and biochemical studies.

How do genes affect us?

Genes do not directly affect psychological characteristics but influence physical structures including the brain and neurotransmitters. Subtle differences in the nervous system, particularly in the brain, can predispose people to acquire psychological characteristics, ie they make people more likely to develop them. Most psychological characteristics are the product of several genes affecting the development of different physical structures, and of a number of environmental influences. Some characteristics are highly heritable, others not so at all.

How does the environment affect us?

From the moment of conception our environment impacts on our development. At AS you may have explored how levels of sex hormones affect gender development for example. There are innumerable environmental factors that have the potential to affect development. To understand how these operate we need to distinguish between the biological and psychological environments and between the shared and non-shared environment.

Biological and psychological environments

One important distinction is between the biological environment and the psychological environment. Biological environmental factors may adversely affect development. For example high levels of lead, gamma radiation and vitamin deficiencies can all lead to reduced intelligence. Recreational drugs such as amphetamines can increase the risk of mental disorder. We can sometimes intervene to counter the effects of poor biological environments. For example, vitamin supplements can be used to counter some of the adverse effects of poverty on psychological development. Because they are biological it is tempting to think of these factors as 'nature' rather than 'nurture'. However, they are very much environmental. What is more obviously 'nurture' is the psychological environment. Psychological environmental influences include socio-economic status, quality of relationship with parents, peer and sibling relationships, intellectual stimulation, abuse, neglect, bullying, education, exposure to role models and experiences of reinforcement and punishment.

Figure 6.43 These children share the same environment but their differing positions in the family mean they have some non-shared aspects too.

Shared and non-shared environments

Logically, we need to distinguish between two ideas about the environment; firstly that growing up in the same environment will make two children develop alike, and secondly that raising two children in different environments will make them different. This might seem like an odd distinction, but actually the two ideas are quite different. Remember, it is really a child's experiences that affect their development. If children grow up in quite different environments then they are very likely to have quite different experiences, and so their environment will cause them to develop differently. However, just because two children are raised in the same environment – for example, in the same home with the same family – this does not necessarily mean that they will have similar experiences. Parents may bring up a second child quite differently from the first, and two children with different interests and personalities may seek out different environments and be treated quite differently by adults.

Gene–environment interaction

Although it is convenient to think of genes and environment as separate influences on psychological development, in reality it is impossible to separate the two and they always work together. Even in cases where there is a strong genetic predisposition towards a characteristic, it is often possible to manipulate the environment in such a way as to alter it. In addition, our individual responses to an environment are influenced by our genetic make-up, meaning that a given environment will not have the same impact on different individuals. This is because we evoke different behaviour from other people and opt for different formative activities that exist within the same environment.

Theoretical approaches and the nature–nurture debate

In the above examples of environmental influences you might have recognised some that are emphasised by particular theoretical perspectives, thus quality of family relationships are important in the psychodynamic approach whereas reinforcement and punishment are associated with the learning approach. We will now look at each approach in turn.

The social approach is concerned almost entirely with the nurture aspects of the debate. Our social experiences are a major source of environmental input. If you recall, the factors affecting our attitudes (such as prejudices) and our acceptance of authority are social; they are determined by the effects of other people and our culture. Even areas that we consider to be governed at least partly by other factors, such as our gender development, are also affected by the social environment – such as the presence of same gender models and social norms.

The cognitive approach draws on factors from both sides of the debate. The role of the brain, especially areas such as the hippocampus, in memory is clearly nature. Furthermore even some changes in our ability to remember are governed genetically, for example, we recall little of our early childhood as our brains need to mature. The influence of experience in producing actual memories and on our capacity to remember, however, are influenced by experience. We can literally 'train' our brains to remember.

The biological approach includes the study of genes, and this is the approach that places the greatest emphasis on genetic influences. Twin studies have established that monozygotic twins are more likely than dizygotic twins to share certain mental disorders, and that separated identical twins remain remarkably similar in personality. Biochemical studies have begun to demonstrate genes that are involved in vulnerability to schizophrenia, depression and drug addiction. The biological approach is also concerned with biological aspects of the environment such as the effect that drugs have on long-term cognitive ability or mental illnesses.

Interactive angles

Using your AS notes or textbook if you need to, decide which approach is being described and whether each of the following illustrates nature, nurture or a mixture of the two:

- a new behaviour can be learned by shaping

- at the end of the phallic stage a child identifies with the same-sex parent and develops a superego

- brain surgery that damages the hippocampus causes amnesia

- concordance between monozygotic twins for homosexuality is much higher than for dizygotic twins

- if a pairing between a conditioned stimulus and an unconditioned stimulus is not repeated the conditioned response undergoes extinction

- Milgram suggests that we are socialised into the capacity to enter the agentic state as children

- psychic energy builds up spontaneously until it is discharged

- strongly associated words are more effective at priming memories than weakly associated words

- teenagers who identify with sporty or religious groups are less likely to take drugs than those who identify as hippies

- the frontal and temporal lobes of the brain are more active during semantic processing

- the *SRY* gene triggers development of a foetus into a male

- we have innate defence mechanisms to avoid the effects of moral strain when we obey.

The psychodynamic approach also places considerable emphasis on the environment; in this case the main source of environmental influence is the quality of early relationships. However, psychodynamic psychology also sees people as having innate emotional needs and instinctive behaviour – these are nature influences. Early relationships are potent environmental influences because of the ways in which they interact with these instinctive tendencies. In Freudian theory, for example, we have an innate tendency to engage in a three-way family dynamic, the Oedipus complex (nature). However, it is the way that parents cope with this dynamic (nurture) that affects psychological development. In attachment theory, we are seen as being born with a set of instinctive behaviours that predispose us to form an attachment (nature), but it is the behaviour of the primary carer that determines the quality of this attachment (nurture).

The learning approach places focus on environmental influences in the form of conditioning experiences and modelling, and plays down the role of genes. In fact the early behaviourists discounted the possibility of innate characteristics altogether, proposing that we are born a 'blank slate', which is then 'written on' by conditioning experiences. However, modern behavioural research has shown that people in general are predisposed to learning some responses rather than others (for example we are more likely to acquire phobias to animals that posed a real danger in our recent evolutionary history). Some individuals may also be more prone to acquiring conditioned responses than others. Psychologists adopting a behavioural approach nowadays do acknowledge the influence of genetic predisposition although the emphasis of the approach remains on environmental factors.

The nature–nurture debate and applied psychology

The applications draw on aspects of different approaches so reflect a variety of positions in relation to the nature–nurture debate. For example, clinical psychology uses each of the approaches to explain, and to offer therapies for, mental illnesses. Similarly, criminological psychology draws on a range of explanations for criminal behaviour.

We will look at an example from child psychology in detail. Attachment is a particularly interesting area to re-examine as it raises several nature–nurture questions:

- Is the quality of attachment (largely nurture) more important than temperament (nature) in determining individual patterns of social behaviour?

- Is quality of parenting (nurture) more important than temperament (nature) in determining the quality of attachment?

- Is attachment an evolutionary mechanism or a product of culture?

1. Is attachment more important than temperament?

Attachment and temperament are the two major characteristics that can be measured in infancy and which predict later development. Temperament is believed to be a result of genetic make-up (for example identical twins are more similar in temperament measures than fraternal twins), whereas attachment is largely (though not entirely) the product of parenting; the relative importance of temperament and attachment is an important issue in the nature–nurture debate. Actually, it seems that both temperament and attachment type are important predictors of later social development.

Attachment type is highly predictive of childhood and adult relationships in a range of contexts. Securely attached infants (type Bs) typically go on to have the best friendships, romantic relationships and working relationships. Type As (avoidant) have few friends and difficulty in forming romantic relationships. They also tend to avoid work situations requiring frequent or intense social interaction. They are the most likely children and adults to suffer bullying. Type Cs (resistant) have a tendency for stormy romantic relationships and difficulty in maintaining friendships and amicable working relationships. They are the most likely to engage in bullying behaviour.

Temperament is less predictive of relationship patterns than attachment type, but it does predict more general social behaviour. For example, babies classified as irritable tend to remain irritable as adults and those classified as unsociable tend to have less interest in social interaction as adults than others. In general then, attachment and temperament predict subtly different things and it is largely pointless to speculate on which is more important.

2. Is parenting more important than temperament in determining attachment type?

As well as being an influence of social development in its own right, temperament may also influence the formation of attachments. Thus, although securely attached babies come from the whole range of temperament types, unsociable babies are at greater risk of developing type A attachments and irritable babies are most likely to end up type Cs. Although it is likely that temperament is an influence on attachment type, there is also a large body of research linking attachment to caring style, in particular to what Ainsworth called *sensitive responsiveness*, the skill with which a carer picks up and responds to infant signals, thus being able to satisfy their needs.

In a meta-analysis of studies of sensitive responsiveness Atkinson et al. (2000) concluded that it is initially the most important influence on attachment type, but that this relationship becomes less pronounced with age, suggesting that either genes or different parenting skills become important later. This is consistent with behavioural genetics research showing that the influence of genes on individual differences increases with age.

Figure 6.44 Are attachments the product of nature, nurture or both?

3. Is attachment an evolutionary mechanism or the product of culture?

We can also look at attachment in the light of the 'new' nature–nurture debate concerning evolution and culture. According to John Bowlby, who first developed attachment theory, attachment is an evolutionary mechanism designed to increase the probability of infants' survival to adulthood through the maintenance of proximity to protective adults. This is a logical idea and in line with modern evolutionary psychology. Belsky (1999) has added to the evolutionary understanding of attachment by suggesting that different attachment types are adaptive in different types of environment. Thus dangerous environments lead parents to adopt a caring style that produces type A children that are well suited to a high mortality environment in which they are likely to lose many attachment figures.

What evolutionary theory finds it harder to explain are cultural variations in attachment behaviour and the proportion of babies classified as types A, B and C. For example, Germany has a particularly high proportion of type A attachments although it is not a high-mortality

environment. Grossman & Grossman (1990) explain this in cultural terms, suggesting that type A behaviour has a different cultural meaning in Germany, being seen as independent and tough rather than avoidant, and is thus more socially acceptable. It seems then that although attachment is probably the product of evolution, its nature is also affected by cultural factors.

We can conclude that attachment involves a complex interaction of nature and nurture. The tendency to form attachments and the existence of different attachment types are probably products of evolution, although this is difficult to directly test. However, attachment also has different meanings in different cultures and cultural norms influence caring style and hence the proportions of different attachment types. Attachment can thus also be said to be a cultural phenomenon. Whilst caring style appears to be an important predictor of attachment type, temperament is also important and may exert an increasing influence with age. In terms of patterns of adult relationships, caring style and attachment are powerful predictors, but in terms of behavioural dimensions such as irritability, sociability etc attachment may be less important than genetically influenced temperament.

Interactive angles

Draw three tables, one for clinical application and for each of the two other applications that you studied. Present evidence relating to the nurture side of the debate in one column and the nature side in the other. Below are some ideas that will help you to make useful comparisons:

- Criminological psychology: factors affecting the development of criminality – self-fulfilling prophecies and media violence (nurture) and genes, hormones, brain areas and neurotransmitters (nature)

- Health psychology: factors affecting substance misuse – role models in the media, friends and family (nurture) and genetic predisposition (nature)

- Child psychology: Bowlby's evolutionary basis for attachment (nature) and Ainsworth's maternal sensitivity (nurture), the universality of attachment (nature) and cultural variations in attachment (nurture)

- Sports psychology: individual differences and sport – trait theories (nature) and social learning and positive reinforcement (nurture)

- Clinical psychology: genetic predisposition to mental disorders (nature) and the effects of childhood experience (nurture).

Summary and conclusions

Psychological ideas from each of the approaches and applications have made useful contributions to society. These aim to improve the lives of individuals or groups within society, for example, reducing prejudice towards minority groups, providing therapies for people with mental health problems and improving the reliability of testimonies from eyewitnesses. The approaches and applications also raise key issues, such as why people will blindly obey orders, whether interventions with mentally ill people and offenders are effective and recognising the need for family rooms in hospitals.

In order that research is conducted ethically, psychologists follow guidelines relating to research on humans and on animals. For human participants these include obtaining consent, giving participants the right to withdraw, ensuring that they come to no psychological or physical harm, maintaining confidentiality and debriefing them afterwards. Researchers are required by law to have a Home Office licence for experiments on animals that could cause pain or distress. In addition, there are guidelines to help them to ensure the animals suffer as little as possible. These state the need for proper care (for example, in terms of food, water, space and social companions), that the numbers of animals used and the suffering they experience are minimised, that aversive procedures are replaced whenever possible and that alternatives to animal experiments must be considered.

Many different methods are used in psychological research. Experimental studies are typically highly valid and reliable, especially if they are laboratory based. Correlational studies and observations may be used when it would be impractical or unethical to conduct experiments. However, observations present other ethical issues, such as invasion of privacy, and causal conclusions cannot be drawn from correlations. Interviews and questionnaires allow for the collection of both qualitative and quantitative data and unstructured interviews offer the opportunity for obtaining detailed information from open questions. Similarly, case studies enable researchers to obtain in-depth data but this may not generalise from the single participant to others. Content analysis provides a way to explore communications, such as books and TV programmes providing an indirect way to observe patterns such as changes over time.

Psychologists make generalisations from their research and these are often applied to cultures other than their own. An ethnocentric bias prevents one from recognising that cultures differ and that the tools used in research, and the conclusions reached, may not be relevant to other cultural groups.

Scientific study should be objective and the findings should be replicable. Empirical research in psychology uses a range of methods which differ in these respects. For example, experiments, especially rigorously controlled laboratory ones, are highly objective and reliable although they may lack ecological validity. At the other extreme, naturalistic observations have high validity but are less reliable. Methods such as case studies run the risk of being subjective and are unlikely to be replicable. Different approaches to psychology typically use different methods, such as the cognitive and biological approaches using experiments but the psychodynamic approach using case studies. In this sense, the approaches differ in the extent to which they are scientific.

Psychologists design investigations to test hypotheses that can be falsified, satisfying another criterion of scientific study. On the basis of many such investigations, a body of psychological knowledge is built which can produce general laws. However, there are several different approaches each with different explanations so there is not yet a single paradigm, ie psychology lacks an overarching set of principles that are common to the whole discipline.

It is possible to use ideas from psychology to exert social control. Drugs, techniques based on learning theories and the position of a therapist can all be employed to control the behaviour of individuals. Practical and ethical issues are raised by such techniques, for example using medication may be beneficial to patients but they can also have side effects and if they are used to make patients in care easier to manage, this is unethical. Similarly, token economies are also effective with both mentally ill patients and offenders but can also be abused in order to make institutional life easier for the staff rather than to improve the individuals' quality of life. Whilst administering drugs is, in practical terms, very easy for staff, running a token economy programme is much more demanding. Staff have to be vigilant to reward good behaviours immediately and consistent in their reinforcement.

Both biological factors and environmental ones affect the development of psychological characteristics. The extent to which genes and the environment affect particular traits, such as the development of a mental disorder, illustrates the nature–nurture debate. This can be investigated by methods such as twin and adoption studies and more recently through biochemical analysis of genes.

What do I know?

1. (a) Describe what is meant by the nature–nurture debate. [5]

   (b) Describe **one** approach to psychology that you have studied. [4]

   (c) Explain the extent to which the approach you have described in (b) provides evidence for the nature–nurture debate. [6]

2. Psychologists working with animals have a responsibility to care for them.

   Describe **three** ethical guidelines relating to animals and use examples to explain the ways in which they should be followed in psychological research with non-human animals. [12]

3. Describe **two** different approaches to psychology and compare the extent to which each is scientific. [18]

4. Sandra is seven years old. Like her mum, she goes to ballet classes and is a talented dancer.

   Describe any **two** approaches to psychology and explain how each of them could account for Sandra's behaviour and ability. [18]

5. Describe and evaluate **one** contribution to society from the social approach and **one** from the biological approach. [18]

Chapter 7

Examination advice

What's ahead?

By the end of this chapter I should know:

- how my A2 is examined
- what will be assessed
- what to revise
- how to revise
- how to answer questions
- how to tackle sample questions and answers

How is my A2 examined?

As with the AS examination, there are two examinations. The Unit 3 examination can be taken in either January or June. The Unit 4 examination will only be available in June. Both examinations will assess all three Assessment Objectives.

Unit 3: Applications of Psychology

This unit will contain questions on four different options. The options are:

● Criminological Psychology

● Child Psychology

● Health Psychology

● Sport Psychology.

You will have studied two of these options. It is very important that you answer the two you have studied. Never attempt to answer an option you have not covered within your psychology classes. You will not have covered enough psychological theory and research to be able to gain good marks. For example, students studying a child welfare course or sports science may consider they know lots about these topics. However, the material you will have covered and the theories you will have looked at will not match what you would have done in a psychology class.

The examination is 1 hour 30 minutes long and it is important that you treat it as though you are taking two examinations, one for each option, and each 45 minutes long.

Each option will follow exactly the same pattern in having several short answer questions and an essay. Each option will be marked out of 30 marks, giving a total out of 60. These marks contribute 20% of your final A level marks.

Unit 4: How Psychology Works

This unit is made up of two parts, both of which you must answer. The first part is on Clinical Psychology. This is an application and the questions will follow a similar format to the options in Unit 3, though everyone taking Edexcel Psychology will have studied Clinical Psychology and there will be a few more questions.

The second part of the examination is entitled Issues and Debates. In this section, the questions will expect you to draw on information and understanding from everything you have studied throughout the course, including material from the AS year. There will be a series of short answer questions and an essay. The essay will usually give you a choice between two different titles.

The examination is 2 hours long and, again, it is important that you treat it as though you were taking two separate examinations, one for Clinical and one for Issues and Debates, each lasting 1 hour.

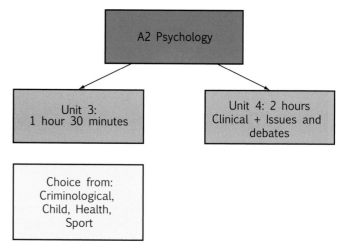

Figure 7.1 What is included in the exam.

What will be assessed?

The course has three Assessment Objectives; each one of these objectives is assessed in each examination. The balance of the marks between the three Assessment Objectives stays the same all the time; however, there is a little leeway because it is not always possible to set questions that exactly fit a certain formula. Under each of the Assessment Objectives there is guidance on the *typical* number of marks available for this skill on each paper.

Assessment Objective 1 (AO1)

This assesses your knowledge and understanding of the course material you have learned. In Unit 3 there will be either 8 or 9 AO1 marks per option. You can expect each option to have the same number of marks. In Unit 4 there will be about 24 AO1 marks; however, these will not be split equally between the two sections. While some of the AO1 marks may be included in the extended writing, many will be short answer questions. These types of questions tend to ask you to 'Describe' or 'Outline' a particular theory, study or part of a study. Describing a key issue is also an AO1 skill.

Assessment Objective 2 (AO2)

This is the most advanced of the skills being assessed. There are therefore more AO2 marks in the second year of the A level than in the AS year. There will be 13 or 14 AO2 marks per option on Unit 3 and about 43 on Unit 4. This skill is mainly evaluation in its various forms, but it also includes practical application of your knowledge. For more on AO2 questions and how to answer them, see the box opposite.

AO2 injunctions, and what they are instructing you to do

Evaluate...

This is the most straightforward AO2 skill. It requires you to write about the strengths and weaknesses of whatever is indicated in the question. You may be asked to evaluate a theory or a study. You can be asked to evaluate in a particular way, for example by looking at issues of reliability and validity, though you should be considering both strengths and weaknesses.

Evaluate using psychological research...

The only difference between this instruction and the previous one is that you must use some named psychological research to back up your evaluation points. If no research is mentioned the number of marks you can gain will be limited, usually to a maximum of 2 marks in a short answer question.

Assess evidence... or Assess 'theory x' ...

This is very similar to an evaluate question, the main difference being that to assess something means you need to comment on the worthiness of an argument. For example, it may be that you can argue that despite flaws in the theory it is still important in helping us to understand an issue.

Compare...

This means you need to explain similarities and differences between the two elements of the question. Remember that for a comparison to be valid there must be a sufficient link between the two points being made. For example, it is fine to compare whether two different theories see nature or nurture as the principal reason for behaviour but not to compare whether one is scientific with whether the other one sees nature as important.

Use your knowledge...

This is an application question. You need to use material you have learned and show how it can be used to solve a problem or produce an answer that is about a real-world experience.

Apply your knowledge...

This is a different way of phrasing an application question.

Explain (one strength/weakness)

Explain can be used to make the question very specific such as explaining strengths, weaknesses or one way a concept could be applied.

Assessment Objective 3 (AO3)

This will apply to questions that ask you about methodological and ethical issues. It includes both description and evaluation of these issues. It will also apply to any questions relating to your own research done under the Evidence in Practice section of the specification. There will usually be 8 AO3 marks per option on Unit 3 and about 22 AO3 marks on Unit 4.

Quality of Written Communication (QWC)

At least one piece of extended writing on each examination paper will be assessed for the standard of your communication skills. This means the answer should hang together as a coherent response to the question asked, with your spelling and grammar being the best you can manage in exam conditions. It is also important that you use relevant psychological terms. If you are concerned that you are not good at writing well because you have spelling difficulties, it is worth working on the terminology. Examiners can operate a trade-off between grammar, spelling and terminology if they are not all good; for someone who struggles with the grammar and spelling you can still do well if your terminology is good. Remember too that even if your spelling, punctuation and grammar are excellent you will not achieve the top level of marks if you do not use psychological terminology.

Any question that is going to be assessed for the quality of your written communication will be marked with an asterisk (*) next to the question number. It will always include an essay and may include a second piece of extended writing.

Figure 7.2 Be sure you are well prepared for your examinations by being clear exactly what you need to know.

What to learn for Evidence in practice

For each of the two applications in Unit 3 and for Clinical psychology in Unit 4 you will have undertaken a piece of work under the heading 'Evidence in practice'. This work will be assessed in examinations. The nature of the questions that can be asked needs to be taken into account when revising. Here we are going to look at the three different tasks that you will have undertaken. In addition to occurring under the relevant application, there could also be questions about what you have done in the Issues and Debates section. You will not be asked to give the results of these tasks as there is no way for an examiner to check whether the answer given is true or false. Questions are likely to ask about the process you followed, what problems you encountered, how these were addressed and what conclusions you drew.

Content analysis

You may well find you are asked to explain how you conducted your content analysis.

This requires you to explain the process of content analysis; it should include specific information such as what categories you chose to use and why these were chosen.

You may be asked to explain a specific problem you encountered and what you did to try and address the problem. This does need to be a realistic and specific problem. Answers which are very general or made up will lose marks because they will not be as focused on a realistic issue. For example, if you had undertaken a content analysis on articles relating to whether criminals are born or made, you may have had categories for evidence used in the articles. Categories might have included 'unsubstantiated assertions' and 'evidence from objective sources' (such as Home Office crime statistics). However, when you looked at the material more closely you may have found that a claim made, apparently using statistics, is making a link not fully supported by the evidence, so making it harder to categorise the statement. Your solution may have been to include an extra category; if so what was it called, and how did you decide when to include a statement in the 'dodgy data' category? Also be prepared to explain what might have happened if you had not made the alteration to the way you collected the data. In contrast, if you stated in your answer that you had problems with the categories you selected for the content analysis without explaining either why you knew they were too broad, what the categories were or the nature of the problem, the marks are unlikely to be awarded.

You are also likely to be asked what your results showed and therefore the conclusions you could draw. An examiner is not able to check whether any figures you give are true or false so these will not gain credit. However, what conclusions could be drawn from the results can be assessed accurately.

Finally a word of warning: examiners are psychology graduates. They will therefore have studied in some

detail evidence that has been shown to be false because the researcher in question has falsified their data. It is surprisingly difficult to produce a 'story' about a study that is convincing when it is made up, so it is really in your interests to make sure that what you learn for the examination is the genuine article!

Summary of articles

For the summary of two articles you should be able to give a brief summary, along with information that allows the articles to be traced. For example, if you put the author's name, and if it is an online newspaper article, which newspaper, this is sufficient to be able to locate the article and you should expect to provide this information to the examiner.

You may be asked to describe which section of the specification the articles relate to and explain how theories and research you have learned about can be used to draw conclusions about the content of the articles. Try to have at least two different theories you can use to explain concepts in an article: there will be points you can make that are positive and others that are negative. You may also be asked to draw some comparisons between the articles. This makes the choice of articles important. It is probably advisable to use two articles that take different views about an issue. For example, you may have two articles that suggest different ways of dealing with the use of illegal drugs (Health Psychology), disagree on the dangers or benefits of pre-school child care (Child Psychology), or differ in their view of whether natural ability or training is of greater importance in determining sporting success (Sport Psychology).

It is important to remember that you need to have revised the conclusions you drew from the article as well as why you drew these conclusions, as this is very likely to be assessed.

Leaflet

In clinical psychology you will have prepared a leaflet for a particular audience. As with Unit 3, there are a range of questions that can be asked so you need to not just recall what the leaflet was about, but also be able to comment on it. You may be asked to identify your target audience and explain briefly why you selected them, be able to explain why the level of information and type of information you included was appropriate given this audience. You need to be able to outline what the main pieces of information in the leaflet were, why they were included and how you tried to get the material across. If you used humour or diagrams, say so and explain why these were used. You should also be able to evaluate the leaflet and its content for both its strengths and its weaknesses, explaining how, if you did the exercise again, you would improve on what you did.

Unit 3 Questions

These questions would be equally applicable to all four topics; just imagine the term Criminological, Health or Sport in the introductory sentence.

1. As part of your course on Child Psychology, you have done either a content analysis or summarised two articles.

Either:

> (a) Describe how you undertook your content analysis. (4)

> Having selected an article on the use of daycare facilities in modern Britain, I chose to divide statements into positive, neutral and negative. ✓ Each of these was subdivided into three categories statements with evidence, those expressing the opinion of the author and those expressing opinions of other people. ✓ I then went through and counted how many statements there were for each of these categories. ✓ Once I had done this, I looked at the nature of the evidence used to see whether it was a reliable source, whether it included statistics and whether the arguments were valid. ✓ 4/4

Comment: From this answer, it is quite clear how the content analysis was conducted and which categories were used. However, the examiner will be looking to ensure that the answers in this part are consistent with the second part of the question. It would be better still if an example was given.

> (b) Using evidence explain what conclusions you drew from your content analysis. (6)

> My content analysis was on the issue of daycare and was in favour of daycare for all children. There were far more positive statements than negative statements; however, very few statements for either side of the argument had any evidence to support the assertion. This tends to suggest that the author had already decided on their viewpoint and selected statements to support an existing view rather than coming to a considered conclusion. ✓ The article used very emotive language and the arguments used in favour of daycare were mainly centred on the rights of parents, particularly mothers being able to return to work. It produced evidence from government statistics to support the idea that daycare is readily available at a reasonable price, but cited no material that looked at the quality of daycare. This again suggested a selective approach to the construction of the article, so that it supported the views of the author. ✓ Given the known importance of quality of care on long-term outcomes as shown by Belsky, this was an interesting omission. ✓ It appeared that the author was avoiding addressing the psychological aspects of daycare and only focusing on the financial and social benefits for parents in the short term, with no consideration for longer term care. ✓ 4/6

Comment: This is a good answer using evidence from the content analysis, material from the specification and blending the two to draw a conclusion.

Or ...

> (a) Give a short summary of one of the articles you studied. (4)

> The article by Simon Barnes in <u>times online</u> is concerned with why people compete, starting with the fact that the crews in the Boat Race get no prize money, no fame and have to fit a gruelling training schedule around academic work. ✓(identification) He uses reinforcement as the primary motive for participation, and that the positive aspects of reinforcement are powerful enough to overcome negative effects. ✓ He argues that taking part is reinforcing because doing a sport well gives satisfaction, explaining how mastery of a sporting technique produces a feeling of pleasure. ✓ He suggests sporting participation is also reinforcing because of the socialising opportunities that participation produces, especially when there is danger or endurance is involved. ✓ He also suggests that endurance events produce an addictive response because of the release of endorphins (✓) 4/4

Comment: While this is quite short and could give much more detail the question is for 4 marks and asks for a short summary, therefore it is sufficient. Remember to judge the amount you write given marks available. At just over 100 words this would be about 10–12 lines of average sized handwriting; you can expect to write about 2 to 3 lines per mark for this type of question.

(b) Using your knowledge of psychological theory explain possible reasons for the opinions expressed in the articles you summarised. (6)

In the Simon Barnes article, he is convinced that the primary reason why people take part in sport is because of reinforcement. He cites a variety of positive aspects to sports participation and even writes about how people taking part in a long-distance rowing event will respond at the end by saying they'll never do it again, but then do. He clearly believes that positive reinforcement is a very powerful aspect to sports participation and that this can be satisfaction of doing something well, of achieving a goal or of sharing a special moment with other people. ✓ However, he dismisses the role of pain and discomfort as punishers. ✓ He also uses the addiction of the endorphin rush as an explanation of why endurance athletes will keep training and competing. Given the knowledge of the addictiveness of endurance training this is a reasonable conclusion; however, he fails to address the issue of whether endorphins may be implicated in sprint sports. ✓

In contrast, the article by Robin Cooke in the San Francisco Times produced biological evidence for sporting performance and success. It uses evidence from the British Heart Foundation that suggests a genetic modification meant some people have superior cardiovascular functioning, which will make them better athletes. However, this article, though it suggests such a biological factor may influence performance, does not provide any evidence that such people are more likely to participate in sport, merely that if they do they will probably outperform those who do not have this gene. ✓ 4/6

Comment: The comments on the first article are generally good, if a little lengthy, showing how reinforcement theory is used, though somewhat selectively. It also mentions how the endorphin explanation only explains some participation. By contrast, the second article is only dealt with briefly, probably because this is not an ideal choice of article as it contains only one core idea and that is very briefly explained. The criticism that having a gene that improves performance does not mean participation will ensue is an important one and an issue that is important within the specification.

Unit 4 Questions

Section A: Clinical Psychology

As part of your course, you designed a leaflet about your key issue.

Describe who the target audience were for your leaflet and why this group were selected. (3)

My target audience were the families of those recently diagnosed with anorexia nervosa. ✓ They were chosen as they are an important group as the people most likely to be able to support the sufferer in her/his attempts to overcome the disorder and avoid hospitalisation. ✓ 2/3

Comment: This needs a little more information for the third mark. For example, why the family are the most able to support the sufferer or comment on the leaflet offering strategies for monitoring/encouraging/persuading the sufferer in their attempts to change eating patterns.

Explain one way in which the nature of the target audience was taken into account when constructing the leaflet. (2)

As the audience is unlikely to have any psychology training, the strategies were described in simple terms without any jargon. ✓ For example, instead of referring to reinforcing eating terms such as praise, pleasure, and sometimes rewards were used. ✓ 2/2

Comment: Clearly *explained*, and sounds realistic. The second sentence demonstrates the student's understanding by giving a relevant example.

Once you had completed the leaflet you will have assessed it for how successfully it achieved the intended outcome. Explain what your conclusions were and why you considered these conclusions were appropriate. (4)

The leaflet was very informative as it gave families several clear strategies for encouraging eating and monitoring food intake in anorexics. I think it would have been useful as it explained how to use positive reinforcement, though this was explained in simple lay terms so that it would be easy to follow. ✓ I think I also suggested some useful reinforcers that could be used to encourage eating and weight gain, such as a new expensive outfit. ✓ However, this might not be appropriate for some people, and boys in particular may prefer something such as a sports treat like tickets to a big match. ✓ 3/4

Comment: A good answer showing some understanding of both positive and negative points. However, there is insufficient here for full marks. Remember when you are preparing your leaflet to really think hard about the positive and negative aspects of the work you produced.

Section B: Issues and Debates

As part of your A2 course you undertook a content analysis.

> Explain how you undertook your content analysis. (4)
>
> Evaluate the use of content analysis in understanding how people may explain their views about an issue you considered in one of the applications you studied in Unit 3. (6)

A question such as this one would ask you to identify the approach you are using and then would be similar to the earlier question. Questions on this are unlikely to come up frequently in the Issues and Debates section, but because this section taps into all of the specification and will assess research methods such a question is likely to come up at some stage. This emphasises the importance of fulfilling all the requirements of the specification.

What to revise

The very short answer here is 'everything'! However, let's try to be more specific and rather more helpful.

Below is a checklist that provides a list of what the specification states you need to know, interpreted for you with guidance on the number of marks' worth of material you should be aiming to learn in each case. You will find it helpful to refer to the relevant sections of the specification. You will probably have been given a photocopy of this, but it is also available on the Edexcel website (http://www.edexcel.com/quals/gce/gce08/psych/Pages/default.aspx).

It is important to appreciate how much 'doubling up' can be achieved in terms of revision, so once you have had a look at the checklist have a look at the What to revise tips.

Unit 3: For each of the options you have covered you will need to know the following:

Definition of the application	Brief definitions/explanations, 3 marks for each of the terms listed. Be able to amalgamate the concepts covered by the list to explain what the application is concerned with (4 marks).
Methodology/ How science works	Be able to describe each of the research methods and concepts in this section (6 marks). Be able to evaluate each method in this section in terms of at least two strengths, two weaknesses, at least three issues of reliability and three of validity. You should be able to supply sufficient detail and elaboration to gain 2 marks for most of these points and be able to include evidence from research for at least some of the points.
Content	Learn six descriptive points for each item that you are asked to describe. Make sure each point is accurate and in sufficient detail to gain credit. (Remember there are some choices here so for example you do not have to learn more than two different ways of controlling anger.) Be able to explain and elaborate two strengths and two weaknesses for each item you learn to describe. This means enough detail for each strength or weakness to gain 2 marks. Be able to produce a study or theory that supports and another that is critical of the material. Be able to show how the material is relevant to the application by being able to explain how it might be used.
Studies in detail	Be able to identify each of the two studies accurately. Give an aim and describe the procedure in detail (6 marks). Describe the findings, including at least some statistics such as scores, means or significance levels and the conclusions (6 marks). Be able to evaluate each study in terms of strengths and weaknesses (6 marks). Points should include both practical and ethical issues and must be specific to the study, not generic points made because for example it is a laboratory study.
Evidence in practice	You need to be able to describe a key issue. Explain what the issue is and why it is of importance (3 marks minimum). Use concepts and theories covered in the application and possibly also in the AS course to explain the key issue. If you can show how different theories disagree this will be very useful (8 marks). For the practical you conducted be able to describe what you did in the content analysis/article summary (5 marks), give a description of the source material for the articles (5 marks) and explain how you did the content analysis (5 marks). Remember a relevant example can gain you a mark in these types of questions as long as it is in sufficient detail. In each case explain the conclusions you came to and why (6 marks).

Unit 4: For Clinical Psychology

Definition of the application	Explain what clinical psychology is and what each of the listed terms means (3 marks).
Methodology/ How science works	Explain the difference between primary and secondary data (3 marks) and give a clear example of each for a fourth mark.
	Evaluate the use of primary and secondary data using evidence from studies (6 marks).
	Explain the importance of reliability and validity in clinical psychology (8 marks). Be able to produce evidence illustrating issues of reliability and validity.
	For each of two different research methods used to study schizophrenia be able to:
	Explain how the research method is conducted (4 marks);
	Explain at least two strengths (4 marks) and two weaknesses (4 marks) for each method;
	Describe and evaluate one study for each method. Know sufficient detail that you can use it to illustrate both how it demonstrates the method used and can be used to evaluate the research method.
Content	Describe the statistical and social norms definitions of abnormality for 4 marks each. Evaluate how suitable these definitions are in helping us to understand abnormality in terms of at least two strengths and two weaknesses. Ensure any examples are related to clinically abnormal behaviour.
	Describe (4 marks) and evaluate the issue of diagnosis in terms of reliability (4 marks) and validity (4 marks).
	Describe (4 marks) and evaluate (4 marks) the use of DSM.
	Describe the symptoms and features of schizophrenia (5 marks).
	Describe a biological explanation for schizophrenia (5 marks).
	Evaluate the biological explanation using research (5 marks).
	Describe an explanation for schizophrenia from one of the other approaches (5 marks) and evaluate it using research (5 marks).
	Describe the symptoms and features of one other disorder from the list in the specification (5 marks).
	For this disorder you must be able to describe two different explanations from two different approaches from among the five approaches studied in the AS specification (5 marks for each explanation).
	Evaluate each explanation including strengths and weaknesses and using evidence from research (6 marks for each).
	For each disorder you must be able to describe two different therapies/treatments from two different approaches from among the five approaches studied in the AS specification (5 marks).
	For each of the chosen therapies/treatments from the different approaches, be able to describe the way the therapy is conducted (5 marks).
	Evaluate each therapy using evidence from research, in terms of effectiveness and ethical and practical issues (6 marks).
Studies in detail	Be able to accurately describe the procedure and the findings of the Rosenhan study (6 marks for each).
	Evaluate Rosenhan's study in terms of strengths and weaknesses and what it tells us about reliability and validity (8 marks in total).
	For each of the other two studies be able to describe the aim and procedure (6 marks), the findings (6 marks) and evaluate (6 marks).
Evidence in practice	You need to be able to describe a key issue in clinical psychology. Explain what the issue is and why it is of importance (3 marks).
	Be able to use concepts and theories you have covered in clinical psychology to explain the key issue (6 marks minimum).
	Describe the topic you prepared a leaflet for, including who the target audience were and the nature of the information included (5 marks).
	Explain what decisions were taken about content and why (5 marks).
	Explain what the purpose of the leaflet was in terms of outcomes (4 marks).

Remember: you need to revise the material you covered in the AS year for this Section as questions based on AS material will be included in the Unit 4 examination.

Unit 4: Issues and Debates

Contributions to society	You need to be able to describe (5 marks), and evaluate (5 marks) in terms of strengths and weaknesses, two ways in which each of the Approaches studied at AS (Social, Cognitive, Psychodynamic, Biological and Learning) have contributed to society *(be careful here that the contributions are to society rather than to psychology)*. Describe and evaluate one contribution from the two Applications options you studied in Unit 3 and one from Clinical (5 marks each for the description and the evaluation).
Ethical issues	Make sure you can identify and describe the five main ethical principles for human research as laid out by the British Psychological Society (3 marks for explaining each principle). Know the five main ethical principles that relate to animal research (3 marks for explaining each principle). You should be able to describe why ethical principles are important, for both human and animal research (6 marks), comment on whether the principles are effective in safeguarding participants and/or animals used in psychological research, and evaluate current ethical standards compared to the historical situation (6 marks). Be able to describe and evaluate two different studies in terms of ethical considerations, including their strengths and weaknesses. (Know the study as well as for a study in detail; 4 marks for strengths and 4 marks for weaknesses.) Remember it is best to use two very different studies. It is sometimes useful to demonstrate knowledge of a study that has very good ethical standards as well as one that does not. Similarly the contrast between human and animal ethical issues can sometimes be best explained if you can demonstrate this with knowledge of relevant studies.

Research methods
(research methods you need to know are:
i experiments:
  a laboratory
  b field
  c natural
ii observations
iii questionnaires
iv interviews
v content analysis
vi correlations
vii case studies)
	For each of the research methods encountered during the course, and listed to the left, you need to be able to describe what the main features of each method are (4 marks), explain two strengths and two weaknesses of each method (each strength and each weakness in enough detail for 2 marks) and be able to describe a psychological study that illustrates the method and can be used to illustrate some of the strengths and weaknesses.
	
	Be able to plan a study for any of the specified methods. Such a plan would need to include all aspects from the context of the research and its aim through to analysis of data (12 marks).
	
	Be able to evaluate research studies in terms of their methodology, including suggestions for how improvements could be made in specific areas such as implementation of controls and other design flaws, or how reliability and validity might be improved.

Key issues	For each of the five AS topics and each of the Applications, be able to describe a key issue (minimum 3 marks) and explain the key issue using theories and concepts from the relevant approach or application (6 marks).
Cultural issues	Describe and give examples of ethnocentrism in psychological research (4 marks). Describe (4 marks) and evaluate (4 marks) possible bias in the application and interpretation of cross-cultural studies.
Psychology and science	Describe what is considered to define a science (4 marks), and describe how well psychology fits this description (4 marks). Evaluate whether psychology can be called a science (6 marks). Describe (5 marks) and evaluate using evidence (5 marks) each of the five Approaches in terms of how scientific they are. Be able to make comparisons across the approaches for how scientific they are.
Social control	Describe issues of social control relating to use of psychological knowledge. Description should include detailed information on drug therapy, token economy, classical conditioning and the effect of the practitioner on therapy/treatment (4 marks for each). Assess each of these topics in terms of both ethical (4 marks for each topic) and practical (4 marks for each topic) issues raised by such control.
Nature–nurture	Define the terms nature and nurture including where these influences originate from (4 marks each). Describe the view of each Approach in terms of nature and nurture (4 marks each). Evaluate the relative merits and demerits of nature and nurture as explanations of behaviour using psychological evidence (8 marks).
Applying knowledge	You should be able to apply any of the skills listed in this section to a novel situation.

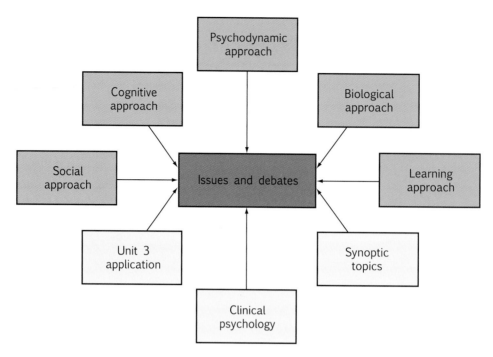

Figure 7.3 What you need to learn for the Unit 4 exam.

What to revise: some tips

A great deal of the material in the Issues and Debates section is material you have already learned for other sections. In addition, in all the Applications there are circumstances where material can be used in more than one place.

As an example, when learning about schizophrenia in Clinical Psychology you will have read about the Rosenhan study. In the Issues and Debates section you can use your knowledge of this study to consider the following:

Ethical issues: Was the study ethical? Is it reasonable to criticise the medical profession for diagnosing someone as schizophrenic when the pseudo-patient lied about their symptoms?

Methodology: The study is an example of a field experiment. What were the independent and dependent variables? What can you say about the methodology of this study?

Figure 7.4 Be sure to revise all the material from the AS year. It will be needed for Unit 4 Issues and Debates.

A good way to ensure that you do not have to learn more studies than you need to is to produce a table with 3 columns. The first column is the topic, the second is the name of one study you can use to illustrate this issue and the third column is a second, back-up study. This strategy is ideal for the Issues and Debates section, but can also be useful in the Applications too.

An example of how to create a studies checklist:

Topic	Study 1	Study 2
Ethical issues – human	Watson & Rayner 'Little Albert'	Money 'Ablatio penis'
Social control	Watson & Rayner 'Little Albert'	
Nature	Money 'Ablatio penis'	De Bellis et al. 'Sex differences in brains'
Nurture	Watson & Rayner 'Little Albert'	Picken & Thompson 'Cocaine reinforcement in rats'

Note that studies can easily be used for several different topics. It is worth thinking carefully about which studies you are going to use. This means you can learn these studies thoroughly so you have in your head the details of studies that are likely to be most useful. It means that you will be going into the exam with a clear idea of which studies are useful to illustrate particular points. If you do not do this as part of your revision programme, you will have to think this through during the examination; that takes up time that could be used for writing answers and you are more likely to forget the 'ideal' study under stress.

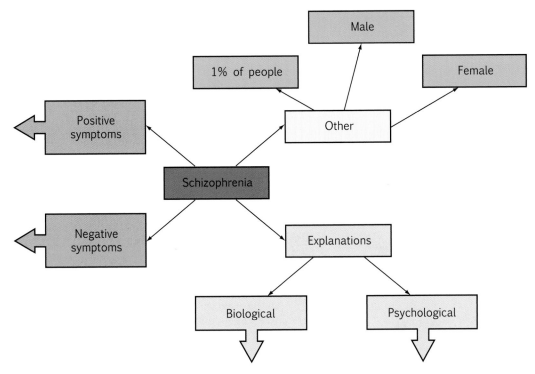

Figure 7.5 Using concept maps or spider diagrams can often help people revise.

How to revise

By the second year of your course you should have moved beyond GCSE revision strategies and be aware that merely memorising information is not enough.

You will also be aware from studying the Cognitive Approach last year that transferring information into long-term memory can be achieved using a variety of techniques.

Your learning style will affect how easily you can learn using different strategies, but you are always going to be producing your examination answers by writing them so it is important that you practise this.

Try to vary the way you learn material by reading, note taking, making spider diagrams, highlighting and any other ways that you have found effective. But it is also important to use methods that make you process information. Answering practice questions is one strategy, but another excellent method is to write your own 'exam questions' then write the mark scheme for the questions – use your notes, text books and even the Internet for this task. You might, if you are working with friends, once you have done this try answering each other's questions. Then you can use the mark schemes to see how well you did!

One final and very important aspect of how best to revise is the issue of 'spaced learning'. Your brain needs time to create memory traces; if you give it time to establish the connections needed to learn the material for your exams it will remember far more effectively than if you try and fit it all in shortly before the exam, when all you will end up with is

brain ache! So start revising early; doing a little on a regular basis over a couple of months will produce memories that are easier to recall than if you leave it all till the last ten days.

How to answer questions

The A2 year of an A level demands a higher standard of performance than an AS. This includes what you need to write in order to achieve the marks in examinations.

Remember to ensure that each point you make is fully made and as clearly expressed as you can manage to make it. You can assume that the examiner is a psychologist, so you can write for a knowledgeable audience. However, the examiner does not know you, nor what you have learned about in class, so try to make points clear.

If you want to use an abbreviation to save time, that is permitted. After all it takes quite a while to keep writing out the word schizophrenia, but it is important to ensure that the first time you use the term you give it in full with the abbreviation in brackets after it. After that, you can just use the abbreviation:

> One explanation for schizophrenia (sz) is that it is caused by an excess of dopamine in the brain. A study into sz by ......

Another issue that causes problems and costs marks is identification of studies. You can only gain credit if the names and/or title are correct. Snappy 'headline' titles are fun to read and help learning but should be avoided in an examination. So if describing a study that raises issues on the nature–nurture debate you identify:

> The study into whether 'Boys will be boys' showed that when one of twin boys had a surgical accident that damaged his penis beyond repair it was decided to rear him as a girl …

This is not acceptable. Examiners will happily accept either the name and date or the title as sufficient. It must be absolutely clear which study you are referring to.

A similar problem can arise when describing a study by a researcher who has published large amounts of research. Bandura has over 300 publications so identifying a study as Bandura does not help a great deal. While not all of his studies are on Bobo dolls, there are still a lot of those so you need to be precise, give the date and if there are co-authors give those too.

When you are describing a study it is very useful to remember APRC. So write something about the **A**im, then the **P**rocedure, this followed by the **R**esults and finally the **C**onclusions.

You will find that often you are asked about just one part of a study, so ensure you know sufficient detail.

In questions that ask you to evaluate in some way, it is important that you never use symbols to indicate that something is a positive or negative point. One problem is that the use of a symbol tempts you into writing in a more note like form. This may not get a mark because it fails to make the point fully enough.

Compare these two points:

> + diagnosis reliable as 7/8 pseudo-patients got the same diagnosis
>
> Rosenhan's study showed good reliability for DSM as out of eight pseudo-patients all reporting the same 'symptoms' seven were admitted with a diagnosis of schizophrenia.

The first statement may be fine as a reminder in your revision notes but the second statement is the one that gets a mark in the examination. If you write several points in this abbreviated, note form an examiner will probably bracket them together and just give you a single mark.

Remember too that the moment you put a plus or minus sign in front of a comment it becomes note form rather than essay style. This is penalised in any questions that assess 'Quality of Written Communication' (QWC); you will know this because the questions will have an asterisk against them on the examination paper. In these questions, sentences should be properly written and abbreviating to symbols avoided.

Always use the number of marks allocated to short answer questions as a guide to how much to write. If the question is for 4 marks then you need to have four things there that can get credit. As it is sometimes difficult for you to judge whether something is worth a mark or not in an examiner's

eyes, it is always a good idea to write one more point than you think you need to get full marks. It is very important that you do not write a lot more than there are marks available. If a question asks you to outline an example of social control for 3 marks, keep it brief as a long detailed description of token economy will take a long time and you probably got all the marks with the first three sentences.

Essays are marked slightly differently. This is because they are marked using levels. This means an examiner will read the whole essay first to gain an impression of what you have written rather than marking it point by point. This means the structure of the essay matters, so it is worth spending a little time planning. An essay with good coherence takes the reader from the introduction of the issues to the conclusions without being repetitive. As already mentioned, an examiner will consider your spelling, punctuation, grammar and use of terminology, and will also consider whether you have successfully addressed the question that you are answering. In addition, on the Issues and Debates essay there are an additional 6 marks awarded separately for how well structured, focused and coherent your answer is. It is important you are aware of this difference in the way essays are marked as it means that a 12-mark essay does not necessarily have to have 12 points made to gain full marks.

Figure 7.6 Be sure you read questions carefully and answer the question that has been asked.

Sample questions and answers

This section is designed to highlight the types of question you may encounter with an indication of how to, and how not to, answer each question. Look for where points you feel should get a mark do not, and find out from the comments sections why not.

In examinations there are two main reasons why candidates do much worse than they thought they had. The first is when they have not read the question carefully enough and answer a different question than the one set; the second is when they have not provided enough detail to get the mark. This is a very common problem at A2 and one that is avoidable.

Short answer questions

> 1. Describe the features of schizophrenia. (4 marks)

This is a typical AO1 question from Clinical. Here questions can ask for **symptoms**: those things used by clinicians to diagnose whether someone has the disorder or not, and **features**: those non-symptom factors that characterise the disorder and may inform a clinician but are not in themselves symptoms. Alternatively, the question could ask for symptoms and/or features, in which case any combination of the two would be permissible.

Sample answers

i

> Schizophrenia is a mental disorder that is diagnosed using DSM. Symptoms of schizophrenia include hallucinations and delusions; these are positive symptoms. Negative symptoms include poverty of speech. It affects 1% of the population. ✓
>
> 1/4

ii

> Schizophrenia is caused by your genes because monozygotic twins are more likely to get it than dizygotic twins. It affects 1% of the population ✓ but your chances of getting it if you have a parent who suffers from schizophrenia is 10%. ✓   2/4

iii

> Schizophrenia is a mental disorder that affects about 1% of the population. ✓ Onset in males is most likely to be in the late teens or early 20s, whereas in females onset is later, typically from 25 up to 30. ✓ It affects men and women equally. ✓ There are both positive and negative symptoms; both the level and balance of symptoms varies greatly from one patient to another. ✓   4/4

Comments: The first answer here focuses on symptoms and diagnosis rather than features. In the second answer the first comment, even if it had been correctly expressed, would still not get a mark as it is an explanation for the cause of the disorder not a feature. The final answer is exactly right. Incidence in the population, typical age of onset and gender differences in onset are all straightforward features. Finally, the last comment is moving towards symptoms, but because it is commenting on the fact that there are both positive and negative symptoms that is a feature.

> 2. Token economies are a means of exerting social control over people. Describe an example of a token economy programme. (4 marks)

Again this is an AO1 question. This would be an Issues and Debates question so the token economy could be from any of the Applications you have studied.

i

> A token economy programme would help people in mental hospitals. The nurses will give the patients tokens for good behaviour and the patients will be able to use these to get privileges. ✓   1/4

ii

> The first thing a token economy programme has to do is decide what behaviour is being targeted and what standard has to be achieved to earn a token. Staff will then implement the programme so the patients can earn the tokens.   0/4

iii

> An example of a token economy programme is one where patients in a mental hospital can earn tokens by improving their personal hygiene. ✓ All the staff would be involved and a clear programme of what earned tokens would be laid out. ✓ So washing or showering each day without having to be told would get tokens, ✓ though there might still be a smaller level of token available if a patient washed after being reminded to do so. ✓ Patients would be able to exchange their tokens for treats such as being able to watch extra television, get sweets or extra 'phone tokens. (✓)   4/4

Comment: The first answer is poorly focused; what sort of good behaviour is not specified – there is enough for a single mark but no more. In contrast, the second answer seems to get off to a good start; however, it fails to answer the question that has been asked. This means that the answer gets no credit. The third answer is so good it could have got an extra mark if there had been one available. This answer gave five marks for a four mark answer – the best strategy if you want to get the best marks.

> 3. Evaluate Rosenhan's (1973) study. (4 marks)

The injunction for this question is evaluate, so this is an AO2 question. It is therefore important not to waste effort describing the Rosenhan study as that cannot get credit. The only description should be that which is essential for you to make a creditworthy point. You can assume the examiner knows the study.

i

> Rosenhan and seven of his colleagues presented themselves at different mental hospitals saying they could hear voices saying thud, hollow and empty. They were all admitted with a diagnosis of schizophrenia and when released they were released as having schizophrenia in remission. Their normal behaviour was regarded as abnormal by the doctors and nurses but the real patients knew they were not ill. 0/4

ii

> Rosenhan's study showed that DSM was reliable because seven out of the eight patients were given a diagnosis of schizophrenia so it has good application. ✓ However, it is not a valid study as people don't normally tell lies to a psychiatrist to get themselves admitted to a mental hospital, ✓ so it's not a very ethical study either. Also Rosenhan only used eight participants so the study can't be generalised. 2/4

iii

> Rosenhan's study is important as it demonstrated that the DSM classification system was reliable as pseudo-patients with the same alleged symptoms were diagnosed in seven out of eight cases with the same disorder. ✓ Another strength of the study is that it demonstrated that there were problems with the validity of diagnosis as all the pseudo-patients were in fact mentally healthy. ✓ However, a weakness of the study is that all the pseudo-patients lied to their psychiatrists and a psychiatrist would not normally expect someone to lie in order to get admitted to a mental hospital. ✓ Rosenhan did keep the names of the hospitals and the psychiatrists confidential so he did ensure their anonymity. ✓ Because Rosenhan used a variety of different hospitals his results can be reasonably well generalised as experiences were similar in all cases. (✓) 4/4

Comment: Answer (i) is a description (AO1) of the study, not an evaluation (AO2) which the question requests. Therefore it gets no marks. This is a common problem in examinations and one you should work hard to avoid by practising what each injunction requires. Answer (ii) is much better. The reliability and validity points gain marks but saying 'it's not a very ethical study' is not sufficient for an extra mark. More detail would be required. The final comment is not worth a mark for two reasons. Firstly, the nature of the study means it would be very difficult to use a larger sample; secondly, as the results are so consistent then the need for a larger sample is clearly not essential. The third answer looks at a variety of evaluation points, each fully made. If you read the last point this is a much better comment relating to the scale of the study than the negative point in the previous answer.

> 4. Use evidence from **one** approach you have studied to evaluate the view that nature is more important than nurture in explaining human behaviour. (6 marks)

This is an AO2 question as it asks you to use evidence from one approach. Evidence can be research studies or theories. As the question asks you to evaluate the view that nature is more important than nurture, you need to present evidence that suggests it is more important and evidence that suggests this is not true.

i

> In the Psychodynamic Approach the belief is that the mind is divided up into the conscious, preconscious and unconscious and these are our nature. However, Freud believed that although we are born with our id the ego and superego develop as a result of experience so our personality is a result of both nature and nurture. In contrast the Learning Approach believes that everything is down to our biology, that is our genes and our hormones, and this is why we are programmed to be the way we are. However, a study by some psychologists showed that not everything is a result of our genes as sometimes people who are genetically male want to be female. ✓ 1/6

Figure 7.7 Examiners want to give you marks if possible but cannot give you credit for material that does not answer the question.

ii

The Biological Approach is the approach I am using. It states that behaviour is mainly to do with nature and our genes. This means that certain characteristics run in families. This has been shown as monozygotic twins are more likely to both get schizophrenia than dizygotic twins. However, monozygotic twins are more likely to be treated the same compared to dizygotic twins so this could be the reason why they are more alike and not down to genetics at all. ✓ But a study by Heston showed when children of mothers with schizophrenia raised in normal homes were checked they had a 10% chance of getting it compared to a control group where none got schizophrenia. ✓ This shows a genetic influence as these children were more likely to get schizophrenia than the general population, but not as likely as if it was all genetic. ✓

3/6

iii

The Biological Approach supports the nature viewpoint. Twin studies into schizophrenia show that the incidence of the second twin getting the disorder if the first one has it is very different in monozygotic twins at 48% compared to dizygotic twins at 17% (Gottesman and Shields). ✓ This supports the role of genetics in schizophrenia as monozygotic twins share all their genes while dizygotic twins only share half. ✓ However, if the disorder was entirely genetic the concordance rate for monozygotic twins should be 100% as they are genetically identical, so this shows other factors must play a part. ✓ If our nature is most important in determining our gender then all people born with a Y chromosome would be male and those with no Y chromosome would be female. Evidence from the attempt to reassign the gender of David Reimer supports the idea that gender is genetically determined as though, despite attempts to rear him as a girl, he always felt he was a boy. ✓ However, other case studies such as Daphne West demonstrate that this is very variable as 'she' always felt female despite having a Y chromosome. ✓

5/6

Comments: The first answer has a problem with the rubric of this question which asks for one approach. It starts off with the Psychodynamic and describes a biological feature. It then proceeds to identify the Learning Approach before going on to provide an evaluation of the Biological Approach. This evaluation gets credit as it is correct, even though the approach has not been identified. This is an example of how, even though this answer has a lot of incorrect material, that will be ignored and the answer gets the mark it can get. The second answer spends a lot of time describing before getting onto the evaluation. However, once it starts on evaluation it produces some relevant points that gain credit. Note that the first marking point is general; however, it is correct and so long as some research is mentioned in the answer this type of comment can gain credit.

The final answer is a good answer and gives a range of material. See if you can come up with another couple of marking points to ensure *you* could get all the marks!

5. Describe the case study method as used in psychology. (4 marks)

This is an AO3 question as it is about methodology and how science works. Remember these questions may be description or evaluation; they are testing your understanding of science.

i

A case study is a detailed study of one person where the researcher finds out a lot about one person. ✓ They are good for studying brain damaged patients as there are not a lot of these people and they need lots of help.

1/4

ii

A case study is an in depth study of one or a small number of people. ✓ A case study will use lots of different techniques such as observations, interviews and sometimes cognitive tests. ✓ Because they are so very detailed they can provide a lot of very rich, detailed data about the person(s). ✓ They produce a lot of qualitative data; the amount of quantitative data will depend on the reason for the study. Case studies are used to collect data in the psychodynamic approach (e.g. little Hans) and on brain damaged patients such as HM. ✓

4/4

Comments: The first answer here makes a good, but repetitive, point in the first sentence which is certainly worth a mark. However, the second sentence is not quite enough. It is correct to say they are used for studying brain damaged patients but the elaboration offered in the sentence is evaluation: 'they are good' and 'they need lots of help'. The question asks for description so the elaboration cannot be credited; this means that the only relevant part is 'studying brain damaged patients' and it is not sufficient.

It is worth comparing this with the second example. Here the last sentence shows appropriate elaboration, giving two different approaches that use it and examples of studies. The first two points in the second example are clear and unambiguous. The third point is a little bit more problematic. The rich, detailed data comment can often be an evaluation; however, here because the answer is linking the richness of the data to the detail in the study it is fine. The qualitative and quantitative sentence is almost a mark; a little more detail such as the source of the types of data or the reason why some studies produce more quantitative data than others would have been sufficient for a mark.

> 6. Laboratory studies are widely used in psychology.
>
>   (a) Outline two strengths of laboratory experiments.
>
>   (4 marks)
>
>   (b) Outline two weaknesses of laboratory experiments.
>
>   (4 marks)

This is also an AO3 question, but here you are asked for strengths and weaknesses, so that makes it an evaluation question. Also note the use of the word 'outline'; this means each item should be quite brief. For 8 marks this means there are 2 marks for each strength and 2 marks for each weakness.

i

> (a) A strength of lab experiments is that they are easy to replicate because they take place in a lab and everything is controlled. ✓ Another strength is that the IV and the DV are controlled so cause and effect can be seen.   1/4
>
> (b) One weakness of lab experiments is experimenter effects; this is where the experimenter might influence the results because of what they want to find. ✓ My second weakness is that lab experiments lack ecological validity.   1/4

ii

> (a) One strength of laboratory experiments is that they allow the researchers to have tight control over extraneous variables so they can be sure it is only the independent variable that is causing a change in the dependent variable. ✓✓
>
>   Another good thing about laboratory experiments is that they have controls and standardised instructions that means it is easy to replicate them and be sure the results are reliable. ✓✓   4/4
>
> (b) A weakness of laboratory experiments is that the conditions they are conducted under make them very artificial, therefore the results lack ecological validity as they are not applicable to real-life situations. ✓✓
>
>   A second weakness of laboratory experiments is that human participants will know they are part of an experiment and are likely to respond to demand characteristics. ✓ This means their results may not be valid as they have changed their behaviour in order to fulfil what they believe is the aim of the researcher. ✓ 4/4

Comments: The first answer is an example of writing material that is too brief and unexplained as well as not always being accurate. 'Easy to replicate' + 'everything is controlled' is just about enough for a mark. The first comment is correct but some indication of what makes it

replicable is required. Everything being controlled is not wonderfully accurate but sufficient to ensure that one mark can be given. The second comment is just too unexplained to gain credit. The claim about the independent and dependent variables is not accurate, but even if it were it is not enough to explain cause–effect relationships. More importantly, there is no indication of why it is an advantage to demonstrate a cause–effect relationship.

The disadvantages do not fare much better. The comment on experimenter effects is accurate and creditworthy but needs more information to gain a second mark. For example making a comment about unconsciously or consciously influencing the way that participants behave when the results start going as expected. The second weakness is a classic point made by candidates in the hope of getting a mark. Issues of ecological validity are important but there needs to be some indication of why or how ecological validity matters and what effect this is likely to have to gain the marks.

By comparison answer (ii) is a model answer with each point properly made.

> 7. Outline one way in which a researcher conducting a survey might collect qualitative data and one way that quantitative data might also be collected by the same survey.
>
>   (4 marks)

This question is one of the practical application questions; again it is on methodology so is an AO3 question.

i

> A way to collect qualitative data on a survey is to give people open ended questions so they can answer as they wish. ✓
>
> A way to collect quantitative data is to have options to choose from, such as with a Likert scale where they have to say how much they agree or disagree with a statement. ✓   2/4

ii

> One way to collect qualitative data when conducting a survey is to ask people to answer a question in their own words. ✓ These are open ended questions and can be used to get people to explain their views which can then be analysed for content. ✓ Other questions in the same survey could be closed questions; these could be statements that the person has to decide whether they agree with or not so they could be given a score. ✓✓   4/4

Comments: The first answer here is correct, but lacks sufficient elaboration and detail to get the second marks. These could be achieved as in the second one with expanding on the first point; an alternative would be to give an example to demonstrate the point you are making.

Extended writing questions

For all of the Applications in Unit 3, and for Clinical Psychology and Issues and Debates in Unit 4, there is a part of the question paper that is referred to as extended writing. This means that most of the questions here will be worth more marks and some are marked rather differently.

Some questions, such as those on a key issue, may be in two parts with the first part being quite brief. For example:

> (a) Describe one key issue you have learned about in Clinical Psychology. (3 marks)
>
> (b) Evaluate the issue you have described in (a) using psychological concepts. (6 marks)

Other questions will be more challenging and demanding as they could be worth anything up to 12 marks. Such questions are unlikely to be AO1 questions but could easily be either AO2 or AO3.

Here are two questions that could be in an extended writing section along with answers to show how to answer and how not to answer such questions.

> 8. Assess the diagnosis of mental disorders in terms of reliability and validity. (8 marks)

This is a popular AO2 question and one that is quite challenging. With such a question, remember to try and keep the balance between reliability and validity points as you need to cover both topics to get all the marks. Often there will be a maximum of either 4 or 5 marks for either one of the issues.

i

> Reliability of diagnosis of mental disorders is very important. For a diagnosis to be reliable it should be repeatable; that means the same person should be diagnosed with the same disorder. This can be either over time or different clinicians coming to the same diagnosis. Beck et al. (1961) got only 54% agreement when two clinicians were asked to diagnose the same patients, showing this is not very reliable. ✓ Another study showed that clinicians in Britain were more likely to diagnose someone with depression compared to American clinicians who diagnosed the same patients with schizophrenia. ✓ Rosenhan showed that diagnosis is not always valid because his eight pseudo-patients were diagnosed with schizophrenia when they were mentally healthy. ✓ Sometimes there are cultural issues that can make diagnosis unreliable, for example in Japan a diagnosis of schizophrenia may not be made because it is not considered an acceptable disorder. 3/8

ii

> Reliability of diagnosis is not always good as has been shown by studies such as Beck et al. (1961). They gave clinicians the same cases but agreement on diagnosis was only found in 54% of cases. ✓ However, this is an old study that used DSM-II and it has since been updated and is now on DSM-IV TR. However, a more recent study looked at the diagnosis of eating disorders in children and showed that neither ICD10 nor DSM-IV are particularly reliable in diagnosing children (Nicholls et al., 2000), so perhaps the improvement in diagnosis depends on the disorder. ✓✓ Lipton and Simon (1985) also found poor reliability when clinicians were asked to re-diagnose patients using the same information that had been used in the initial diagnosis. Under 20% of patients retained the same diagnosis as originally given. ✓ One problem is that patients may not always report the same symptoms to a clinician so rather than it being poor validity it might be poor reliability. ✓ However, Robins and Guze have said that for a diagnosis to be valid it should be the case that people diagnosed with a disorder share the same symptoms. ✓ While this is sometimes the case it can be a problem. This is because many people who attend for diagnosis are suffering from more than one disorder so their symptoms are a mixture from these disorders. ✓ Nonetheless Rosenhan showed that diagnosis can be reliable as seven out of the eight pseudopatients were given a diagnosis of schizophrenia when they had reported identical symptoms. ✓ 8/8

Comments: The first answer wastes time defining reliability before giving the evidence from the Beck study which is creditworthy. The evidence from the Cooper study is accurate and gets credit even though the name has been forgotten. As long as a study is recognisable an examiner will give you credit in this sort of situation. It is therefore in your interests to make sure you identify the studies and make sure you use well known ones wherever possible. If you cite a very obscure study and cannot recall the names of the researchers it is unlikely to gain credit. This is because without any names the examiner has no evidence that you have not made it up so it cannot be credited with a mark. The Rosenhan point is creditworthy. Make sure you remember which way round the Rosenhan study is; it shows good reliability and poor validity. The cross-cultural material does not gain credit. Some cross-cultural material can be used to assess reliability and validity but this does not make a clear point. You are probably safer steering away from cross-cultural issues except where they are asked for.

The second answer is well focused and uses the material effectively. Not only does it use the Beck study, it goes on to consider the fact that the study uses an old version of DSM and perhaps things have moved on, or not. There is very nearly a fourth mark here because the material has been so well used. The other points are fairly straightforward, each using relevant material.

> 9. Evaluate case studies as a research method within psychology.
> (8 marks)

This is an AO3 question because it is on methodology. Again the answer needs to show a balance to be sure of getting all the marks.

i

> Case studies are when one or a small number of participants are studied in detail. Case studies are very good at getting a very detailed account of the person as the researcher spends a lot of time interviewing them so there is a lot of data. ✓ However, they often rely on information being recalled from the past, especially in the psychodynamic approach, and this information may not always be accurate. ✓ This means that the conclusions the researchers come to may be incorrect or misguided because the person hasn't been truthful. This might not be the person's fault; it may just be that they have forgotten because it was a long time ago, or it might be that the information has been planted in their minds by the way they have been questioned as in hypnosis. One of the problems with a case study is the researcher may get to study the person so much they have no privacy left and that is wrong. ✓
>
> 3/8

ii

> In the psychodynamic approach therapists will often undertake a detailed case study of an interesting client (e.g. little Hans, Anna O). One problem with this type of case study is that they rely heavily on clients recalling information, often from many years before. ✓ The therapist treats the information as accurate which it may not be as memories change with time, or distorted by the problems the client is experiencing. ✓ However, the degree of detail that the lengthy therapy sessions provide means the therapist has a rich and detailed view of the person and this will help the therapist to understand the client much better. ✓ Case studies are used in the Biological Approach, e.g. David Reimer. This is a unique case so a case study is appropriate as it is desirable to get as much data as possible if the conclusions that are drawn are to be of any value. ✓ The distorted conclusions made by Money that the reassignment of gender had been successful do not reflect on the case study as a method; this is because it was clear later with sufficient additional data that there was evidence that the gender reassignment was not working even pre-puberty. ✓ It was the detailed material available because it was a case study that allowed this to be done. ✓ In some instances where case studies go on for a long time the researcher may become so involved in the participant's condition that the researcher ceases to be neutral. ✓ This is a major problem as it is only through being objective about the information gathered that an unbiased conclusion can be drawn. ✓
>
> 8/8

Comments: The first answer is good, as far as it goes, but for an extended writing question you will need to draw more widely, using examples from different approaches and even examples of studies as in the second answer.

You will find that often on an examination paper a particular question will include some prompts to help you answer the question. These are designed to help you and are well worth using to guide what you write. So you may find an evaluation question may suggest you use practical issues, ethical issues and generalisability as prompts. This does not mean these are the only things you can write about. Prompts of this type are designed to help you.

Essays

Essay questions are marked differently as they use Levels instead of ticking the number of points you have made. Essays may be either a mixture of AO1 and AO2 or they may be AO3. All essays are marked initially using four different levels, and a zero level if there is nothing that can be given credit at all.

In summary:

- Level 1 is usually brief and not very relevant
- Level 2 is on the right lines but limited in what it covers
- Level 3 is a good essay but may miss out something rather important or not be wonderfully organised
- Level 4 is well organised, relevant and well focused, and uses terminology well.

One difference between the essay in Issues and Debates compared to all the other essays throughout the course is that it has an additional 6 AO2 marks that are awarded for the overall impression the essay gives in terms of its structure and content. Both the titles here are Issues and Debates titles so you can see how this 'extra' layer works.

The first essay is AO1 plus AO2 so there are 6 marks for each of these plus 6 marks for overall impression. However, because the essay is not marked using a tick per mark there does not have to be an exact match in the number of AO1 and AO2 points, so long as the balance is reasonable. The second essay is an AO3 essay.

When you go through the essays match up the content and comments – this will allow you to understand what is meant by 'limited' or 'effective'. Note also that these questions and their mark schemes indicate that they also assess the quality of written communication. This is shown by the asterisk against the question number on the exam paper and by the letters QWC in the mark scheme.

Describe and evaluate two ways in which the
Cognitive Approach in psychology has contributed to
society. (18 marks)

Answer

One way in which the Cognitive Approach has contributed to
society is by helping to understand problems when witnesses
to events cannot remember things clearly. This is particularly
important when the event is a crime and witnesses to a crime
cannot recall what happened, or what the perpetrator looked
like very clearly. This may be because they genuinely didn't
get a good look but more often it is because of the nature
of the events. This has been demonstrated by work such as
that by Loftus who has shown that when a weapon is present
the witness tends to focus on the weapon instead of the
face of a criminal. Often this means that the weapon details
can be remembered very clearly but person details are very
sketchy. Loftus has demonstrated this in several studies (e.g.
1985) and it is now sufficiently recognised as a problem in
eyewitness testimony that court room evidence often takes
it into account. One explanation for weapons focus is arousal
level. The inverted U theory explains that as arousal increases
performance improves but then as arousal continues to
increase performance gets worse. If a weapon causes very high
arousal levels because the person is scared then recall will be
affected. However, Pickel (1998) showed that it may not be the
threat of the weapon but rather the unusualness that causes
poor recall. In experiments that tested for both unusualness
and threat it was unusualness that tended to affect recall
more than threat. Pickel et al. (2006) has also shown that
if potential witnesses are aware of the weapons focus effect
their ability to recall information when a weapon is present is
unimpaired whereas control participants who do not know of the
effect will have much worse recall when a weapon is present. This
suggests that if the dangers of weapons focus is more widely
publicised then the effect on witnesses will diminish making
court room evidence better.

My second contribution to society is the improvement of
learning and revision techniques in schools as a result of
memory research. Evidence from Craik and Tulving's Levels
of Processing theory suggests that processing information
more deeply enhances learning. This means revision
techniques such as reading and summarising material or
writing answers to questions are more effective as the
learner is processing the information for meaning. Research
has also shown that using a variety of different input
methods also helps. There is also information on where you
should revise as if you take the exam in a room you don't
normally revise in you might find that you can't remember
things. However, if you can imagine yourself back in the room
this may trigger the memory.

Mark scheme

This is an indication of what type of material could be
included here and is divided up into AO1 and AO2 points.

The first topic in the answer – on understanding the
inaccuracy of eyewitness testimony – is quite well done;
the issue of weapons focus and how it affects eyewitness
testimony is described, research studies and theory are
used to explain what is happening and the explanation is
evaluated. Below is a mark scheme that could be used to
mark this contribution. Remember that mark schemes only
indicate the type of material that is creditworthy. The symbol
'/eq;' at the end of a point tells an examiner that equivalent
points are also creditworthy. The sample answer gives two
social contributions; can you think of a third?

Example of how the indicative content might be shown in a
mark scheme for this question:

Indicative content
AO1 points:
Understanding why eyewitnesses tend to make errors when asked about events such as a robbery/eq;
The presence of a weapon may mean witnesses cannot recall details about the scene/perpetrator/eq;
The witness will focus on the weapon and be able to give detail about that/eq;
They may not even encode material on what the criminal looks like as they are looking at the weapon/eq;
If there is a time delay from witnessing the event and being interviewed other material may have been incorporated into the memory/eq;
The longer the time delay the more likely this is to have occurred/eq;
AO2 points:
Evidence from Pickel et al. (1998) suggests it is unusualness that is critical, not that it is a weapon/eq;
Loftus suggests the high arousal level caused by seeing a weapon interferes with the ability to create memories/eq;
This can be explained using the inverted U hypothesis as the witness may be over-aroused because of the threat involved/eq;
Pickel (2006) showed warning participants of weapon's focus reduces the effect it has on recall/eq;
Look for any other relevant material.

Level	Mark	Descriptor
Level 0	0	No rewardable material.
Level 1	1–3	Candidates will produce brief answers, make simple statements, show some relevance to the question.
		Only description or evaluation present.
		May only use commonsense psychology.
		Little attempt at the analytical/evaluation demands of the question. Lack of relevant evidence. The skills needed to produce effective writing will not normally be present. The writing may have some coherence and will be generally comprehensible, but lack both clarity and organisation. High incidence of syntactical and/or spelling errors.
Level 2	4–6	Candidates will produce statements with some development in the form of evaluation, with limited success.
		May have only attempted one application, but done fairly well **or** made an attempt at both.
		Will have attempted both description and evaluation with either both reasonable or one good and the other attempted.
		Limited evidence will be presented.
Level 3	7–9	Candidates' answers will show some good knowledge with understanding of the focus of the question and will include both description and evaluation.
		Two applications will be described reasonably well, or one very good and the other somewhat weaker.
		Evaluation will include research evidence for at least one of the applications.
		Points made may not be fully treated critically though there may be some evidence of judgement and of reaching conclusions where this is relevant. Use of a range of evidence.
Level 4	10–12	Candidates will offer a response which is relevant and focused on the question, and addresses the main issues contained in it.
		Both applications will be described with reasonable detail with a range of evidence presented to evaluate the contributions.
		In addition to evaluation of the application there will be some assessment of the relative merit to society of the application.
		There will be evidence of reasoned argument and of judgement when relevant to the question. The analysis will be supported by accurate factual material, which is relevant to the question. Good use of evidence.

Comments: This essay falls into Level 3. It fits the criteria here quite well as one of the applications is done quite well while the other is much weaker. In both cases there is an attempt at evaluation though again the second application is not so well thought-through as the first. The descriptive parts of the essay suggest it should be in the middle of the band while the evaluation at the bottom and the quality of written communication puts it at the top. So 8 out of 12 for this component is a fair mark.

Now look at the structure levels. This is the final part of the mark scheme and is awarded separately after giving the content level. Read through the descriptions for each level and decide where you think it should go.

Guidance – 6 AO2 marks rewarding structure, focus of description and evaluation using two approaches.

Level	Mark	Descriptor
Level 0	0	No rewardable material.
Level 1	1–2	Response lacks focus and structure. Points are disparately made with little cohesion and flow. Some appropriate use of terminology.
Level 2	3–4	Response is generally focused and cohesive but may be lacking in some evaluation and judgement as some points are not relevant to the overall structure. The response is presented in a legible style using appropriate terminology.
Level 3	5–6	Response is coherent, well structured and focused.

Now you have seen how weapons focus has been dealt with try and do the same for the second contribution identified in the essay, improvement of learning and revision. This time the answer is not so good so you will need to think of some extra points of your own. Use the weapons focus answers as a guide. Try and ensure you have a reasonable number of both AO1 and AO2 marks.

Finally, try the same strategy for a contribution to society you have identified that does not feature in the essay. Be careful though: something like the development of Cognitive Therapy does not count as a contribution to society; because it is used by professional psychologists, it is a contribution to psychology.

This technique is a very useful revision strategy. Devising possible questions and then writing the mark scheme to go with them enables you to think how much you need to know as well as what you need to know.

For essays in this final section – Issues and Debates – the way you use the levels is slightly different. There are two sets of levels. The first is for content, the second for communication.

Read through the essay carefully, keeping in mind the question, then decide which of the Levels best reflects its content. Once you have identified the level, decide whether it is a good, bad or middle score within that level. You can then award a mark for this component.

Comment: This essay is either a top Level 2 or a low Level 3. If we compare the two let us first go through the Level 2 criteria. Though it is slightly lacking in some evaluation, it is not because there is any irrelevancy. It is omission rather than irrelevancy that causes the weakness here. It is certainly legible and uses appropriate terminology. Now compare the essay with Level 3. Is the response coherent? – yes. Is it well structured? – yes, not wonderful, but fairly good. Is it focused? – again, reasonable but not wonderful. This suggests it is more like a 5 than a 4. So the overall mark for the essay is 13/18.

Now let us have a look at an essay that could come up and which would be an AO3 essay.

*11. Describe qualitative and quantitative data and evaluate their use within psychological research.

(18 marks)

Answer

Qualitative data are those data that refer to information that is not in a numerical form. Qualitative data often come from open questions on surveys where people are asked to give their views on an issue. Another type of qualitative data can be produced from content analysis. For example, research into the effects of violence in the media on children's behaviour often want to look at the type as well as the amount of violence portrayed on television and in computer games. This highlights one of the major problems for qualitative data because the decisions about how to classify the violence are subjective. This means that different researchers may have different views on how to interpret information. It can also lead to information being coded incorrectly.

Participants expressing their views often use very varied language; this can make it hard to compare responses. One strategy is to code the responses into similar groups. There is also a problem if there are a large number of words as these become unwieldy. Again the only realistic way to deal with this amount of data is to put similar words together. This is a problem because one of the advantages of qualitative data is its richness and variety and by lumping lots of things together the advantage disappears. It is often possible to generate quantitative data from qualitative which can be useful at times.

The opportunity for participants to express themselves in an open ended way can often produce information that would not be acquired any other way. This is a major plus for qualitative methods. It may lead to new avenues of inquiry and new ideas about the reasons for people's behaviour.

In contrast, quantitative data is where the information is found in numerical form. This may be in terms of the number of items or time taken but it could also be nominal data where people are placed into a category. Whereas qualitative data are subjective, quantitative data are objective; this means that the researcher is not interpreting the data. This makes it more reliable and more accurate in terms of the data set. However, there is a loss of information when only numerical data are collected as the richness of human experience is reduced to a number. This means that the information being analysed may be at best superficial and at worst meaningless.

It is easier to ensure quantitative data are reliable than is the case with qualitative data and because these data are normally collected in conjunction with objective research tools such as experiments a new set of data that can be compared with the original can be collected fairly readily. The ease with which quantitative data can be collected and analysed compared to qualitative data means that it is usually possible to obtain a good amount of data from a wide range of people, making the results more generalisable. The objective nature of quantitative data means it is seen as more scientific and conclusions that are drawn are less inclined to be an interpretation of the researcher's views and less subject to bias.

However, the range and type of data collected can be very narrow; this means the data may not truly reflect how people behave but only some superficial aspect of behaviour. For example a study into memory processes may use an artificial task using lists of nonsense syllables recalled under controlled conditions, nothing like real world experiences of memory. This means some people question the ability of results derived from quantitative data to throw light on human behaviour as they are so narrowly focused.

The techniques used to collect quantitative data can also be a source of bias as the development of a research instrument is subject to the understanding and interpretation of the researcher.

Mark scheme

Read through the whole answer before attempting to award any marks.

Go to the content levels and award a mark appropriate to the content and quality of the answer.

Once the content mark has been awarded refer to the structure levels and award those marks separately.

Remember that this essay is about methodology so it is AO3 and there are no AO1 or AO2 marks. However, the essay asks the candidate to both describe and to evaluate, and these injunctions apply to both qualitative and quantitative data.

Level	Mark	Descriptor
Level 0	0	No rewardable material.
Level 1	1–3	Candidates will produce brief answers, making simple statements, showing some relevance to the question.
		Only description or evaluation present.
		May confuse qualitative and quantitative data.
		Little attempt at the analytical/evaluation demands of the question. Lack of relevant evidence.
Level 2	4–6	Candidates will produce statements with some development in the form of analysis/evaluation, with limited success.
		Either attempts to describe both and evaluate one or describes and evaluates one type of data well.
		Limited evidence will be presented.
Level 3	7–9	Candidates' answers will show some good knowledge with understanding of the focus of the question and will include analysis and evaluation.
		Both qualitative and quantitative data will be explained though one may be brief.
		Both qualitative and quantitative data evaluated, though one may be weak if the other is very strong.
		Likely to comment on use/application.
		Points made may not be fully treated critically though there may be some evidence of judgement and of reaching conclusions where this is relevant. Use of a range of evidence.
Level 4	10–12	Candidates will offer a response which is relevant and focused on the question, and addresses the main issues contained in it.
		Descriptions of qualitative and quantitative data will be clear and likely to include comments on source or nature of such data.
		Both strengths and weaknesses will be considered for each type of data.
		Some comparisons or links between the two types of data are likely though not necessary.
		There will be evidence of reasoned argument and of judgement when relevant to the question. The analysis will be supported by accurate factual material, which is relevant to the question. Good use of evidence.

Interactive angles

Use the essay as a starting point to produce your own mark scheme of indicative content. This time use headings such as description and evaluation to help you to identify the different aspects of the question that need to be addressed.

Comments: This essay is a Level 4. It covers all the relevant issues giving an effective description and evaluation of both qualitative and quantitative data and makes some useful points linking the two types of data. You may find it useful to create a list of indicative content from this essay. It is a little weak in terms of development of reasoned argument, so 11 is appropriate for content.

Structure levels: Now focus on the structure of the essay. Does it hold together well? Does it use language effectively? Remember that an essay written under exam conditions is never going to be as beautifully written as one in other circumstances. However, you should be looking for good spelling, grammar and punctuation, appropriate use of psychological terminology and a flow and coherence to the essay that means you feel the writer has been 'in command' and is telling you a story.

Level	Mark	Descriptor
Level 0	0	No rewardable material.
Level 1	1–2	Response lacks focus and structure. Points are disparately made with little cohesion and flow. Some appropriate use of terminology.
Level 2	3–4	Response is generally focused and cohesive but may be lacking in some evaluation and judgement as some points may be irrelevant to the overall structure. The response is presented in a legible style using appropriate terminology.
Level 3	5–6	Response is coherent, well structured and focused.

This is clearly a Level 3 for structure and is worthy of a 6. Combining marks for content and structure means the essay gets 17/18.

In the exam

Remember to make each point full and clear. You will gain more marks by making one point clearly and fully than writing a list of three or four things 'I would have covered if I had time'. If you think you could make a point more clearly by using an example, then do so as this can often gain credit. But remember, several examples will not gain you more marks.

- Read carefully through the questions. Think about the wording; what is the examiner expecting you to write?

- Take time to think about what to write. Rushing into a question may mean you end up crossing out material when you realise there is a better way of answering it.

- Use a plan when writing essays. A plan allows you to create a better structured essay, something which is rewarded in the levels marking system.

- Manage time carefully. The marks and time are calculated to allow enough but not lots of time. The paper will recommend times; use this advice!

- Indicate clearly when prompted which option you are selecting. It is always easier for an examiner to give you marks if they know what you are writing about!

- Answer a question you feel comfortable with first to get yourself into the right frame of mind. It is common to look at an exam paper and get a blank, but once you start answering questions information will start to fall into place.

And finally…

- Do make sure you cover all the relevant material. Don't assume something won't be on the exam paper.

- Do revise material and different ways of answering questions. But don't memorise model answers.

- Do target the material carefully so you write exactly what is needed. But don't put in everything you know about a topic.

- Do try to make as many points as there are marks for the answer, plus one. Don't leave a question unanswered.

- Do use your time carefully, managing it in terms of marks and minutes. Don't believe you can make up lots of marks on one topic that compensate for not properly answering a question on another topic.

- Do start revising early so you can space it out over time. Don't cram everything in at the last minute.

- Do use different techniques to revise such as answering past questions, setting questions and writing mark schemes. Don't rely on just reading through notes.

References

Abikoff, H., Hechtman, L. & Klein, R. (2004) 'Social functioning in children with ADHD treated with long-term methylphenidate and multimodal psychosocial treatment.' *Journal of the American Academy of Child & Adolescent Psychiatry*, 43: 812–19.

Adityanji, M.J. & Kaizad, R.M. (2005) 'Neuropsychiatric sequelae of Neuroleptic Malignant Syndrome.' *Clinical Neuropharmacology*, 28: 197–203.

Ageton, S.S. & Elliott, D.S. (1974) 'The effects of legal processing on delinquent orientations.' *Social Problems*, 22(1): 87–100.

Aggleton, J.P. (1993) 'The contribution of the amygdala to normal and abnormal emotional states.' *Trends in Neuroscience*, 16: 328–33.

Agrawal, A., Neale, M.C., Prescott, C.A. & Kendler, K.S. (2004) 'A twin study of early cannabis use and subsequent use and abuse/dependence of other illicit drugs.' *Psychological Medicine*, 34(7): 1227–37.

Ahnert, L., Gunnar, M.R., Lamb, M.E. & Barthel, M. (2004) 'Transition to child care: associations with infant–mother attachment, infant negative emotions and elevated cortisol levels.' *Child Development*, 75: 639–50.

Ainsworth, M.D.S. (1967) *Infancy in Uganda: infant care and the growth of love*. Baltimore: Johns Hopkins University Press.

Ainsworth, M.D.S. (1989) 'Attachments beyond infancy.' *American Psychologist*, 44: 709–16.

Ainsworth, M.D.S. & Wittig, B.A. (1969) 'Attachment theory and the exploratory behaviour of one-year-olds in a strange situation.' In Foss, B.M. (ed) *Determinants of infant behaviour vol 4*. London: Methuen.

Allardyce, J., Gaebel, W., Zielasek, J. & Van Os, J. (2007) 'Deconstructing Psychosis Conference February 2006: the validity of schizophrenia and alternative approaches to the classification of psychosis.' *Schizophrenia Bulletin*, 33: 863–7.

Allhusen, V. & NICHD (2003) 'Does quality of day care affect child outcomes at age 4½?' *Developmental Psychology*, 39: 451–9.

American Psychiatric Association (2000) *Diagnostic and Statistical Manual of Mental Disorders-IV with test revisions (DSM-IV-TR)*. Arlington, Vancouver: APA.

Amorose, A.J. & Horn, T.S. (2001) 'Intrinsic motivation: relationships with collegiate athletes' gender, scholarship status and perceptions of coaches' behaviour.' *Journal of Sport & Exercise Psychology*, 22: 6 –84.

Andersson, B.E. (1996) 'Children's development related to day care, type of family and other home factors.' *European Child and Adolescent Psychiatry*, 5: 73–5.

Antshel, K.M. & Remer, R. (2003) 'Social skills training in children with attention deficit hyperactivity disorder: a randomized-controlled clinical trial.' *Journal of clinical child and adolescent psychology: the official journal for the Society of Clinical Child and Adolescent Psychology*, American Psychological Association, Division 53, 32(1):153–65

Armfield, J. (2007) 'Manipulating perceptions of spider characteristics and predicted spider fear: evidence for the cognitive vulnerability model of the etiology of fear.' *Journal of Anxiety Disorders*, 21: 691–703.

Arroll, B., Macgillivray, S., Ogston, S., Reid, I., Sullivan, F., Williams, B. & Crombie, I. (2005) 'Efficacy and tolerability of tricyclic antidepressants and SSRIs compared with placebo for treatment of depression in primary care: a meta-analysis.' *Annals of Family Medicine*, 3: 449–56.

Ashford, B., Biddle, S. & Goudas, M. (1993) 'Participation in community sport centres: motives and predictors of enjoyment.' *Journal of Sport Sciences*, 11: 249–56.

Atkin, C. & Block, M. (1981) *Content and Effects of Alcohol Advertising*, prepared for the Bureau of Alcohol, Tobacco & Firearms, no PB82–123142, Springfield, VA: National Technical Information Service.

Atkinson, L., Niccols, A., Paglia, A., Cool bear, J., Parker, K.C.H., Poulton, L., Guger, S. & Sitarenios, G. (2000) 'A meta-analysis of time between maternal sensitivity and attachment assessments: implications for internal working models in infancy/toddlerhood.' *Journal of Social & Personal Relationships*,17: 791–810.

Bahr, S.J., Hoffmann, J.P. & Yang, X. (2005) 'Parental and peer influences on the risk of adolescent drug use.' *Journal of Primary Prevention*, 26(6): 529–51.

Bailey, A., Le Couteur, A., Gottesman, I., Bolton, P., Simonoff, E. & Yuzda, E. (1995) 'Autism as a strongly genetic disorder: evidence from a British twin study.' *Psychological Medicine*, 25: 63–77.

Bailey, H.N., Moran, G., Pederson, G.R. & Bento, S. (2007) 'Understanding the transmission of attachment using variable- and relationship-centred approaches.' *Development and Psychopathology*, 19: 313–43.

Baldwin, S. & Cooper, P. (2000) 'How should ADHD be treated?' *The Psychologist*, 13: 598–662.

Bandura, A. (1965) 'Influence of a model's reinforcement contingencies on the acquisition of imitative responses.' *Journal of Personality & Social Psychology*, 36: 589–95.

Bandura, A. (1977) *Social learning theory*. Englewood Cliffs, NJ: Prentice Hall.

Bandura, A. (1982) 'Self-efficacy mechanisms in human agency.' *American Psychologist*, 37: 122–47.

Bandura, A., Ross, D. & Ross, S.A. (1961) 'Transmission of aggression through imitation of aggressive models.' *Journal of Abnormal and Social Psychology*, 63: 575–82.

Bandura, A., Ross, D. & Ross, S.A. (1963) 'Imitation of film-mediated aggressive models.' *Journal of Abnormal and Social Psychology*, 66: 3–11.

Banse, R. (2004) 'Adult attachment and marital satisfaction: evidence for dyadic configuration effects.' *Journal of Social & Personal Relationships*, 21: 273–82.

Bard, P. (1929) 'The central representation of the sympathetic nervous system.' *Archives of Neurology & Psychiatry*, 22: 230–46.

Baron-Cohen, S. (2001) 'Theory of mind and autism: a review.' *Special Issue of the International Review of Mental Retardation*, 23: 169.

Baron-Cohen, S. (2005) 'Testing the extreme male brain theory of autism: let the data speak for themselves.' *Cognitive Neuropsychiatry*, 10: 77–81.

Baron-Cohen, S. (2008) 'Hypersystematising, autism and truth.' *Quarterly Journal of Experimental Psychology*, 61: 64–75.

Baron-Cohen, S. & Wheelwright, S. (2003) 'The Friendship Questionnaire: an investigation of adults with Asperger syndrome or high-functioning autism, and normal sex differences.' *Journal of Autism and Developmental Disorders*, 33: 509–17.

Baron-Cohen, S., Wheelwright, S., Burtenshaw, A. & Hobson, E. (2007) 'Mathematical talent is linked to autism.' *Human Nature*, 18: 115–21.

Bartlett F.C. (1932) *Remembering*. Cambridge, Cambridge University Press.

Bassett, J.E. & Blanchard, E.B. (1977) 'The effect of the absence of close supervision on the use of response cost in a prison token economy.' *Journal of Applied Behavior Analysis*, 101(3): 375–9.

Bates, J., Marvinney, D., Kelly, T., Dodge, K., Bennett, R. & Pettit, G. (1994) 'Childcare history and kindergarten adjustment.' *Developmental Psychology*, 30: 690–700.

Bateson P. (1986) 'When to experiment on animals.' *New Scientist*, 1496:30–2.

Beck, A.T. (1976) *Cognitive Therapy and the Emotional Disorders*. New York: International Universities Press.

Beeman, E.A. (1947) 'The effect of male hormone on aggressive behaviour in mice.' *Physiological Zoology*, 20: 373–405.

Belsky, J. (1986) 'Infant day care: a cause for concern?' *Zero to Three*, 6: 1–9.

Belsky, J. (1999) 'Modern evolutionary theory and patterns of attachment.' In Cassidy, J. & Shaver, P. (eds) *Handbook of attachment: theory, research and clinical applications*. New York: Guilford Press.

Belsky, J. (2002) 'Quantity counts: amount of child care and children's socio-emotional development.' *Developmental & Behavioural Pediatrics*, 23: 167–70.

Belsky, J. & Fearon, R.M.P. (2002) 'Infant–mother attachment security, contextual risk and early development: a moderational analysis.' *Development & Psychopathology*, 14: 293–310.

Belsky, J. & Rovine, M.J. (1988) 'Non-maternal care in the first year of life and the security of infant–parent attachment.' *Child Development*, 59: 157–67.

Benedetti, G. (1987) *Psychotherapy of schizophrenia*. New York: New York University Press.

Benjamin, J., Ben-Zion, P., Karbofsky, E. & Dannon, P. (2000) 'Double-blind placebo-controlled pilot study of paroxetine for specific phobia.' *Psychopharmacology*, 149: 194–6.

Bental, R., Baker, G.A. & Havers, S. (1991) 'Reality monitoring and psychotic hallucinations.' *British Journal of Clinical Psychology*, 30: 213–22.

Best, D., Gross, S., Manning, V., Gossop, M., Witton, J. & Strang, J. (2005) 'Cannabis use in adolescents: the impact of risk and protective factors and social functioning.' *Drug & Alcohol Review*, 24(6): 483–8.

Bettencourt, B.A. & Miller, N. (1996) 'Gender differences in aggression as a function of provocation: a meta-analysis.' *Psychological Bulletin*, 119(3): 422–47.

Bion, W.R. (1967) *Second thoughts*. London: William Heinemann.

Blacker, J., Watson, A. & Beech, A.R. (2008) 'A combined drama-based and CBT approach to working with self-reported anger aggression.' *Criminal Behaviour & Mental Health*, 18(2): 129–37.

Blättler, R., Dobler-Mikola, A., Steffen, T. & Uchtenhagen, A. (2002) 'Decreasing intravenous cocaine use in opiate users treated with prescribed heroin.' *Sozial und Praventimedizin*, 47(1): 24–32.

Bolla, K.I., Lesage, S.R., Gamaldo, C.E., Neubauer, D.N., Funderburk, F.R., Cadet, J.L., David, P.M., Verdejo-Garcia, A. & Benbrook, A.R. (2008) 'Sleep disturbance in heavy marijuana users.' *Sleep*, 31(6): 901–8.

Boon, S.D. & Lomore, C.D. (2001) 'Admirer–celebrity relationships among young adults: explaining perceptions of celebrity influence on identity.' *Human Communication Research*, 27: 432–65.

Bowen, A.M. & Bourgeois, M.J. (2001) 'Attitudes towards lesbian, gay and bisexual college students: the contribution of pluralistic ignorance, dynamic social impact and contact theories.' *Journal of America College Health*, 50: 91–6.

Bowlby, J. (1946) *Forty-four juvenile thieves*. London: Bailliere, Tindall & Cox.

Bowlby, J. (1951) *Maternal care and mental health*. Geneva: World Health Organization.

Bowlby, J. (1955) 'Mother–child separation.' In Soddy, K. (ed) *Mental health and infant development*. London: Routledge.

Bowlby, J. (1957) 'Symposium on the contribution of current theories to an understanding of child development.' *British Journal of Medical Psychology*, 30: 230–40.

Bowlby, J. (1969) *Attachment and loss vol I*. London: Pimlico.

Boyatzis, C.J., Matillo, G.M. & Nesbit, K.M. (1995) 'Effects of *The Mighty Morphin Power Rangers* on children's aggression with peers.' *Child Study Journal*, 25(1): 45–55.

Boyd, J. & Munroe, K.J. (2003) 'The use of imagery in climbing.' *Athletic Insight*, 5: 15–30.

Bozarth, M.A. & Wise, R.A. (1985) 'Toxicity associated with long-term intravenous heroin and cocaine self-administration in the rat.' *Journal of the American Medical Association*, 254: 81–3.

Bradshaw, W. (1998) 'Cognitive-behavioral treatment of schizophrenia: a case study.' *Journal of Cognitive Psychotherapy: An International Journal*, 12: 13–25.

Brazelton, T.B., Tronick, E., Adamson, L., Als, H. & Wise, S. (1975) 'Early mother–infant reciprocity.' Parent–infant Interaction. *Ciba Symposium*, 33: 137–54.

Brennan, M. & Brennan, R. (1988) 6–15 year olds failed to understand one third of questions asked by lawyers in court.

Brennan, M. & Brennan (1988) *Stranger Language*. Wagga Wagga, New South Wales, Australia: Riverina Murry Institute of Higher Education.

British Association for Behavioural & Cognitive-behavioural therapies (BABCP) (2002).

British Psychological Society (2006) *Ethical Principles for conducting Research with Human Participants: Introduction to the revised principles*. Leicester: BPS.

British Psychological Society Scientific Affairs Board (1985) 'Guidelines for the use of animals in research.' *Bulletin of The British Psychological Society*, 38: 289–91.

Broadcasting Standards Commission (2002) *Briefing update: depiction of violence on terrestrial television.* London: BSC.

Broberg, B.V., Glenthøj, B.Y., Dias, R., Larsen, D.B. & Olsen, C.K. (2009) 'Reversal of cognitive deficits by an ampakine (CX516) and sertindole in two animal models of schizophrenia-sub-chronic and early postnatal PCP treatment in attentional set-shifting.' *Psychopharmacology*, April 24. [epub ahead of print]

Brook, J.S., Richter, L., Whiteman, M. & Cohen, M. (1999) 'Consequences of adolescent marijuana use: incompatibility with the assumption of adult roles.' *Genetic, Social & General Psychology Monographs*, 125(2): 193–207.

Brooner, R.K., King, V.L. & Kindorf, M. (1997) 'Psychiatric and substance abuse comorbidity among treatment-seeking opioid abusers.' *Archives of General Psychiatry*, 54: 71–80.

Brosnan, M.J. & Thorpe, S.J. (2006) 'An evaluation of two clinically-derived treatments for technophobia.' *Computers in Human Behavior*, 22: 1080–95.

Brown, A.S., Schaefer, C.S., Wyatt, R.J. & Susser, E. (2002) 'Paternal age and risk of schizophrenia in adult offspring.' *American Journal of Psychiatry*, 159: 1528–33.

Brown, G.W., Andrews, B., Harris, T., Adler, Z. & Bridge, L. (1986) 'Social support, self-esteem and depression.' *Psychological Medicine*, 16: 813–31.

Brunner, H.G., Nelen, M., Breakfield, X.O., Ropers, H.H. & van Oost, B.A. (1993) 'Abnormal behaviour associated with a point mutation in the structural gene for monoamine oxidase A.' *Science*, 262: 578–80.

Buss, D.M., Larsen, R.J., Westen, D. & Semmelroth, J. (1992) 'Sex differences in jealousy: evolution, physiology and psychology.' *Psychological Science*, 3: 251–5.

Butler, A.C., Chapman, J.E., Forman, E.M. & Beck, A.T. (2006) 'The empirical status of cognitive-behavioral therapy: a review of meta-analyses.' *Clinical Psychology Review*, 26: 17–31.

Cadoret, R.J., Yates, W.R., Troughton, E., Woodworth, G. & Stewart, M.A. (1995) 'Genetic-environmental interaction in the genesis of aggressivity and conduct disorders.' *Archives of General Psychiatry*, 52: 916–24.

Caine, S.B. & Koob, G.F. (1994) 'Effects of mesolimbic dopamine depletion on responding maintained by cocaine and food.' *Journal of the Experimental Analysis of Behavior*, 61: 213–21.

Campbell, J.M. & Marino, C.A. (2009) 'Sociometric status and behavioural characteristics of peer-nominated buddies for a child with autism.' *Journal of Autism & Developmental Disorders*. In Press.

Campbell, J.M., Ferguson, J.E., Herzinger, C.V., Jackson, J.N. & Marino, C. (2005) 'Peers attitudes towards autism vary across sociometric groups: an exploratory investigation.' *Journal of Developmental & Physical Disabilities*, 17: 281–98.

Carmichael, L.C., Hogan, H.P. & Walter, A.A. (1932) 'An experimental study of the effect of language on the reproduction of visually perceived forms.' *Journal of Experimental Psychology*, 15: 73–86.

Carter, C.A., Bottom, B.L. & Levine, M. (1996) 'Linguistic and socioemotional influences on the accuracy of children's reports.' *Law & Human Behavior*, 20: 335–58.

Castle, D., Scott, K., Wessley, S. & Murray, R.M. (1993) 'Does social deprivation during gestation and early life predispose to schizophrenia?' *Social Psychiatry and Psychiatric Epidemiology*, 25: 210–15.

Chalabaev, A., Sarrazin, P. & Fontayne, P. (2009) 'Stereotype endorsement and perceived ability as mediators of the girls' gender orientation–soccer performance relationship.' *Psychology of Sport and Exercise*, 10: 297–9.

Champion, L. (2000) 'Depression.' In Champion, L. & Power, M. (eds) *Adult psychological problems*. Hove: Taylor & Francis.

Champion, L. & Power, M. (2000) *Adult psychological problems*. Hove: Taylor & Francis.

Charlton, A. (1986) 'Children's advertisement awareness related to their views on smoking.' *Health Education Journal*, 45: 75–9.

Charlton, T. & O'Bey, S. (1997) 'Links between television and behaviour: students' perceptions of TV's impact in St Helena, South Atlantic.' *Support for Learning*, 12(3): 130–6.

Charlton, T., Coles, D., Panting, C. & Hannan, A. (1999) 'Nursery children's behaviour across the availability of broadcast television: a quasi-experimental study of two cohorts in a remote community.' *Journal of Social Behaviour & Personality*, 14: 1–10.

Charlton, T., Gunter, B. & Hannan, A. (2002) *Broadcast television effects in a remote community*. London: Lawrence Earlbaum Associates

Charlton, T., Panting, C., Davie, R., Coles, D. & Whitmarsh, L. (2000) 'Children's playground behaviour across five years of broadcast television: a naturalistic study in a remote community.' *Emotional & Behavioural Difficulties*, 54: 4–12.

Chen, C., Rainnie, D.G., Greene, R.W. & Tonegawa, S. (1994) 'Abnormal fear response and aggressive behaviour in mutant mice deficient for α-calcium-calmodulin kinase II.' *Science*, 266: 291–4.

Cinnirella, M. & Loewenthal, K.M. (1999) 'Religious and ethnic group influences on beliefs about mental illness: a qualitative interview study.' *British Journal of Medical Psychology*, 72: 505–525.

Childress, A.R., Mozley, P.D., McElgin, W., Fitzgerald, J., Reivich, M. & O'Brien, C.P. (1999) 'Limbic activation during cue-induced cocaine craving.' *American Journal of Psychiatry*, 156(1): 11–18.

Clarke, A.D.B. & Clarke, A.M. (1998) 'Early experience and the life path.' *The Psychologist*, 11: 433–6.

Clifford, B.R. & Lloyd-Bostock, S.M.A. (1983) 'Witness evidence: conclusion and prospect.' In Lloyd-Bostock, S.M.A. & Clifford, B.R. (eds) *Evaluating witness evidence*, 285–90. New York: Wiley.

Clough, P., Earle, K. & Sewell, D. (2002) 'Mental toughness: the concept and its measurement.' In Cockerill, I. (ed) *Solutions in sport psychology*. London: Thomson Learning.

Cockett, M. & Tripp, D. (1994) 'Children living in re-ordered families.' *Social Policy Research Findings*, 45. York: Joseph Rowntree Foundation.

Cohen, H. & Filipczak, J. (1971) *A new learning environment.* San Francisco: Jossey-Bass.

Cook, M. & Mineka, S. (1989) 'Observational conditioning of fear to fear-relevant versus fear-irrelevant stimuli in rhesus monkeys.' *Journal of Abnormal Psychology*, 98: 448–59.

Corrigan, P.W. (1995) 'Use of a token economy with seriously mentally ill patients: criticisms and misconceptions.' *Psychiatric Services*, 46(12): 1258–63.

Cottrell, B. (1968) 'Performance in the presence of other human beings: presence, audience and affiliation effects.' In Summell, E., Hoppe, R. & Milton, G. (eds) *Social facilitation and imitative behaviour*. Boston: Allyn & Bacon.

Courtois, R., Caudrelier, N., Legay, E., Lalande, G., Halimi, A. & Jonas, C. (2007) 'Influence of parental tobacco dependence and parenting styles on adolescents' tobacco use.' *Presse Médicale*, 36(10 Pt 1): 1341–9.

Craft, L.L., Magyar, T.M., Becker, B.J. & Feltz, D.L. (2003) 'The relationship between the Competitive State Anxiety Inventory-2 and sports performance: a meta-analysis.' *Journal of Sport & Exercise Psychology*, 25: 44–65.

Craik F.I.M. & Lockhart B. (1972) 'Levels of processing.' *Journal of Verbal Learning & verbal Behaviour*, 11, 671–84.

Crust, L. & Clough, P. (2005) 'Relationship between mental toughness and physical endurance.' *Perceptual & Motor Skills*, 100: 192–4.

Cumberbatch, G. & Woods, S. (1996) 'Content analyses.' *Broadcasting Standards Commission Monitoring Report 5*. London: John Libbey and Broadcasting Standards Council.

Curtiss, B., Simpson, D.D. & Cole, S.G. (1976) 'Rapid puffing as a treatment component of a community smoking program.' *Journal of Community Psychology*, 4(2): 186–93.

Curtiss, S. (1977) *Genie: a psycholinguistic study of a modern day 'wild child'*. London: Academic Press.

Dabbs, J.M. Jr & Hargrove, M.F. (1997) 'Age, testosterone, and behavior among female prison inmates.' *Psychosomatic Medicine*, 59(5): 477–80.

Dabbs, J.M. Jr, Bernieri, F.J., Strong, R.K., Campo, R. & Milun, R. (2001) 'Going on stage: testosterone in greetings and meetings.' *Journal of Research in Personality*, 35(1): 27–40.

Dabbs, J.M. Jr, Carr, T.S., Frady, R.L. & Riad, J.K. (1995) 'Testosterone, crime and misbehaviour among 692 male prison inmates.' *Personality & Individual Differences*, 18: 627–33.

Danaher, B.G. (1977) 'Rapid smoking and self-control in the modification of smoking behavior.' *Journal of Consulting & Clinical Psychology*, 45(6): 1663–75.

Danforth, S. & Navarro, V. (2001) 'Hyper talk: sampling the social construction of ADHD in everyday language.' *Anthropology & Education Quarterly*, 32: 167–90.

Demas, G.E., Kriegsfeld, L.J., Blackshaw, S., Huang, P., Gammie, S.C., Nelson, R.J. & Snyder, S.H. (1999) 'Elimination of aggressive behavior in male mice lacking endothelial nitric oxide synthase.' *Journal of Neuroscience*, 19: RC30.

Department of Health (1997) *The spectrum of care: local services for people with mental health problems*. London: HMSO.

Depatie, L. & Lal, S.L. (2001) 'Apomorphine and the dopamine hypothesis of schizophrenia: a dilemma?' *Journal of Psychiatry & Neuroscience*, 26: 203–20.

Devlin, Lord (1976) *Report to the Secretary of State for the Home Department of the Departmental Committee on evidence of identification in criminal cases*. London: HMSO.

Di Ciano, P., Coury, A., Depoortere, R.Y., Egilmez, Y., Lane, J.D., Emmett-Oglesby, M.W., Lepiane, F.G., Phillips, A.G. & Blaha, C.D. (1995) 'Comparison of changes in extracellular dopamine concentrations in the nucleus accumbens during intravenous self-administration of cocaine or d-amphetamine.' *Behavioural Pharmacology*, 6: 311–22.

Dick, D.M. & Bierut, L.J. (2006) 'The genetics of alcohol dependence.' *Current Psychiatry Reports*, 8: 151–7.

Dielman, T.E., Butchart, A.T., Shope, J.T. & Miller, M. (1991) 'Environmental correlates of adolescent substance use and misuse: implications for prevention programs.' *International Journal of the Addictions*, 25(7A–8A): 855–80.

Donohew, R.L., Hoyle, R.H., Clayton, R.R., Skinner, W.F., Colon, S.E. & Rice, R.E. (1999) 'Sensation seeking and drug use by adolescents and their friends: models for marijuana and alcohol.' *Journal of Studies on Alcohol*, 60(5): 622–31.

Donovan, W., Leavitt, L., Taylor, N. & Broder, J. (2007) 'Maternal sensory sensitivity, mother–infant 9-month interaction, infant attachment status: predictors of mother–toddler interaction at 24 months.' *Infant Behavior & Development*, 30: 336–52.

Driscoll, J.W. & Bateson, P. (1988) 'Animals in behavioural research.' *Animal Behaviour*, 36: 1569–74.

Duda, J. & Pensgard, A.M. (2002) 'Enhancing the quality and quantity of motivation: the promotion of task involvement in a junior football team.' In Cockerill, I. (ed) *Solutions in sport psychology*. London: Thomson.

Duff, D.C., Levine, T.R., Beatty, M., Woolbright, J. & Park, H.S. (2007) 'Testing public anxiety treatments against a credible placebo control.' *Communication Education*, 56: 72–88.

Dupaul, G.J., McGoey, K.E., Eckert, T.L. & Vanbrakle, J. (2001) 'Preschool children with attention-deficit/hyperactivity disorder: impairments in behavioral, social, and school functioning.' *Journal of the American Academy of Child & Adolescent Psychiatry*, 40: 508–15.

Egloff, B. & Gruhn, A.J. (1996) 'Personality and endurance sports.' *Personality & Individual Differences*, 21: 223–9.

Ehrenreich, H., Rinn, T., Kunert, H.J., Moeller, M.R., Poser, W., Schilling, L., Gigerenzer, G. & Hoehe, M.R. (1999) 'Specific attentional dysfunction in adults following early start of cannabis use.' *Psychopharmacology*, 142: 295–301.

Eitle, D. (2005) 'The moderating effects of peer substance use on the family structure–adolescent substance use association: quantity versus quality of parenting.' *Addictive Behavior*, 30(5): 963–80.

Eranti, S., Mogg, A., Pluck, G., Landau, S., Purvis, R., Brown, R.G., Howard, R. & Knapp, M. (2007) 'A randomized, controlled trial with 6-month follow-up of repetitive transcranial magnetic stimulation and electroconvulsive therapy for severe depression.' *American Journal of Psychiatry*, 164: 73–81.

Eron, L.D. & Huesmann, L.R. (1986) 'The role of television in the development of antisocial and prosocial behavior.' In Olweus, D., Block, J. & Radke-Yarrom, M. (eds) *Development of Antisocial and Prosocial Behaviour, Theories and Issues*. New York: Academic Press.

Eron, L.D., Huesmann, L.R., Leftowitz, M.M. & Walder, L.O. (1972) 'Does television violence cause aggression?' *American Psychologist*, 27: 253–63.

European Federation of Sport Psychology (1996) 'Position statement of the FEPSAC: 1. Definition of sport psychology.' *The Sport Psychologist*, 10: 221–3.

Eysenck, H.J. (1952) *The scientific study of personality*. London: Routledge & Kegan Paul.

Eysenck, H.J., Nias, D.K.B. & Cox, D.N. (1982) 'Sport and personality.' *Advances in Behavioural Research and Therapy*, 4(1): 1–56.

Eysenck, M.W. (1992) *Anxiety*. Hove: Psychology Press.

Fan, P. (1995) 'Cannabinoid agonists inhibit the activation of 5-HT3 receptors in rat nodose ganglion neurons.' *Journal of Neurophysiology*, 73: 907–10.

Faraone, S.V., Doyle, A.E., Mick, E. & Biederman, J. (2001) 'Meta analysis of the association between the 7-repeat allele of the Dopamine D4 receptor gene and attention deficit hyperactivity disorder.' *American Journal of Psychiatry*, 158: 1052–7.

Farzin, F., Perry, H., Hessl, D., Loesch, D., Cohen, J., Bacalman, S., Gane, L., Tassone, F., Hagerman, P. & Hagerman, R. (2006) 'Autism spectrum disorders and attention-deficit/hyperactivity disorder in boys with the Fragile X premutation.' *Developmental and Behavioral Pediatrics*, 27: 137–44.

Fazey, J. & Hardy, L. (1988) 'The inverted U hypothesis: a catastrophe for sport psychology?' *British Association of Sport Sciences Monograph 1*. Leeds: National Coaching Foundation.

Feher, P., Meyers, M.C. & Skelly, W.A. (1998) 'Psychological profiles of rock climbers: state and trait attributes.' *Journal of Sport Behaviour*, 21: 167–80.

Fergusson, D.N., Horwood, L.J. & Lynskey, M.T. (1992) 'Family change, discord and early offending.' *Journal of Child Psychology and Psychiatry*, 33: 1059–75.

Fletcher, J.M., Page, J.B., Francis, D.J., Copeland, K., Naus, M.J., Davis, C.M., Morris, R., Krauskopf, D. & Satz, P. (1996) 'Cognitive correlates of long-term cannabis use in Costa Rican men.' *Archives of General Psychiatry*, 53: 1051–7.

Foll, D.L., Rascle, O. & Higgins, N.C. (2006) 'Persistence in a putting task during perceived failure: the influence of attributions.' *Applied Psychology*, 55: 586–605.

Fowler, T., Shelton, K., Lifford, K., Rice, F., McBride, A., Nikolov, I., Neale, M.C., Harold, G., Thapar, A. & van den Bree, M.B.M. (2007) 'Genetic and environmental influences on the relationship between peer alcohol use and own alcohol use in adolescents.' *Addiction*, 102(6): 894–903.

Francis, L.J., Kelly, P. & Jones, S.J. (1998) 'The personality profile of female students who play hockey.' *Irish Journal of Psychology*, 19: 394–9.

Freeman, H. (1994) 'Schizophrenia and city residence.' *British Journal of Psychiatry*, 23: 39–50.

Freeman, M.A., Hennessey, E.V. & Marzullo, D.M. (2001) 'Defensive evaluation of anti-smoking messages among college-age smokers: the role of possible selves.' *Health-Psychology*, 20: 424–33.

Freud, S. (1917) 'Mourning and melancholia.' *Collected works volume 14*. London: Hogarth.

Fride, E., Foox, A., Rosenberg, E., Faigenboim, M., Cohen, V., Barda, L., Blau, H. & Mechoulam, R. (2003) 'Milk intake and survival in newborn cannabinoid CB1 receptor knockout mice: evidence for a "CB3" receptor.' *European Journal of Pharmacology*, 461(1): 27–34.

Fride, E., Ginzburg, Y., Bruer, A., Bisogno, T., Di Marzo, V. & Mechoulam, R. (2001) 'Critical role of the endogenous cannabinoid system in mouse pup suckling and growth.' *European Journal of Pharmacology*, 419(2–3): 207–14.

Frith, C.D. (1992) *The cognitive neuropsychology of schizophrenia*. Hove: Psychology Press.

Fromm-Reichmann, F. (1948) 'Notes on the development of treatment of schizophrenics by psychoanalytic psychotherapy.' *Psychiatry*, 11: 263–73.

Fuertes, M., Santos, P.L., Beeghly, M. & Tronick, E. (2006) 'More than maternal sensitivity shapes attachment: the role of infant coping and temperament.' *Annals of the New York Academy of Science*, 1094: 292–6.

Galynker, I.I., Watras-Ganz, S., Miner, C., Rosenthal, R.N., Des Jarlais, D.C., Richman, B.L. & London, E. (2000) 'Cerebral metabolism in opiate-dependent subjects: effects of methadone maintenance.' *Mount Sinai Journal of Medicine*, 67(5–6): 381–7.

Garland, D.J. & Barry, J.R. (1990) 'Personality and leader behaviors in collegiate football: a multidimensional approach to performance.' *Journal of Research in Personality*, 24: 355–70.

Garrido, V. & Morales, L.A. (2007) 'Serious (violent and chronic) juvenile offenders: a systematic review of treatment effectiveness in secure corrections.' In The Campbell Collaboration Reviews of Intervention and Policy Evaluations (C2-RIPE), July 2007. Philadelphia, Pennsylvania: Campbell Collaboration.

Gibbs, J.P. (1974) 'The effects of juvenile legal procedures on juvenile offenders' self-attitudes.' *Journal of Research in Crime & Delinquency*, 11: 51–5.

Gill, D. (1992) *Psychological dynamics of sport*. Champagne: Human Kinetics.

Godden D.R. & Baddeley A.D. (1975) 'Context-dependent memory in two natural environments: on land and underwater.' *British Journal of Psychology*, 66, 325–31.

Golby, J., Sheard, M. & Lavallee, D. (2003) 'A cognitive-behavioural analysis of mental toughness in national rugby league football teams.' *Perceptual & Motor Skills*, 96: 455–62.

Goldberg, A.S. (1998) 'Sports slump busting: 10 steps to mental toughness and peak performance.' Chpgn, IL: H. Kinetics.

Goldstein, J.M. (1988) 'Gender differences in the course of schizophrenia.' *American Journal of Psychiatry*, 145: 684–9.

Gottdiener, W.H. (2006) 'Individual psychodynamic psychotherapy of schizophrenia: empirical evidence for the practising physician.' *Psychoanalytic Psychology*, 23: 583–9.

Gottdiener, W.H. & Haslam, N. (2002) 'A critique of the methods and conclusions in the Patient Outcome Research Team (PORT) report on psychological treatments for schizophrenia.' *Journal of the American Academy of Psychoanalysis & Dynamic Psychiatry*, 31: 191–208.

Gottesman, I. (1991) *Schizophrenia genesis: the origins of madness*. New York: Freeman.

Gould, R. A., Buckminster, S., Pollack, M. H., Otto, M.W.,& Yap, L. (1997) 'Cognitive-behavioral and pharmacological treatment for social phobia: A meta-analysis.' *Clinical Psychology*: Science and Practice 4: 291–306.

Grant, S., London, E.D., Newlin, D.B., Villemange, V.L., Lui, X., Contoreggi, C., Phillips, R.L., Kimes, A.S. & Margolin, A. (1996) 'Activation of memory circuits during cue-elicited cocaine craving.' *Proceedings of the National Academy of Sciences, USA*, 93: 12040–5.

Gregg, M., Hall, C. & Nederhof, E. (2005) 'The imagery ability, imagery use, and performance relationship.' *Sport Psychologist*, 18: 363–75.

Grossman, K.E. & Grossman, K. (1990) 'The wider concept of attachment in cross-cultural research.' *Human Development*, 33: 31–47.

Grouios, G. (1992) 'Mental practice: a review.' *Journal of Sport Behaviour*, 15: 42–59.

Guillet, E., Sarrazin, P. & Fontayne, P. (2000) '"If it contradicts my gender role I'll stop". Introducing survival analysis to study the effects of gender typing on the time of withdrawal from sport practice: a 3-year study.' *European Review of Applied Psychology*, 50: 417–21.

Gunsekera, H., Chapman, S. & Campbell, S. (2005) 'Sex and drugs in popular movies: an analysis of the top 200 films.' *Journal of the Royal Society of Medicine*, 9(8): 464–70.

Gunter, B. & Harrison, J. (1996) *Violence on television in Britain: a content analysis – 1995–96*. Report to the Broadcasting Standards Council, British Broadcasting Corporation, British Sky Broadcasting, Channel Four Television, ITV Association and Independent Television Commission.

Hagell, A. & Newbury, T. (1994) *Young offenders and the media*. London: Policy Studies Institute.

Hajek, P. & Stead, L.F. (2004) 'Aversive smoking for smoking cessation.' *Cochrane Database of Systematic Reviews*, 3: CD000546.

Hall, H.K. & Kerr, A.W. (1998) 'Predicting achievement anxiety: a social-cognitive perspective.' *Journal of Sport & Exercise Psychology*, 20: 98–111.

Hammad, T.A. (2007) 'Benefits of anti-depressants outweigh risks of suicidal ideation and attempts in children and adolescents.' *Evidence-based Mental Health*, 10: 108.

Hammen, C. (1997) *Depression*. Hove: Psychology Press.

Hampson, R.E. & Deadwyler, S.A. (2000) 'Cannabinoids reveal the necessity of hippocampal neural encoding for short-term memory in rats.' *Neuroscience*, 20(23): 8932–42.

Han, C., McGue, M.K. & Iacono, W.G. (1999) 'Lifetime tobacco, alcohol and other substance use in adolescent Minnesota twins: univariate and multivariate behavioral genetic analyses.' *Addiction*, 94(7): 981–93.

Haney, M., Ward, A.S., Comer, A.D., Foltin, R.W. & Fischman, M.W. (1999) 'Abstinence syndrome following smoked marijuana in humans.' *Psychopharmacology*, 141(4): 395–404.

Haninger, K. & Thompson, K.M. (2004) 'Content and ratings of teen-rated video games.' *Journal of the American Medical Association*, 291: 856–65.

Hanssen, A. (1988) 'Alcohol, television and young people.' *Brewing Review*, summer.

Hardy, L. (1996) 'Testing the predictions of the cusp catastrophe model of anxiety and performance.' *Sport Psychologist*, 10: 140–56.

Hardy, L., Parfitt, G. & Pates, J. (1994) 'Performance catastrophes in sport: a test of the hysteresis hypothesis.' *Journal of Sport Sciences*, 12: 327–34.

Harrison, G.P. Jr, Gruber, A.J., Hudson, J.I., Huestis, M.A. & Yurgelun-Todd, D. (2002) 'Cognitive measures in long-term cannabis users.' *Journal of Clinical Pharmacology*, 42(11 Suppl): 41S–47S.

Harrison, L.J. & Ungerer, J.A. (2002) 'Maternal employment and infant–mother attachment security and 12 months post-partum.' *Developmental Psychology*, 38: 758–73.

Hay, G., Gannon, M., MacDougall, J., Millar, T., Eastwood, C. & McKeganey, N. (2007) 'National and regional estimates of the prevalence of opiate use and/or crack cocaine use 2005/06: a summary of key findings.' Home Office Online Report 21/07. London: Home Office.

Hetterna, J.M., Neale, M.C. & Kendler, K.S. (2001) 'A review and meta-analysis of the genetic epidemiology of anxiety disorders.' *American Journal of Psychiatry*, 158: 1568–78.

Higley, J.D., Mehlman, P.T., Higley, S.B., Fernald, B., Vickers, J., Lindell, S.G., Taub, D.M., Suomi, S.J. & Linnoila, M. (1996) 'Excessive mortality in young free-ranging male nonhuman primates with low cerebrospinal fluid 5-hydroxyindolacetic acid concentrations.' *Archives of General Psychiatry*, 53: 537–43.

Hills, P. & Argyle, M. (1998) 'Positive moods derived from leisure and their relationship to happiness and personality.' *Personality & Individual Differences*, 25: 523–35.

Hobbs, T.R. & Holt, M.M. (1976) 'The effects of token reinforcement on the behaviour of delinquents in cottage settings.' *Journal of Applied Behavior Analysis*, 9(2): 189–98.

Hochbaum, G.M. (1958) *Public participation in medical screening: a sociopsychological study* (Public Health Service Publication 572). Washington DC: US Government Printing Office.

Holbrook, M.I. (1997) 'Anger management training in prison inmates.' *Psychological Reports*, 81(2): 623–6.

Hollin, C.R. (1989) *Psychology and Crime: An Introduction to Criminological Psychology*. London: Routledge.

Holmes, J. (2002) 'All you need is cognitive therapy?' *British Medical Journal*, 342: 288–94.

Hopf, W.H., Huber, G.L. & Wei, R.H. (2008) 'Media violence and youth violence: a 2-year longitudinal study.' *Journal of Media Psychology: Theories, Methods, & Applications*, 20: 79–96.

Hopper, K., Harrison, G., Janca, A. and Sartorius, N. (2007) *Recovery from schizophrenia: an international perspective. A report from the WHO Collaborative Project, the International Study of Schizophrenia*. Oxford: Oxford University Press.

Houston, C. & Milby, J.B. (1983) 'Drug-seeking behavior and its mediation: effects of aversion therapy with narcotic addicts on methadone.' *International Journal of the Addictions*, 18: 1171–7.

Howard, M.O. (2001) 'Pharmacological aversion treatment of alcohol dependence. I. Production and prediction of conditioned alcohol aversion.' *American Journal of Drug and Alcohol Abuse*, 27(3): 561–85.

Huesmann, R. (1986) 'Psychological processes promoting the relation between exposure to media violence and aggressive behaviour by the viewer.' *Journal of Social Issues*, 42(3): 125–40.

Hunter, D. (1993) 'Anger management in the prison: an evaluation.' *Research on Offender Programming Issues*, 5(1): 3–15.

Iacono, W.G., Malone, S.M. & McGue, M. (2003) 'Substance use disorders, externalizing psychopathology, and P300 event-related potential amplitude.' *International Journal of Psychophysiology*, 48(2): 147–78.

Ireland, J.L. (2004) 'Anger management therapy with young male offenders: an evaluation of treatment outcome.' *Aggressive Behavior*, 30(2): 174–85.

Jahoda, G. (1954) 'A note on Ashanti names and their relationship to personality.' *British Journal of Psychology*, 45: 192–5.

Jambor, E.A. (1999) 'Parents as children's socialising agents in youth soccer.' *Journal of Sport Behaviour*, 22: 350–9.

Janis, I.L. & Feshbach, S. (1953) 'Effects of fear-arousing communications.' *Journal of Abnormal & Social Psychology*, 48: 78–92.

Jarvis, M. (2006) *Sport psychology: a student handbook.* London: Routledge.

Jenkins, W.O., Witherspoon, A.D., DeVine, M.D., deValera, E.K., Muller, J.B., Barton, M.C. & McKee, J.M. (1974) *Post-prison analysis of criminal behaviour and longitudinal follow-up evaluation of institutional treatment.* Springfield, Virginia: National Technical Information Service.

Jiménez-Ruiz, C.A., Miranda, J.A., Hurt, R.D., Pinedo, A.R., Reina, S.S. & Valero, F.C. (2008) 'Study of impact of laws regulating tobacco consumption on the prevalence of passive smoking in Spain.' *European Journal of Public Health*, 18(6): 622–5.

Jones, G. (1991) 'Recent developments and current issues in competitive state anxiety research.' *The Psychologist*, 4: 152–5.

Juliano, L.M., Houtsmuller, E.J. & Stitzer, M.L. (2006) 'A preliminary investigation of rapid smoking as a lapse-responsive treatment for tobacco dependence.' *Experimental & Clinical Psychopharmacology*, 14(4): 429–38.

Julien, R.M. (2001) *A primer of drug action.* New York: Worth Publishers.

Kagan, J., Kearsley, R.B. & Zelazo, P.R. (1980) *Infancy: its place in human development.* Cambridge, MA: Harvard University Press.

Karen, R. (1994) *Becoming attached: unfolding the mystery of the infant–mother bond and its impact on later life.* New York: Warner Books.

Kazdin, A.E. (1982) 'The token economy: a decade later.' *Journal of Applied Behavior Analysis*, 15(3): 431–45.

Kebbell, M.R., Johnson, S.D., Froyland, I. & Ainsworth, M. (2002) 'The influence of belief that a car crashed on witnesses' estimates of civilian and police car speed.' *Journal of Psychology*, 136(6): 597–607.

Keen, J. (2000) 'A practitioner's perspective: anger management work with young offenders.' *Forensic Update*, 60: 20–5.

Keenan, H.T., Hall, G.C. & Marshall, S.W. (2009) 'Early head injury and attention deficit/hyperactivity disorder.' *British Medical Journal*, 337: 1–4.

Keith, S.J., Regier, D.A. & Rae, D.S. (1991) 'Schizophrenic disorders.' In Robins, L.N. & Regier, D.S. (eds) *Psychiatric Disorders in America: the Epidemiological Catchment Area Study.* New York: Free Press.

Kendler, K.S., Jacobson, K.C., Prescott, C.A. & Neale, M.C. (2003) 'Specificity of genetic and environmental risk factors for use and abuse/dependence of cannabis, cocaine, hallucinogens, sedatives, stimulants, and opiates in male twins.' *American Journal of Psychiatry*, 160: 687–95.

Kendler, K.S., Thornton, L.M. & Pederson, N.L. (2000) 'Tobacco consumption in Swedish twins reared apart and reared together.' *Archives of General Psychiatry*, 57: 886–92.

Kershaw, C., Nicholas, S. & Walker, A. (2008) *Crime in England and Wales 2007/08: findings from the British Crime Survey and police recorded crime.* Home Office Statistical Bulletin. London: Home Office.

Khroyan, T.V., Barrett-Larimore, R.L., Rowlett, J.K. & Spealman, R.D. (2000) 'Dopamine D1- and D2-like receptor mechanisms in relapse to cocaine-seeking behavior: effects of selective antagonists and agonists.' *Journal of Pharmacology and Experimental Therapeutics*, 294(2): 680–7.

Kindt, M. & Brosschot, J.F. (1997) 'Phobia-related cognitive bias for pictorial and linguistic stimuli.' *Journal of Abnormal Psychology*, 106: 644–8.

Kirigin, K.A., Braukman, C.J., Atwater, J.D. & Wolf, M.M. (1982) 'An evaluation of teaching-family (Achievement Place) group homes for juvenile offenders.' *Journal of Applied Behavior Analysis*, 15(1): 1–16.

Kirkby, R.J. & Whelan, R.J. (1996) 'The effects of hospitalisation and medical procedures on children and their families.' *Journal of Family Studies*, 2: 56–77.

Kirley, A., Hawi, Z., Daly, G., McCarron, M., Mullins, C., Millar, N., Waldman, I., Fitzgerald, M. & Gill, M. (2002) 'Dopaminergic system genes in ADHD: toward a biological hypothesis.' *Neuropsychopharmacology*, 27: 608–19.

Klein, G., Juni, A., Waxman, A.R., Arout, C.A., Inturrisi, C.E. & Kest, B. (2008) 'A survey of acute and chronic heroin dependence in ten inbred mouse strains: evidence of genetic correlation with morphine dependence.' *Pharmacology, Biochemistry & Behavior*, 90(3): 447–52.

Klein, M. (1946) *Envy & gratitude.* New York: Simon & Schuster.

Klimek, V., Stockmeier, C., Overholser, J., Meltzer, H.Y., Kalka, S., Dilley, G. & Ordway, G.A. (1997) 'Reduced levels of norepinephrine transporters in the locus coeruleus in major depression.' *Journal of Neuroscience*, 17: 8451–8.

Kniveton, B.H. (1976) 'Social learning and imitation in relation to television.' In Brown, R. (ed) *Children and television.* London: Collier Macmillan, 237–66.

Kobasa, S.C. (1979) 'Stressful life events, personality & health: an inquiry into hardiness.' *Journal of Personality & Social Psychology*, 37: 1–11.

Koivula, N. (1995) 'Ratings of gender-appropriateness of sports participation: effects of gender-based schematic processing.' *Sex Roles*, 33: 543–57.

Koluchova, J. (1972) 'Severe deprivation in twins: a case study.' *Journal of Child Psychology and Psychiatry*, 13: 107–11.

Koluchova, J. (1991) 'Severely deprived twins after 22 years' observation.' *Studia Psychologica*, 33: 23–8.

Konijn, E.A., Bijvank, M.N. & Bushman, B.J. (2007) 'I wish I were a warrior: the role of wishful identification in the effects of violent video games on aggression in adolescent boys.' *Developmental Psychology*, 43: 1038–44.

Koren-Karie, N. (2001) 'Mothers' attachment representations and choice of infant care: centre care vs home.' *Infant & Child Development*, 10: 117–27.

Koster, E.H., De Raedt, R., Goeleven, E., Franck, E. & Crombez, G. (2005) 'Mood-congruent attentional bias in dysphoria: maintained attention to and impaired disengagement from negative information.' *Emotion*, 5: 446–55.

Krackow, E. & Lynn, S.J. (2003) 'Is there touch in a game of Twister? The effects of innocuous touch and suggestive questions on children's eyewitness memory.' *Law and Human Behavior*, 27(6): 589–604.

Kremer, J. & Scully, D. (1994) *Psychology in sport*. London: Taylor & Francis.

Kurzthaler, I., Hummer, M., Miller, C., Sperner-Unterweger, B., Günther, V., Wechdorn, H., Battista, H.J. & Fleischhacker, W.W. (1999) 'Effect of cannabis use on cognitive functions and driving ability.' *Journal of Clinical Psychiatry*, 60(6): 395–9.

Lagerspetz, K. & Wuorinen, K. (1965) 'A cross-fostering experiment with mice selectively bred for aggressiveness and non-aggressiveness.' Reports of the Institute of Psychology of the University of Turku, 17: 1–6.

Lagerspetz, K.M.J. (1979) 'Modification of aggressiveness in mice.' In Feshbach, S. & Fraçzek, A. (eds) *Aggression and behavior change: biological and social processes*. New York: Praeger Publishers.

Lamb, R.J., Preston, K.L., Schindler, C.W., Meisch, R.A., Davis, F., Katz, J.L., Henningfield, J.E. & Goldberg, S.R. (1991) 'The reinforcing and subjective effects of morphine in post-addicts: a dose-response study.' *Journal of Pharmacology & Experimental Therapeutics*, 259: 1165–73.

Law, K. (1997) 'Further evaluation of anger-management courses at HMP Wakefield: an examination of behavioural change.' *Inside Psychology: The Journal of Prison Service Psychology*, 3(1): 91–5.

Ledent, C., Valverde, O., Cossu, G., Petitet, F., Aubert, J.F., Beslot, F., Böhme, G.A., Imperato, A., Pedrazzini, T., Roques, B.P., Vassart, G., Fratta, W. & Parmentier, M. (1999) 'Unresponsiveness to cannabinoids and reduced addictive effects of opiates in CB_1 knock-out mice.' *Science*, 283: 401–3.

Leff, J. (1997) *Care in the community – illusion or reality?* Chichester: Wiley.

Leichsenring, F., Rabung, S. & Leibing, D. (2004) 'The efficacy of short-term psychodynamic psychotherapy in specific psychiatric disorders.' *Archives of General Psychiatry*, 61: 1208–16.

Levin, H., Hanten, G., Jeffrey, M., Li, X., Swank, P., Ewing-Cobbs, L., Dennis, M., Menefee, D. & Schachar, R. (2007) 'Symptoms of attention deficit hyperactivity disorder following traumatic brain injury in children.' *Journal of Developmental & Behavioural Pediatrics*, 28: 108–18.

Levy, P. & Hartocollis, P. (1976) 'Nursing aides and patient violence.' *American Journal of Psychiatry*, 133: 429–35.

Lewine, R.R.J., Gulley, L.R., Risch, C., Jewart, R. & Houpt, J.L. (1990) 'Sexual dimorphism, brain morphology and schizophrenia.' *Schizophrenia Bulletin*, 16: 195–203.

Lewis, C., Wilkins, R., Baker, L. & Woobey, A. (1995) '"Is this man your daddy?" Suggestibility in children's eyewitness identification of a family member.' *Child Abuse and Neglect*, 19(6): 739–44.

Lindsay, D.S. (1990) 'Misleading suggestions can impair eyewitnesses' ability to remember event details.' *Journal of Experimental Psychology: Learning, Memory & Cognition*, 16: 1077–83.

Lindstroem, L.H., Gefvert, O., Hagberg, G., Lundberg, T., Bergstroem, M., Harvig, P. & Langstroem, B. (1999) 'Increased dopamine synthesis rate in medial prefrontal cortex and striatum in schizophrenia indicated by L-DOPA and PET.' *Biological Psychiatry*, 46: 681–8.

Lipton, D.S., Pearson, F.S., Cleland, C.M. & Yee, D. (2002) 'The effectiveness of cognitive-behavioural treatment methods on offender recidivism: meta-analytic outcomes from the CDATE project.' In McGuire, J. (ed) *Offender rehabilitation and treatment: effective programmes and policies to reduce re-offending*, 79–112. Chichester: John Wiley & Sons.

Lisanby, S.H., Maddox, J.H., Prudic, J., Devanand, D.P. & Sackeim, H.A. (2000) 'The effects of electroconvulsive therapy on memory of autobiographical and public events.' *Archives of General Psychiatry*, 57: 581–90.

Littlewood, R. & Lipsedge, M. (1997) *Aliens and alienists: ethnic minorities and psychiatry*. London: Routledge.

Locke, E.A. (1996) 'Motivation Through Conscious Goal Setting.' *Applied and Preventive Psychology*, 5: 117–24

Loftus, E.F. (1979a) *Eyewitness memory*. Cambridge, MA: Harvard University Press.

Loftus, E.F. (1979b) 'Reactions to blatantly contradictory information.' *Memory & Cognition*, 7: 368–74.

Loftus, E.F. & Palmer, J.C. (1974) 'Reconstruction of automobile destruction: an example of the interaction between language and memory.' *Journal of Verbal Learning and Verbal Behavior*, 13: 585–9.

Loftus, E.F. & Zanni, G. (1975) 'Eyewitness testimony: The influence of the wording of a question.' *Bulletin of the Psychonomic Society*, 5(1): 86-8.

Logan, F.A. (1965) 'Decision making by rats: delay versus amount of reward.' *Journal of Comparative & Physiological Psychology*, 59: 1–12.

Lorenz, K. (1935) 'The companion in the bird's world. *Auk*, 54: 245–73.

Lorenz, K. (1952) *King Solomon's ring*. London: Methuen.

Lou, H.R., Hou, Z.F., Wu, J., Zhang, Y.P. & Wan, Y.J. (2005) 'Evolution of the DRD2 gene haplotype and its association with alcoholism in Mexican Americans.' *Alcohol*, 36(2): 117–25.

Loza, W. & Loza-Fanous, A. (1999) 'The fallacy of reducing rape and violent recidivism by treating anger.' *International Journal of Offender Therapy and Comparative Criminology*, 43(4): 492–502.

Lubman, D.I., Peters, L.A., Moog, K., Bradley, B.P. & Deaking, J.F.W. (2000) 'Attentional bias for drug cues in opiate dependence.' *Psychological Medicine*, 30(1):169–75.

Lucchini, R. (1985) 'Young drug addicts and the drug scene.' *Bulletin on Narcotics*, 37(2–3): 135–48.

Lunddqvist, T. (1995) 'Chronic cannabis use and the sense of coherence.' *Life Sciences*, 56: 2145–50.

Lupyan, G. (2008) 'From chair to "chair"; a representational shift account of object labeling effects on memory.' *Journal of Experimental Psychology: General*, 137(2): 348–69.

Lyons, M.J., True, W.R., Eisen, S.A., Goldberg, J., Meyer, J.M., Faraone, S.V., Eaves, L.J. & Tsuang, M.T. (1995) 'Differential heritability of adult and juvenile antisocial traits.' *Archives of General Psychiatry*, 52: 906–15.

Madon, S., Guyll, M., Spoth, R.L., Cross, S.E. & Hilbert, S.J. (2003) 'The self-fulfilling influence of mother expectations on children's underage drinking.' *Journal of Personality and Social Psychology*, 84: 1188–205.

Maedgen, J.W. & Carlson, C.L. (2000) 'Social functioning and emotional regulation in the attention deficit hyperactivity disorder subtypes.' *Journal of Clinical Child Psychology*, 29: 30–42.

Maes, H.H., Woodard, C.E., Murrelle, L., Meyer, J.M., Silberg, J.L., Hewitt, J.K., Rutter, M., Simonoff, E., Pickles, A., Carbonneau, R., Neale, M.C. & Eaves, L.J. (1999) 'Tobacco, alcohol and drug use in eight- to sixteen-year-old twins: the Virginia Twin Study of Adolescent Behavioral Development.' *Journal of Alcohol Studies*, 60(3): 293–305.

Maldonado, R., Blendy, J.A., Tzavara, E., Gass, P., Roques, B.P., Hanoune, J. & Shütz, G. (1996) 'Reduction of morphine abstinence in mice with a mutation in the gene coding CREB.' *Science*, 273: 657–9.

Mason, D.A. & Frick, P.J. (1994) 'The heritability of antisocial behaviour: a meta-analysis of twin and adoption studies.' *Journal of Psychopathology & Behavioral Assessment*, 16: 301–23.

Massie H. & Szanberg N. (2002) 'The relationship between mothering in infancy, childhood experience and adult mental health.' *International Journal of Psychoanalysis*, 83, 35–55.

Matochik, J.A., Eldreth, D.A., Cadet, J.L. & Bolla, K.I. (2005) 'Altered brain tissue composition in heavy marijuana users.' *Drug & Alcohol Dependence*, 77(1): 23–30.

Matthes, H.W.D., Maldonado, R., Simonin, F., Valverde, O., Slowe, S., Kitchen, I., Befort, K., Dierch, A., Le Meur, M., Dolle, P., Tzavara, E., Hanoune, J., Roques, B.P. & Kieffer, B.L. (1996) 'Loss of morphine-induced analgesia, reward effect and withdrawal symptoms in mice lacking the Mu-opioid-receptor gene.' *Nature*, 383: 819–23.

McClelland, D.C., Atkinson, J.W., Clark, R.W. & Lowell, E.J. (1961) *The achievement motive*. New York: Appleton Century Crofts.

McGuffin, P., Katz, R., Watkins, S. & Rutherford, J. (1996) 'A hospital-based twin register of the heritability of DSM-IV unipolar depression.' *Archives of General Psychiatry*, 53: 129–36.

McNeal, E.T. & Cimbolic, P. (1986) 'Antidepressants and biochemical theories of depression.' *Psychological Bulletin*, 99: 361–74.

Medina, K.L., Hanson, K.L., Schweinsburg, A.D., Cohen-Zion, M., Nagal, B.J. & Tapert, S.F. (2007) 'Neuropsychological functioning in adolescent marijuana users: subtle deficits detectable after a month of abstinence.' *Journal of the International Neuropsychological Society*, 13(5): 807–20.

Memon, A. & Wright, D.B. (1999) 'Eyewitness testimony and the Oklahoma bombing.' *The Psychologist*, 12: 292–5.

Memon, A., Holliday, R. & Hill, C. (2006) 'Pre-event stereotypes and misinformation effects in young children.' *Memory*, 14: 104–14.

Menzies, R.G. (1996) 'The origins of specific phobias in a mixed clinical sample: classificatory differences between two origins instruments.' *Journal of Anxiety Disorders*, 10: 347–54.

Mezulis, A.H., Hyde, J.S. & Abramson, L.Y. (2006) 'The developmental origins of cognitive vulnerability to depression: temperament, parenting, and negative life events in childhood as contributors to negative cognitive style.' *Developmental Psychology*, 42: 1012–25.

Middleton, S.C., Marsh, H.W., Martin, A.J., Richards, G.E., Savis, J., Perry, C. Jr & Brown, R. (2004) 'The Psychological Performance Inventory: is the mental toughness test tough enough?' *International Journal of Sport Psychology*, 35: 91–108.

Milin, R., Manion, I., Dare, G. & Walker, S. (2008) 'Prospective assessment of cannabis withdrawal in adolescents with cannabis dependence: a pilot study.' *Journal of the American Academy of Child & Adolescent Psychiatry*, 47(2): 174–8.

Miller, J.L. & Levy, G.D. (1996) 'Gender role conflict, gender-typed characteristics, self-concept and sports socialisation in female athletes and non-athletes.' *Sex Roles*, 35: 111–12.

Mitchell, M. (2008) *FRANK campaign: performance & development*. London: Home Office. [accessed online: http://drugs.homeoffice.gov.uk/publication-search/frank/frankpresentation?view=Binary]

Moeller, F.G., Dougherty, D.M., Swann, A.C., Collins, D., Davis, C.M. & Cherek, D.R. (1996) 'Tryptophan depletion and aggressive responding in healthy males.' *Psychopharmacology*, 126: 97–103.

Moore, P.J., Ebbesen, E.B. & Konecni, V.J. (1994) *What does real eyewitness testimony look like? An archival analysis of witnesses to adult felony crimes*. Technical Report. San Diego, CA: University of California San Diego, Law and Psychology Program.

Morgan, L.K., Griggin, J. & Heywood, V.H. (1996) 'Ethnicity, gender and experience effects on attributional dimensions.' *Sport Psychologist*, 10: 4–16.

Morgan, M. & Grube, J.W. (1991) 'Closeness and peer group influence.' *British Journal of Social Psychology*, 30(2): 159–69.

Morrison, A.P., French, P., Walford, L., Lewis, S.W., Kilcommons, A., Green, J., Parker, S. & Bentall, R.P. (2004) 'Cognitive therapy for prevention of psychosis in people of ultra-high risk: a random control trial.' *British Journal of Psychiatry*, 185: 291–7.

Musty, R.E. & Kaback, L. (1995) 'Relationships between motivation and depression in chronic marijuana users.' *Life Sciences*, 56: 2151–8.

Myers, N.D., Payment, C.A. & Feltz, D.L. (2004) 'Reciprocal relationships between collective efficacy and team performance in women's ice hockey.' *Group Dynamics: Theory, Research, and Practice*, 8: 182–95.

National Institute for Clinical Excellence (2002) *Schizophrenia: core interventions in the treatment and management of schizophrenia in primary and secondary care.* London: NICE.

National Institute for Clinical Excellence (2003) *The clinical management of depression.* London: NICE.

National Institute for Clinical Excellence (2004) *Depression: management of depression in primary and secondary care. Clinical guideline 23.* London: NICE.

National Institute for Health and Clinical Excellence (2007) Public Health Intervention Guidance, Draft Scope: Preventing the uptake of smoking by children and young people, including point of sale measures. London: NIHCE.

National Institute for Health and Clinical Excellence (2008) *Attention deficit hyperactivity disorder: diagnosis and management of ADHD in children, young people and adults.* London: NCCMH.

Nicholls, D., Chater, R. & Lask, B. (2000) 'Children into DSM don't go: a comparison of classification systems for eating disorders in childhood and adolescence.' *International Journal of Eating Disorders*, 28: 317–24.

Nicholls, J. (1984) 'Concepts of ability and achievement motivation.' In Ames, R. & Ames, C. (eds) *Research on motivation in education: student motivation*, vol 1: 39–73. New York: Academic Press.

Nielsen, D.A., Ji, F., Yuferov, V., Ho, A., Chen, A., Levran, O., Ott, J. & Kreek, M.J. (2008) 'Genotype patterns that contribute to increased risk for or protection from developing heroin addiction.' *Molecular Psychiatry*, 13(4): 417–28.

Office for National Statistics (2008) 'Drug poisoning deaths.' http://www.statistics.gov.uk/cci/nugget.asp?id=806 [accessed 18/4/09]

Olds, J. (1958) *Self-stimulation of the brain.* Science, 127:315-24.

Olds, J. & Milner, P. (1954) 'Positive reinforcement produced by electrical stimulation of septal area and other regions of rat brain.' *Journal of Comparative & Physiological Psychology*, 47:419–27.

Olmstead, T.A., Sindelar, J.L. & Petry, N.M. (2007) 'Cost-effectiveness of prize-based incentives for stimulant abusers in outpatient psychosocial treatment programs.' *Drug & Alcohol Dependence*, 87(2–3): 175–82.

Olweus, D., Mattsson, A., Schalling, D. & Low, H. (1980) 'Testosterone, aggression, physical, and personality dimensions in normal adolescent males.' *Psychosomatic Medicine*, 42(2): 253–69.

Omoaregba, J.O., James, B.O. & Eze, G.O. (2009) 'Schizophrenia spectrum disorders in a Nigerian family: 4 case reports.' *Cases Journal*, 2(1): 14 [accessed electronically ahead of print].

Orbach, I., Singer, R. & Price, S. (1999) 'An attribution programme and achievement in sport.' *Sport Psychologist*, 13: 69–82.

Owen, L. & Youdan, B. (2006) '22 years on: the impact and relevance of the UK No Smoking Day.' *Tobacco Control*, 15: 19–25.

Owens, G., Granader, Y., Humphrey, A. & Baron-Cohen, S. (2008) 'LEGO® Therapy and the Social Use of Language Programme: an evaluation of two social skills interventions for children with high functioning autism and Asperger syndrome.' *Journal of Autism & Developmental Disorders*, 38: 1944–57.

Paivio, A. (1986) *Mental representations: a dual coding approach.* Oxford: Oxford University Press.

Paquette, V., Levesque, J., Mensour, B., Leroux, J.M., Beaudoin, G., Bourgouin, P. & Beauregard, M. (2003) 'Effects of cognitive behavioural therapy on the neural correlates of spider phobia.' *Neuroimage*, 18: 401–9.

Paterson, H.M. & Kemp, R.I. (2006) 'Comparing methods of encountering post-event information: the power of co-witness suggestion.' *Applied Cognitive Psychology*, 20: 1083–99.

Pennington, D.C. (1986) *Essential social psychology.* London: Edward Arnold.

Pert, C.B. & Snyder, S.H. (1973) 'The opiate receptor: demonstration in nervous tissue.' *Science*, 179: 1011–14.

Pickens, R. & Thompson, T. (1968) 'Cocaine-reinforced behaviour in rats: effects of reinforcement magnitude and fixed-ratio size.' *The Journal of Pharmacology and Experimental Therapeutics*, 161(1): 122–9.

Pilling, S., Bebbington, P., Kuipers, E., Garety, P., Geddes, J., Orbach, G. & Morgan, C. (2002) 'Psychological treatments in schizophrenia: I. Meta-analysis of family intervention and cognitive behaviour therapy.' *Psychological Medicine*, 32: 763–82.

Pinquart, M., Duberstein, P.R. & Lyness, J.M. (2006) 'Treatments for later-life depressive conditions: a meta-analytic comparison of pharmacotherapy and psychotherapy.' *American Journal of Psychiatry*, 163: 1493–501.

Pontizovsky, A.M., Grinshpoon, A., Poogachev, I., Ritsner, M. & Abramowitz, M.Z. (2006) 'Changes in stability of first-admission psychiatric diagnoses over 14 years, based on cross-sectional data at three time points.' *Israeli Journal of Psychiatry and Related Sciences*, 43: 34–9.

Pope, H. (1998) 'Marijuana: special report.' In Acheson, D. & Mullin, T. (1998) *New Scientist*, 2122: 24–34.

Potegal, M. (1994) 'Aggressive arousal: the amygdala connection.' In Potegal, M. & Knutson, J.F. (eds) *The dynamics of aggression*, 73–111. Hillsdale, NJ: Lawrence Erlbaum.

Potegal, M., Ferris, C., Herbert, M., Meyerhoff, J.M. & Skaredoff, L. (1996a) 'Attack priming in female Syrian golden hamsters is associated with a *c-fos* coupled process within the corticomedial amygdala.' *Neuroscience*, 75: 869–80.

Potegal, M., Herbert, M., DeCoster, M. & Meyerhoff, J.L. (1996b) 'Brief, high-frequency stimulation of the corticomedial amygdala induces a delayed and prolonged increase of aggressiveness in male Syrian golden hamsters.' *Behavioral Neuroscience*, 110: 410–12.

Quinsey, V.L. & Sarbit, B. (1975) 'Behavioral changes associated with the introduction of a token economy in a maximum security psychiatric institution.' *Canadian Journal of Criminology and Corrections*, 17: 177–82.

Raine, A., Buchsbaum, M. & LaCasse, L. (1997) 'Brain abnormalities in murderers indicated by positron emission tomography.' *Biological Psychiatry*, 42: 495–508.

Rathod, S. & Turkington, D. (2005) 'Cognitive-behaviour therapy for schizophrenia: a review.' *Current Opinion in Psychiatry*, 18: 159–63.

Read, J., Van Os, J., Morrison, A.P. & Ross, C.A. (2005) 'Childhood trauma, psychosis and schizophrenia: a literature review with theoretical and clinical implications.' *Acta Psychiatrica*, 112: 330–50.

Reif, A., Jacob, C.P., Rujescu, D., Herterich, S., Lang, S., Gutknecht, L., Baehne, C.G., Strobel, A., Freitag, C.M., Giegling, I., Romanos, M., Hartmann, A., Rösler, M., Renner, T.J., Fallgatter, A.J., Retz, W., Ehlis, A.C. & Lesch, K.P. (2009) 'Influence of functional variant of neuronal nitric oxide synthase on impulsive behaviors in humans.' *Archives of General Psychiatry*, 66(1): 41–50.

Retz, W., Retz-Junginger, P., Supprian, T., Thome, J. & Rösler (2004) 'Association of serotonin transporter promoter gene polymorphism with violence: relation with personality disorders, impulsivity, and childhood ADHD psychopathology.' *Behavioral Sciences and the Law*, 22(3): 415–25.

Rice, M.E., Quinsey, V.L. & Houghton, R. (1990) 'Predicting treatment outcome and recidivism among patients in a maximum security token economy.' *Behavioral Sciences and the Law*, 8: 313–26.

Richards, M. (1995) 'The international year of the family – family research.' *The Psychologist*, 8: 17–20.

Roberts, D.F., Christenson, P.G., Henriksen, L., Bandy, E., Jessup, H.D., Abdul-Wahid, J., Carbone, S., Wilson, A.B. & Johnson, B. (2002) *Substance use in popular music videos*. Washington, DC: Office of National Drug Control Policy.

Robertson, J. & Bowlby, J. (1952) 'Responses of young children to separation from their mothers.' *Courier Centre International d'enfance*, 2: 131–42.

Robinson, T.E. & Berridge, K.C. (1993) 'The neural basis of drug craving: an incentive-sensitization theory of addiction.' *Brain Research Reviews*, 18: 247–91.

Rocha, B.A., Scearce-Levie, K., Lucas, J.J., Hiroi, N., Castanon, N., Crabbe, J.C., Nestler, E.J. & Hen, R. (1998) 'Increased vulnerability to cocaine in mice lacking the serotonin-1B receptor.' *Nature*, 393(6681): 175–8.

Rosenhan, D.L. (1973) 'On being sane in insane places.' *Science*, 179: 250–8.

Ross, R.P., Campbell, T., Wright, J.C., Huston, A.C., Rice, M.L. & Turk, P. (1984) 'When celebrities talk, children listen: an experimental analysis of children's responses to TV ads with celebrity endorsement.' *Journal of Applied Developmental Psychology*, 5: 185–202.

Ross, R.R. & MacKay, H.B. (1976) 'A study of institutional treatment programs.' *International Journal of Offender Therapy & Comparative Criminology*, 20: 165–73.

Rounsville, B.J., Anton, S.F., Carroll, K., Budde, D., Prusoff, B.A. & Gawin, F. (1991) 'Psychiatric diagnosis of treatment-seeking cocaine abusers.' *Archives of General Psychiatry*, 48(1): 43–51.

Rung, J.P., Carlsson, A., Markinhuhta, R. & Carlsson, M.L. (2005) '(+)-MK-801 induced social withdrawal in rats; a model for negative symptoms in schizophrenia.' *Progress un neuropsychopharmacology and Biological Psychiatry*, 29(5): 827–32.

Rutter, M. (1981) *Maternal deprivation reassessed*. Harmondsworth: Penguin.

Rutter, M. (2006) 'The psychological effects of institutional rearing.' In Marshall, P. & Fox, N. (eds) *The development of social engagement: neurobiological perspectives*. New York: Oxford University Press.

Rutter, M. & the English & Romanian Adoptees Study Team (1998) 'Developmental catch up and deficit after severe global early privation.' *Journal of Child Psychology and Psychiatry*, 39: 465–76.

Rychtarik, R.G., Fairbank, J.A., Allen, C.M., Fay, D.W. & Drabman, R.S. (1983) 'Alcohol use in television programming: effects on children's behaviour.' *Addictive Behaviour*, 8: 19–22.

Sanchez-Villegas, A., Schlatter, J., Ortuno, F., Lahortiga, F., Pla, J., Benito, S. & Martinez-Gonzalez, M.A. (2008) 'Validity of a self-reported diagnosis of depression among participants in a cohort study using the Structured Clinical Interview for DSM-IV (SCID-I).' *BMC Psychiatry*, 8: np.

Schlaepfer, T.E., Pearlson, G.D., Wong, D.F., Marenco, S. & Dannals, R.F. (1997) 'PET study of competition between intravenous cocaine and [11C]raclopride at dopamine receptors in human subjects.' *American Journal of Psychiatry*, 154(9): 1209–13.

Schooler, N., Rabinowitz, J., Davidson, M., Emsley, R., Harvey, P.D., Kopala, L., McGorry, P.D., Van Hove, I., Eerdekens, M., Swyzen, W. & De Smedt, G. (2005) 'Risperidone and haloperidol in first-episode psychosis: a long-term randomized trial.' *American Journal of Psychiatry*, 162: 947–53.

Schunk, D.H. (1991) 'Self-efficacy and academic motivation.' *Educational Psychologist*, 26: 207–32.

Schurr, K.T., Ashley, M.A. & Joy, K.L. (1977) 'A multivariate analysis of male athlete personality characteristics; sport type and success.' *Multivariate Experimental Clinical Psychology*, 3: 53–68.

Self, D.W., Barnhart, W.J., Lehman, D.A. & Nestler, E.J. (1996) 'Opposite modulation of cocaine-seeking behaviour in D_1-like and D_2-like dopamine receptor agonists.' *Science*, 271: 1586–9.

Semple, D.M., McIntosh, A.M. & Lawrie, S.M. (2005) 'Cannabis as a risk factor for psychosis: systematic review.' *Journal of Psychopharmacology*, 19(2): 187–94.

Sewell, R.A., Ranganathan, M. & D'Souza, D.C. (2009) 'Cannabinoids and psychosis.' *International Review of Psychiatry*, 21(2): 152–62.

Shaham, Y. & Stewart, J. (1995) 'Stress reinstates heroin-seeking in drug-free animals: an effect mimicking heroin, not withdrawal.' *Psychopharmacology*, 119: 334–41.

Sheese, B.E. & Graziano, W.G. (2005) 'Deciding to defect: the effects of video game violence on cooperative and competitive behavior.' *Psychological Science*, 16(5): 391–6.

Shepherd, G. (1998) 'Models of community care.' *Journal of Mental Health*, 7: 165–77.

Siegel, A. & Pott, C.B. (1988) 'Neural substrates of aggression and flight in the cat.' *Progress in Neurobiology*, 31(4): 261–83.

Simons-Morton, B., Haynie, D.L., Crump, A.D., Eitel, S.P. & Saylor, K.E. (2001) 'Peer and parent influences on smoking and drinking among early adolescents.' *Health Education & Behavior*, 28(1): 95–107.

Sim-Selley, L.J. & Martin, B.R. (2002) 'Effect of chronic administration of R-(+)-[2,3-Dihydro-5-methyl-3-[(morpholinyl)methyl]pyrrolo[1,2,3-de]-1,4-benzoxazinyl]-(1-naphthalenyl)methanone mesylate (WIN55,212-2) or delta(9)-tetrahydrocannabinol on cannabinoid receptor adaptation in mice.' *Journal of Pharmacology & Experimental Therapeutics*, 303(1): 36–44.

Sindelar, J., Elbel, B. & Petry, N.M. (2007) 'What do we get for our money? Cost-effectiveness of adding contingency management.' *Addiction*, 102(2): 309–16.

Skre, I., Onstad, S., Torgersen, S. & Kringlen, E. (2000) 'The heritability of common phobic fear: a twin study of a clinical sample.' *Journal of Anxiety Disorders*, 14: 549–62.

Smallbone, S.W. & Dadds, M.R. (2000) 'Attachment and coercive sexual behaviour.' *Sexual Abuse*, 12: 3–15.

Smith, G. & Sweeny, E. (1984) *Children and television advertising: an overview*. London: Children's Research Unit.

Smith, J.W. (1988) 'Long-term outcome of clients treated in a commercial stop smoking program.' *Journal of Substance Abuse & Treatment*, 5(1): 33–6.

Smith, P.B. & Bond, M.H. (1993) *Social Psychology Across Cultures: Analysis and Perspectives*. Hemel Hempstead: Harvester Wheatsheaf.

Solowij, N. (1995) 'Do cognitive impairments recover following cessation of cannabis use?' *Life Sciences*, 56: 2119–26.

Stacy, A.W., Newcomb, M.D. & Bentler, P.M. (1993) 'Cognitive motivations and sensation seeking as long-term predictors of drinking problems.' *Journal of Clinical & Social Psychology*, 12(1): 1–24.

Staude-Muller, F., Bliesener, T. & Luthman, S. (2008) 'Hostile and hardened? An experimental study on (de-)sensitization to violence and suffering through playing video games.' *Swiss Journal of Psychology*, 67: 41–50.

Stein, M., Liebowitz, M., Lydiard, R., Pitts, C., Bushnell, W. & Gergel, I. (1998) 'Paroxetine treatment of generalized social phobia (social anxiety disorder): a randomized controlled trial.' *Journal of the American Medical Association*, 280: 708–13.

Stewart, L.A. (1993) 'Profile of female firesetters. Implications for treatment.' *British Journal of Psychiatry*, 163: 248–56.

Sturman, T.S. & Thibodeau, R. (2001) 'Performance-undermining effects of baseball free-agent contracts.' *Journal of Sport & Exercise Psychology*, 23: 23–36.

Swaffer, T. & Hollin, C. (2001) 'Anger and general health in young offenders.' *Journal of Forensic Psychiatry*, 12: 90–103.

Takahashi, K. (1990) 'Affective relationships and their lifelong development.' In Baltes, P.B. (ed) *Lifespan development and behaviour*, vol 10. Hillsdale, NJ: Lawrence Erlbaum.

Thelwell, R.C. & Maynard, I.W. (2000) 'Professional cricketers' perceptions of the importance of antecedents influencing repeatable good performance.' *Perceptual & Motor Skills*, 90: 649–58.

Thornicroft, G. & Sartorius, N. (1993) 'The course and outcome of depression in different cultures: a 10 year follow-up of the WHO collaborative study on the assessment of depressive disorders.' *Psychological Medicine*, 23: 1023–32.

Timimi, S. (2004) 'A critique of the International Consensus Statement on ADHD.' *Clinical Child and Family Psychology Review*, 7: 59–63.

Trauer, T., Farhall, J., Newton, R. & Cheung, P. (2001) 'From long-stay psychiatric hospital to community care unit: evaluation at 1 year.' *Social Psychiatry and Psychiatric Epidemiology*, 36: 416–19.

Tucker, L.A. (1985) 'Television's role regarding alcohol use among teenagers.' *Adolescence*, 20(79): 593–8.

Turkington, D., Dudley, R., Warman, D.M. & Beck, A.T. (2004) 'Cognitive-behavioral therapy for schizophrenia: a review.' *Journal of Psychiatric Practice*, 1: 5–16.

Turkington, D., Kingdon, D. & Turner, T. (2002) 'Effectiveness of a brief cognitive-behavioural therapy intervention in the treatment of schizophrenia.' *British Journal of Psychiatry*, 180: 523–7.

Tutko, T.A. & Ogilvie, B.C. (1966) *Athletic motivation inventory*. San Jose, CA: Institute for the Study of Athletic Motivation.

Valliant, P.M. & Raven, L.M. (1994) 'Management of anger and its effect on incarcerated assaultive and nonassaultive offenders.' *Psychological Reports*, 75(1): 275–8.

Valzelli, L. (1973) 'The "isolation syndrome" in mice.' *Psychopharmacologia*, 31: 305–20.

Valzelli, L. & Bernasconi, S. (1979) 'Aggressiveness by isolation and brain serotonin turnover changes in different strains of mice.' *Neuropsychobiology*, 5: 129–35.

Van de Poll, N.E., Taminiau, M.S., Endert, E. & Louwerse, A.L. (1988) 'Gonadal steroid influence upon sexual and aggressive behaviour of female rats.' *International Journal of Neuroscience*, 41: 271–86.

Van Ijzendoorn, M.H. & Kroonenberg, P.M. (1988) 'Cross-cultural patterns of attachment: a meta-analysis of the Strange Situation.' *Child Development*, 59: 147–56.

Vealey, R.S. & Walter, S.M. (1993) 'Imagery training for performance enhancement and personal development.' In Williams, J. (ed) *Applied sport psychology*. Mountain View, CA: Mayfield.

Virkkunen, M., DeJong, J., Bartko, J., Goodwin, F.K. & Linnoila, M. (1989) 'Relationship of psychobiological variables to recidivism in violent offenders and impulsive fire setters.' *Archives of General Psychiatry*, 46: 600–3.

Virkkunen, M., Nuutila, A., Goodwin, F.K. & Linnoila, M. (1987) 'Cerebrospinal fluid monoamine metabolite levels in male arsonists.' *Archives of General Psychiatry*, 44: 241–7.

Wareing, M., Fisk, J.E. & Murphy, P.N. (2000) 'Working memory deficits in current and previous users of MDMA ("ecstasy").' *British Journal of Psychology*, 91: 181–8.

Watson, J.B. & Rayner, R. (1920) 'Conditioned emotional responses.' *Journal of Experimental Psychology*, 3: 1–14.

Weinberg, R.S., Butt, J. & Knight, B. (2001) 'High school coaches' perceptions of the process of goal setting.' *Sport Psychologist*, 15: 20–47.

Weinberg, R.S., Bruya, L., Jackson, A., & Garland, H. (1987) 'Goals difficulty and endurance performance: A challenge to the goal attainability assumption.' *Journal of Sport Behavior*, 10(2): 82–92.

Weinberg, R.S., Yukelson, D., Burton, S. & Weigand, D. (2000) 'Perceived goal setting practices of Olympic athletes: an exploratory investigation.' *Sport Psychologist*, 14: 279–95.

Weiner, B. (1974) *Achievement motivation and attribution theory*. Morristown, NJ: General Learning Press.

Wells, C.M., Collins, D. & Hale, B.D. (1993) 'The self-efficacy-performance link in maximum strength performance.' *Journal of Sport Sciences*, 11: 167–75.

Westerberg, H., Hirvikovsky, T., Forssberg, H. & Klingberg, T. (2004) 'Visuo-spatial working memory span: a sensitive measure of cognitive deficits in children with ADHD.' *Child Neuropsychology*, 10: 155–61.

White, F.J. & Kalivas, P.W. (1998) 'Neuroadaptations involved in amphetamine and cocaine addiction.' *Drug & Alcohol Dependence*, 51: 141–53.

White, N.M. & Hiroi, N. (1993) 'Amphetamine conditioned cue preference and the neurobiology of drug seeking.' *Seminars in the Neurosciences*, 5: 329–36.

Wilhelm, K., Mitchell, P.B., Niven, H., Finch, A., Wedgewood, L., Scimone, A., Blair, I.P., Parker, G. & Schofield, P. (2006) 'Life events, first depression onset and the serotonin transporter gene.' *British Journal of Psychiatry*, 188: 210–15.

Williams, T.M. (1981) 'How and what do children learn from television?' *Human Communication Research*, 7(2): 180–92.

Wilson, T.W., Neuendorff, D.A., Lewis, A.W. & Randel, R.D. (2002) 'Effect of zeranol or melengestrol acetate (MGA) on testicular and antler development and aggression in farmed fallow bucks.' *Journal of Animal Science*, 80: 1433–41.

Wise, R.A., Leone, P., Rivest, R. & Leeb, K. (1995) 'Elevations of nucleus accumbens dopamine and DOPAC levels curing intravenous heroin self-administration.' *Synapse*, 21: 140–8.

Wood, G.K., Tomasiewicz, H., Rutihauser, U., Magnuson, T., Quierion, R., Rochford, J. & Srivastava, L.K. (1998) 'NCAM-knockout mice display increased lateral ventricle size and reduced prepulse inhibition of startle.' *Neuroreport*, 9: 461–6.

Wynn V.E. & Logie R.H. (1998) 'The veracity of long-term memory: did Bartlett get it right?' *Applied Cognitive Psychology*, 12, 1–20.

Xu, B., Roos, J.L., Levy, S., van Rensberg, E.J., Gogos, J.A. & Karayiorgou, M. (2008) 'Strong association of de novo copy number mutations with sporadic schizophrenia.' *Nature Genetics*, 40: 880–5.

Yeates, K.O., Taylor, H.G., Drotar, D., Wade, S., Stancin, T. & Klein, S. (1997) 'Preinjury family environment as a determinant of recovery from traumatic brain injury in school-age children.' *Journal of the International Neuropsychological Society*, 3: 617–30.

Yerkes, R.M. & Dodson, J.D. (1908) 'The relation of strength of stimulus to rapidity of habit formation.' *Journal of Comparative Neurology and Psychology*, 18: 459–82.

Yuille, J.C. & Cutshall, J.L. (1986) 'A case study of eyewitness memory of a crime.' *Journal of Applied Psychology*, 71(2): 291–301.

Zahariadis, P.N. & Biddle, S.J.H. (2000) 'Goal orientations and participation motives in physical education and sport: their relationships in English schoolchildren.' *Athletic Insight*, 2: np.

Zamble, E. & Quinsey, V.L. (1997) *The criminal recidivism process.* Cambridge: Cambridge University Press.

Zeanah, C.H., Smyke, A.T., Koga, S.F. & Carlson, E. (2005) 'Attachment in institutionalised and community children in Romania.' *Child Development*, 76: 1015–28.

Zebrowitz, L.A. & Andreoletfi, C. (1998) 'Bright, bad, babyfaced boys: appearance stereotypes do not always yield self-fulfilling prophecy effects.' *Journal of Personality & Social Psychology*, 75(5): 1300–20.

Zillman, D. (1993) 'Mental control of angry aggression.' In Wegner, D. & Pennebaker, J. (eds) *Handbook of mental control*, vol 5: 370–92. Englewood Cliffs, NJ: Prentice Hall.

Zuckerman, M. (1979) *Sensation seeking: beyond the optimal level of arousal.* Hillsdale, NJ: Lawrence Erlbaum.

Index

Abnormality; defining 134–6
Abreaction 160
Abstinence syndrome 72
Achievement motivation theory 118
Additive principle 118
ADHD 56–9; diagnostic criteria 57
Adolescents; and marijuana 97, 98
Adopted children; and crime 14
Affectionless psychopathy 50, 51
Ageton, S.S. & Elliot, D.S. 18, 178–9
Aggression 13, 14–17, 37
Agonist 71, 75
Ahnert, L. et al. 65
Ainsworth, M. 44–8
Alcohol misuse 89, 90–2
Allardyce, J. et al. 138
Allhusen, V. et al. 65
Amorose, A.J. & Horn, T.S. 117
Amy, event recall study 28
Amygdala; and aggression 15
Andersson, B.E. 64
Androgyny; and sport 115, 116
Anger management 33–4
Animal studies 84, 189–92; and
    schizophrenia 142
Antabuse 103
Antagonist 71
Antidepressant drugs 156–7, 163
Antipsychotics 146–7
Antisocial behaviour 4; disorder 134
Anxiety 120, 121, 123
Appetite stimulant 85
Applications of Psychology (Unit 3);
    examination of 226; questions
    228–30
Approach-avoidance conflict 118
Armfield, J. 162
Arousal 120, 121–2
Arroll, B. et al. 157
Ashanti people 18
Ashford, B. et al. 117
Asperger syndrome 60
Assessment Objectives; AO1 226; AO2
    226–7; AO3 227
Athletic motivation inventory 113
Attachment 40–56; culture
    49–50; deprivation 50–3;
    institutionalisation 55–6; and
    nature-nurture debate 220–1;
    privation 53–6; types of 45–8;
Attributional retraining 127–8
Atypical development 56–62
Audience effects 121

Autism 59–62; diagnostic criteria 60
Aversion therapy 102–3, 175, 180–1
Avoidance-conditioning model 161–2

Bailey, H.N. et al. 43, 62
Bandura, A. 4–5, 6, 7, 8, 119
Banse, R. 179
Bard, P. 15
Baron-Cohen, S. 61, 62
Bartlett, F.C. 171
Bassett, J.E. & Blanchard, E.B. 30–1
Beck, A.T. 154–5
Behaviour therapy 175–6
Behavioural (learning) theory 161–2
Belsky, J. & Rovine, M.J. 63–4, 197–8
Belsky, J. 41, 49, 221
Benedetti, G. 148
Benjamin, J. et al. 161
Bental, R. et al. 143
Benzodiazepines 162
Beta-blockers 163
Biological approach; and crime 13–17,
    37; to depression 152–4; drug
    misuse 88–98; heroin dependence
    100; and nature-nurture debate
    219; to schizophrenia 140–2
Bion, W.R. 144
Blacker, J. et al. 34
Blättler, R. et al. 101, 102, 185
Bobo doll study 5
Boon, S.D. & Lomore, C.D. 96
Bowen, A.M. & Bourgeois, M.J. 170
Bowlby, J. 41–4, 50–1, 62–3, 179, 221
Boyatzis, C.J. et al. 7
Boyd, J. & Monroe, K.J. 126
BPS guidelines, animal use 189–90
Bradshaw, W. 147, 183, 209
Brain; and ADHD 58; and aggression
    15–17; in murderers 16; scanning
    76–7
Brazleton, T.B. et al. 43
Brief dynamic therapy (BDT) 159–60
Broberg, B.V. et al. 191
Brook, J.S. et al. 97, 98
Brosnan, M.J. & Thorpe, S.J. 164
Brown, A.S. et al. 150–1
Brunner, H.G. 17
Butler, A.C. et al. 159, 164

Caine, S.B. & Koob, G.F. 82
Calvin, case of 135, 212
Campbell, J.M. et al. 61
Cannabis 83–8

Car accident study 20–1; and speed
    26–7
Carli 171
Carol, case study 147–8
Carter, C.A. et al. 27
Case study 54, 193, 209–210
Castle, D. et al. 145
Catastrophe model 122–3
Catharsis 160
Cattell's personality factors 112, 114
CBT 183–4, 217–8
Central control 143
Cerebrospinal fluid 154
Chalabaev, A. et al. 116, 181–2
Charlton, A. 197
Charlton, T. et al. 9, 177
Child psychology 39–67; contributions
    to society 179–80
Child witnesses 27–9
Childress, A.R. et al. 83
Chi-squared test 195
Clanging 143
Classical conditioning 161, 217;
    and drug use 73; treating drug
    dependence 102–3
Clinical psychology 133–164;
    contributions to society 182–4;
    questions 230–1; revision checklist
    232
Closed questions 127, 202
Clough, P. 114
Cocaine 81–3
Cockett, M. & Tripp, D. 52, 180
Cognitive approach; contributions to
    society 171–2; and nature-nurture
    debate 219
Cognitive behavioural therapy (CBT)
    147–8, 158–9, 164
Cognitive development; and ADHD
    58; and autism 60–1
Cognitive imagery 126
Cognitive model of depression 154–5
Cognitive motivation 91
Cognitive preparation 33
Cognitive theory 162
Cognitive triad 154–5
Cohen's Kappa 137
Columbine massacre 11
Community care; and schizophrenia
    149–50
Compensatory reaction hypothesis 73
Competence 185
Competitive State Anxiety Inventory 120

Confidentiality 187
Conflict view 4
Consensus view 4
Consent 185–6
Consistency 30
Construct validity 138
Content analysis 193, 206–7
Content analysis exercise 36, 66, 108,
    128, 228
Correlational analysis 193, 207–9
Correlational studies 8
Correlations 120–1
Corrigan, P.W. 32–3
Counterbalancing 194
Craft, L.L. et al. 120
Craik, F.I.M. & Lockhart, B. 171
Criminal behaviour; causes of 4–6
Criminal psychology 3–36;
    contributions to society 177–9
Criterion validity 138
Critical period 40
Cross-cultural studies 49, 50
Cross-dependence 73
Cross-tolerance 73
Culture 211–2; and attachment 49–50,
    221; and socialisation 115; and
    social norms 115
Culture bound 49
Curtiss, B. et al. 103
Curtiss, S. 53–4
Czech twins, case of 54, 56

Dabbs, J.M. et al. 15
Danaher, B.G. 103
Daycare 62–6
Debates in psychology 211–21
Debriefing participants 186
Deception 186
Demand characteristics 195–6
Dependence 71–2
Dependent variable 23, 29, 194–5
Depressants 78
Depression 174, 183; biological
    explanations 152–4; biological
    treatments 156–8; clinical
    characteristics 151–2;
    psychological explanations 154–6;
    psychological treatments 158–60
Deprivation 51–3
Despair 52
Detachment 52
Developmental retardation 50
Devlin report 22
Diagnosis; of depression 151, 152; of
    mental disorder 136–7; phobias
    161; of schizophrenia 140
Discord 52

Discrimination 169–70
Disinhibited attachment 55
Donohew, R.L. et al. 94
Donovan, W. et al. 47
Dopamine; and cocaine 81–2; reward
    system 88; and schizophrenia 142,
    146
Dose effect, daycare 64, 65
Double blind 157, 196
Down regulation 73
Dream analysis 149
Drinking, teenage 19
Drug abuse; campaigns 104–7
Drugs; classifying 77; effects of 77–88;
    and neurotransmitters 70–1;
    therapies 182–3, 216; users of
    71–3
Duff, D.C. 164
Dysthymic disorder 152

ECT (electroconvulsive therapy) 157–8
Egloff, B. & Gruhn, A.J. 113
Empirical methods 213, 214, 215
Environment, influence of 218–9
Eranti, S. et al. 158
Eron, L.D. et al. 8
Ethical issues 46, 55, 84, 184–90
Ethnocentrism 211–2
Etic approach 212
Evidence in practice 35–6, 65–6, 106–8,
    128–9, 228–31
Evolution; and attachment 40–1, 221
Examination; criteria 226; technique
    247
Excellence; in sport 112
Exchange system 30
Experimenter effects 195
Experiments 193, 194–8
External imagery 125
Extreme male brain theory 62
Extrinsic motivation 117, 118
Extroversion 113
Eye-witness testimony 19–29, 171
Eysenck, H. 113, 162

Falsifiability 213
Family reordering 52, 180
Farzin, F. et al. 62
Fazey, J. & Hardy, L. 122
Feher, P. et al. 114
Fergusson, D.N. et al. 52–3
Field experiment 25–6, 28, 29, 193,
    196–7, 199
Foll, D.L. et al. 127
Forty-four thieves study 50–1
Fowler, T. et al. 89
Francis, L.J. et al. 113

FRANK, Talk to 104–6, 180
Free-association 149
Freud, S. 149, 156
Fride, E. et al. 85
Frith, C.D. 143
Fromm-Reichmann, F. 144

GABA 70, 71, 77; and phobias 161
Garland, D.J. & Barry, J.R. 114
Garrido, V. & Morales, L.A. 32
Gender 115; and schizophrenia 139,
    141
Genes; and ADHD 58–9; and autism
    62; and crime 13–14; and
    depression 152–3; and drug use
    89–91; and environment 219;
    influence of 218; and phobias
    160–1; and schizophrenia 140–1
Genie, case of 53–4, 56
Gibbs, J.P. 19
Goal-setting 124
Godden, D.R. & Baddeley, A.D. 171
Goldberg, A.S. 114
Goldstein, J.M. 139
Goths, attack on 169
Gottdiener, W.H. & Haslam, N. 149
Gottesman, I. 140, 208
Gould, R.A. et al. 164
Grant, S. et al. 75
Guillet, E. et al. 115, 181
Gunsekera, H. et al. 96

Hagell, A. & Newbury, T. 8
Hallucination 78
Hammad, T.A. 163
Haney, M. et al. 88
Haninger, K. & Thompson, K.M. 11, 207
Hardy, L. et al. 123
Harrison, L.J. & Ungerer, J.A. 64
Harrison, L.J. et al. 86
Health belief model 105–6
Health psychology 69–108;
    contributions to society 180–1
Heroin 77–9; effects of 80–81; treating
    dependence to 100–4
Hetterna, J.M. et al. 161
Hills, P. & Argyle, M. 113
Hobbs, T.R. & Holt, M.M. 31
Hollin, C.R. 4
Holmes, J. 159
Homeostatic theory 73
Hopf, W.H. et al. 11
Hormones; and aggression 14–15
How Psychology Works (Unit 4);
    examination of 226; questions
    230–1
Howard, M.O. 102–3

Huesmann, R. 7
Hypersystematising 61
Hypothalamus; and aggression 15
Hypothesis, testing 214–5

Identification 11–12
Imagery techniques 125–6
Imprinting 40–1
Independent groups design 194
Independent variable 23, 29, 194–5
Induction 214
Inhibitory synapses 71
Innate 40
Institutionalisation 55
Interactional synchrony 42, 43
Interactionist view 4
Internal imagery 125
Internal working model 42–3
Inter-rater reliability 137
Interview 193, 203–6
Intrinsic motivation 117, 118
Inverted U-hypothesis 121–2, 123
IQ; and abnormality 134

Jahoda, G. 18
Jambor, E.A. 115
Janis, I.L. & Feshbach, S. 106
Jean Charles de Menezes 19
Jenkins, W.O. et al. 31–2
Juliano, L.M. et al. 103

Kebbell, M.R. et al. 26–7
Keen, J. 33
Keenan, H.T. et al. 58
Kendler, K.S. et al. 90
Key issues 36, 67, 108, 130, 165,
    168–84, 210–1
Kindt, M. & Brosschot, J.F. 162
Kirigin, K.A. et al. 32
Kirkby, R.J. & Whelan, R.J. 52
Kirley, A. et al. 58–9
Klein, G. 144
Klimek, V. et al. 154, 196
Kniveton, B.H. 8
Knock out mice 14, 78, 85
Koivula, N. 115, 181
Koluchova, J. 54, 198
Konijn, E.A. et al. 11–12
Koren-Karie, N. 64
Koster, E.H. et al. 155, 195–6
Krackow, E. & Lynn, S.J. 28, 29, 197
Kuhn, T. 214
Kurzthaler, I. et al. 85

Laboratory experiments 7–8, 23, 193,
    195–6, 199
Lagerspetz, K. 13
Lamb, R.J. et al. 88

L-DOPA 142
Leading questions 20, 26, 27, 28–9
Leaflet 228
Learning approach; contributions to
    society 175–7; and crime 4–13;
    and drug misuse 74–5, 93–8;
    and nature-nurture debate 219;
    treating drug misuse 102–3
Ledent, C. et al. 85
Leff, J. 150
Legalese 27
LEGO therapy 61–2
Leichsenring, F. et al. 160
Levels of processing theory 171
Levin, H. et al. 58
Levy, P. & Hartocollis, P. 18
Lewine, R.R.J. et al. 141
Lewis, C. et al. 27
Likert scale 127, 203
Lindsay, D.S. 24
Lipton, D.S. et al. 32
Lisanby, S.H. et al. 158
Little Albert 161
Locke, E.A. 124
Loftus, E.F. & Palmer, J.C. 20–3, 171, 214
Loftus, E.F. & Zanni, G. 20
Logan, F.A. 73
Longitudinal studies 48, 65
Long-term deprivation 52–3
Lorenz, K. 40–1
Lou, H.R. et al. 90
Loza, W. & Loza-Fanous, A. 34
Lucchini, R. 94
Lyons, M.J. et al. 13

Madon, S. et al. 19
Maedgen, J.W. & Carlson, C.L. 58
Maes, H.H. et al. 90
Major depressive disorder 151
Mann Whitney test 195
MAOIs (monoamine oxidase inhibitors)
    156
Marijuana 83–8, 97
Mason, D.A. & Frick, P.J. 13
Massie, H. & Szajnberg, N. 173
Matched pairs design 194
Maternal deprivation 50–1
Maternal sensitivity hypothesis 47
Matthes, H.W.D. et al. 78
McClelland, D.C. 118
McGuffin, P. 208
McGuffin, P. et al. 152
Media influence; and drug misuse 96
Media violence 6–13, 35, 176
Medina, K.L. et al. 86
Memory 171; and cannabis 85–6;
    and Ecstasy 99
Mental disorder, classification of 136–7

Mental retardation 134
Mental toughness questionnaire 114
Meta-analysis 42
Metarepresentation 143
Methadone 100
Mezulis, A.H. et al. 155, 156
Milgram, S. 168, 185, 186
Milin, R. et al. 88
Mitchell, M. 180
Monoamines 154
Monotropy 41, 42
Morgan, L.K. et al. 115
Morgan, M. & Grube, J.W. 95
Motivation; and sport 117–20
Motivational imagery 126
MRI scanning 76–7
Musty, R.E. & Kaback, L. 86
Myers, N.D. et al. 119–20

Natural experiment 193, 197–8, 199
Nature–nurture debate 218–21
Negative reinforcement 73, 74–5; and
    sporting behaviour 116
Negative self-schemas 155
Neuroleptic malignant syndrome 146
Neuroticism 113
Neurotransmitters 174; and ADHD
    59; and aggression 16–17; and
    depression 154; and drugs 70–1;
    and schizophrenia 142
NICE 100, 147, 148, 149, 158, 160
Nicholls, J. 119
Nicholls, D. et al. 137
Nielsen, D.A. et al. 89
No Smoking Day 106
Normal distribution 134
NOS gene 14
NRIs (noradrenalin reuptake inhibitors)
    157
Nucleus accumbens 89

Objectivity 213
Observation 46, 193, 198–201; and
    privacy 187
Offenders, treating 30–5
Olds, J. & Milner, P. 89
Olmstead, T.A. et al. 104
Olweus, D. et al. 14
Omoaregba, J.O. et al. 188
Open questions 202
Operant conditioning 161–2; and drug
    use 73–7, 103–4
Opiate 78
Optimal arousal 182
Orbach, I. et al. 128
Outcome goals 124–5
Owens, G. 61–2

Paivio, A. 126
Paquette, V. et al. 164
Paradigm 214
Participation; in sport 112–13
Paul & Lentz 176
Pennington, D.C. 5
Performance catastrophe 122
Performance goals 124–5
Personality; and sport 112–15
Pert, C.B. & Snyder, S.H. 77
PET scanning 76–7
Phobias 160–4; explanations for 160–2; treatments for 162–4
Phonemic processing 171
Physical dependence 72
Pilling, S. et al. 148
Pinquart, M. et al. 157
Placebo 157
Pontizovsky, A.M. et al. 137
Pope, H. 85
Popper, K. 213
Positive reinforcement 73, 74; and sporting behaviour 116
Potegal, M. et al. 15–16
PPV (positive predictive value) 137
Predictive validity 138
Prejudice 169–70
Primary reinforcers 30
Primary socialisation 115
Prisoners, maltreatment of 168–9
Prisons; and token economy 30–2
Privation 51, 53–6
Protection from harm 186–7
Protest 52
Proximity seeking 40
Psychoactive drug 71
Psychodynamic approach; contributions to society 172–4; and nature-nurture debate 219
Psychodynamic model; of depression 156; of schizophrenia 144
Psychodynamic therapies; for depression 159–60; for schizophrenia 148–9
Psychological dependence 71
Psychological explanations; for depression 154–6; for phobias 160–2; for schizophrenia 143–5
Psychoneuromuscular theory 125
Psychopaths 134

Qualitative data 124
Quality of Written Communication (QWC) 227
Quantitative data 124
Questionnaire 93, 127, 193, 201–3, 205

Questions; answering 235–40; essays 242–7; extended writing 241–2
Quinsey, V.L. & Sarbit, B. 32

RAAD 100
Raine, A. et al. 16
Random control trial 157, 164
Read, J. et al. 144
Recidivism 18, 30
Recording progress 30
Reif, A. et al. 14
Relapse 75
Reliability 29, 46, 54, 137, 192, 213
Repeated measures design 194
Replicability 213
Research methods 192–211
Retz, W. et al. 14
Revision; checklists 231–4; how to revise 235
Reward cards 216–7
Rice, M.E. et al. 32
Right to withdraw 186
Robber's cave study 169
Roberts, D.F. et al. 97
Robertson, J. & Bowlby, J. 51–2
Robinson, T.E. & Berridge, K.C. 75
Rocha, B.A. et al. 82
Role models; and drug misuse 96
Romanian orphanages 55, 56
Rosenhan, D.L. 138, 186, 199
Ross, R.R. & MacKay, H.B. 32
Ross, R.R. et al. 96
Rounsville, B.J. et al. 83
Rung, J.P. et al. 174
Russian Olympic team; and visualisation 125, 126
Rutter, M. 55–6
Rychtarik, R.G. et al. 96

Sanchez-Villegas, A. et al. 138
Savants 60
Schedules and shaping 30
Schizophrenia 182–3, 188; clinical characteristics 139; construct validity 138; diagnosis 140; drugs 174; explanations for 140–5; and gender 139, 141; and neurotransmitters 142; treatment 146–50
Schizophrenogenic mother 144
Schooler, N. et al. 146, 196
Schurr, K.T. et al. 112
Scientific method 213–6
Secondary data 164
Secondary reinforcers 103
Secondary socialisation 115
Secure base behaviour 40

Sedative 78
Self, D.W. et al. 75
Self-attribution 127
Self-efficacy theory 119–20
Self-esteem; and depression 150–1
Self-fulfilling prophecy (SFP) 17–19, 37
Self-medication 75
Self-report techniques 201–6
Semantic processing 172
Semple, D.M. et al. 86
Sensation seeking 91
Sensitive period 55
Sensitive responsiveness 47
Separation anxiety 40
Serotonin 16–17, 153, 154; and phobias 161
Serotonin transporter gene 153
Sewell, R.A. et al. 86
Shaham, Y. & Stewart, J. 75
Shaping 103
Sheese, B.E. & Graziano, W.G. 12–13
Short-term deprivation 51–2
Sindelar, J. et al. 104
Single blind 196
Skill acquisition 33
Skinner boxes; and drug self-administration 79–80
Skre, I. et al. 161
Smith, P.B. & Bond, M.H. 211
Smith, J.W. 103
Social approach; contributions to society 168–70; and crime 17–19; and nature-nurture debate 219; to treating schizophrenia 149–50
Social constructionist; and ADHD 59
Social control 135, 216–8; and CBT 217–8; and classical conditioning 217; and drug therapies 216; and token economies 216–7
Social development; and ADHD 58; and autism 61–2
Social identity theory 169
Social learning theory; and crime 4–6; and drug misuse 93–8; and phobias 162, 163
Social model; of schizophrenia 145
Social norms, deviation from 134
Social releasers 42
Socialisation 115
Spearman test 208
Spiders on drugs 87
Sport psychology 111–130; contributions to society 181–2; and personality traits 112–15
SSRIs (selective serotonin reuptake inhibitors) 157, 174
St Helena TV study 9, 10–11

Stability, daycare 65
Stacy, A.W. *et al.* 91
Statistical abnormality 134
Staude-Muller, F. *et al.* 12
Stein, M. *et al.* 161
Stereotyping 17–19
Stimulants 78
Stimulus-driven behaviour 143
Strange situation 44–5, 47, 215
Stranger anxiety 40
Stroop task 162
Study technique 171
Sturman, T.S. & Thibodeau, R. 118
Subjectivity 213
Substance misuse 69–108; diagnostic criteria 72; treating 98–104
Summary of articles 228
Swaffer, T. & Hollin, C. 156, 202
Synaptic cleft 71
Systematic desensitisation 163–4, 175

Tagged questions 27, 28, 197
Tajfel, H. & Turner, J.C.168, 169
Takahashi, K. 49
Talk to FRANK 104–6, 180
Tardive dyskinesia 146, 147
Target behaviours 30
Television violence 6–11
Temperament 220–1
Testosterone; and aggression 14–15
Test-retest reliability 137

THC 83–4, 85, 87
Thelwell, R.C. & Maynard, I.W. 122
Theory, constructing 214–5
Timimi, S. 59
Token economies 30–3 176, 178, 181, 216–7; treating drug misuse 103–4
Tolerance 73, 88–9
Transference 160
Transition, daycare 65
Trauer, T. *et al.* 150
Tricyclic antidepressants 156
Turkington, D. *et al.* 147, 148
Tutko, T.A. & Ogilvie, B.C. 113
Twin studies; and autism 62; and crime 13; and depression 152–3; and drug use 90; and schizophrenia 145
Types of attachment 45–8

Unipolar depression 151–160
Unit 3 questions 228–30
Unit 4 questions 230–31; revision checklists 232–4

Validity 29, 44, 46, 54, 137, 138, 192–3, 213
Valliant, P.M. & Raven, L.M. 34
Valzelli, L. 16
Van de Poll, N.E. *et al.* 15
Van Ijzendoorn, M.H. & Kroonenberg, P.M. 49, 212

Vicarious reinforcement; and sporting behaviour 116
Video games; and crime 11–12
Virkkunen, M. 17

Wareing, M. *et al.* 98, 99
Watson, J.B. & Rayner, R. 161
Wednesday boys 18
Weinberg, R.S. *et al.* 125
Weiner, B. 127
Wells, C.M. *et al.* 119, 182
Westerberg, H. *et al.* 58
Wilhelm, K. 186
Willed behaviour 143
Williams, T.M. 8
Wilson, T.W. *et al.* 6
WIN-2 85, 87
Withdrawal symptoms 72
Wood, G.K. *et al.* 142
Wynn, V.E. & Logie, R.H. 171

Xu, B. *et al.* 140–1

Yeates, K.O. *et al.* 58
Yerkes, R.M. & Dodson, J.D. 121
Yuille, J.C. & Cutshall J.L. 24–5, 29, 185

Zahariadis, P.N. & Biddle, S.J.H. 119
Zeanah, C.H. *et al.* 56
Zebrowitz, L.A. & Andreoletfi, C. 19

Acknowledgements

Thanks to Rick and everyone at Folens for their ongoing support.

The authors and publishers are grateful to the following for permissions to reproduce copyright material.

p. 2, © Brian A. Jackson/Shutterstock; p. 5, © Albert Bandura; p. 6 (top), © ITV/ Rex Features; p.6 (bottom), © Sipa Press/Rex Features; p. 7 (left), © Photos 12/ Alamy; p. 7 (right), © Content Mine International/Alamy; p. 10 © David Fisher/ Rex Features; p. 11 (left), © GreenGate Publishing; p. 11 (right) © Stewart Cook/ Rex Features; p. 12, © Doug Steley A./Alamy; p.13 (top) © GreenGate Publishing; p. 13 (middle), © Alekss/Fotolia; p. 13, (bottom), © iofoto/Shutterstock; p.14, © Eric Gevaert/Shutterstock; p.15, © Wolfgang Amri/Shutterstock; p. 17, Jason Maehl/Shutterstock; p. 19 (left), © Brendan MacNeill/Alamy; p. 18 (top), © Sally and Richard Greenhill/Alamy; p. 18 (bottom), © Sascha Burkard/Fotolia; p. 19 (top), © Kuttig-People/Alamy; p. 19 (right), © AP/Press Association Images; p. 19 (bottom), © Kent Probation Service; p. 25, © CPS/PA Wire/Press Association Images; p. 27, © ImageState/Alamy; p.28, © Betty LaRue/Alamy; p. 33, © Jason Stitt/Shutterstock; p. 34, © Cyrus Cornell/Fotolia; p. 38, © Maxim Slugin/ Shutterstock; p. 40, © MaleWitch/Shutterstock; p. 41 (top), © Rublev/Fotolia; p 41 (bottom), © Gertjan Hooijer/Shutterstock; p. 42 (left), © Michael William/ Shutterstock; p.42 (right), © Kurhan; p. 43, © iofoto/Shutterstock; p. 44, © Zsolt Nyulaszi/Shutterstock; p. 45, © Peter Baxter/Shutterstock; p. 47 (top), © Dave Arns/ Fotolia; p. 47 (bottom), © Yuri Arcurs/Shutterstock; p. 48, © Tatyana Gladskih/ Fotolia; p. 49, © Supri Suharjoto/Shutterstock; p. 51, © Kelpfish/Shutterstock; p. 52, © Lisa F. Young/Fotolia; p. 53, © Monkey Business Images/Fotolia; p. 55, © Mike Abrahams/Alamy; p. 57, Tomasz Trojanowski/Shutterstock; p. 61 (left), © Pictorial Press Ltd/Alamy; p. 61 (right), © khz/Fotolia; p. 62, © openlens/ Fotolia; p. 63 (top), © Losevsky Pavel/Shutterstock; p. 63 (bottom), © Monkey Business/Fotolia; p. 65 (left), © soupstock/Fotolia; p. 65 (right), © Igor Stepovik/ Shuterstock; p. 68, © Yakobchuk Vasyl/Shutterstock; p. 72, © Jenny/Fotolia; p. 74, © Courtesy of University of Texas; p. 75, © (1996) National Academy of Sciences, U.S.A.; p. 77 (top), Reproduced with the permission of John Wiley & Sons, Inc.; p. 80, © Terex/Fotolia; p. 82, Courtesy of The Advertising Archives; p. 83, © Anna/Fotolia; p. 85, © Arco Images/Reinhard, H.; p. 86, © Avalon Imaging/ Shutterstock; p. 87, © Photo Researchers; p. 89, © Floris Slooff/Shutterstock; p. 90, © Erin Patrice O'brien/Getty Images; p. 91, © Forgiss /Fotolia; p. 92, © Pakhnyushcha/Shutterstock; p. 94, © Duard van der Westhuizen/Shutterstock; p. 95, Simone van den Berg/Shutterstock; p. 96 (left) Courtesy of The Advertising Archives; p. 96 (right), © GreenGate Publishing; p. 97, © John Bailey/Shutterstock; p. 102, © AJ Photo/Hop Americain/Science Photo Library; p. 103, © Victoria Alexandrova/Shutterstock; p. 105 Crown Copyright; p. 106 Crown Copyright; p. 110, © Nizam D/Shutterstock; p. 112, Sirena Designs/Fotolia; p. 113, © Nick R/ Fotolia; p. 114, © Steve Lovegrove/Fotolia; p. 115, © iofoto/Fotolia; p. 116, © Val Thoermer/Fotolia; p. 117, © moodboard/Fotolia; p.118 (left), © eblue/Fotolia; p. 118 (right), © Stephen Coburn/Fotolia; p. 119, © vuk/Fotolia; p. 122, © Michael Flippo/Fotolia; p. 123, © Grandaded/Fotolia; p. 124, © Mitchell Knapton/Fotolia; p. 125, © FloridaStock/Shutterstock; p. 126 (left), © Daniel Krylov/Shutterstock; p. 126 (middle), © Izzet Ugur Can/Fotolia; p. 126 (bottom), © Bruce Yeung/ Shutterstock; p. 132, Yurok/Shutterstock; p. 135, © Nathalie P/Shutterstock; p. 135, © Lucian Coman/Shutterstock; p. 139, © Wrangler; p. 140, © Losevsky Pavel/Shutterstock; p. 142, © Chad Littlejohn/Shutterstock; p. 143, © Emin Ozkan/ Fotolia; p. 144, © Lisa F. Young/Fotolia; p. 145, Ella/Fotolia; p. 146, Alexandre Zveiger/Fotolia; p. 147, © endostock/Fotolia; p. 149, © RichG/Fotolia; p. 151, © Anita Patterson Peppers/Shutterstock; p. 152, Karen Roach/Shutterstock; p. 155